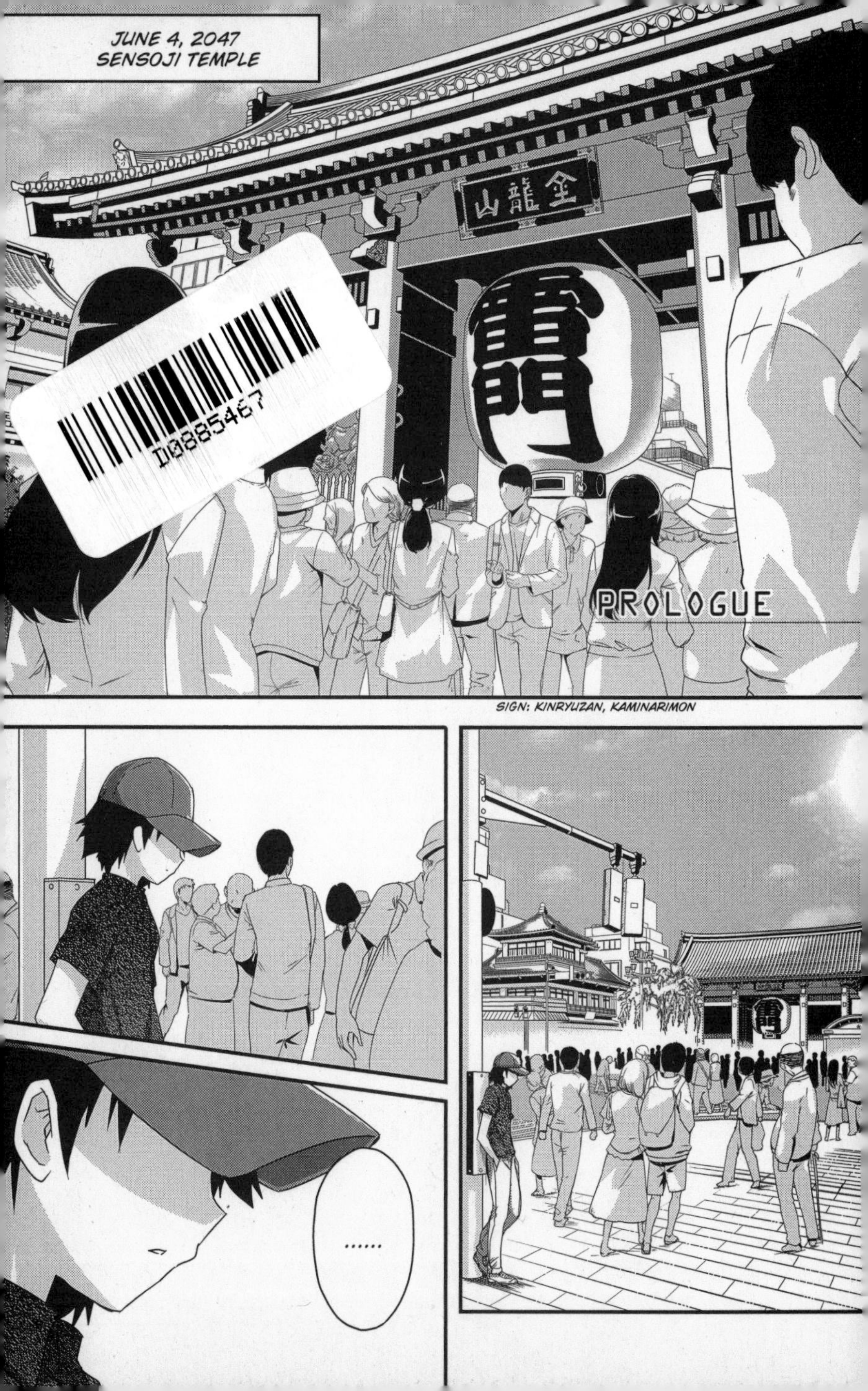
JUNE 4, 2047
SENSOJI TEMPLE
PROLOGUE
SIGN: KINRYUZAN, KAMINARIMON
......

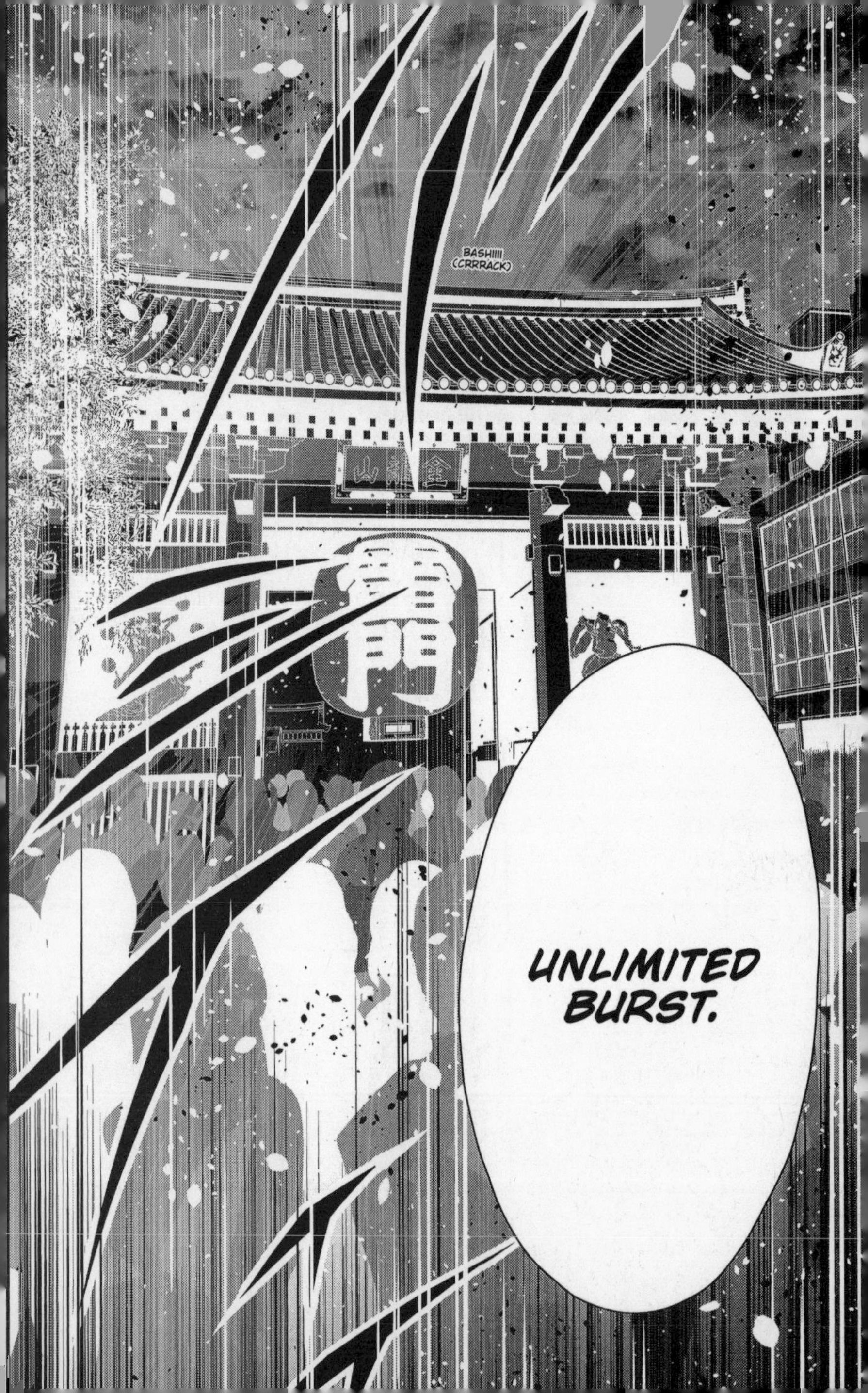
BASHIIII (CRRRACK)
UNLIMITED BURST.

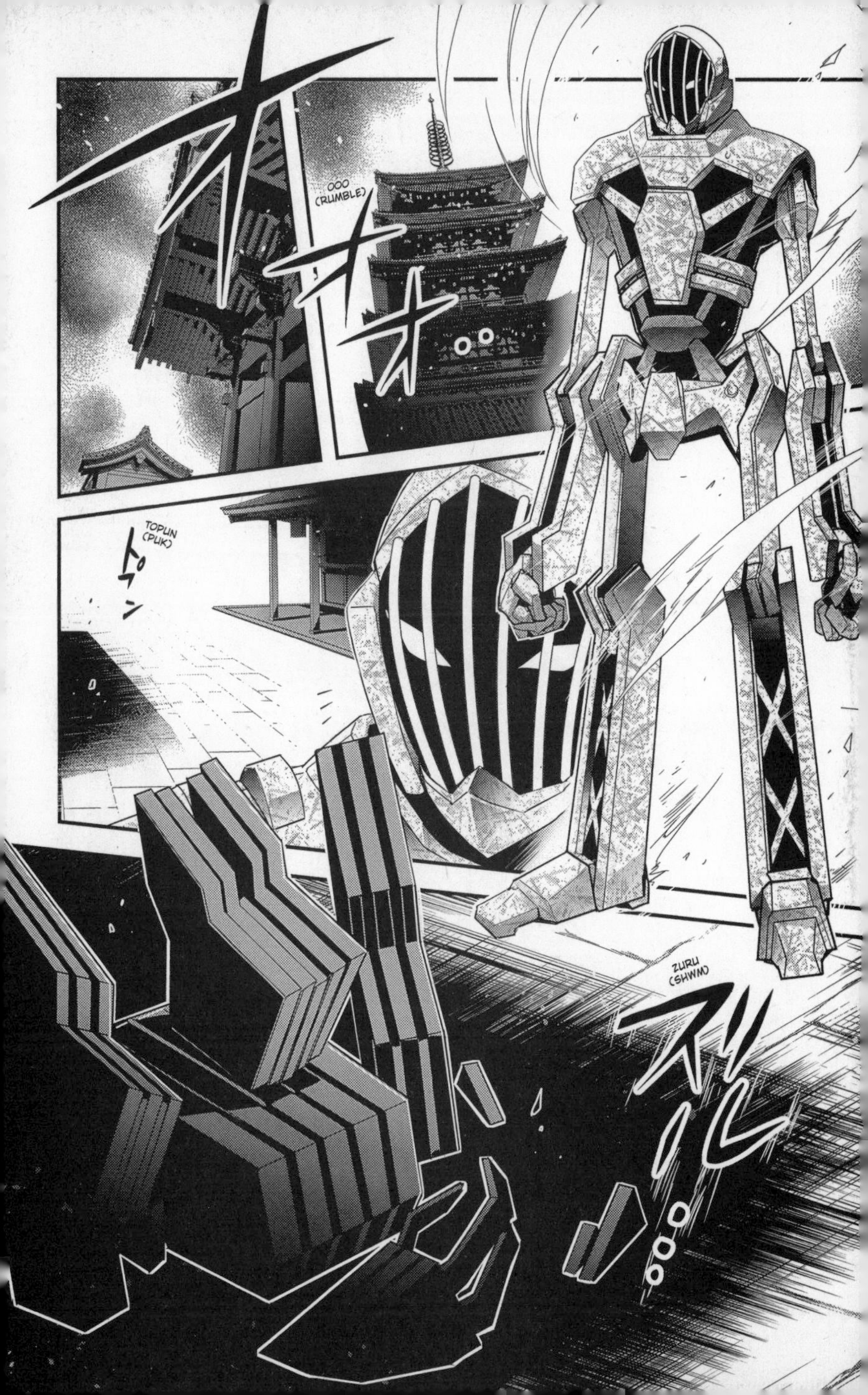

OOO (RUMBLE)
オオオ…
TOPUN (PUK)
トプン
ZURU (SHWM)
ズル…

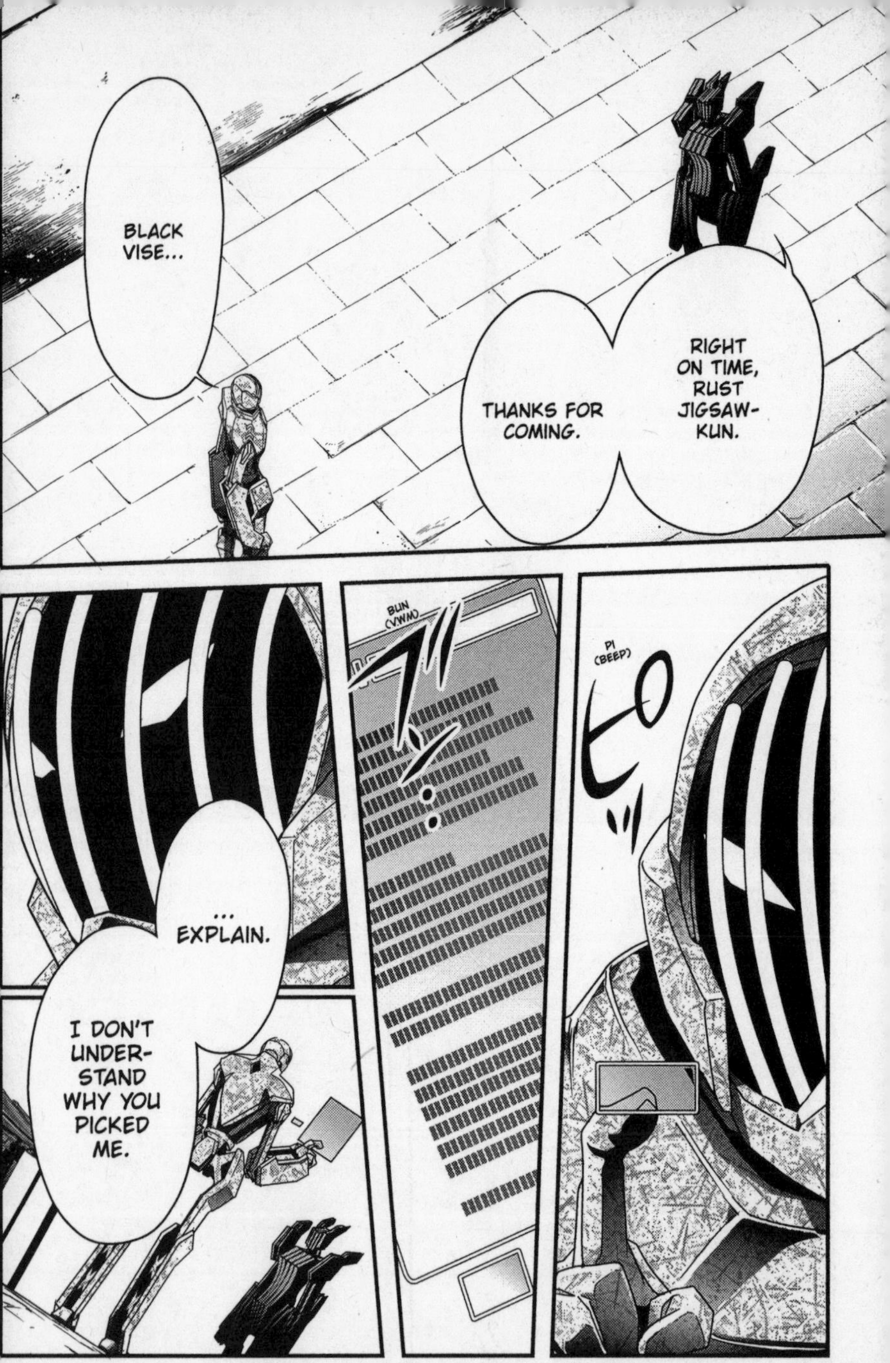

BLACK VISE...
RIGHT ON TIME, RUST JIGSAW-KUN.
THANKS FOR COMING.
PI (BEEP)
BUN (VWM)
... EXPLAIN.
I DON'T UNDER-STAND WHY YOU PICKED ME.

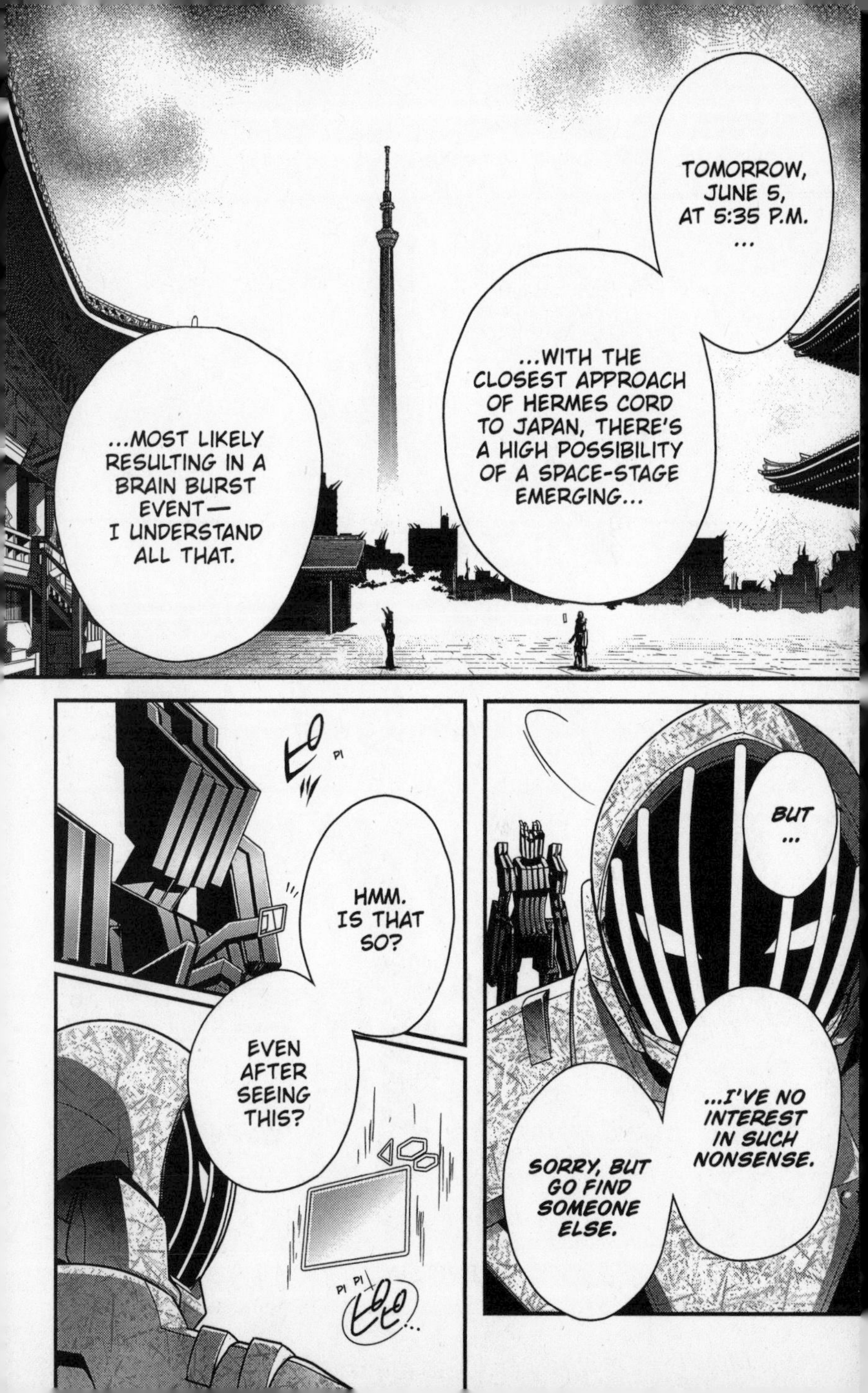
TOMORROW, JUNE 5, AT 5:35 P.M. ...
...WITH THE CLOSEST APPROACH OF HERMES CORD TO JAPAN, THERE'S A HIGH POSSIBILITY OF A SPACE-STAGE EMERGING...
...MOST LIKELY RESULTING IN A BRAIN BURST EVENT— I UNDERSTAND ALL THAT.
BUT ...
...I'VE NO INTEREST IN SUCH NONSENSE.
SORRY, BUT GO FIND SOMEONE ELSE.
PI
HMM. IS THAT SO?
EVEN AFTER SEEING THIS?
PI PI

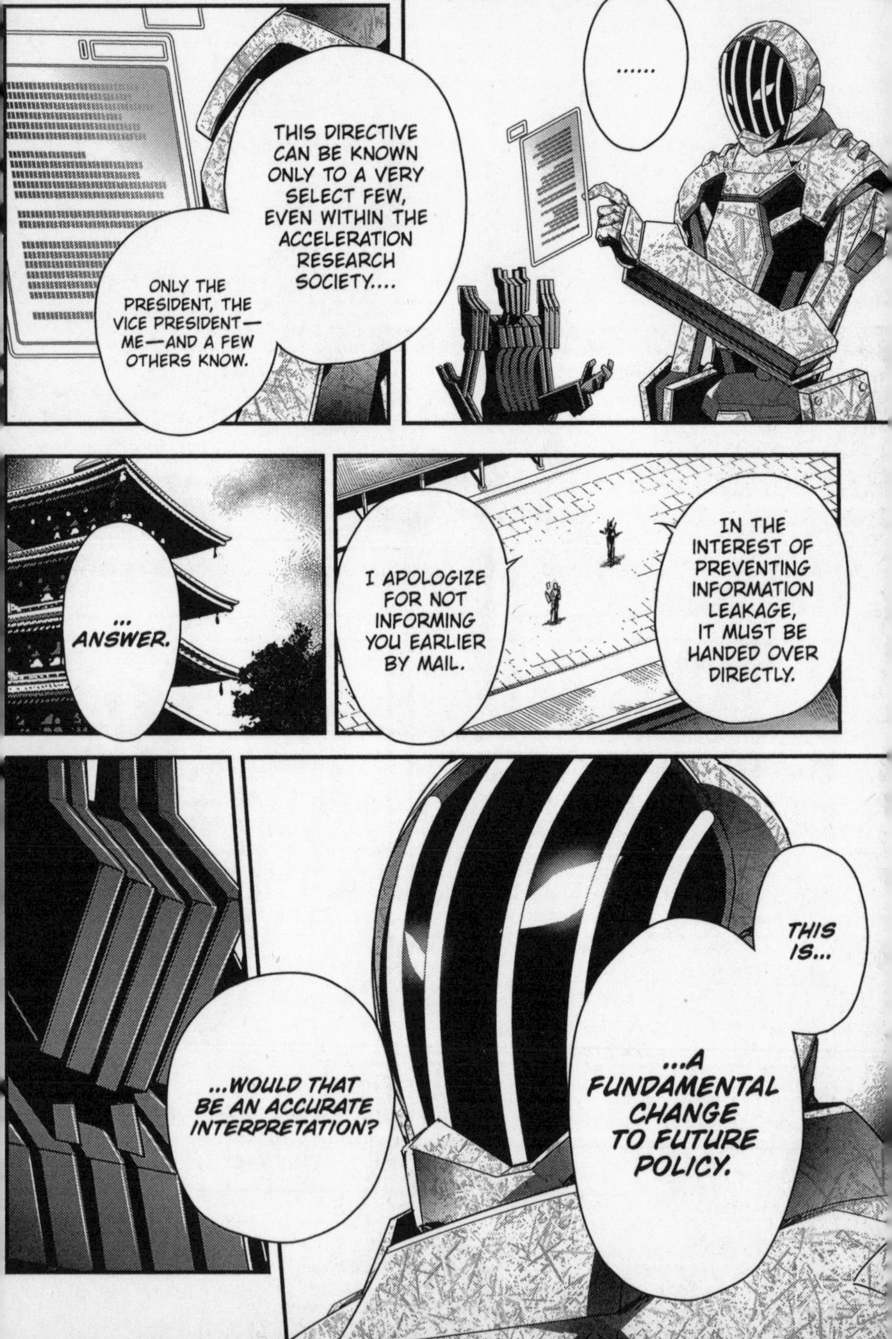
……
THIS DIRECTIVE CAN BE KNOWN ONLY TO A VERY SELECT FEW, EVEN WITHIN THE ACCELERATION RESEARCH SOCIETY....
ONLY THE PRESIDENT, THE VICE PRESIDENT—ME—AND A FEW OTHERS KNOW.
IN THE INTEREST OF PREVENTING INFORMATION LEAKAGE, IT MUST BE HANDED OVER DIRECTLY.
I APOLOGIZE FOR NOT INFORMING YOU EARLIER BY MAIL.
... ANSWER.
THIS IS...
...A FUNDAMENTAL CHANGE TO FUTURE POLICY.
...WOULD THAT BE AN ACCURATE INTERPRETATION?

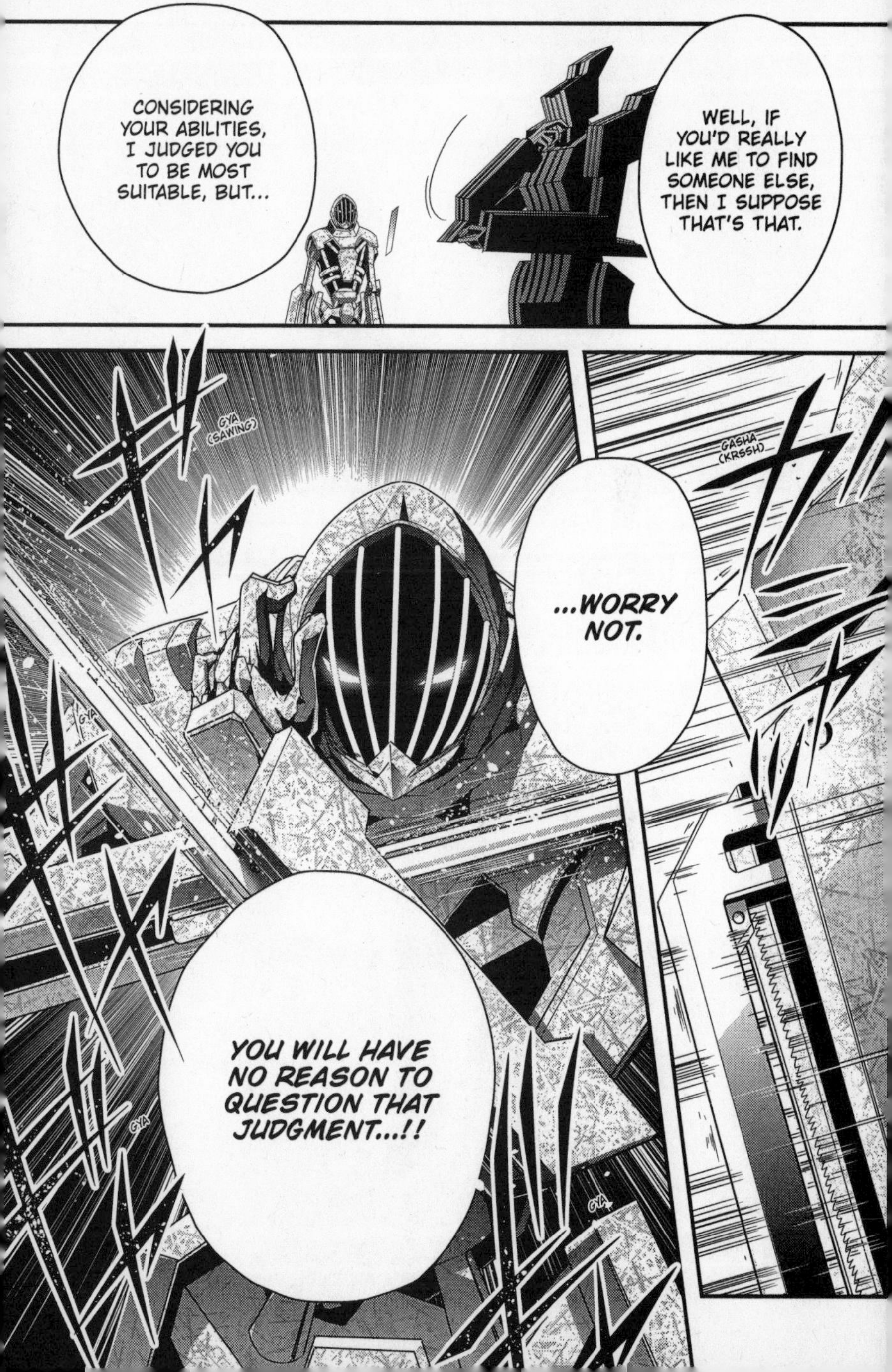
WELL, IF YOU'D REALLY LIKE ME TO FIND SOMEONE ELSE, THEN I SUPPOSE THAT'S THAT.
CONSIDERING YOUR ABILITIES, I JUDGED YOU TO BE MOST SUITABLE, BUT...
GASHA (KRSSH)
GYA (SAWING)
...WORRY NOT.
GYA
YOU WILL HAVE NO REASON TO QUESTION THAT JUDGMENT...!!
GYA
GYA

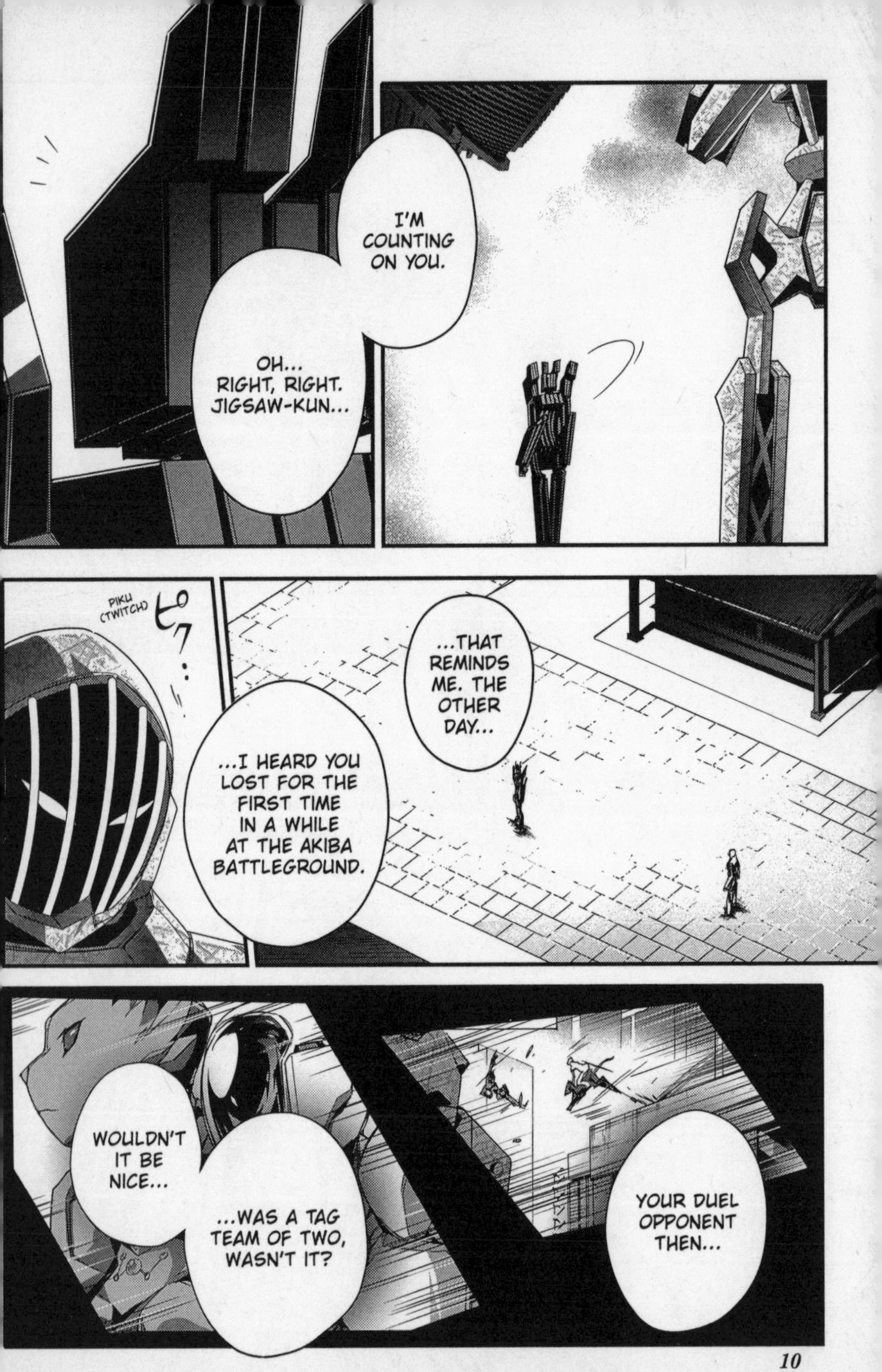
I'M COUNTING ON YOU.
OH... RIGHT, RIGHT. JIGSAW-KUN...
...THAT REMINDS ME. THE OTHER DAY...
PIKU (TWITCH)
...I HEARD YOU LOST FOR THE FIRST TIME IN A WHILE AT THE AKIBA BATTLEGROUND.
YOUR DUEL OPPONENT THEN...
...WAS A TAG TEAM OF TWO, WASN'T IT?
WOULDN'T IT BE NICE...

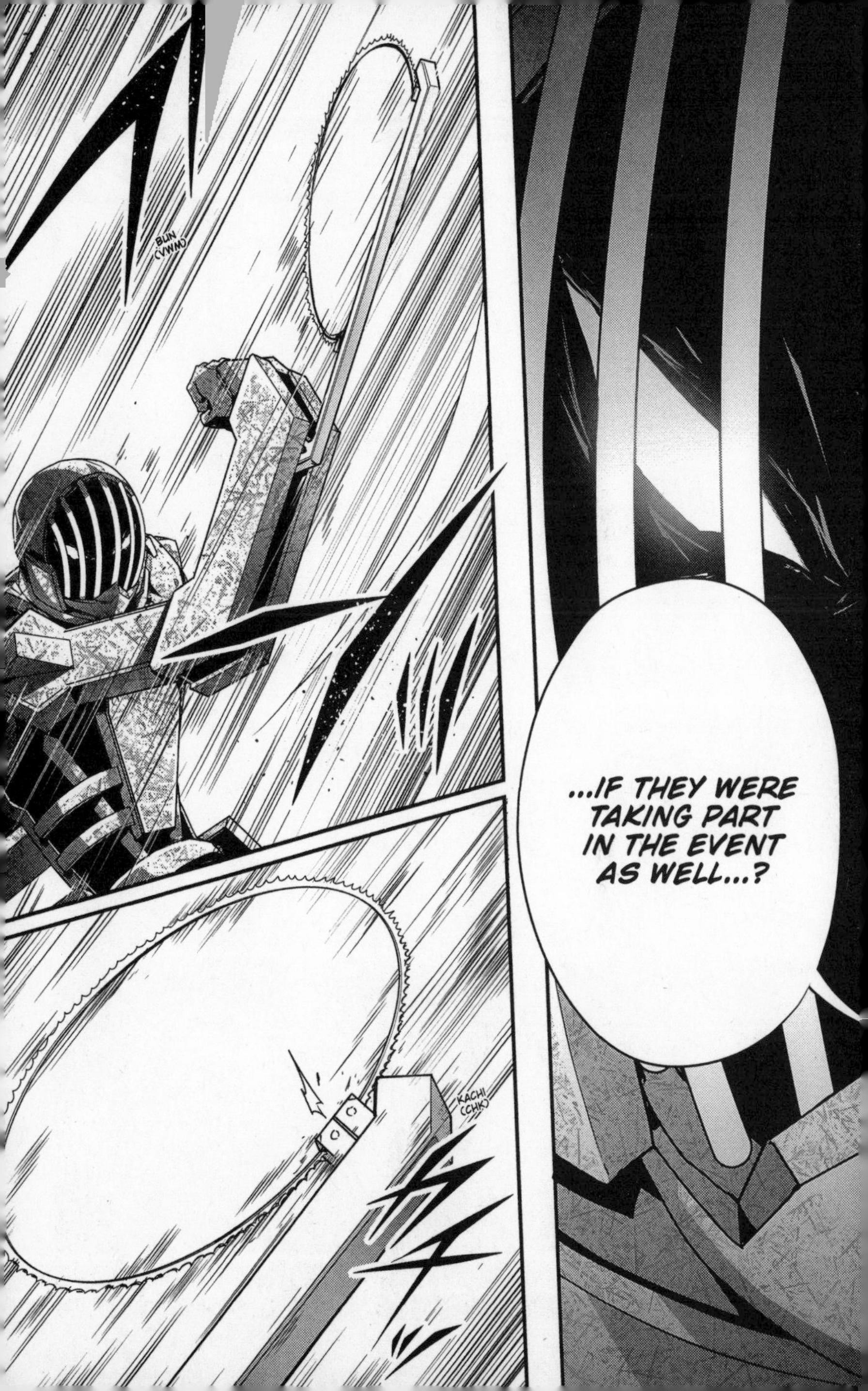
...IF THEY WERE TAKING PART IN THE EVENT AS WELL...?
BUN (VWM)
KACHI (CHK)

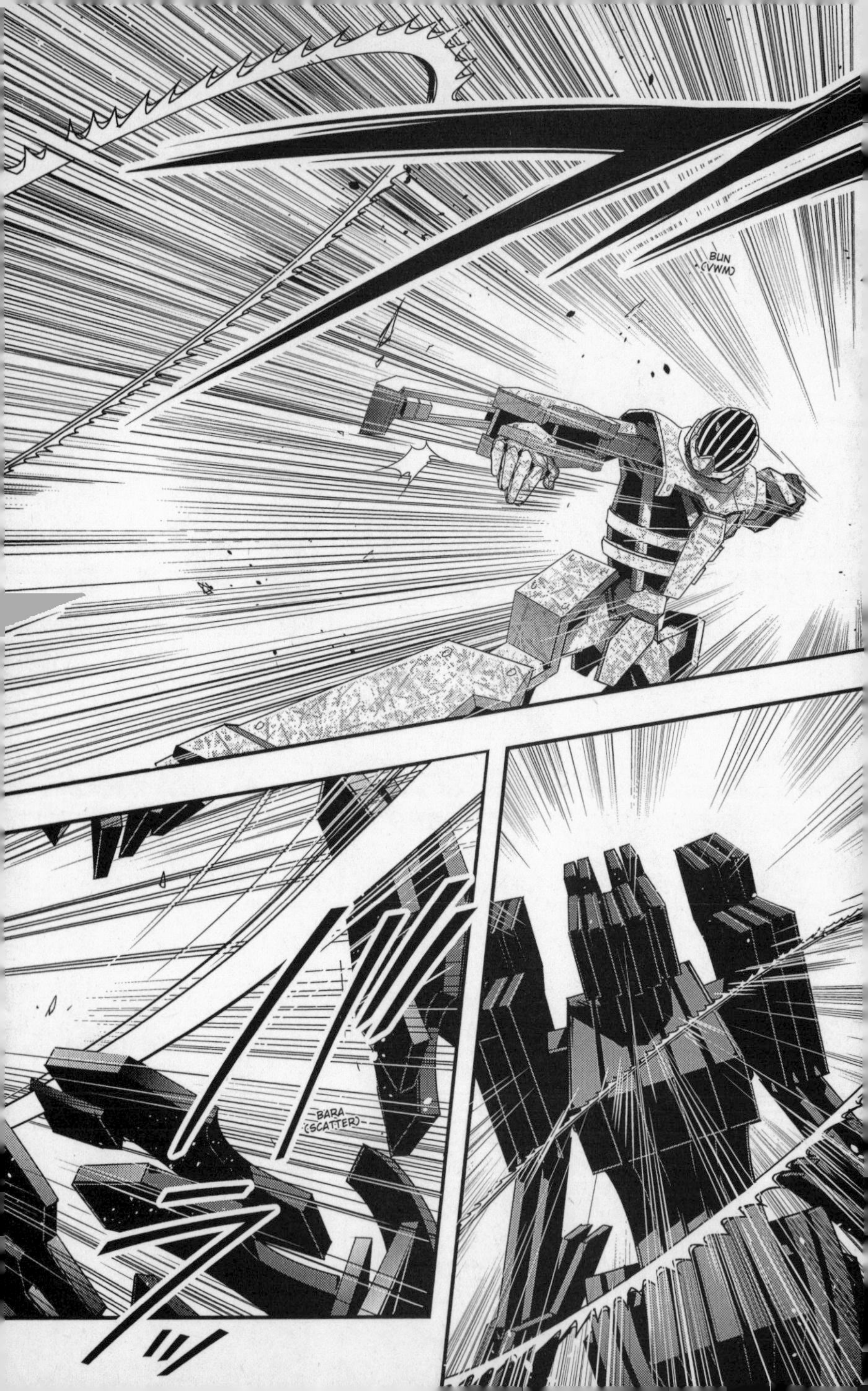
BUN
(VWM)
BARA
(SCATTER)

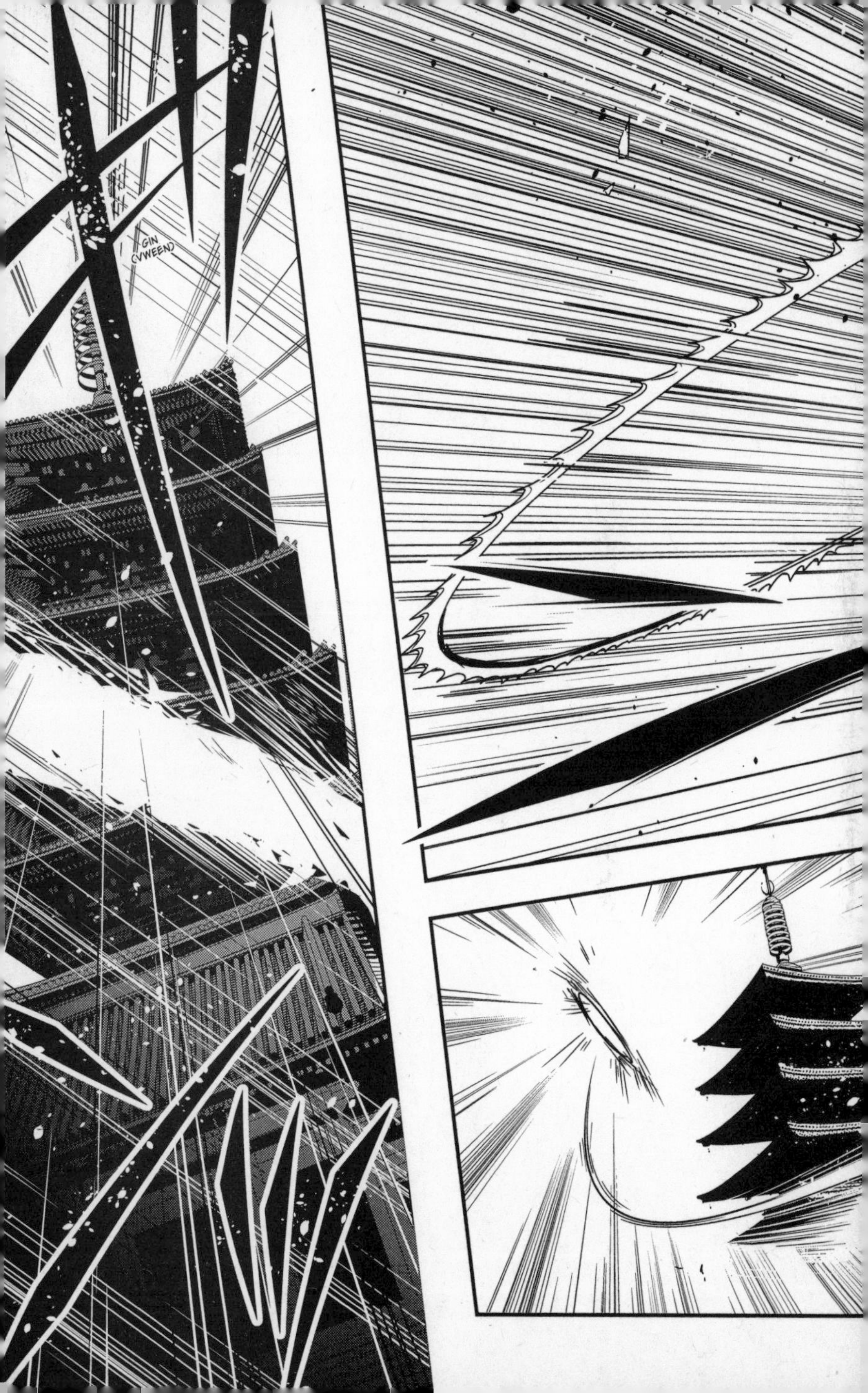
GIN (VWEEN)

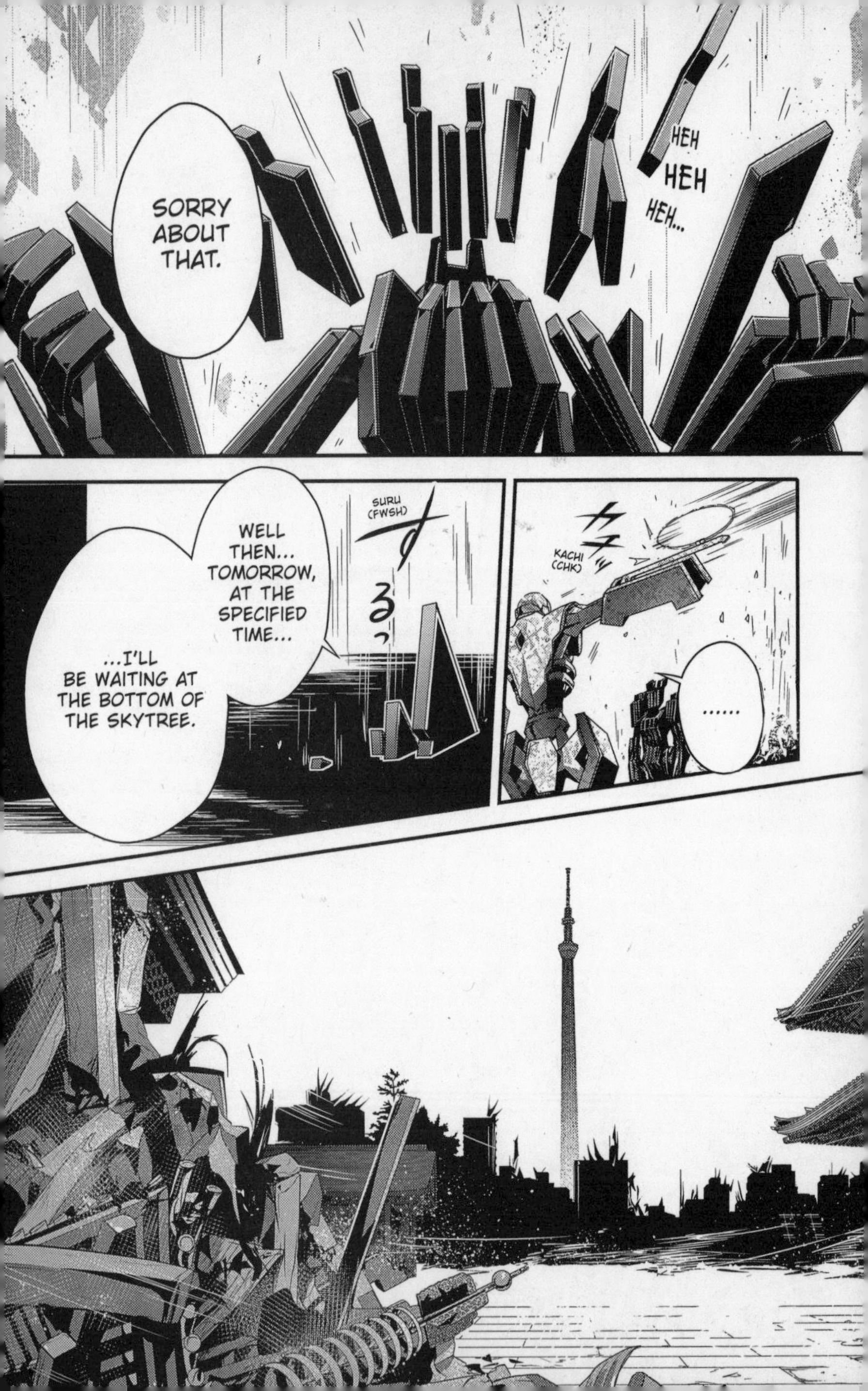
HEH HEH HEH...
SORRY ABOUT THAT.
カチッ
KACHI (CHK)
......
SURU (FWSH)
するっ
WELL THEN... TOMORROW, AT THE SPECIFIED TIME...
...I'LL BE WAITING AT THE BOTTOM OF THE SKYTREE.

►►►*ACCEL•WORLD*

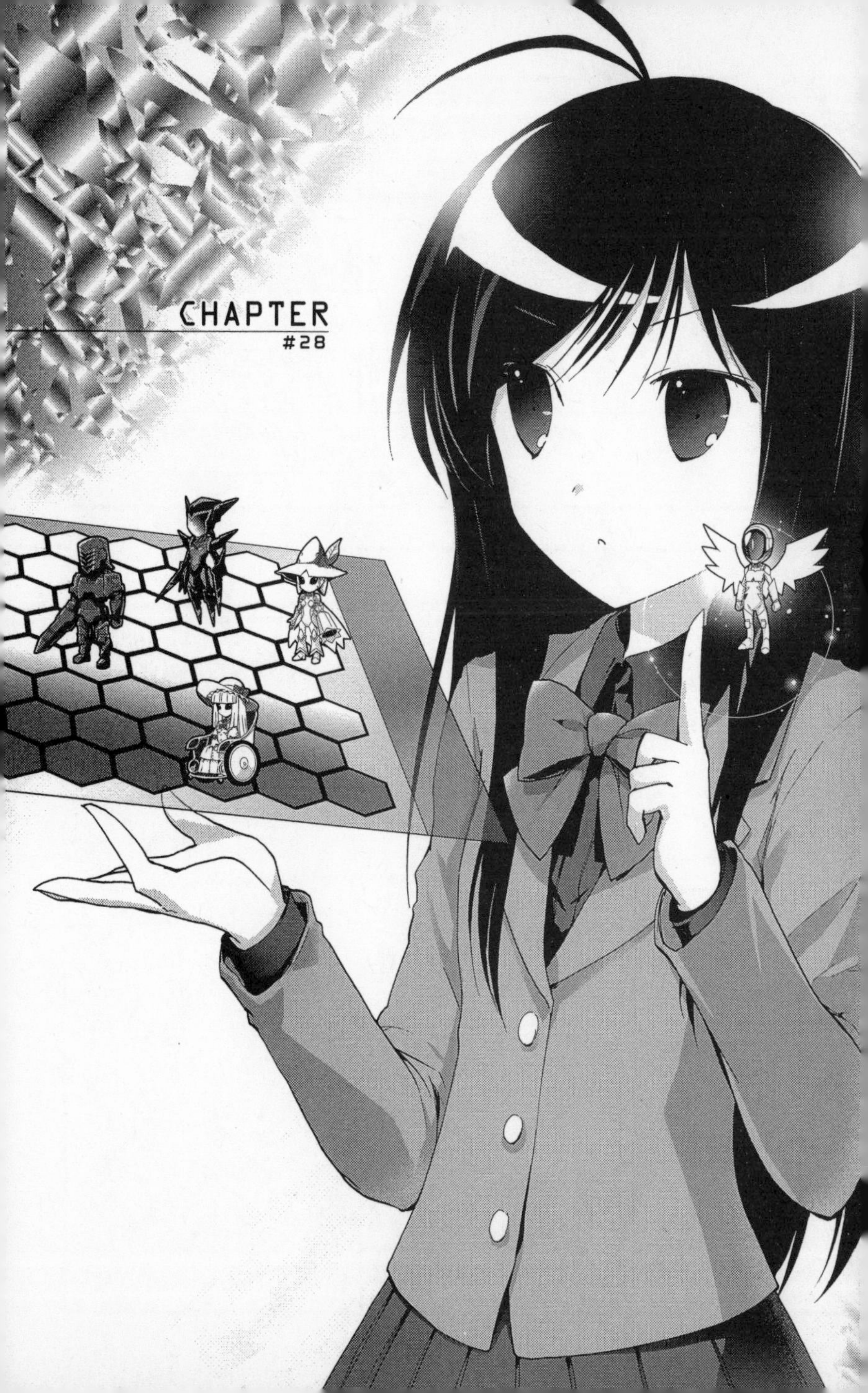
CHAPTER
#28

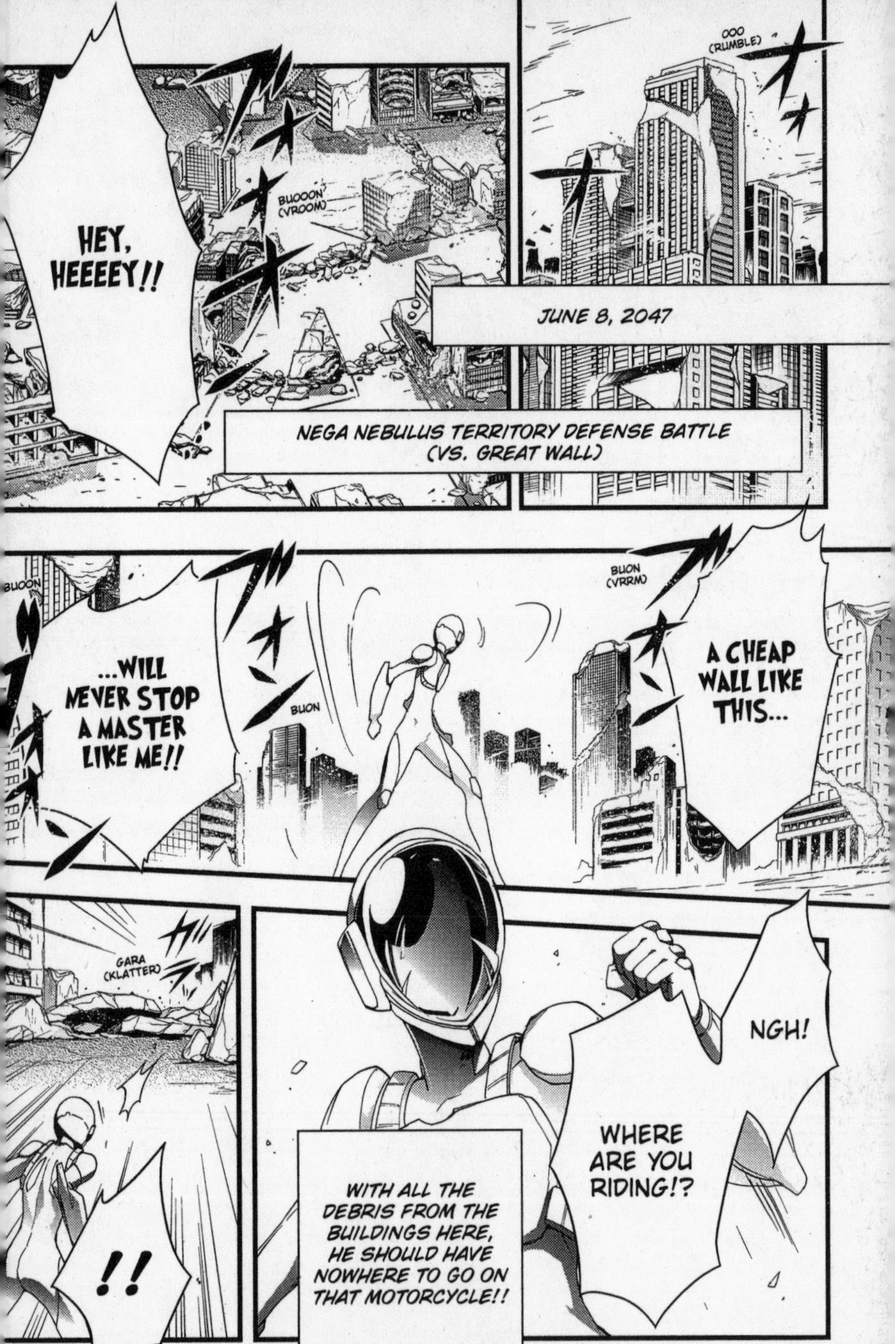
OOO
(RUMBLE)
JUNE 8, 2047
NEGA NEBULUS TERRITORY DEFENSE BATTLE
(VS. GREAT WALL)
BUOOON
(VROOM)
HEY, HEEEEY!!
BUON
(VRRM)
A CHEAP WALL LIKE THIS...
BUON
BUOON
...WILL NEVER STOP A MASTER LIKE ME!!
NGH!
WHERE ARE YOU RIDING!?
WITH ALL THE DEBRIS FROM THE BUILDINGS HERE, HE SHOULD HAVE NOWHERE TO GO ON THAT MOTORCYCLE!!
GARA
(KLATTER)
!!

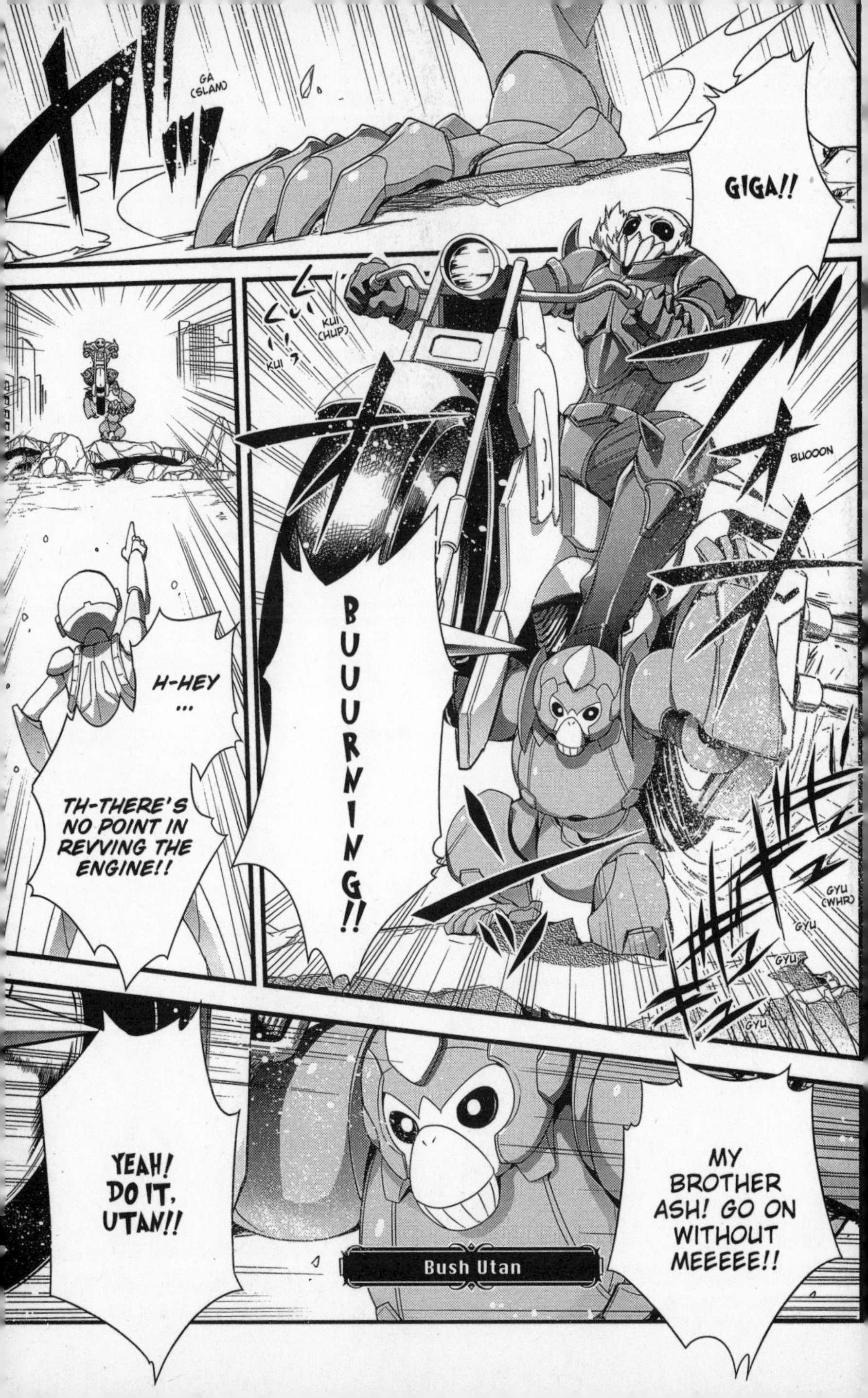
GIGA!!
GA (SLAM)
KUI (HUP)
KUI
BUOOON
BUUURNING!!
GYU (WHR)
GYU
GYU
GYU
H-HEY ...
TH-THERE'S NO POINT IN REVVING THE ENGINE!!
MY BROTHER ASH! GO ON WITHOUT MEEEEE!!
Bush Utan
YEAH! DO IT, UTAN!!

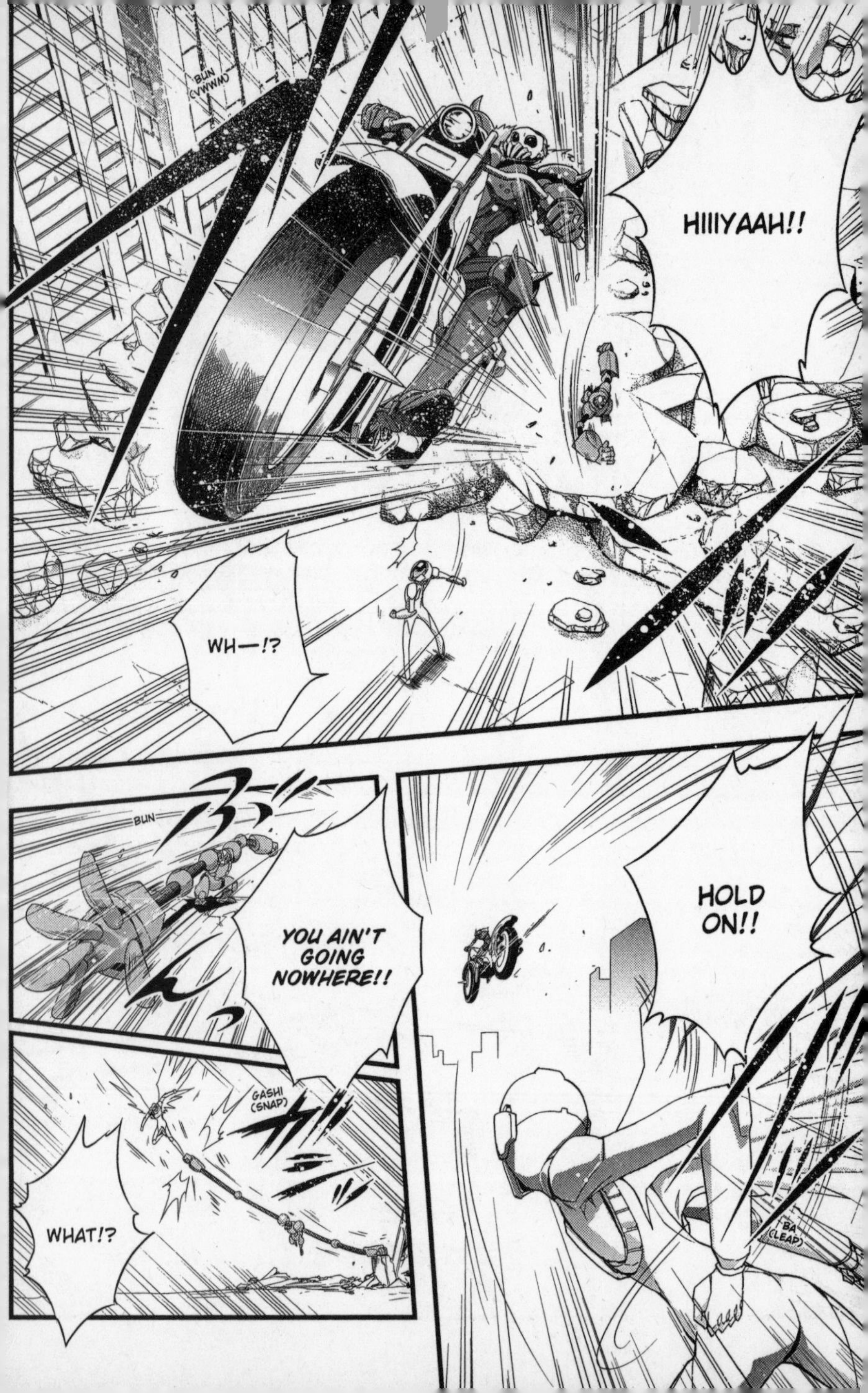
HIIIYAAH!!
BUN (VWWM)
WH—!?
HOLD ON!!
BA (LEAP)
BUN
YOU AIN'T GOING NOWHERE!!
GASHI (SNAP)
WHAT!?

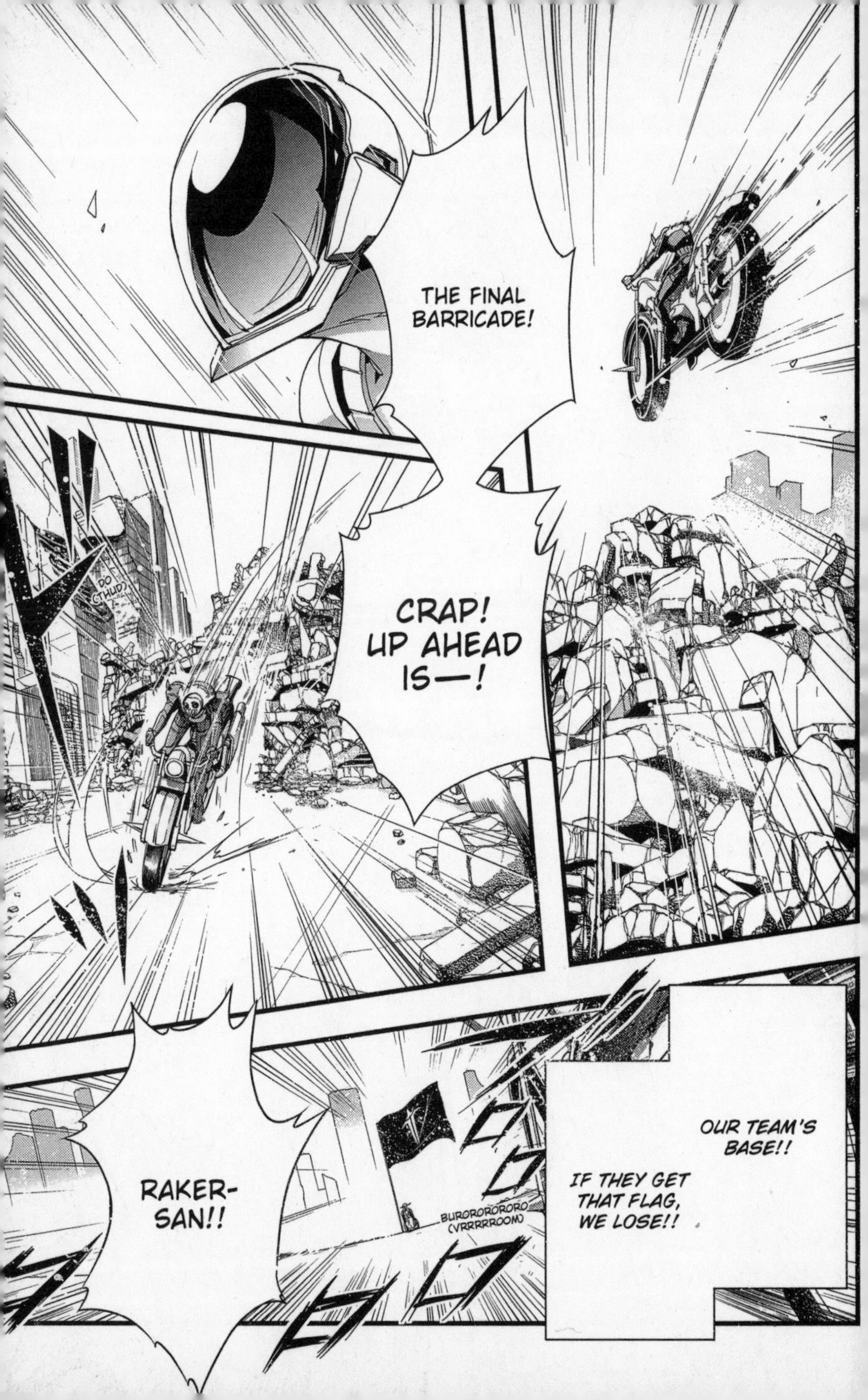
THE FINAL BARRICADE!
CRAP! UP AHEAD IS—!
DO (THUD)
OUR TEAM'S BASE!!
IF THEY GET THAT FLAG, WE LOSE!!
BURORORORORO (VRRRRROOM)
RAKER-SAN!!

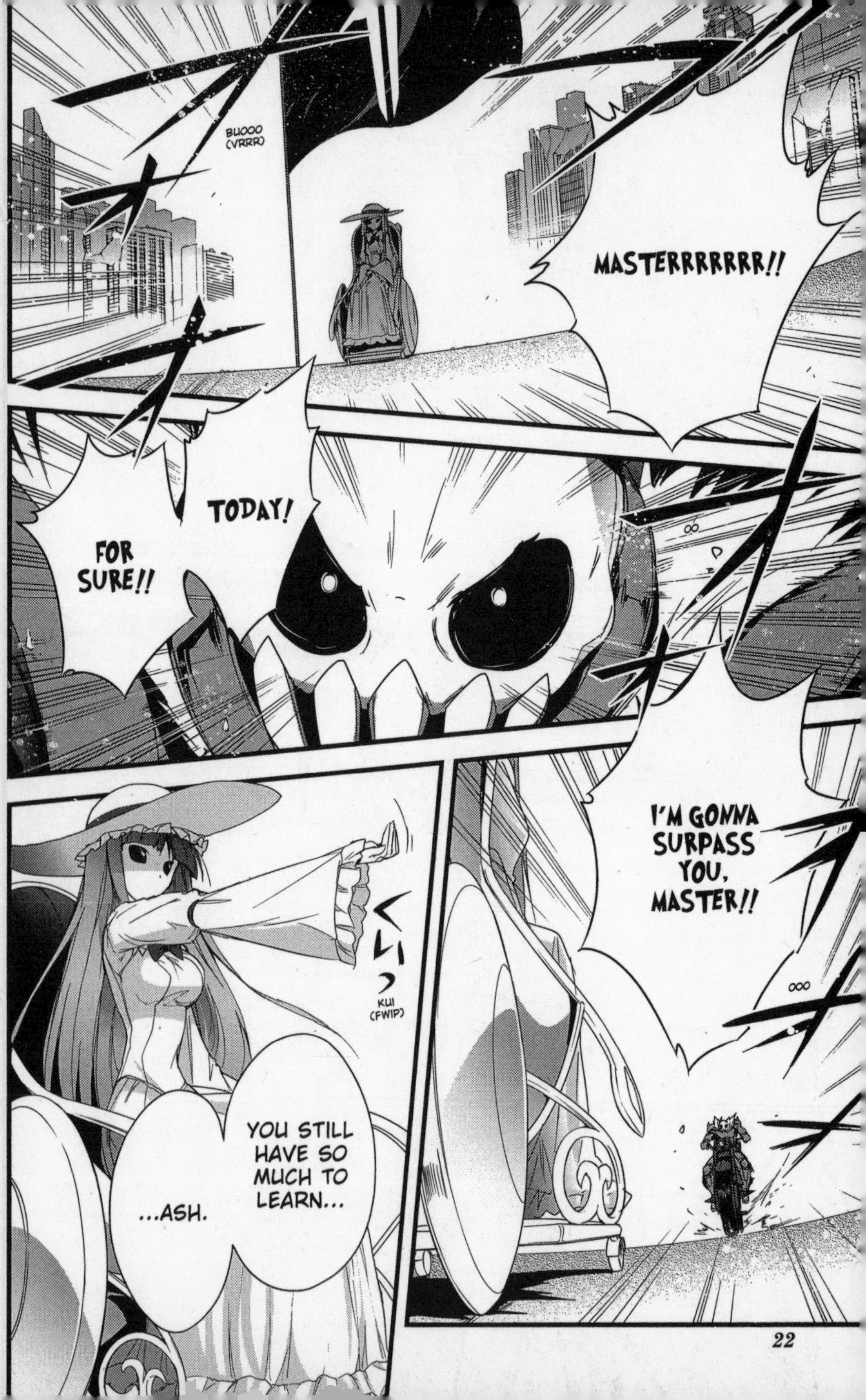
MASTERRRRRRR!!
BUOOO (VRRR)
TODAY!
FOR SURE!!
I'M GONNA SURPASS YOU, MASTER!!
くいっ
KUI (FWIP)
YOU STILL HAVE SO MUCH TO LEARN...
...ASH.

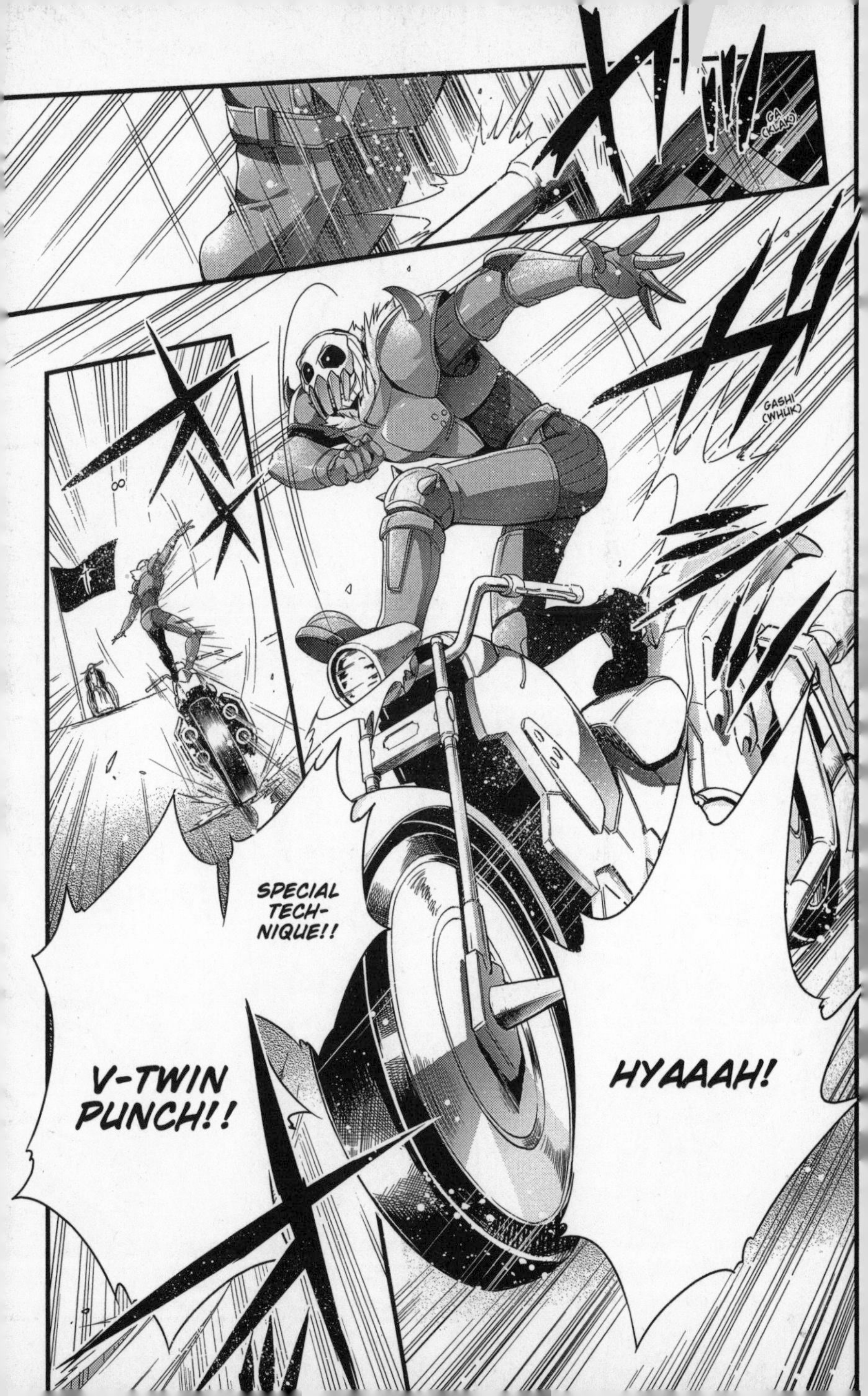
GA (KLAK)
GASHI (WHUK)
SPECIAL TECH-NIQUE!!
HYAAAH!
V-TWIN PUNCH!!

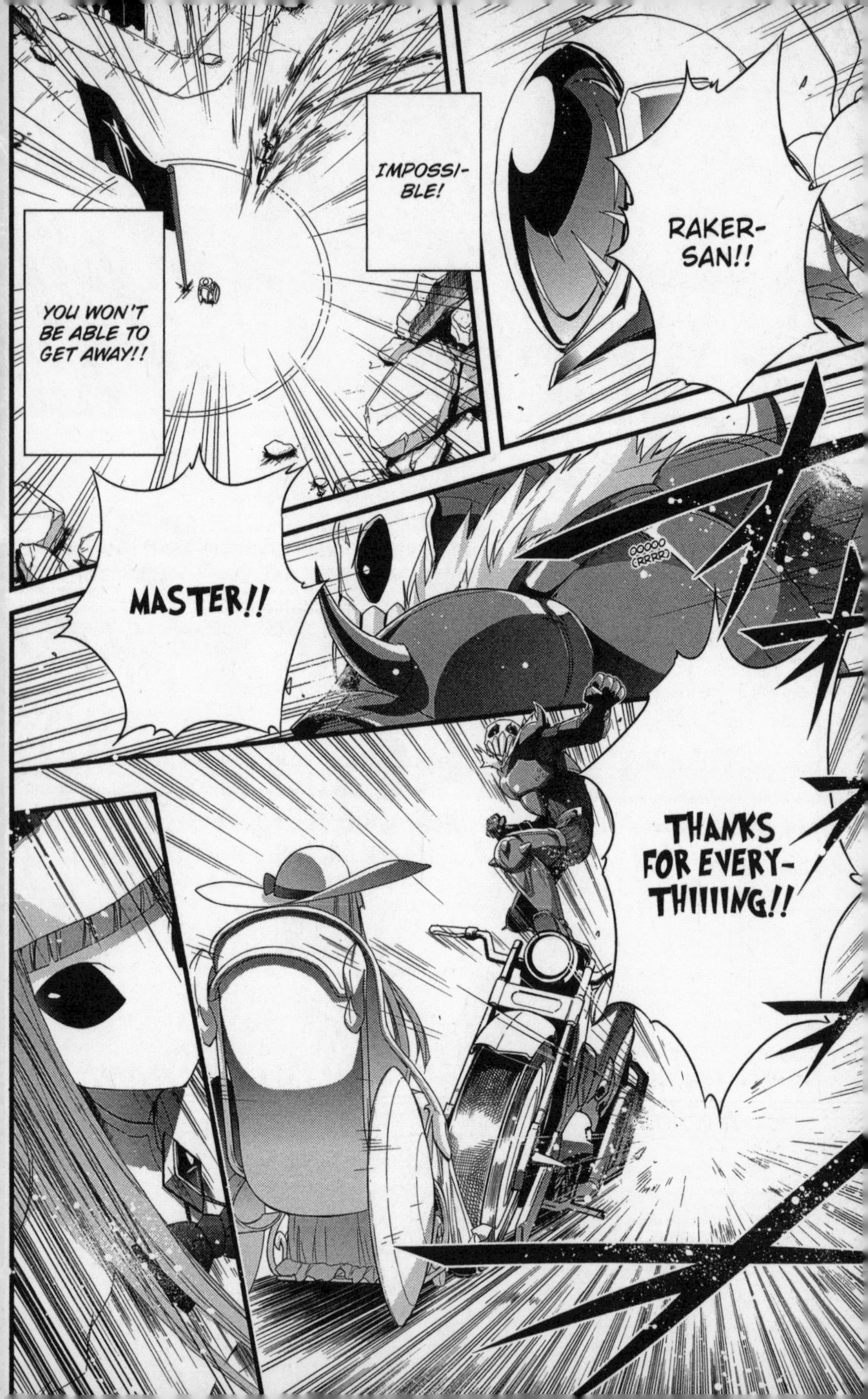
RAKER-SAN!!
IMPOSSIBLE!
YOU WON'T BE ABLE TO GET AWAY!!
(RRRR)
MASTER!!
THANKS FOR EVERYTHIIIIING!!

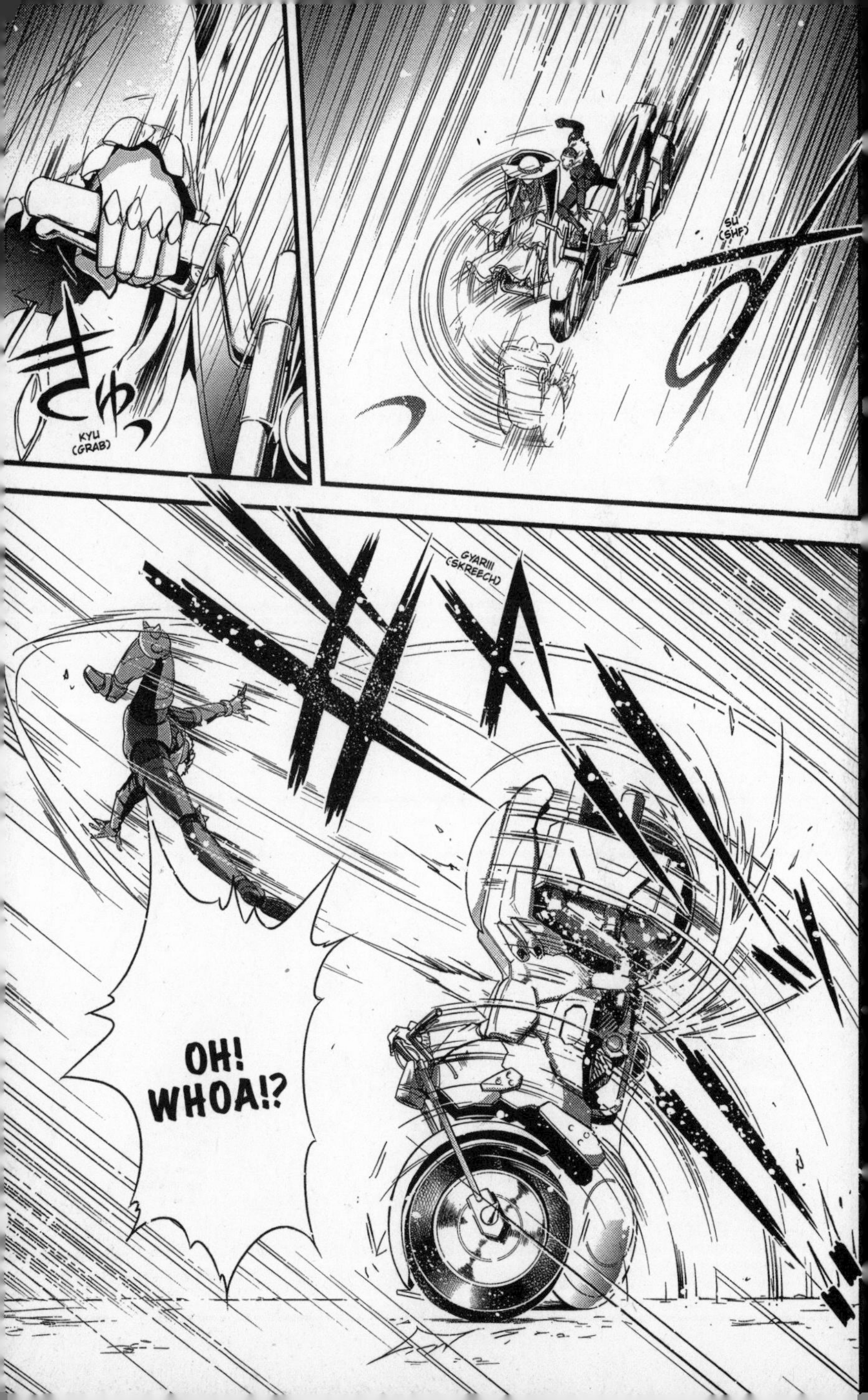
SU
(SHF)
きゅっ
KYU
(GRAB)
GYARIII
(SKREECH)
OH!
WHOA!?

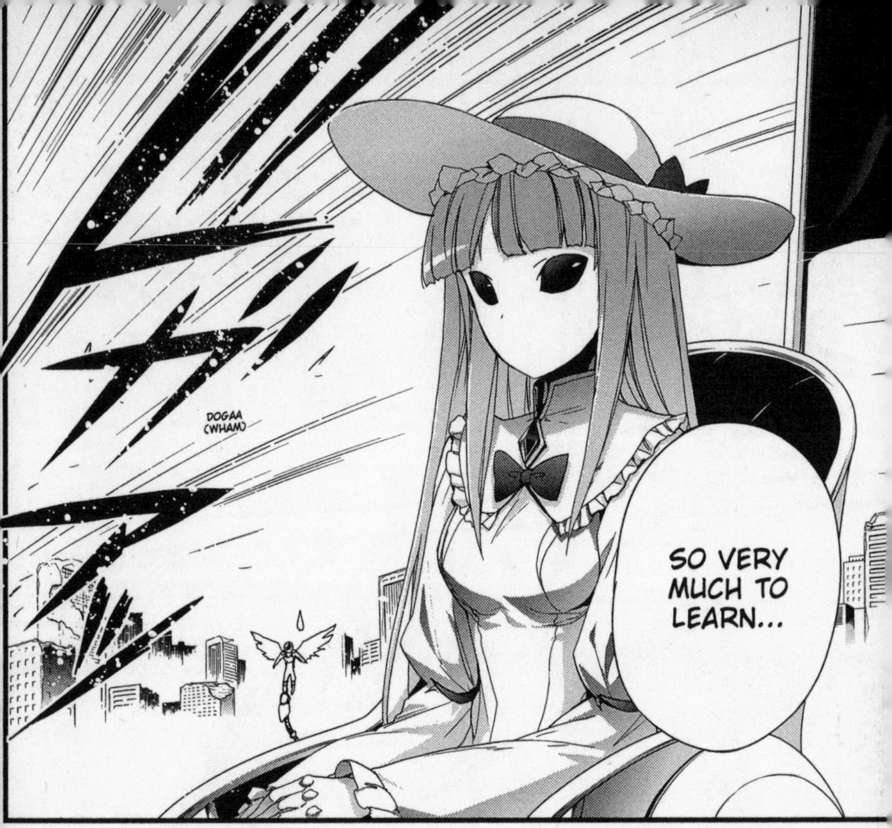
SO VERY MUCH TO LEARN...
DOGAA (WHAM)

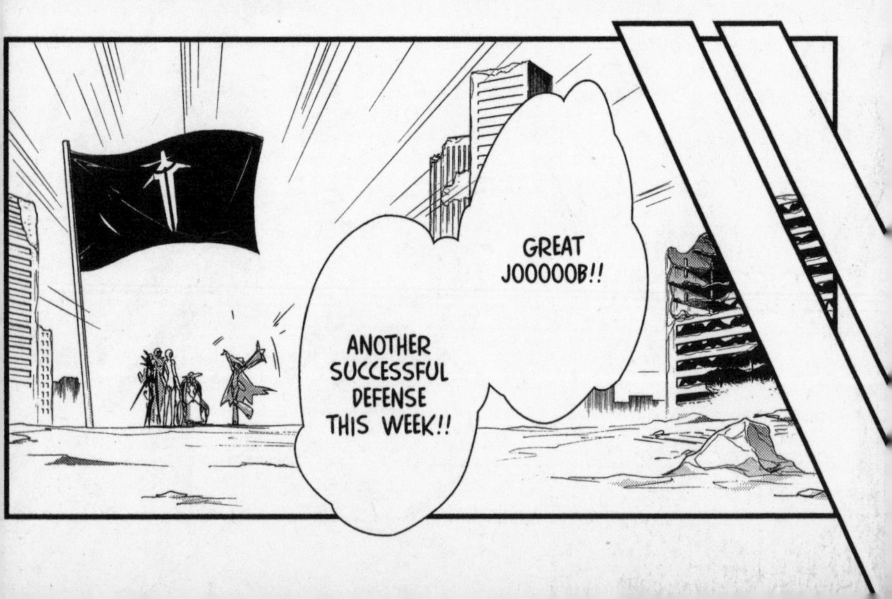
GREAT JOOOOOB!!
ANOTHER SUCCESSFUL DEFENSE THIS WEEK!!

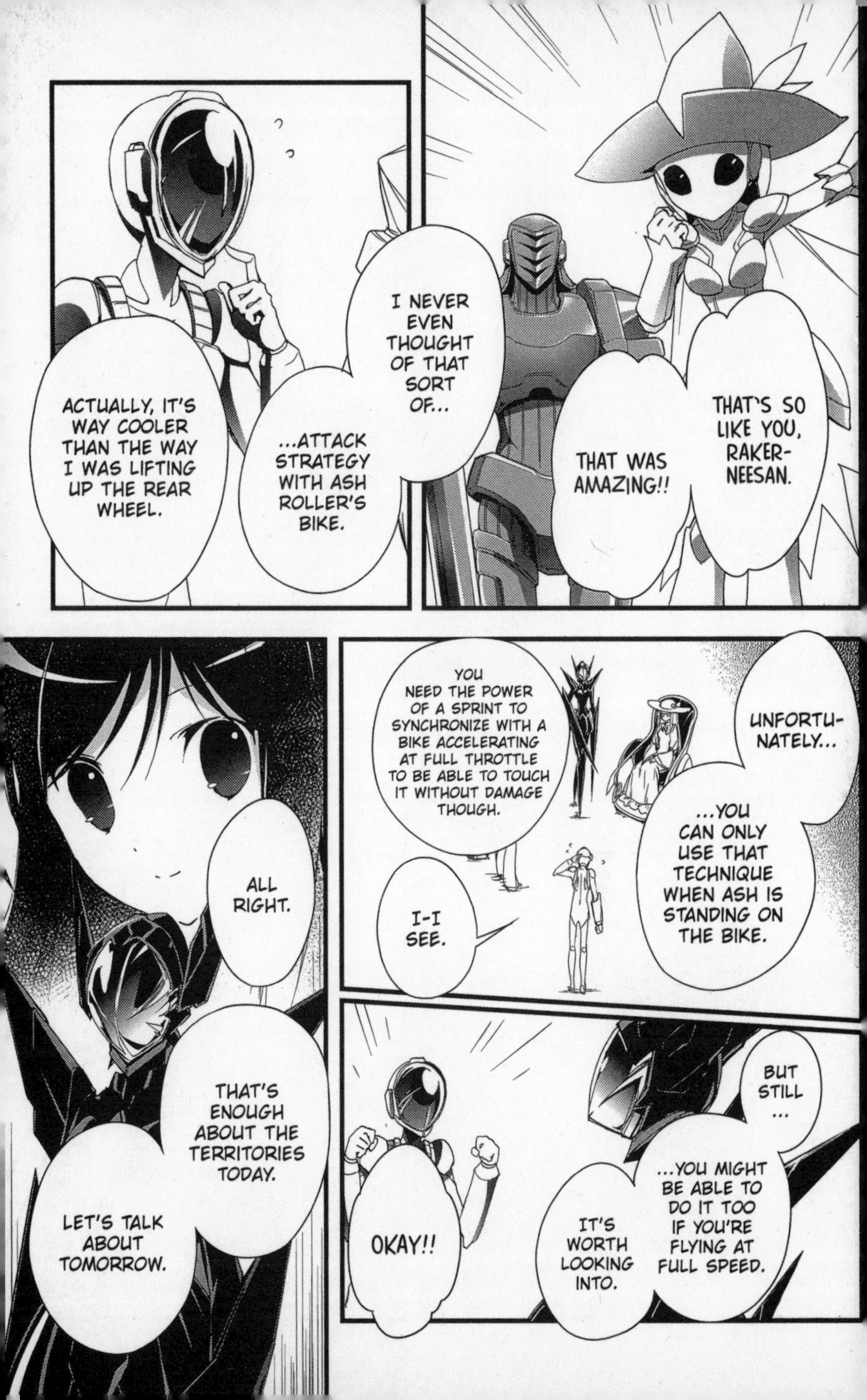
THAT'S SO LIKE YOU, RAKER-NEESAN.
THAT WAS AMAZING!!
I NEVER EVEN THOUGHT OF THAT SORT OF...
...ATTACK STRATEGY WITH ASH ROLLER'S BIKE.
ACTUALLY, IT'S WAY COOLER THAN THE WAY I WAS LIFTING UP THE REAR WHEEL.
UNFORTUNATELY...
...YOU CAN ONLY USE THAT TECHNIQUE WHEN ASH IS STANDING ON THE BIKE.
YOU NEED THE POWER OF A SPRINT TO SYNCHRONIZE WITH A BIKE ACCELERATING AT FULL THROTTLE TO BE ABLE TO TOUCH IT WITHOUT DAMAGE THOUGH.
I-I SEE.
BUT STILL...
...YOU MIGHT BE ABLE TO DO IT TOO IF YOU'RE FLYING AT FULL SPEED.
IT'S WORTH LOOKING INTO.
OKAY!!
ALL RIGHT.
THAT'S ENOUGH ABOUT THE TERRITORIES TODAY.
LET'S TALK ABOUT TOMORROW.

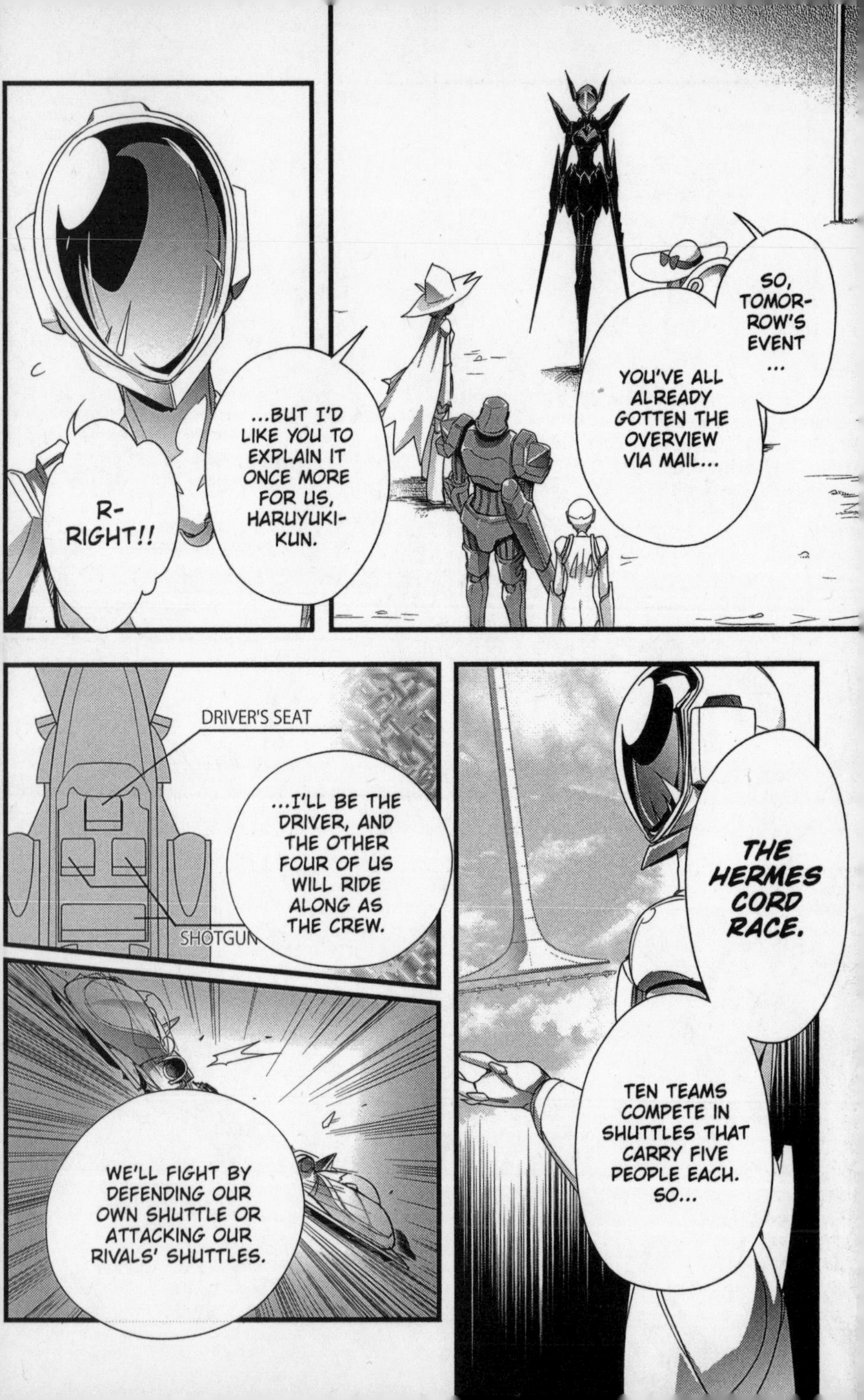
SO, TOMOR-ROW'S EVENT...
YOU'VE ALL ALREADY GOTTEN THE OVERVIEW VIA MAIL...
...BUT I'D LIKE YOU TO EXPLAIN IT ONCE MORE FOR US, HARUYUKI-KUN.
R-RIGHT!!
THE HERMES CORD RACE.
TEN TEAMS COMPETE IN SHUTTLES THAT CARRY FIVE PEOPLE EACH. SO...
DRIVER'S SEAT
SHOTGUN
...I'LL BE THE DRIVER, AND THE OTHER FOUR OF US WILL RIDE ALONG AS THE CREW.
WE'LL FIGHT BY DEFENDING OUR OWN SHUTTLE OR ATTACKING OUR RIVALS' SHUTTLES.

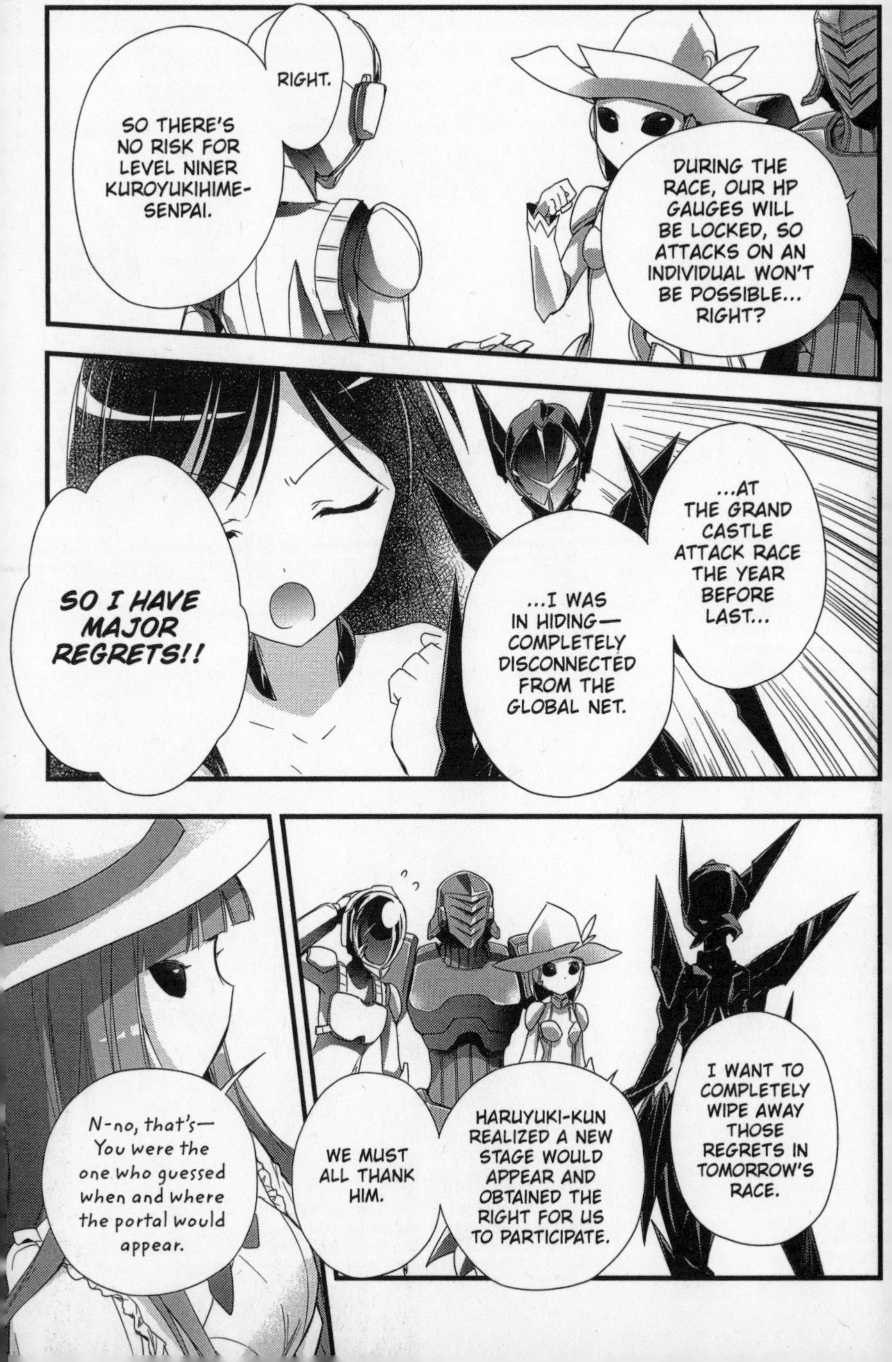
DURING THE RACE, OUR HP GAUGES WILL BE LOCKED, SO ATTACKS ON AN INDIVIDUAL WON'T BE POSSIBLE... RIGHT?
RIGHT.
SO THERE'S NO RISK FOR LEVEL NINER KUROYUKIHIME-SENPAI.
...AT THE GRAND CASTLE ATTACK RACE THE YEAR BEFORE LAST...
...I WAS IN HIDING—COMPLETELY DISCONNECTED FROM THE GLOBAL NET.
SO I HAVE MAJOR REGRETS!!
I WANT TO COMPLETELY WIPE AWAY THOSE REGRETS IN TOMORROW'S RACE.
HARUYUKI-KUN REALIZED A NEW STAGE WOULD APPEAR AND OBTAINED THE RIGHT FOR US TO PARTICIPATE.
WE MUST ALL THANK HIM.
N-no, that's—You were the one who guessed when and where the portal would appear.

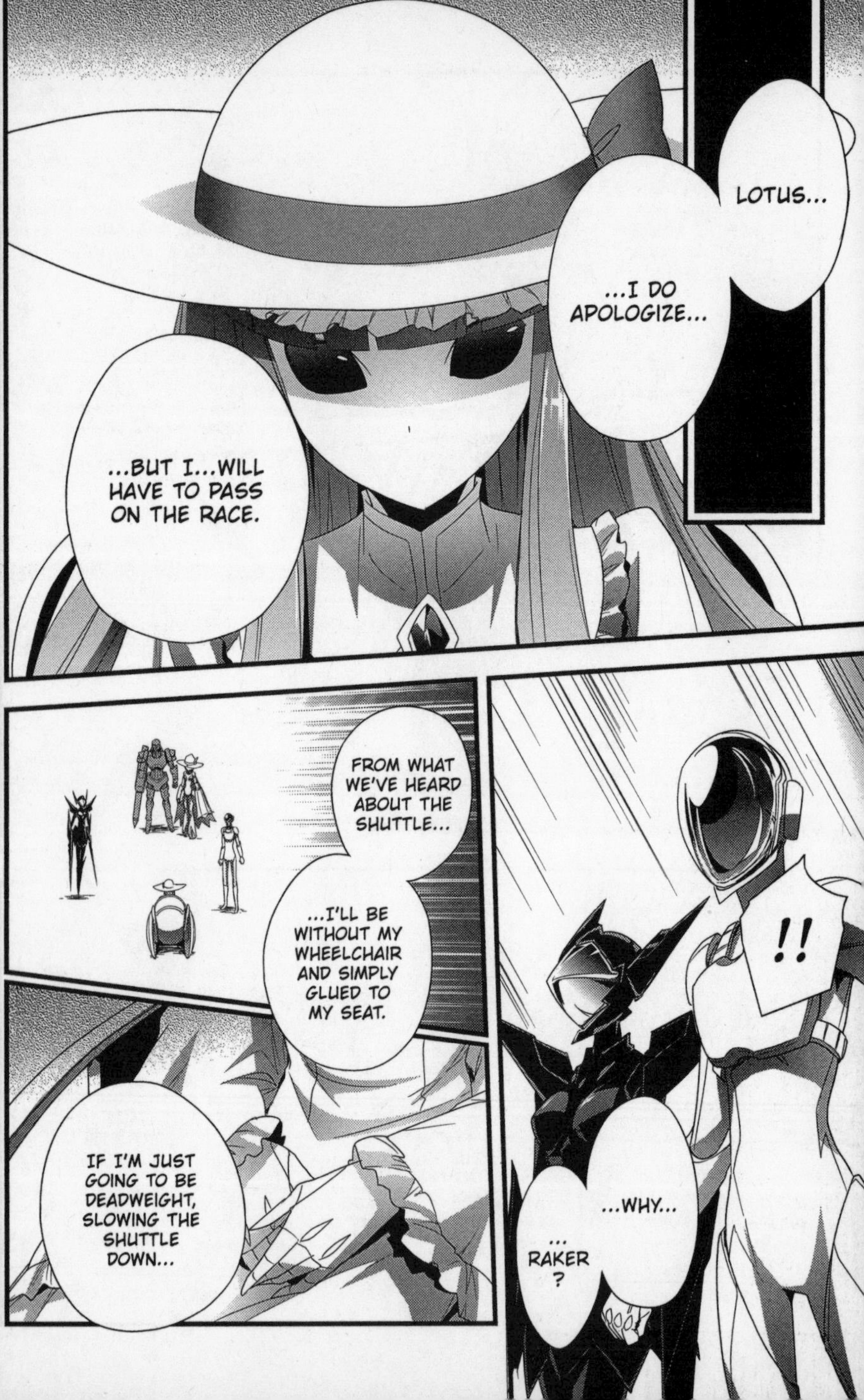
LOTUS...
...I DO APOLOGIZE...
...BUT I...WILL HAVE TO PASS ON THE RACE.
!!
...WHY...
...RAKER?
FROM WHAT WE'VE HEARD ABOUT THE SHUTTLE...
...I'LL BE WITHOUT MY WHEELCHAIR AND SIMPLY GLUED TO MY SEAT.
IF I'M JUST GOING TO BE DEADWEIGHT, SLOWING THE SHUTTLE DOWN...

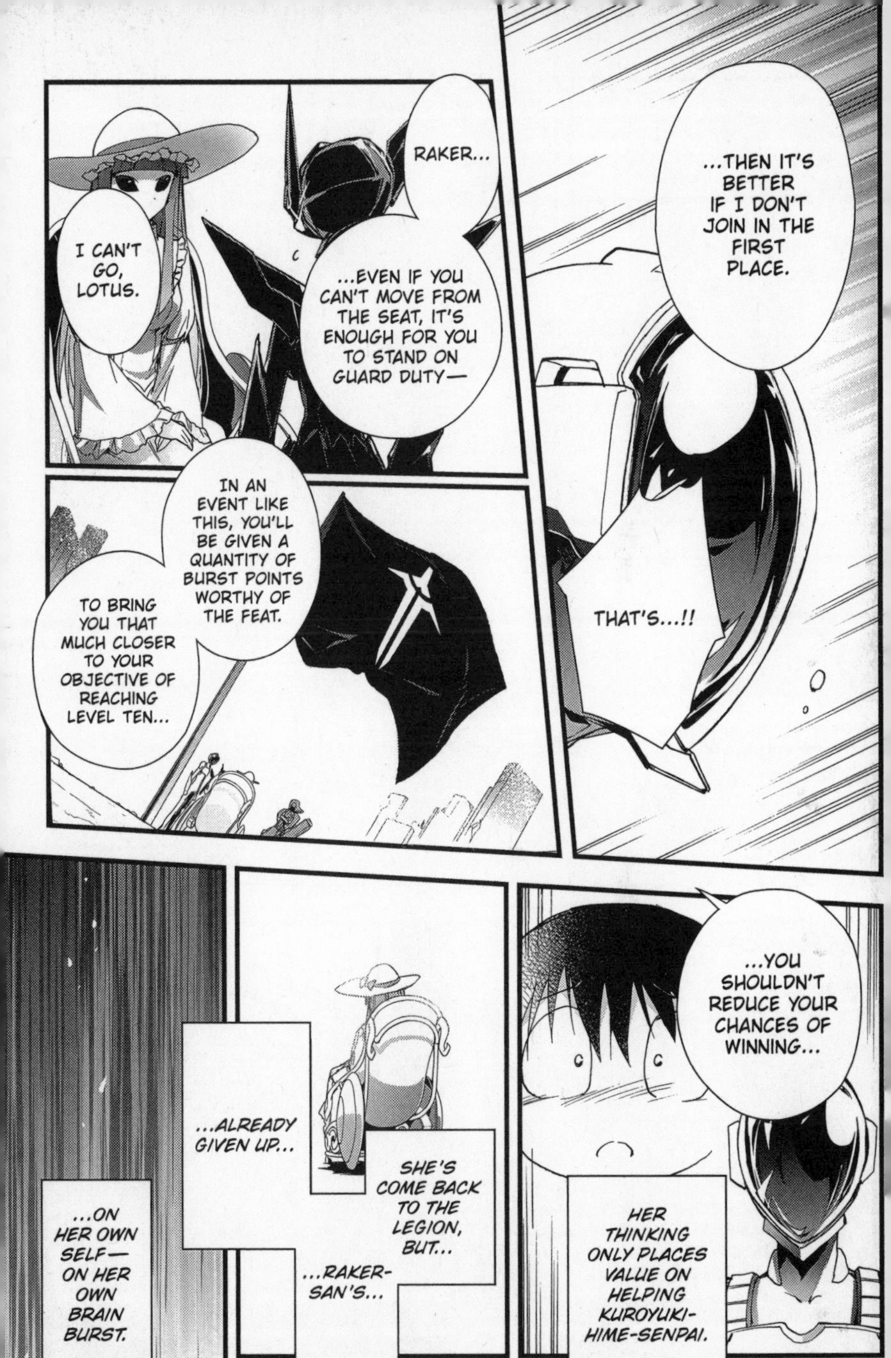
RAKER...
...EVEN IF YOU CAN'T MOVE FROM THE SEAT, IT'S ENOUGH FOR YOU TO STAND ON GUARD DUTY—
I CAN'T GO, LOTUS.
IN AN EVENT LIKE THIS, YOU'LL BE GIVEN A QUANTITY OF BURST POINTS WORTHY OF THE FEAT.
TO BRING YOU THAT MUCH CLOSER TO YOUR OBJECTIVE OF REACHING LEVEL TEN...
...THEN IT'S BETTER IF I DON'T JOIN IN THE FIRST PLACE.
THAT'S...!!
...YOU SHOULDN'T REDUCE YOUR CHANCES OF WINNING...
HER THINKING ONLY PLACES VALUE ON HELPING KUROYUKI-HIME-SENPAI.
SHE'S COME BACK TO THE LEGION, BUT...
...RAKER-SAN'S...
...ALREADY GIVEN UP...
...ON HER OWN SELF—ON HER OWN BRAIN BURST.

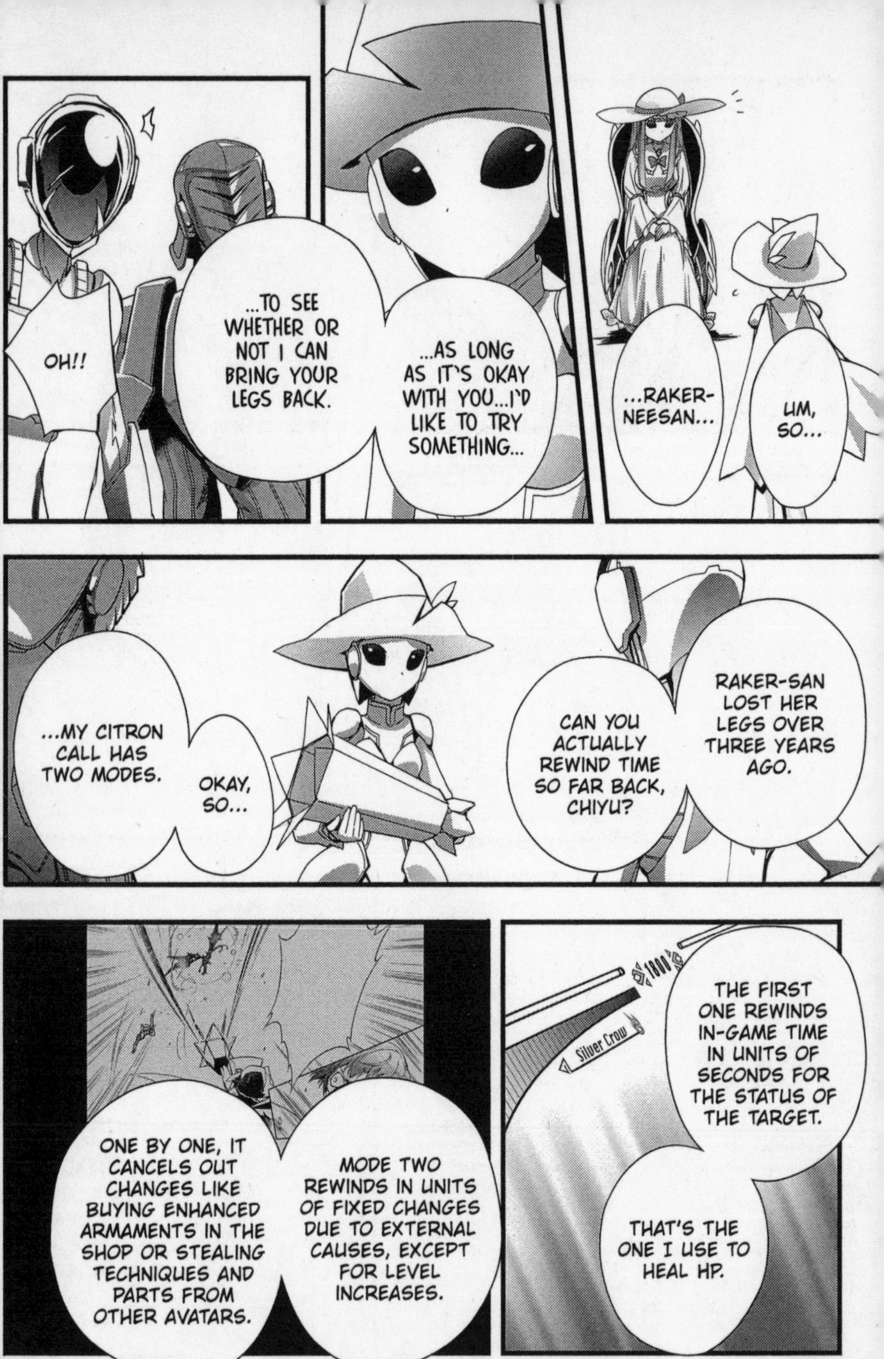
UM, SO...
...RAKER-NEESAN...
...AS LONG AS IT'S OKAY WITH YOU...I'D LIKE TO TRY SOMETHING...
...TO SEE WHETHER OR NOT I CAN BRING YOUR LEGS BACK.
OH!!
RAKER-SAN LOST HER LEGS OVER THREE YEARS AGO.
CAN YOU ACTUALLY REWIND TIME SO FAR BACK, CHIYU?
OKAY, SO...
...MY CITRON CALL HAS TWO MODES.
Silver Crow
THE FIRST ONE REWINDS IN-GAME TIME IN UNITS OF SECONDS FOR THE STATUS OF THE TARGET.
THAT'S THE ONE I USE TO HEAL HP.
MODE TWO REWINDS IN UNITS OF FIXED CHANGES DUE TO EXTERNAL CAUSES, EXCEPT FOR LEVEL INCREASES.
ONE BY ONE, IT CANCELS OUT CHANGES LIKE BUYING ENHANCED ARMAMENTS IN THE SHOP OR STEALING TECHNIQUES AND PARTS FROM OTHER AVATARS.

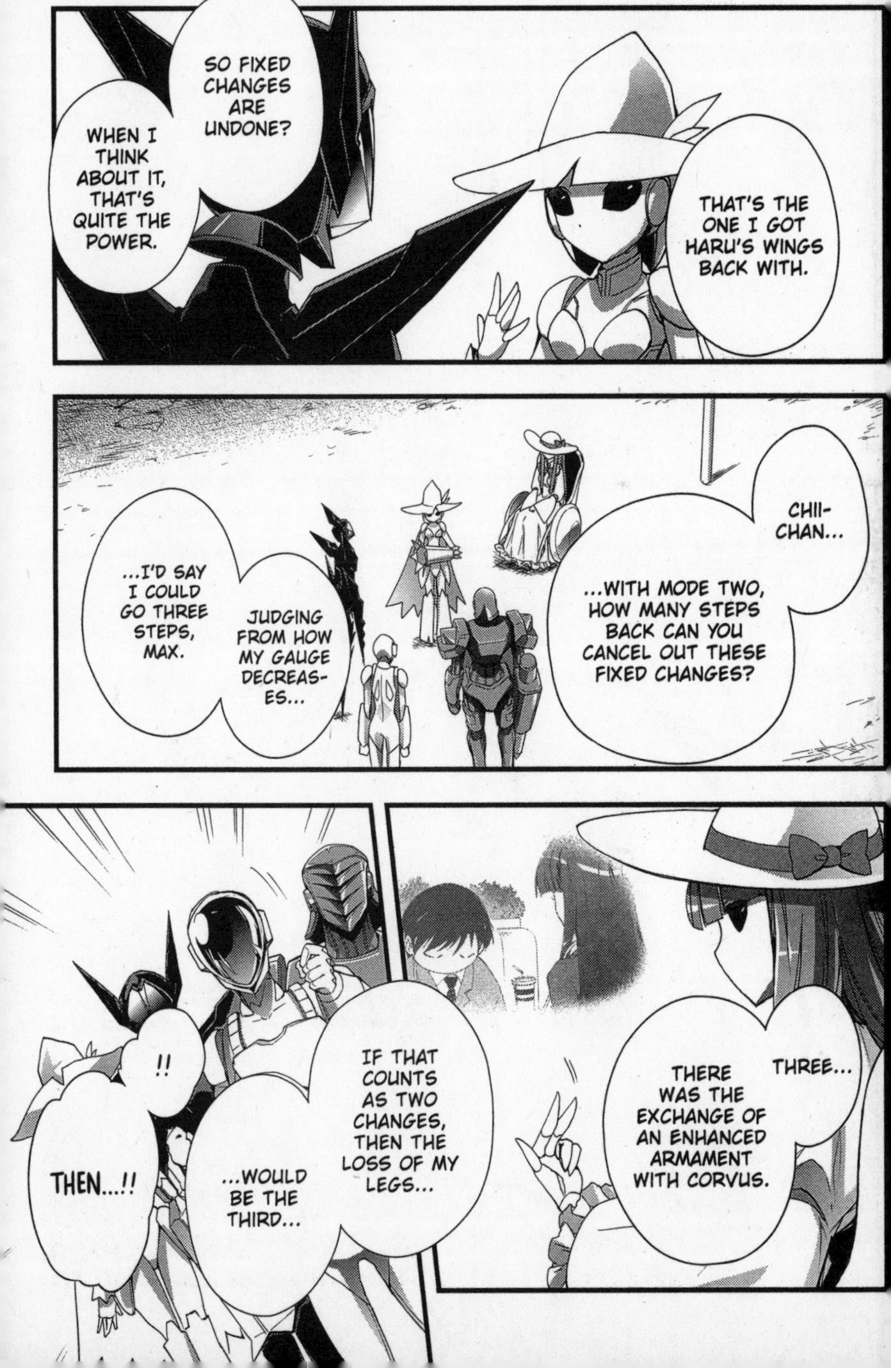
THAT'S THE ONE I GOT HARU'S WINGS BACK WITH.
SO FIXED CHANGES ARE UNDONE?
WHEN I THINK ABOUT IT, THAT'S QUITE THE POWER.
CHII-CHAN...
...WITH MODE TWO, HOW MANY STEPS BACK CAN YOU CANCEL OUT THESE FIXED CHANGES?
JUDGING FROM HOW MY GAUGE DECREAS-ES...
...I'D SAY I COULD GO THREE STEPS, MAX.
THREE...
THERE WAS THE EXCHANGE OF AN ENHANCED ARMAMENT WITH CORVUS.
IF THAT COUNTS AS TWO CHANGES, THEN THE LOSS OF MY LEGS...
...WOULD BE THE THIRD...
!!
THEN...!!

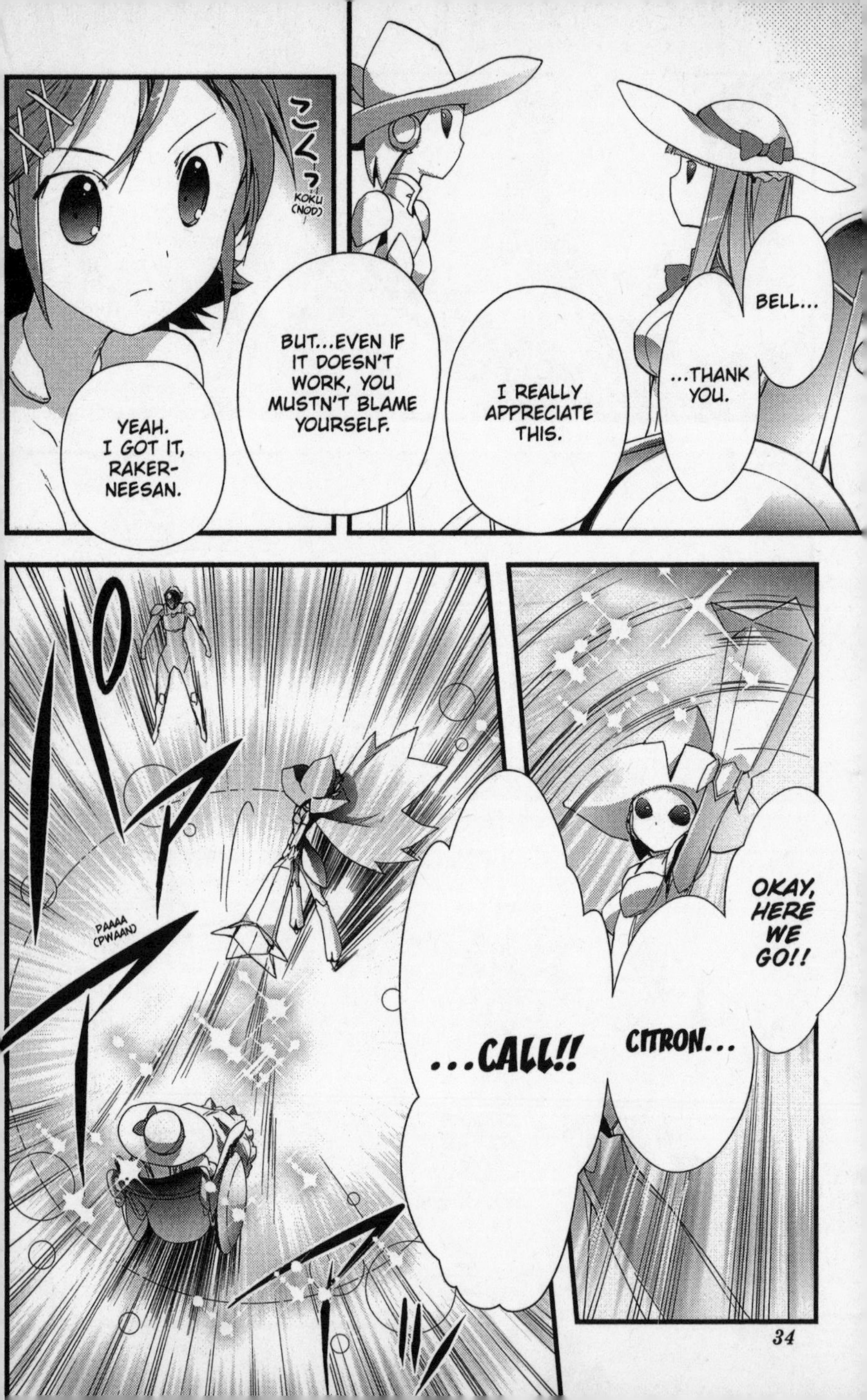
BELL...
...THANK YOU.
I REALLY APPRECIATE THIS.
BUT...EVEN IF IT DOESN'T WORK, YOU MUSTN'T BLAME YOURSELF.
こくっ
KOKU (NOD)
YEAH. I GOT IT, RAKER-NEESAN.
OKAY, HERE WE GO!!
CITRON...
...CALL!!
パァ
PAAAA (PWAAN)

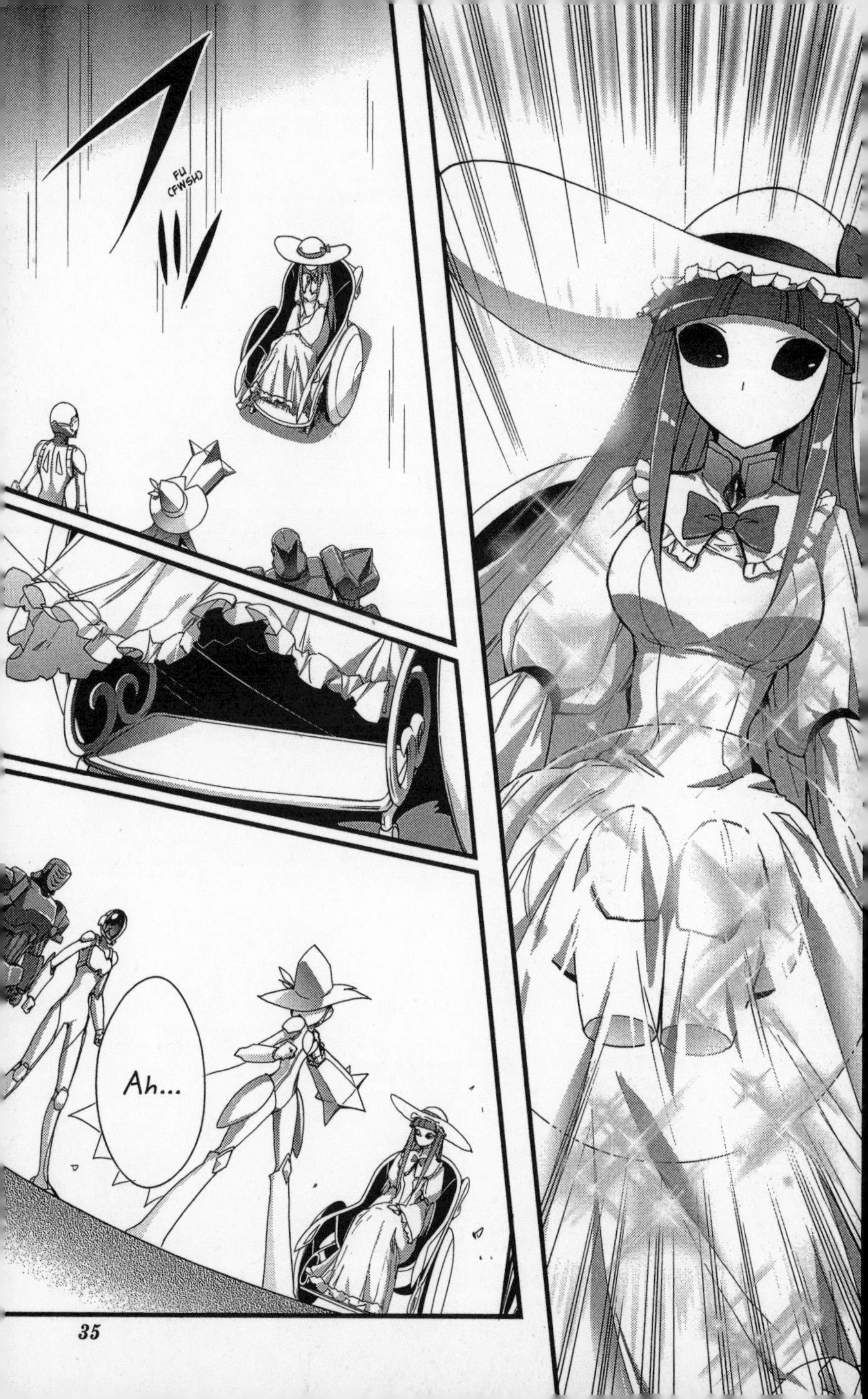
FU (FWSH)
Ah...

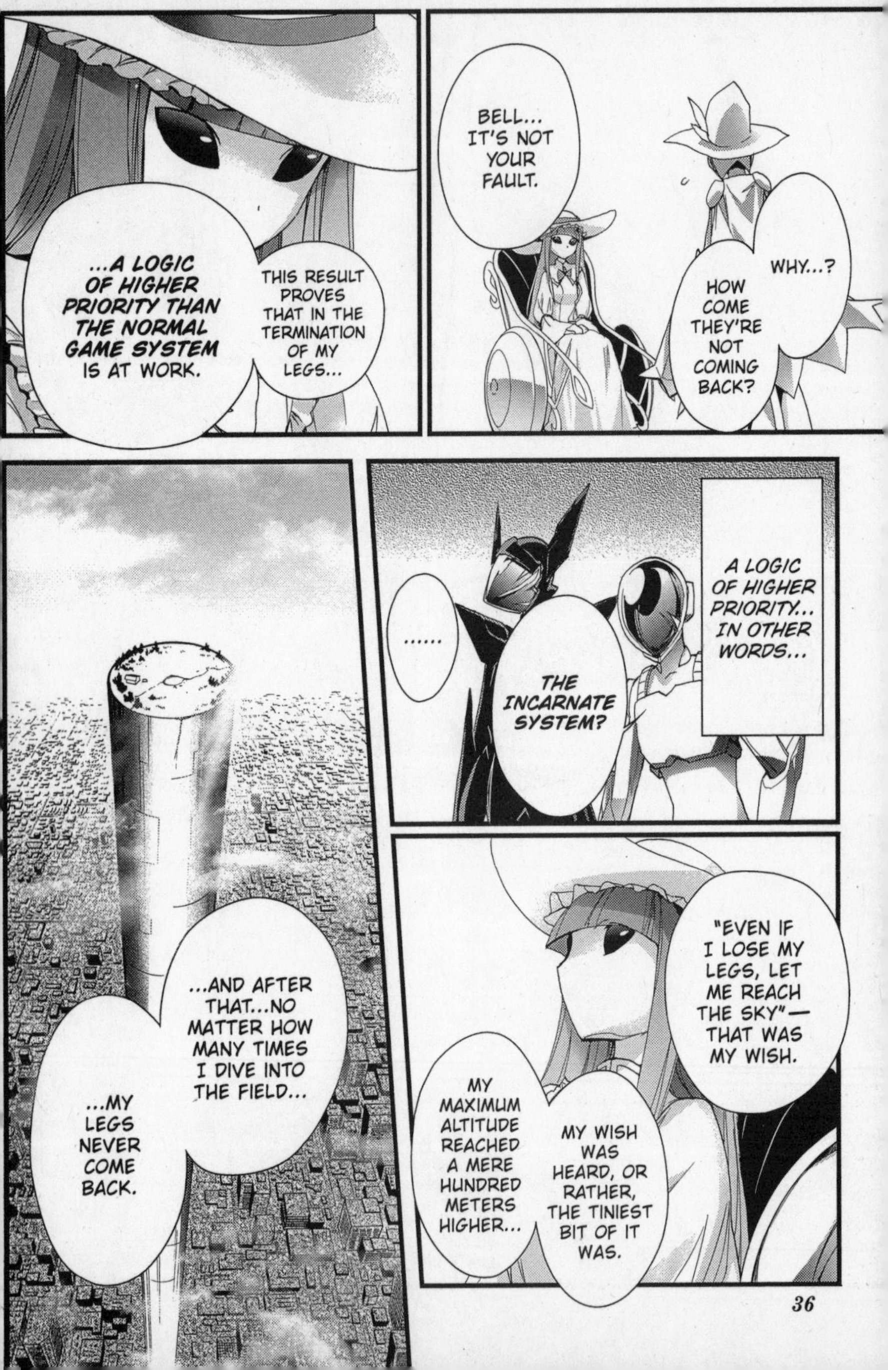

WHY...?
HOW COME THEY'RE NOT COMING BACK?
BELL... IT'S NOT YOUR FAULT.
THIS RESULT PROVES THAT IN THE TERMINATION OF MY LEGS...
...A LOGIC OF HIGHER PRIORITY THAN THE NORMAL GAME SYSTEM IS AT WORK.
A LOGIC OF HIGHER PRIORITY... IN OTHER WORDS...
THE INCARNATE SYSTEM?
......
"EVEN IF I LOSE MY LEGS, LET ME REACH THE SKY"—THAT WAS MY WISH.
MY WISH WAS HEARD, OR RATHER, THE TINIEST BIT OF IT WAS.
MY MAXIMUM ALTITUDE REACHED A MERE HUNDRED METERS HIGHER...
...AND AFTER THAT...NO MATTER HOW MANY TIMES I DIVE INTO THE FIELD...
...MY LEGS NEVER COME BACK.

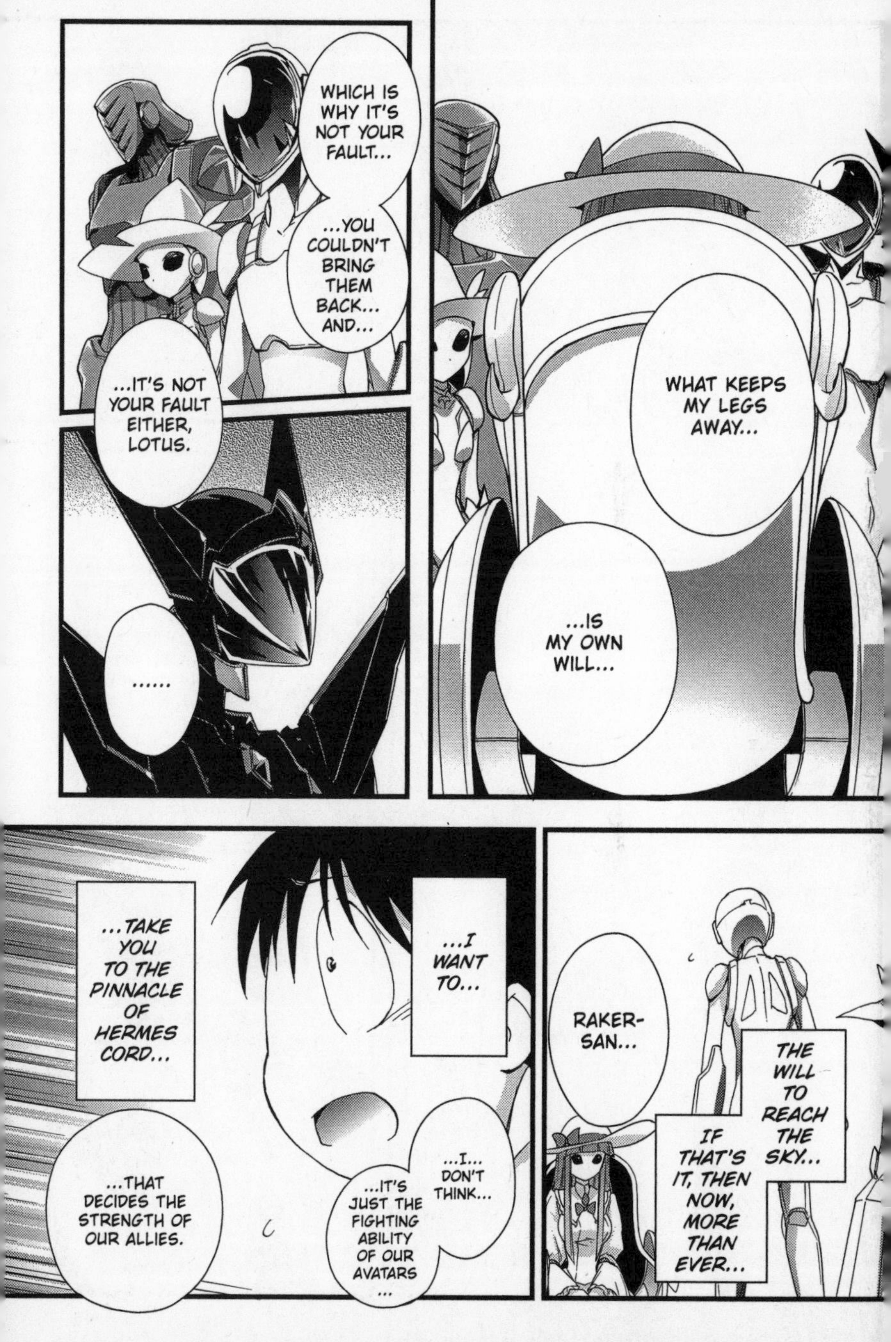
WHAT KEEPS MY LEGS AWAY...
...IS MY OWN WILL...
WHICH IS WHY IT'S NOT YOUR FAULT...
...YOU COULDN'T BRING THEM BACK... AND...
...IT'S NOT YOUR FAULT EITHER, LOTUS.
......
THE WILL TO REACH THE SKY...
IF THAT'S IT, THEN NOW, MORE THAN EVER...
RAKER-SAN...
...I WANT TO...
...TAKE YOU TO THE PINNACLE OF HERMES CORD...
...I... DON'T THINK...
...IT'S JUST THE FIGHTING ABILITY OF OUR AVATARS...
...THAT DECIDES THE STRENGTH OF OUR ALLIES.

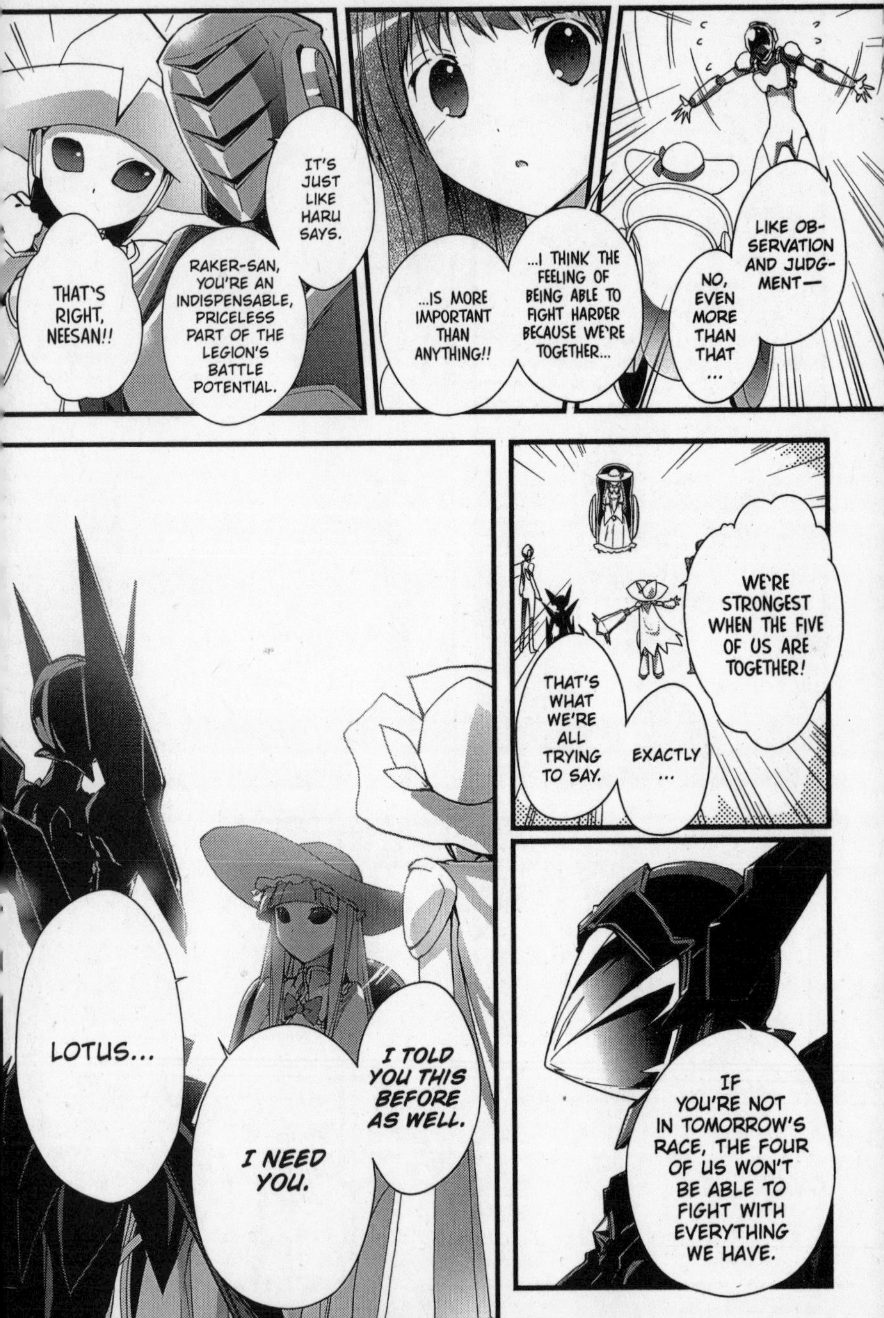
LIKE OB-SERVATION AND JUDG-MENT—
NO, EVEN MORE THAN THAT ...
...I THINK THE FEELING OF BEING ABLE TO FIGHT HARDER BECAUSE WE'RE TOGETHER...
...IS MORE IMPORTANT THAN ANYTHING!!
IT'S JUST LIKE HARU SAYS.
RAKER-SAN, YOU'RE AN INDISPENSABLE, PRICELESS PART OF THE LEGION'S BATTLE POTENTIAL.
THAT'S RIGHT, NEESAN!!
WE'RE STRONGEST WHEN THE FIVE OF US ARE TOGETHER!
EXACTLY ...
THAT'S WHAT WE'RE ALL TRYING TO SAY.
IF YOU'RE NOT IN TOMORROW'S RACE, THE FOUR OF US WON'T BE ABLE TO FIGHT WITH EVERYTHING WE HAVE.
I TOLD YOU THIS BEFORE AS WELL.
I NEED YOU.
LOTUS...

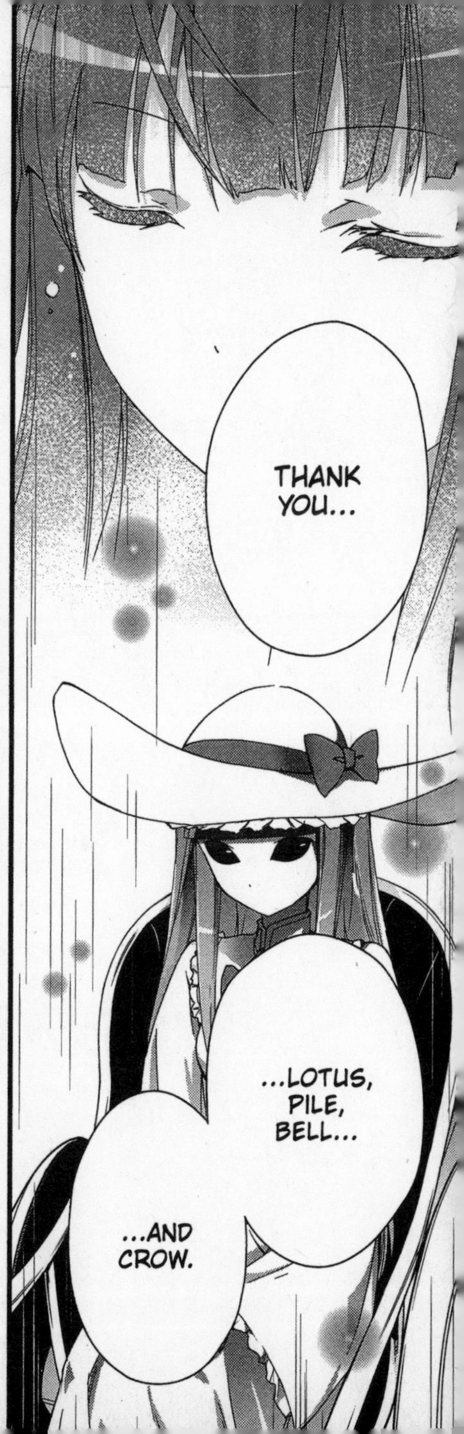
THANK YOU...
...LOTUS, PILE, BELL...
...AND CROW.

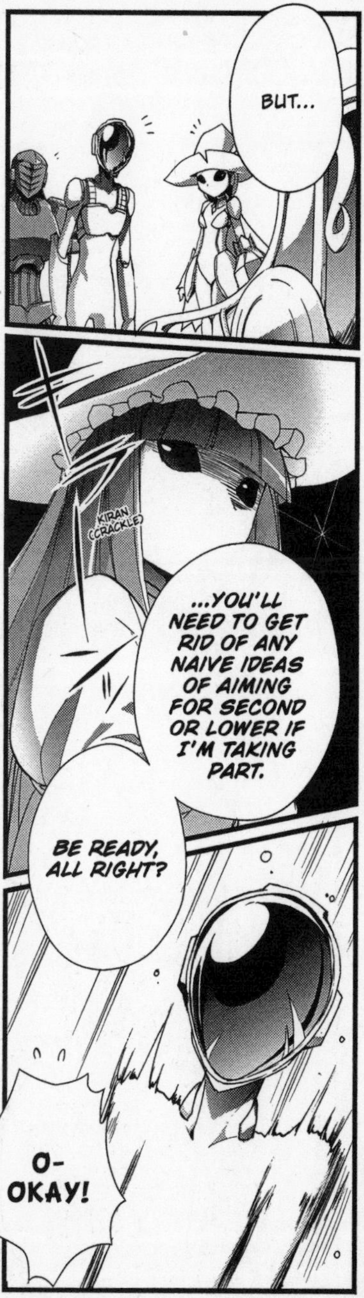
BUT...
KIRAN (CRACKLE)
...YOU'LL NEED TO GET RID OF ANY NAIVE IDEAS OF AIMING FOR SECOND OR LOWER IF I'M TAKING PART.
BE READY, ALL RIGHT?
O-OKAY!

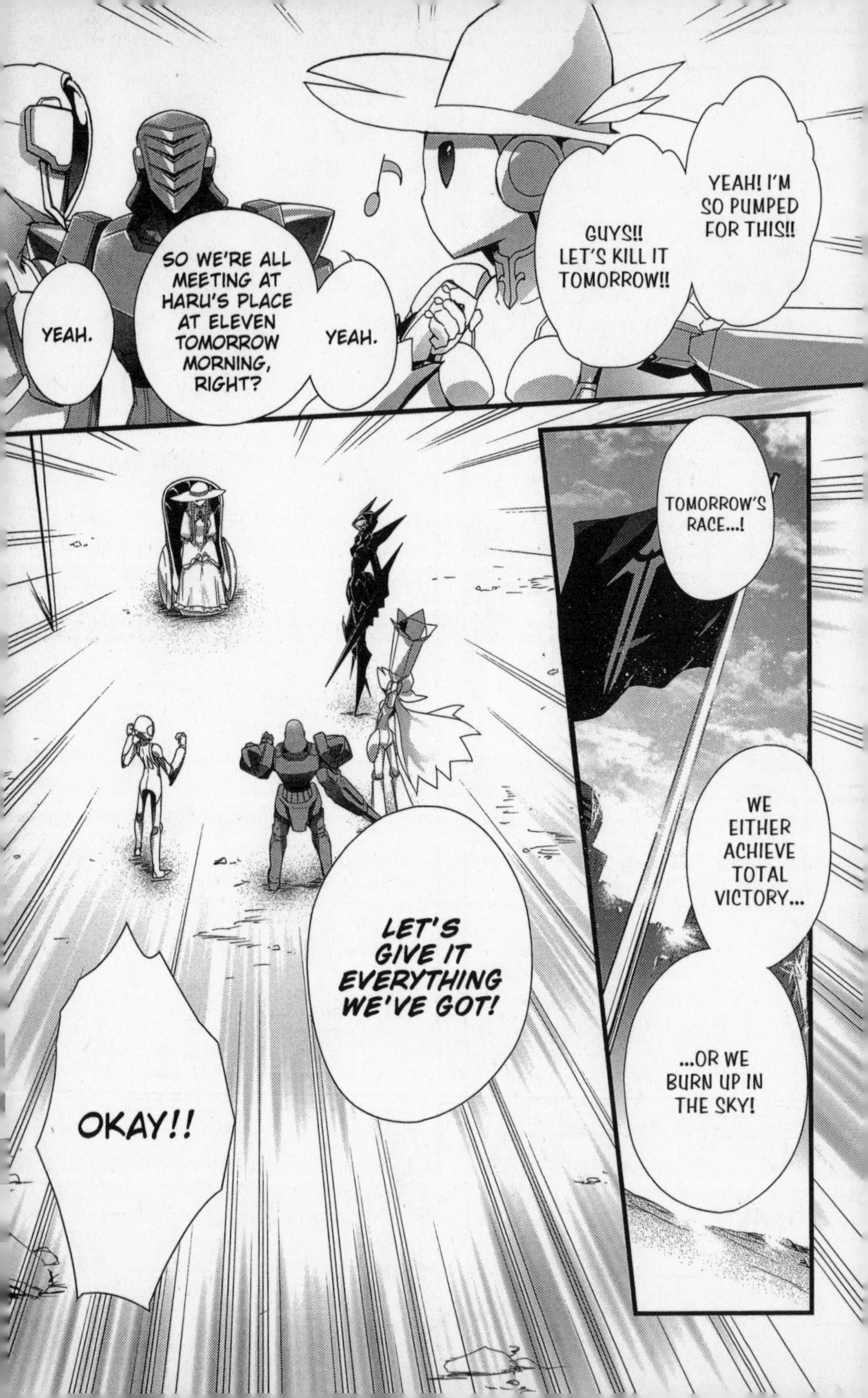
YEAH! I'M SO PUMPED FOR THIS!!
GUYS!! LET'S KILL IT TOMORROW!!
YEAH.
SO WE'RE ALL MEETING AT HARU'S PLACE AT ELEVEN TOMORROW MORNING, RIGHT?
YEAH.
TOMORROW'S RACE...!
WE EITHER ACHIEVE TOTAL VICTORY...
...OR WE BURN UP IN THE SKY!
LET'S GIVE IT EVERYTHING WE'VE GOT!
OKAY!!

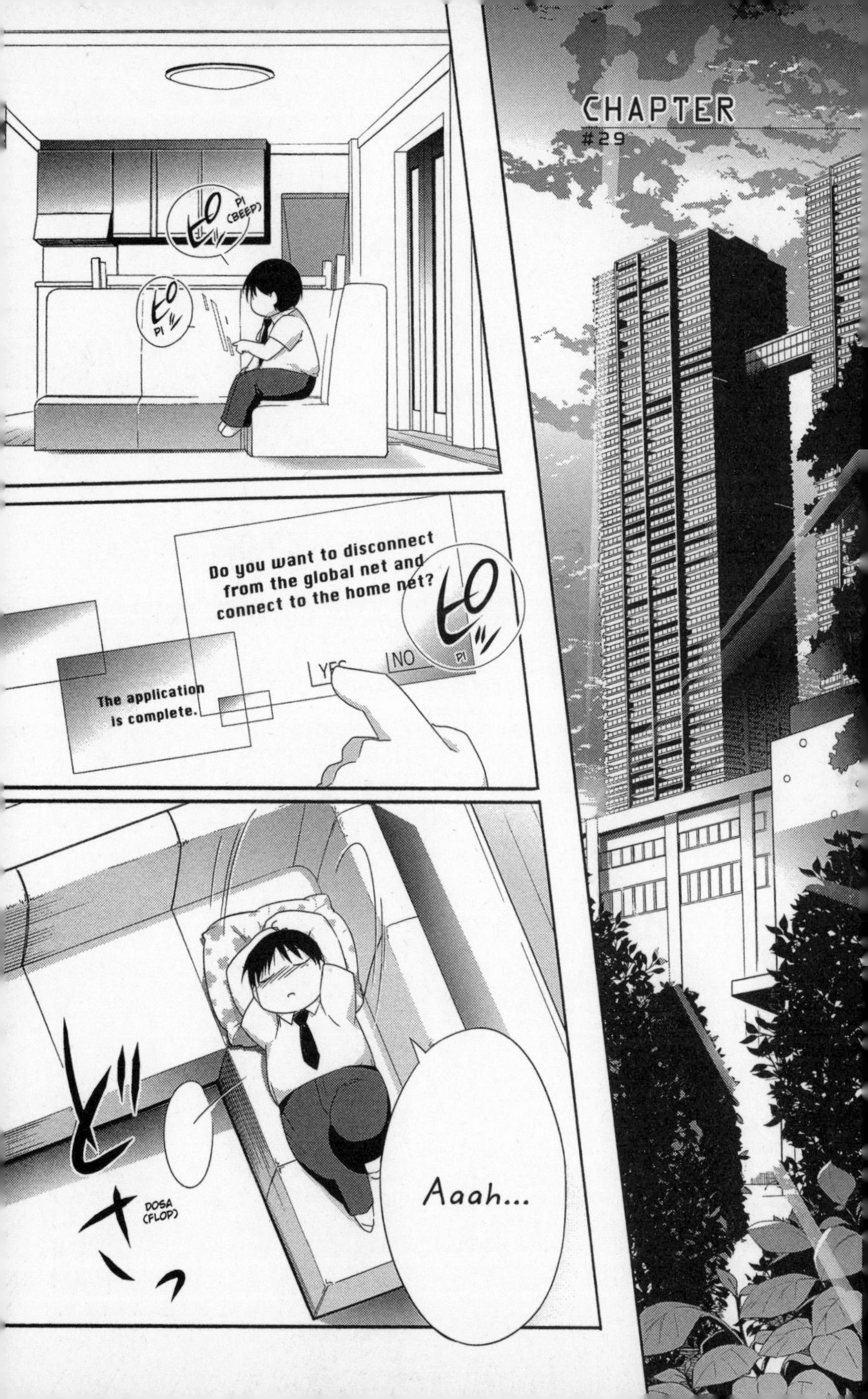
CHAPTER
#29
ピッ
PI (BEEP)
ピッ
PI
Do you want to disconnect from the global net and connect to the home net?
The application is complete.
NO
ピッ
PI
どさっ
DOSA (FLOP)
Aaah...

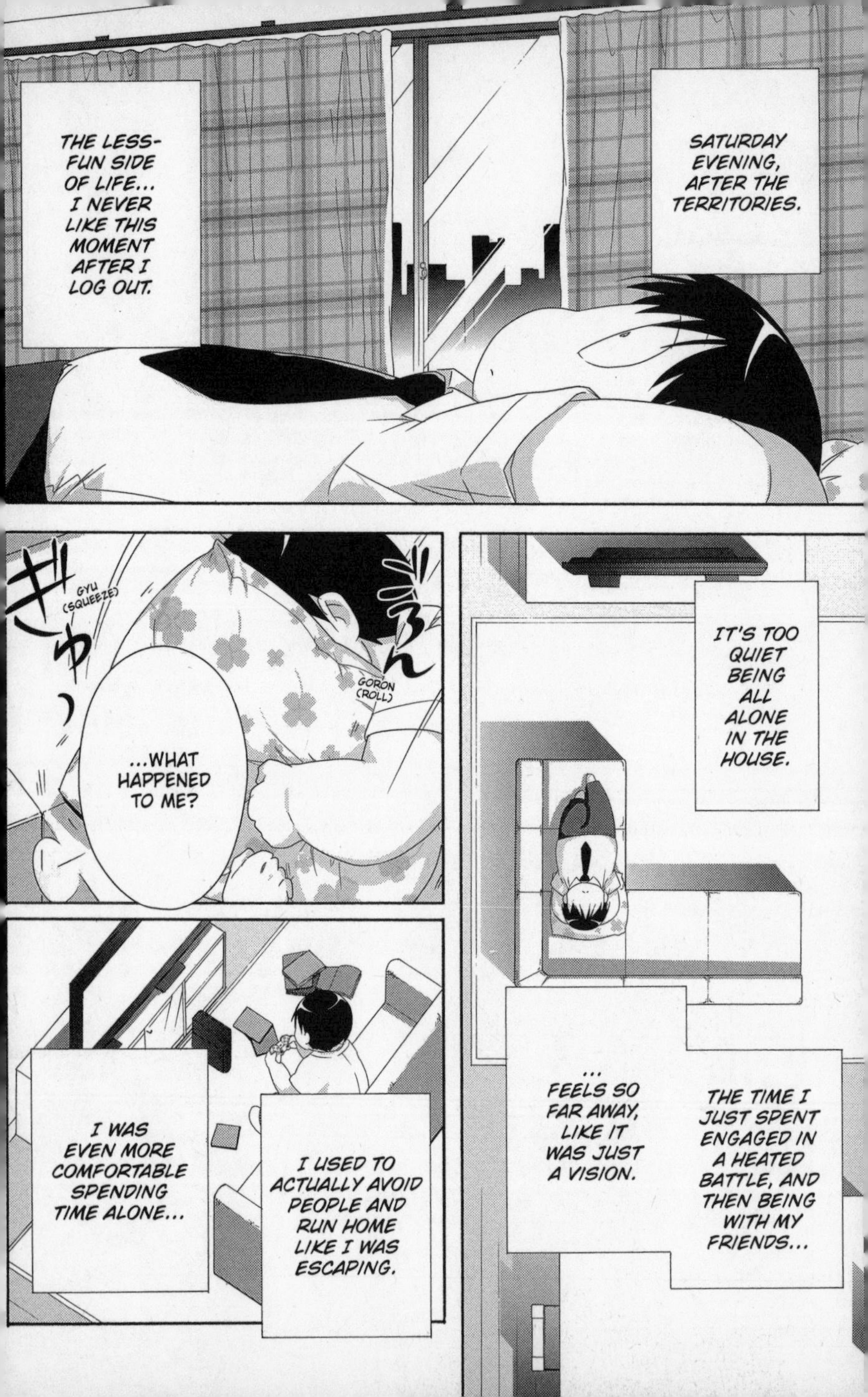
SATURDAY EVENING, AFTER THE TERRITORIES.
THE LESS-FUN SIDE OF LIFE... I NEVER LIKE THIS MOMENT AFTER I LOG OUT.
IT'S TOO QUIET BEING ALL ALONE IN THE HOUSE.
THE TIME I JUST SPENT ENGAGED IN A HEATED BATTLE, AND THEN BEING WITH MY FRIENDS...
...FEELS SO FAR AWAY, LIKE IT WAS JUST A VISION.
GORON (ROLL)
GYU (SQUEEZE)
...WHAT HAPPENED TO ME?
I USED TO ACTUALLY AVOID PEOPLE AND RUN HOME LIKE I WAS ESCAPING.
I WAS EVEN MORE COMFORTABLE SPENDING TIME ALONE...

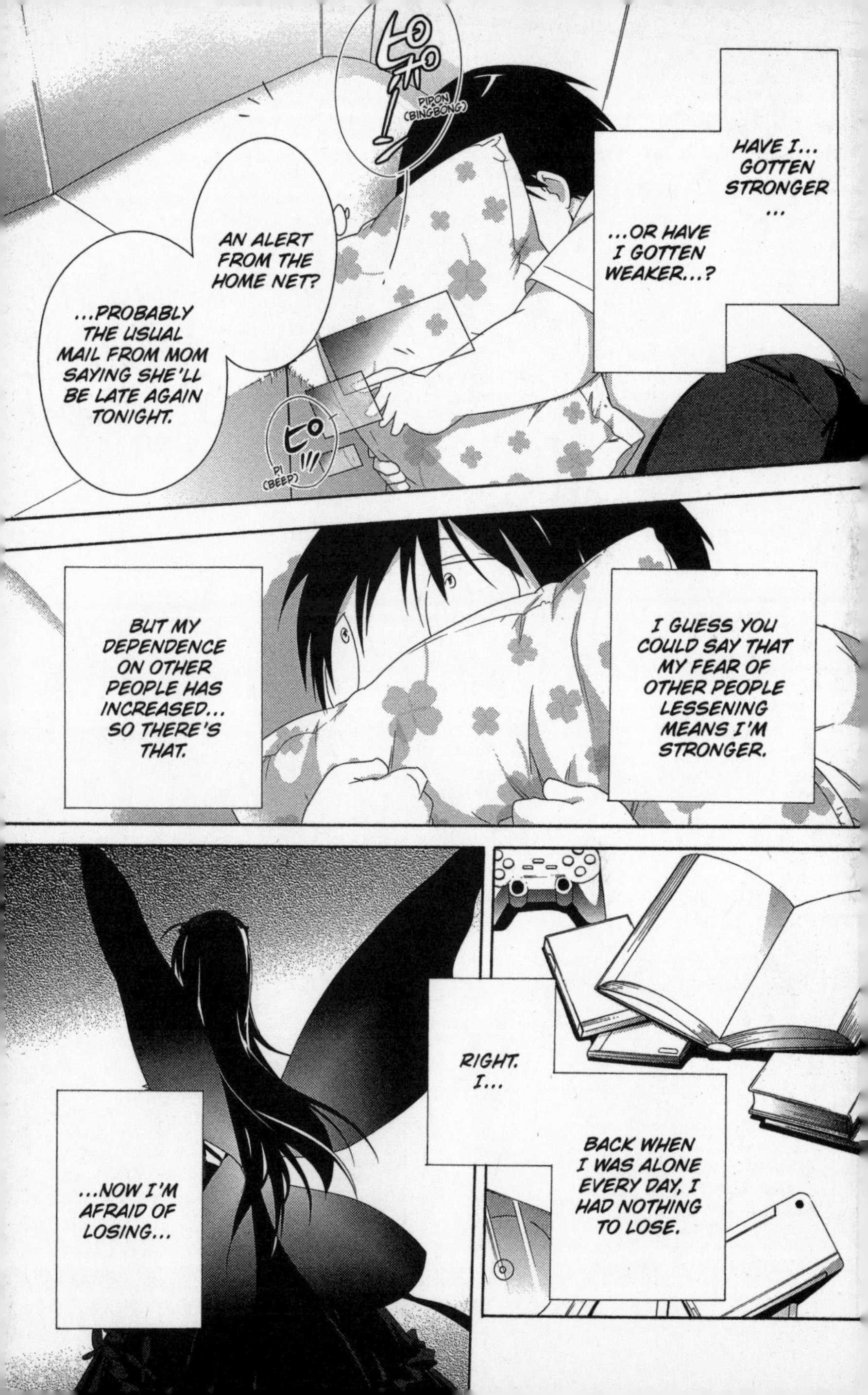
HAVE I... GOTTEN STRONGER ...
...OR HAVE I GOTTEN WEAKER...?
ピポン
PIPON (BINGBONG)
AN ALERT FROM THE HOME NET?
...PROBABLY THE USUAL MAIL FROM MOM SAYING SHE'LL BE LATE AGAIN TONIGHT.
ピッ
PI (BEEP)
I GUESS YOU COULD SAY THAT MY FEAR OF OTHER PEOPLE LESSENING MEANS I'M STRONGER.
BUT MY DEPENDENCE ON OTHER PEOPLE HAS INCREASED... SO THERE'S THAT.
RIGHT. I...
BACK WHEN I WAS ALONE EVERY DAY, I HAD NOTHING TO LOSE.
...NOW I'M AFRAID OF LOSING...

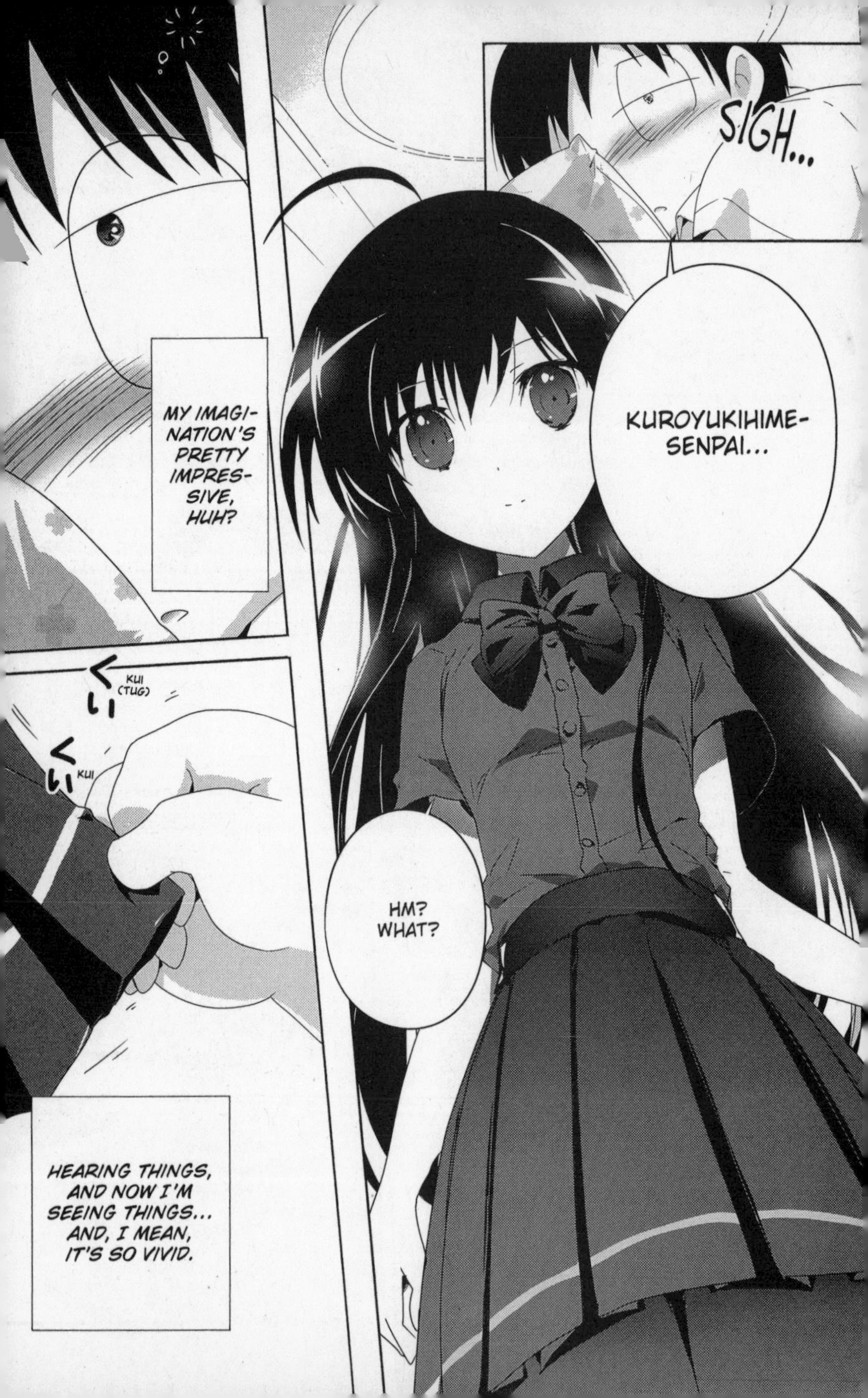
SIGH...
KUROYUKIHIME-SENPAI...
MY IMAGINATION'S PRETTY IMPRESSIVE, HUH?
くい KUI (TUG)
くい KUI
HM? WHAT?
HEARING THINGS, AND NOW I'M SEEING THINGS... AND, I MEAN, IT'S SO VIVID.

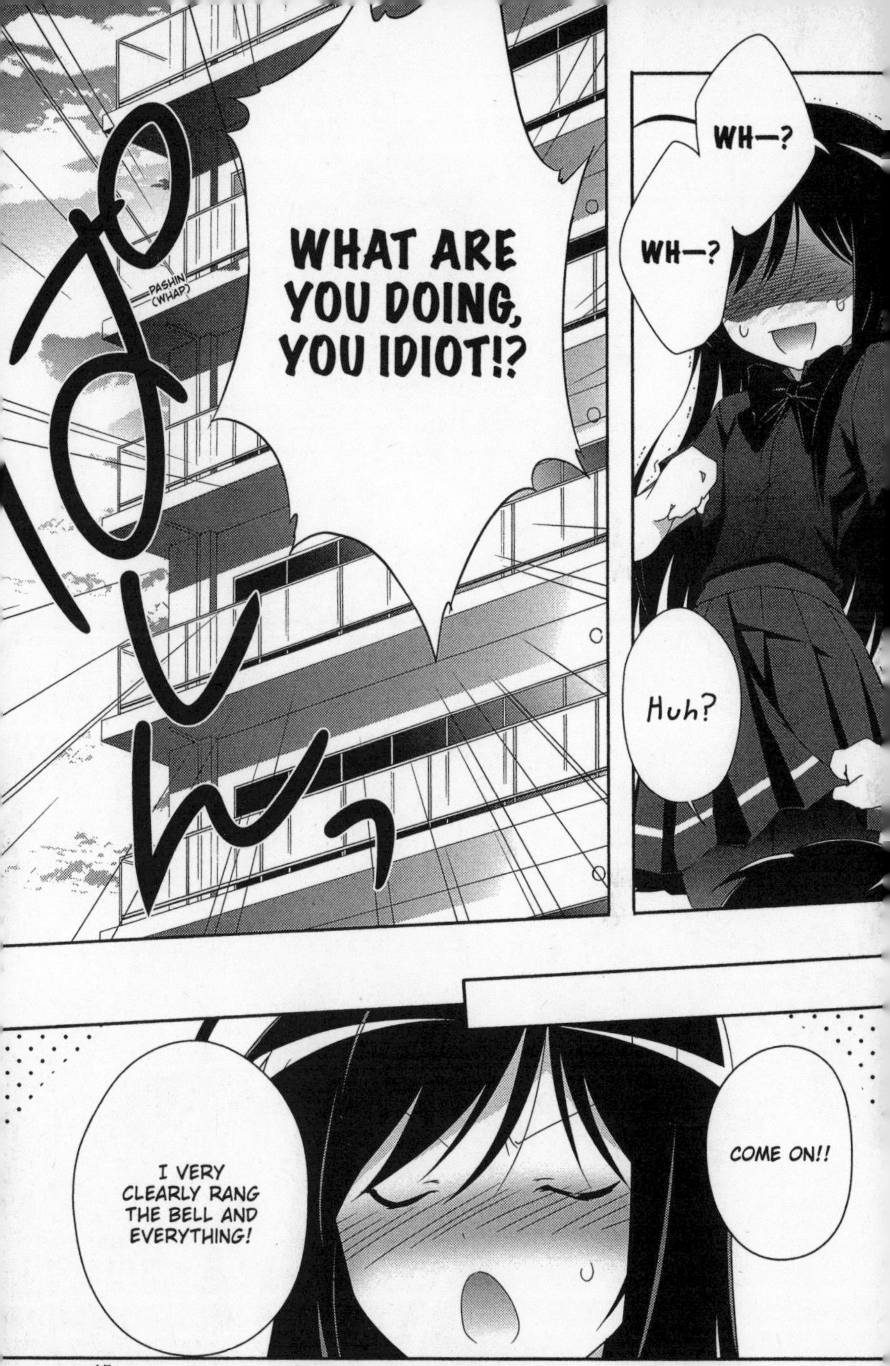
WH—?
WH—?
Huh?
WHAT ARE YOU DOING, YOU IDIOT!?
PASHIN (WHAP)
COME ON!!
I VERY CLEARLY RANG THE BELL AND EVERYTHING!

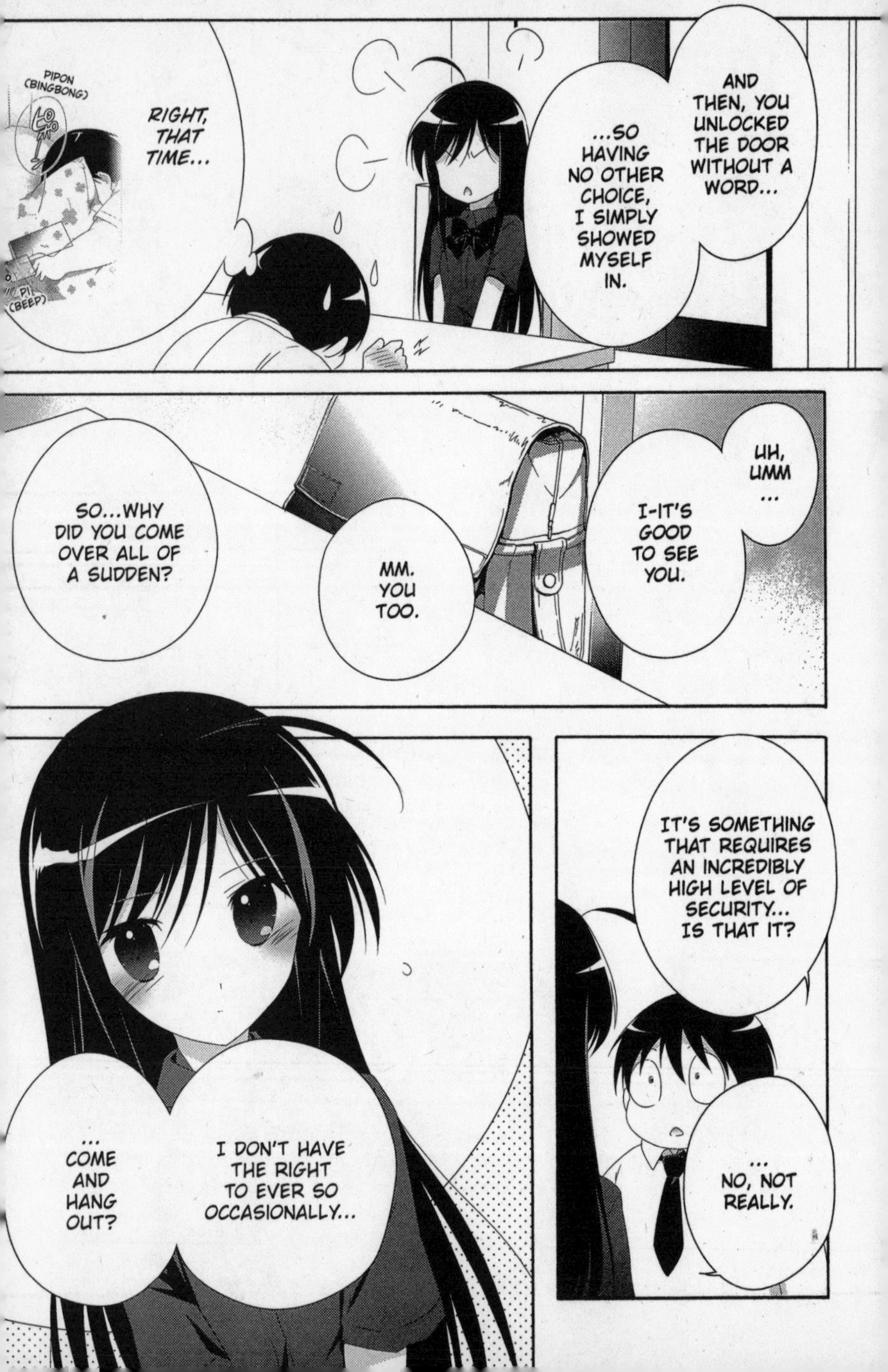
AND THEN, YOU UNLOCKED THE DOOR WITHOUT A WORD...
...SO HAVING NO OTHER CHOICE, I SIMPLY SHOWED MYSELF IN.
RIGHT, THAT TIME...
PIPON (BINGBONG)
PI (BEEP)
UH, UMM ...
I-IT'S GOOD TO SEE YOU.
MM. YOU TOO.
SO...WHY DID YOU COME OVER ALL OF A SUDDEN?
IT'S SOMETHING THAT REQUIRES AN INCREDIBLY HIGH LEVEL OF SECURITY... IS THAT IT?
... NO, NOT REALLY.
I DON'T HAVE THE RIGHT TO EVER SO OCCASIONALLY...
... COME AND HANG OUT?

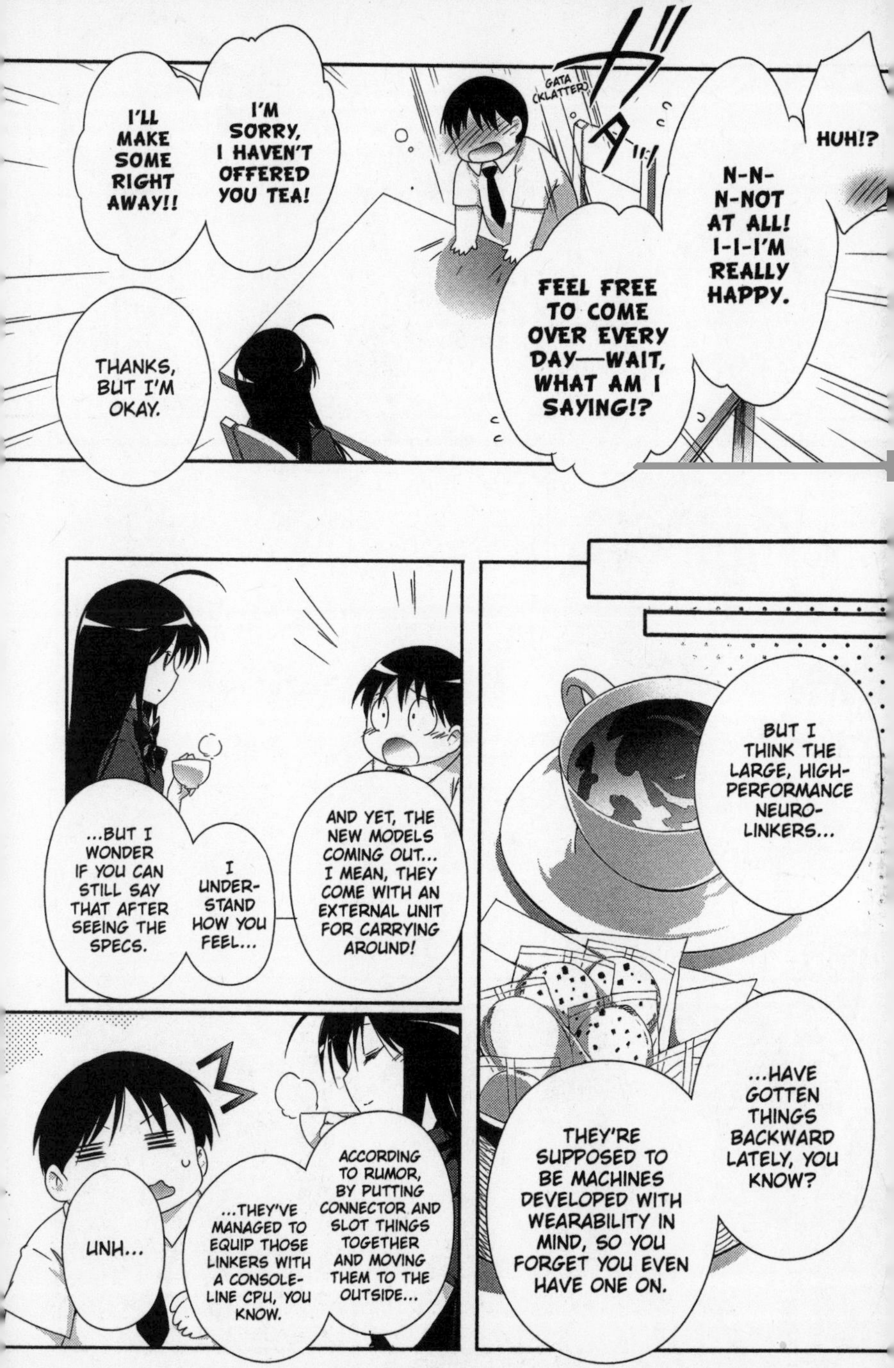
HUH!?
N-N-N-NOT AT ALL! I-I-I'M REALLY HAPPY.
GATA (KLATTER)
FEEL FREE TO COME OVER EVERY DAY—WAIT, WHAT AM I SAYING!?
I'M SORRY, I HAVEN'T OFFERED YOU TEA!
I'LL MAKE SOME RIGHT AWAY!!
THANKS, BUT I'M OKAY.
BUT I THINK THE LARGE, HIGH-PERFORMANCE NEURO-LINKERS...
...HAVE GOTTEN THINGS BACKWARD LATELY, YOU KNOW?
THEY'RE SUPPOSED TO BE MACHINES DEVELOPED WITH WEARABILITY IN MIND, SO YOU FORGET YOU EVEN HAVE ONE ON.
AND YET, THE NEW MODELS COMING OUT... I MEAN, THEY COME WITH AN EXTERNAL UNIT FOR CARRYING AROUND!
I UNDERSTAND HOW YOU FEEL...
...BUT I WONDER IF YOU CAN STILL SAY THAT AFTER SEEING THE SPECS.
ACCORDING TO RUMOR, BY PUTTING CONNECTOR AND SLOT THINGS TOGETHER AND MOVING THEM TO THE OUTSIDE...
...THEY'VE MANAGED TO EQUIP THOSE LINKERS WITH A CONSOLE-LINE CPU, YOU KNOW.
UNH...

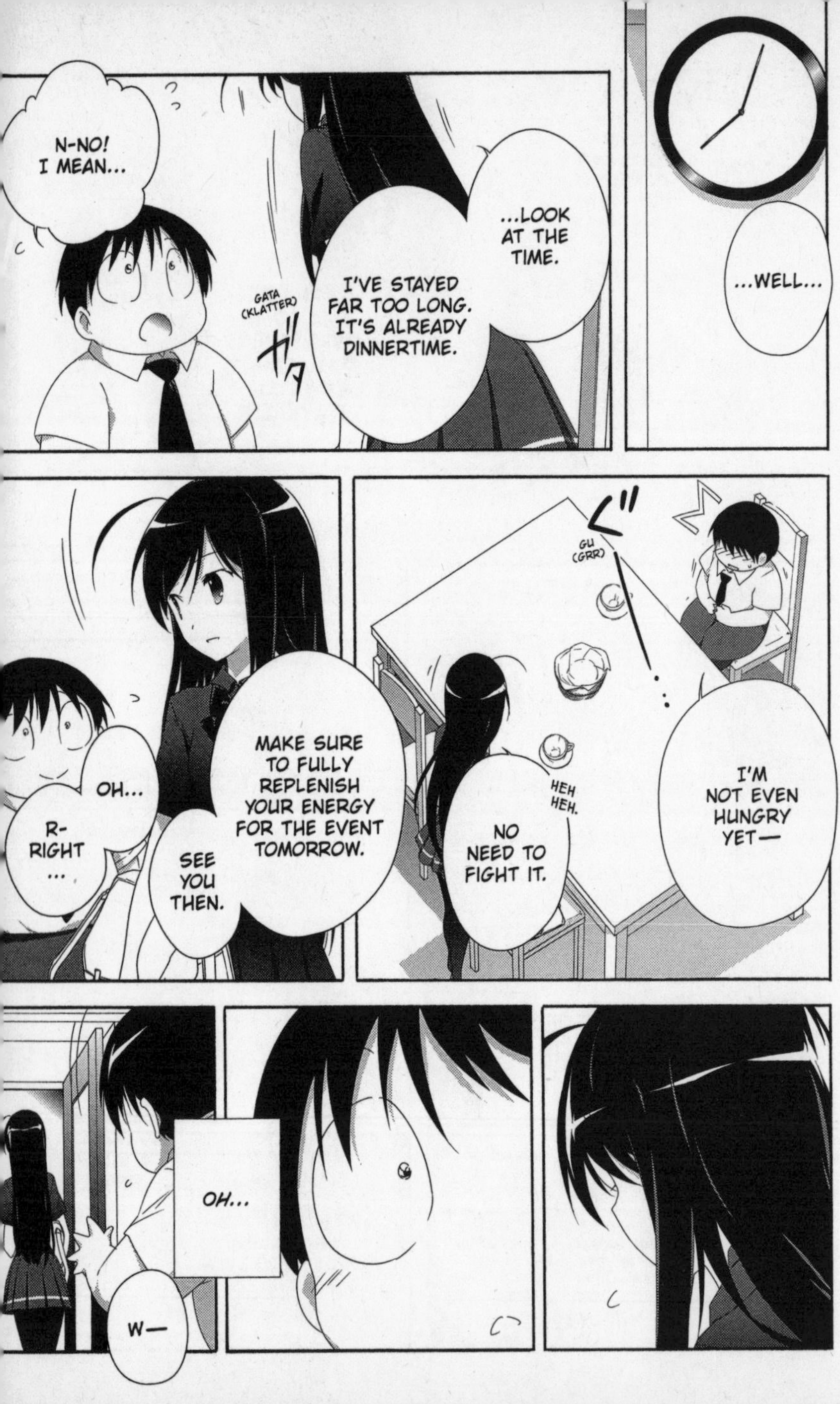
...WELL...
...LOOK AT THE TIME.
I'VE STAYED FAR TOO LONG. IT'S ALREADY DINNERTIME.
GATA (KLATTER)
N-NO! I MEAN...
I'M NOT EVEN HUNGRY YET—
GU (GRR)
HEH HEH.
NO NEED TO FIGHT IT.
MAKE SURE TO FULLY REPLENISH YOUR ENERGY FOR THE EVENT TOMORROW.
SEE YOU THEN.
OH...
R-RIGHT...
OH...
W—

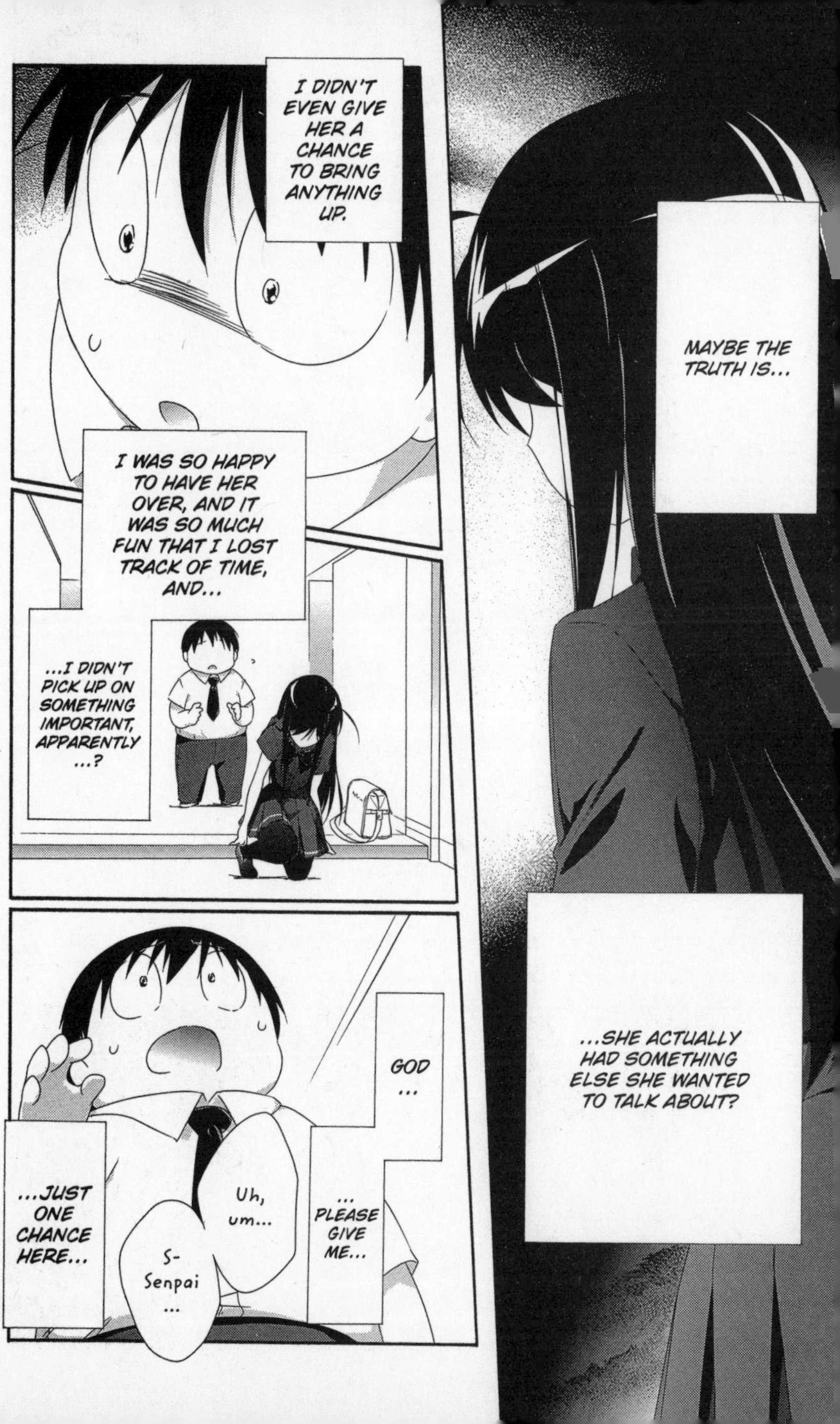
MAYBE THE TRUTH IS...
...SHE ACTUALLY HAD SOMETHING ELSE SHE WANTED TO TALK ABOUT?
I DIDN'T EVEN GIVE HER A CHANCE TO BRING ANYTHING UP.
I WAS SO HAPPY TO HAVE HER OVER, AND IT WAS SO MUCH FUN THAT I LOST TRACK OF TIME, AND...
...I DIDN'T PICK UP ON SOMETHING IMPORTANT, APPARENTLY ...?
GOD ...
... PLEASE GIVE ME...
Uh, um...
...JUST ONE CHANCE HERE...
S-Senpai ...

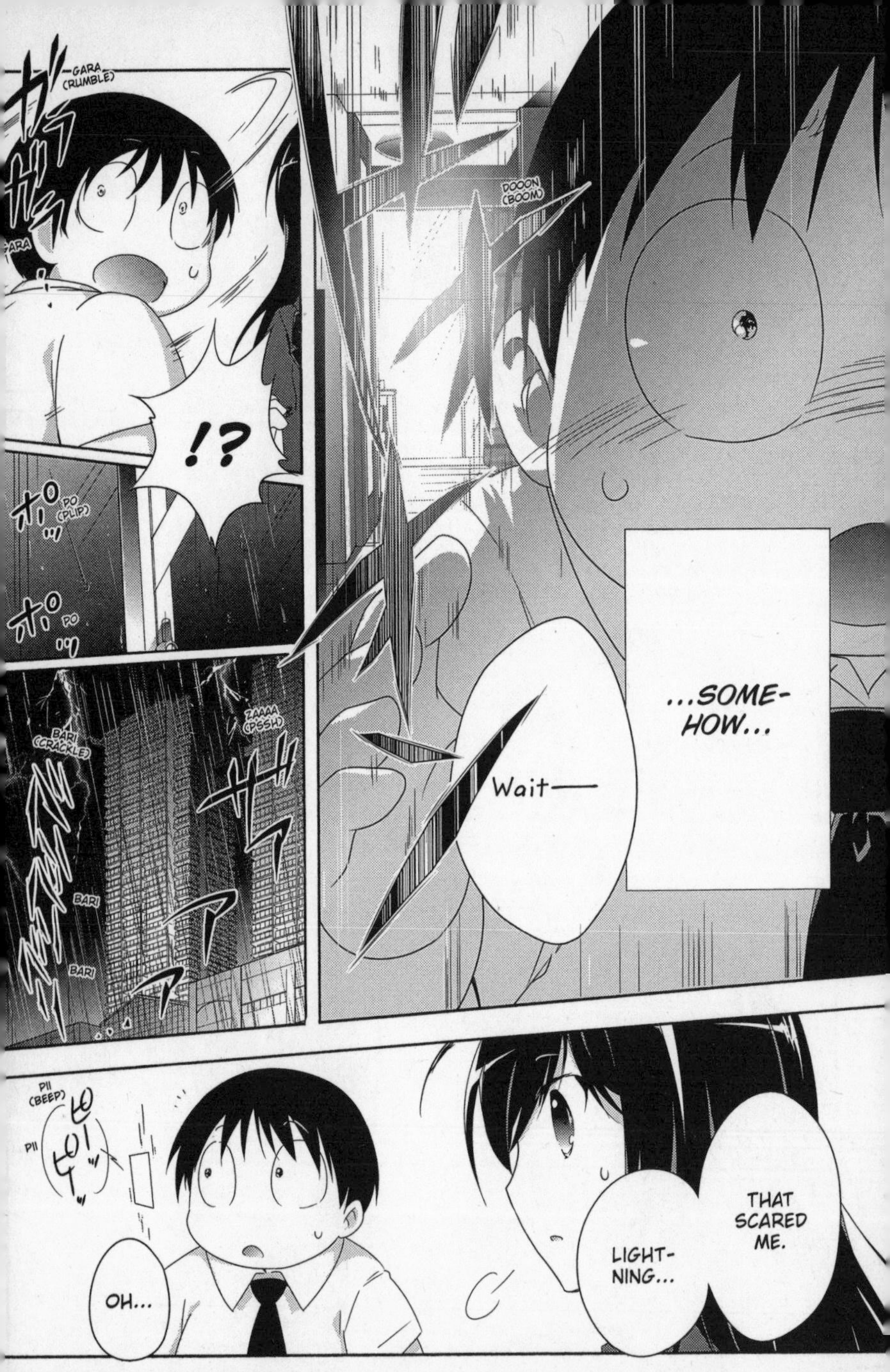

DOOON (BOOM)
...SOME-HOW...
Wait—
GARA (RUMBLE)
GARA
!?
PO (PLIP)
PO
ZAAAA (PSSH)
BARI (CRACKLE)
BARI
BARI
THAT SCARED ME.
LIGHT-NING...
PII (BEEP)
PII
OH...

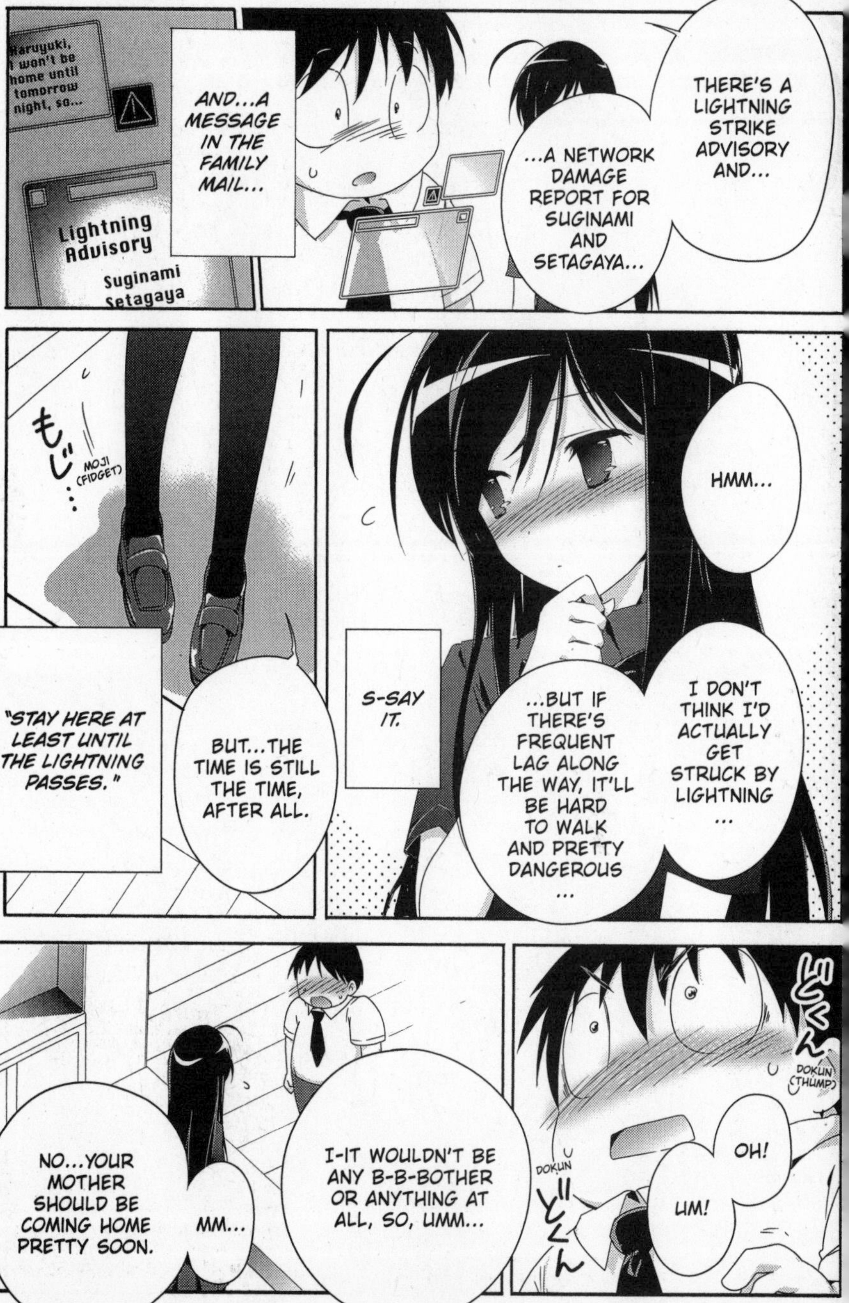
THERE'S A LIGHTNING STRIKE ADVISORY AND...
...A NETWORK DAMAGE REPORT FOR SUGINAMI AND SETAGAYA...
AND...A MESSAGE IN THE FAMILY MAIL...
Haruyuki, I won't be home until tomorrow night, so...
Lightning Advisory
Suginami Setagaya
HMM...
I DON'T THINK I'D ACTUALLY GET STRUCK BY LIGHTNING ...
...BUT IF THERE'S FREQUENT LAG ALONG THE WAY, IT'LL BE HARD TO WALK AND PRETTY DANGEROUS ...
S-SAY IT.
もじ… MOJI (FIDGET)
BUT...THE TIME IS STILL THE TIME, AFTER ALL.
"STAY HERE AT LEAST UNTIL THE LIGHTNING PASSES."
どくん DOKUN (THUMP)
OH!
UM!
どくん DOKUN
I-IT WOULDN'T BE ANY B-B-BOTHER OR ANYTHING AT ALL, SO, UMM...
MM...
NO...YOUR MOTHER SHOULD BE COMING HOME PRETTY SOON.

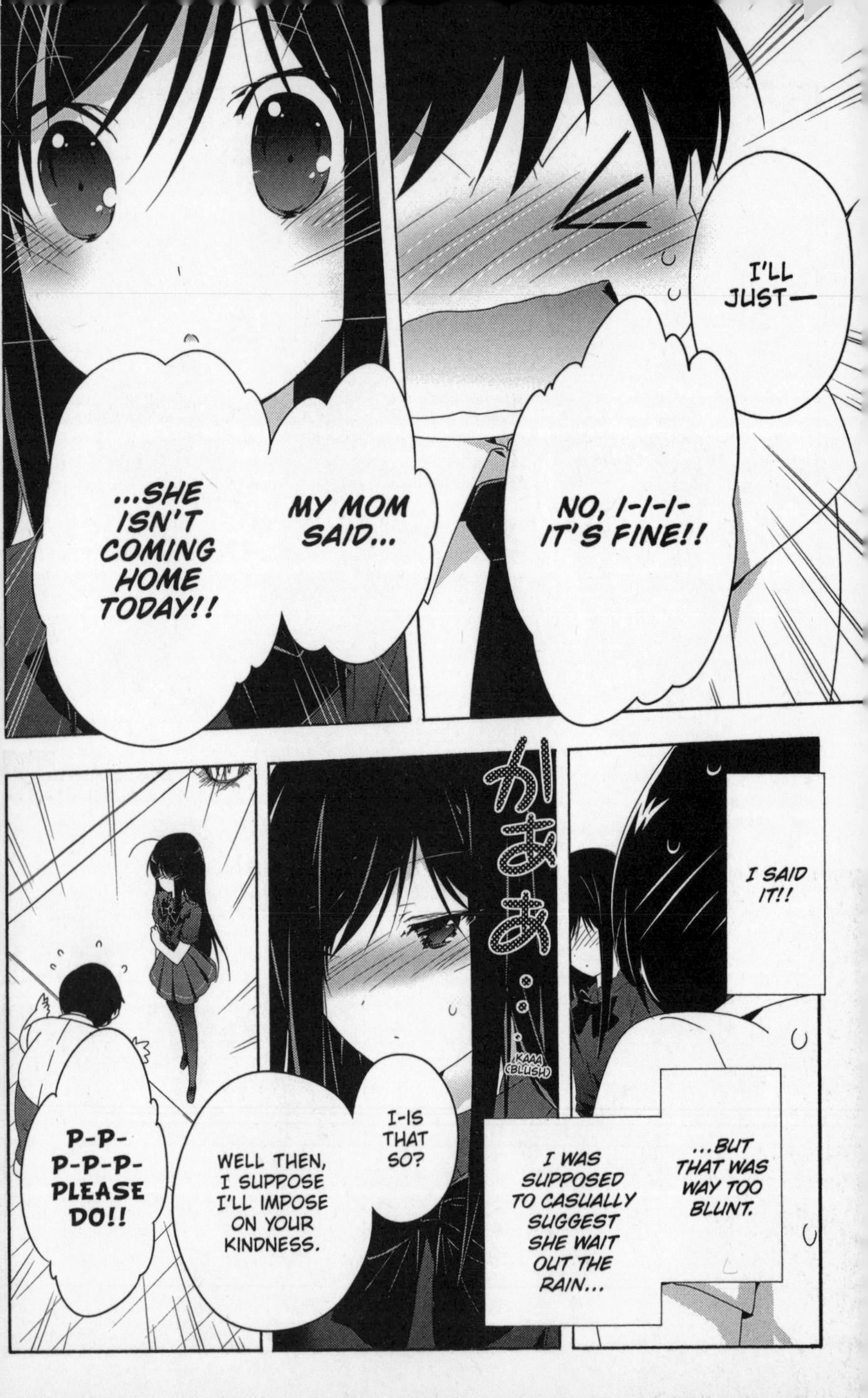
I'LL JUST—
NO, I-I-I- IT'S FINE!!
MY MOM SAID...
...SHE ISN'T COMING HOME TODAY!!
I SAID IT!!
I WAS SUPPOSED TO CASUALLY SUGGEST SHE WAIT OUT THE RAIN...
...BUT THAT WAS WAY TOO BLUNT.
かぁぁ…
KAAA (BLUSH)
I-IS THAT SO?
WELL THEN, I SUPPOSE I'LL IMPOSE ON YOUR KINDNESS.
P-P-P-P-P-PLEASE DO!!

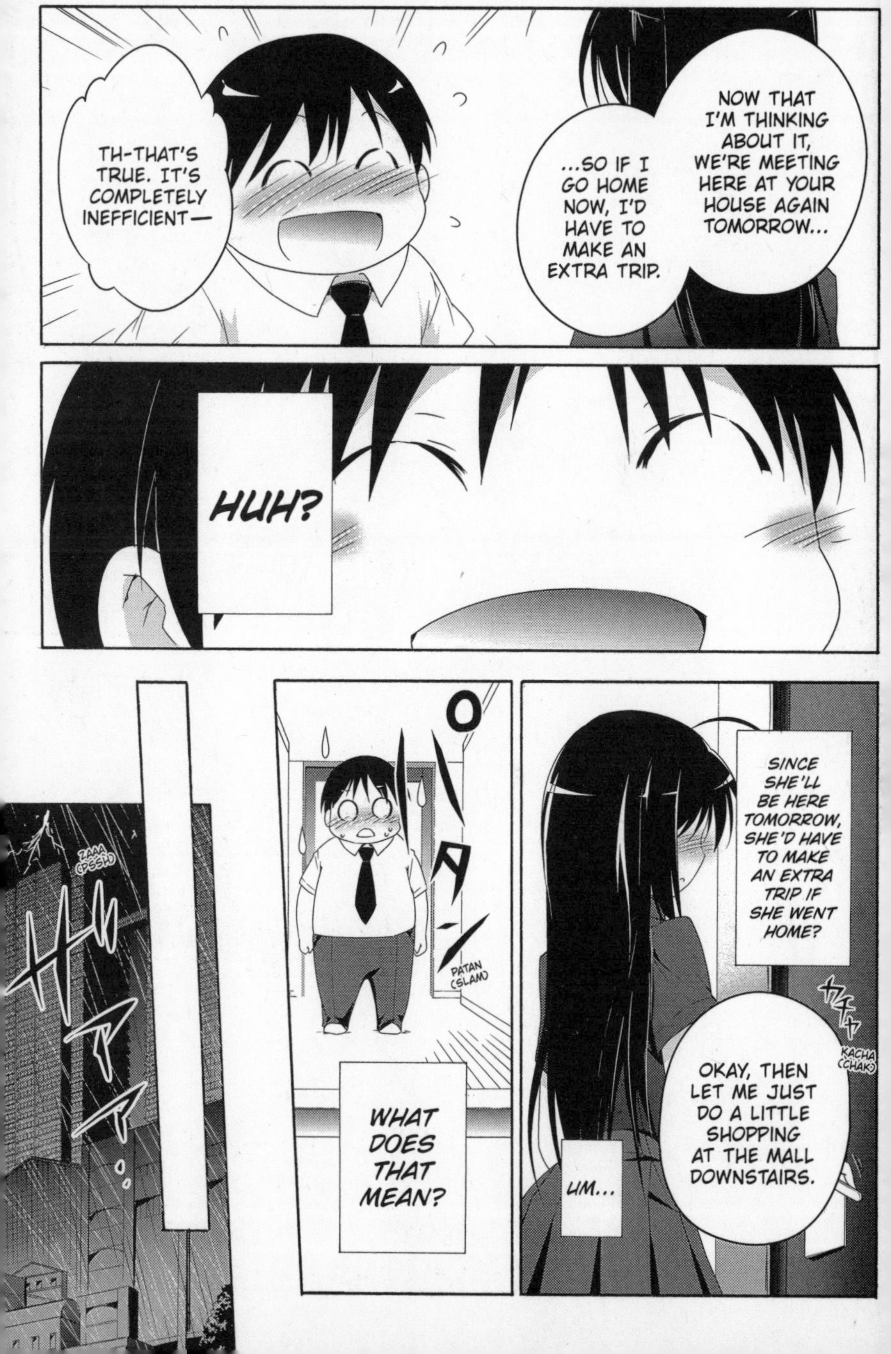
NOW THAT I'M THINKING ABOUT IT, WE'RE MEETING HERE AT YOUR HOUSE AGAIN TOMORROW...
...SO IF I GO HOME NOW, I'D HAVE TO MAKE AN EXTRA TRIP.
TH-THAT'S TRUE. IT'S COMPLETELY INEFFICIENT—
HUH?
SINCE SHE'LL BE HERE TOMORROW, SHE'D HAVE TO MAKE AN EXTRA TRIP IF SHE WENT HOME?
KACHA (CHAK)
OKAY, THEN LET ME JUST DO A LITTLE SHOPPING AT THE MALL DOWNSTAIRS.
UM...
PATAN (SLAM)
WHAT DOES THAT MEAN?
ZAAA (PSSH)

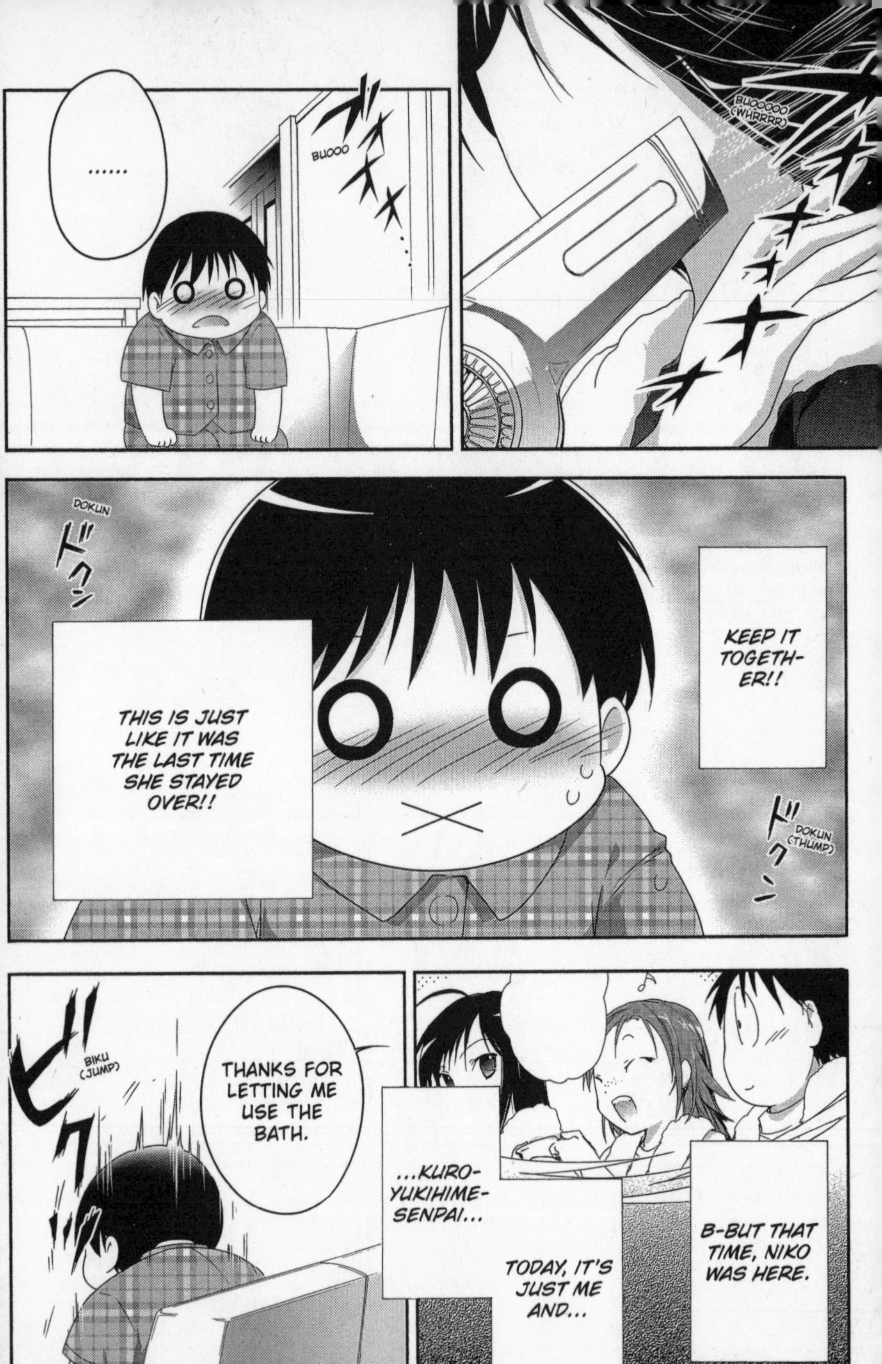

BUOOOOO (WHRRRR)
BUOOO
......
KEEP IT TOGETHER!!
DOKUN (THUMP)
DOKUN
THIS IS JUST LIKE IT WAS THE LAST TIME SHE STAYED OVER!!
B-BUT THAT TIME, NIKO WAS HERE.
TODAY, IT'S JUST ME AND...
...KURO-YUKIHIME-SENPAI...
THANKS FOR LETTING ME USE THE BATH.
BIKU (JUMP)

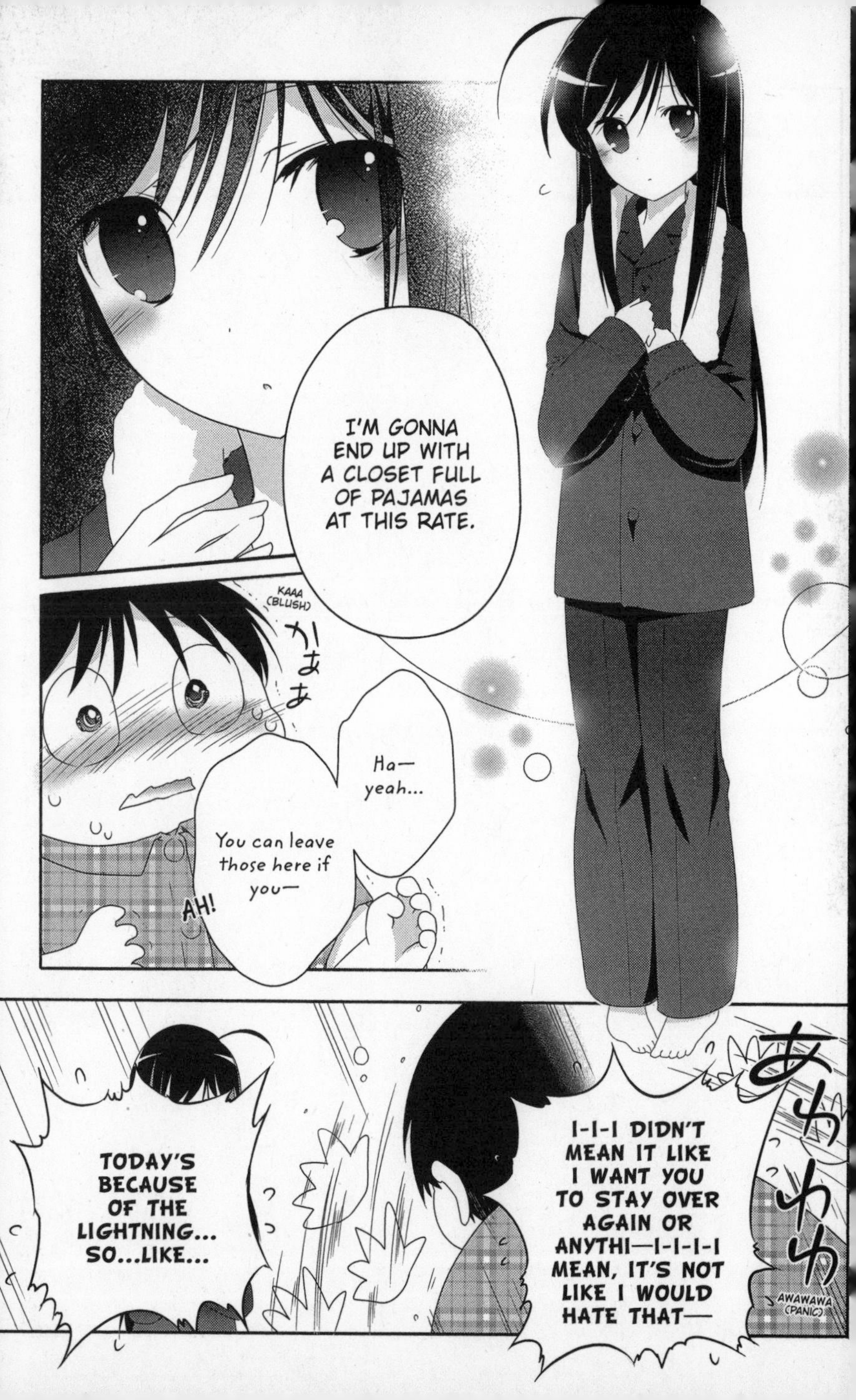

I'M GONNA END UP WITH A CLOSET FULL OF PAJAMAS AT THIS RATE.
KAAA (BLUSH)
かぁぁ
Ha— yeah...
You can leave those here if you—
AH!
あわわ
AWAWAWA (PANIC)
I-I-I DIDN'T MEAN IT LIKE I WANT YOU TO STAY OVER AGAIN OR ANYTHI—I-I-I-I MEAN, IT'S NOT LIKE I WOULD HATE THAT—
TODAY'S BECAUSE OF THE LIGHTNING... SO...LIKE...

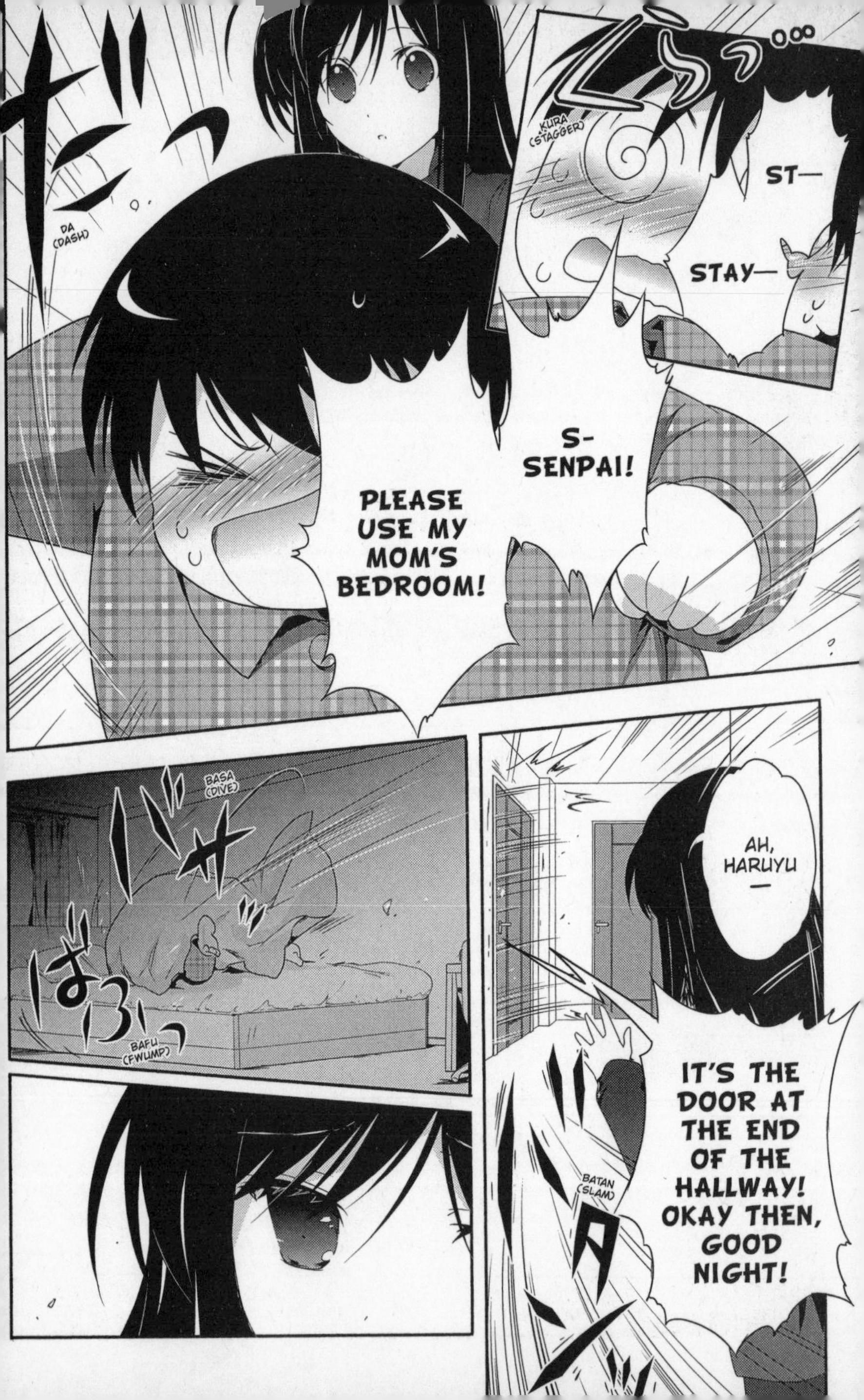
KURA (STAGGER)
ST—
STAY—
DA (DASH)
S- SENPAI!
PLEASE USE MY MOM'S BEDROOM!
AH, HARUYU —
IT'S THE DOOR AT THE END OF THE HALLWAY! OKAY THEN, GOOD NIGHT!
BATAN (SLAM)
BASA (DIVE)
BAFU (FWUMP)

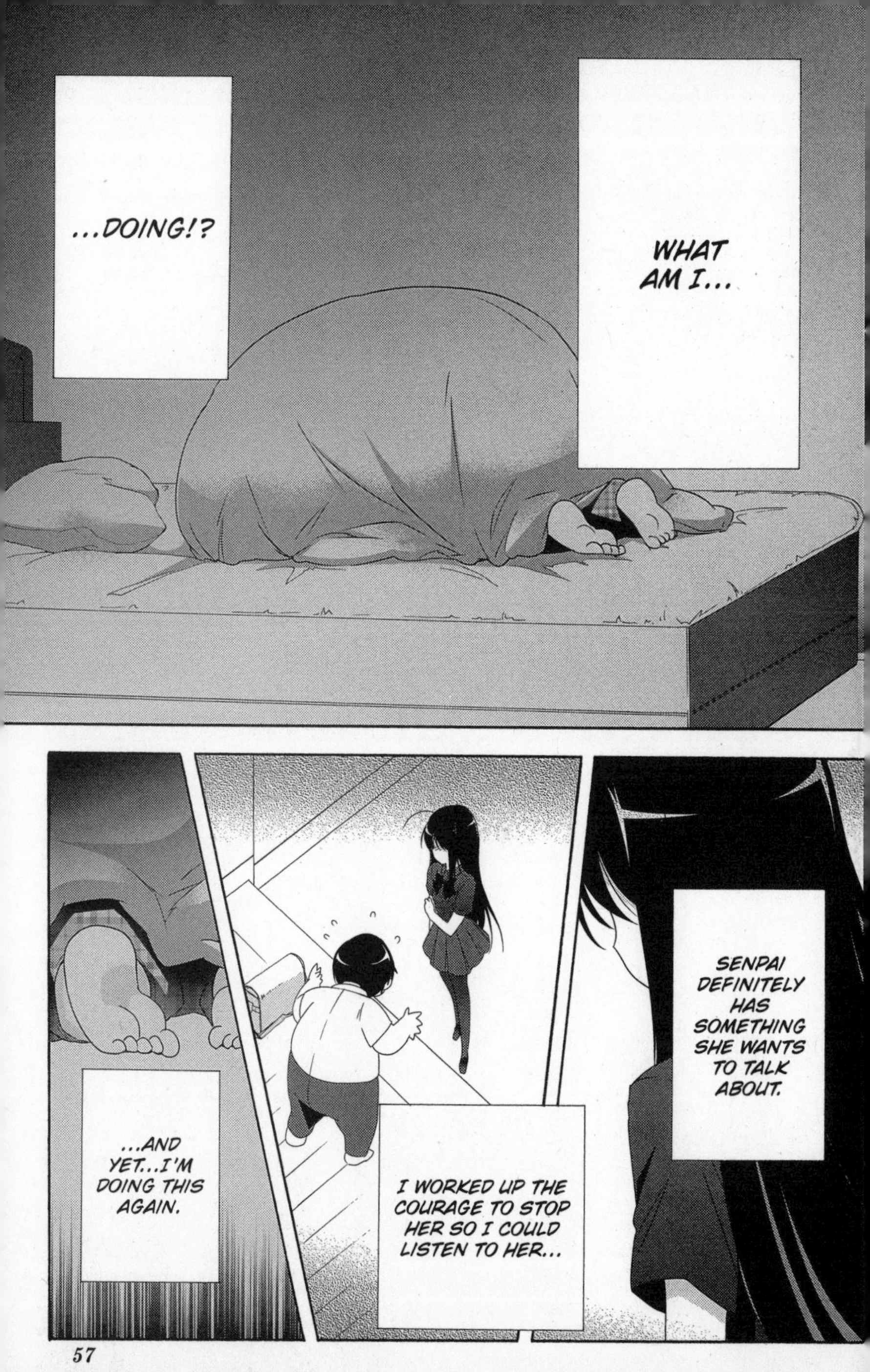
WHAT AM I...
...DOING!?
SENPAI DEFINITELY HAS SOMETHING SHE WANTS TO TALK ABOUT.
I WORKED UP THE COURAGE TO STOP HER SO I COULD LISTEN TO HER...
...AND YET...I'M DOING THIS AGAIN.

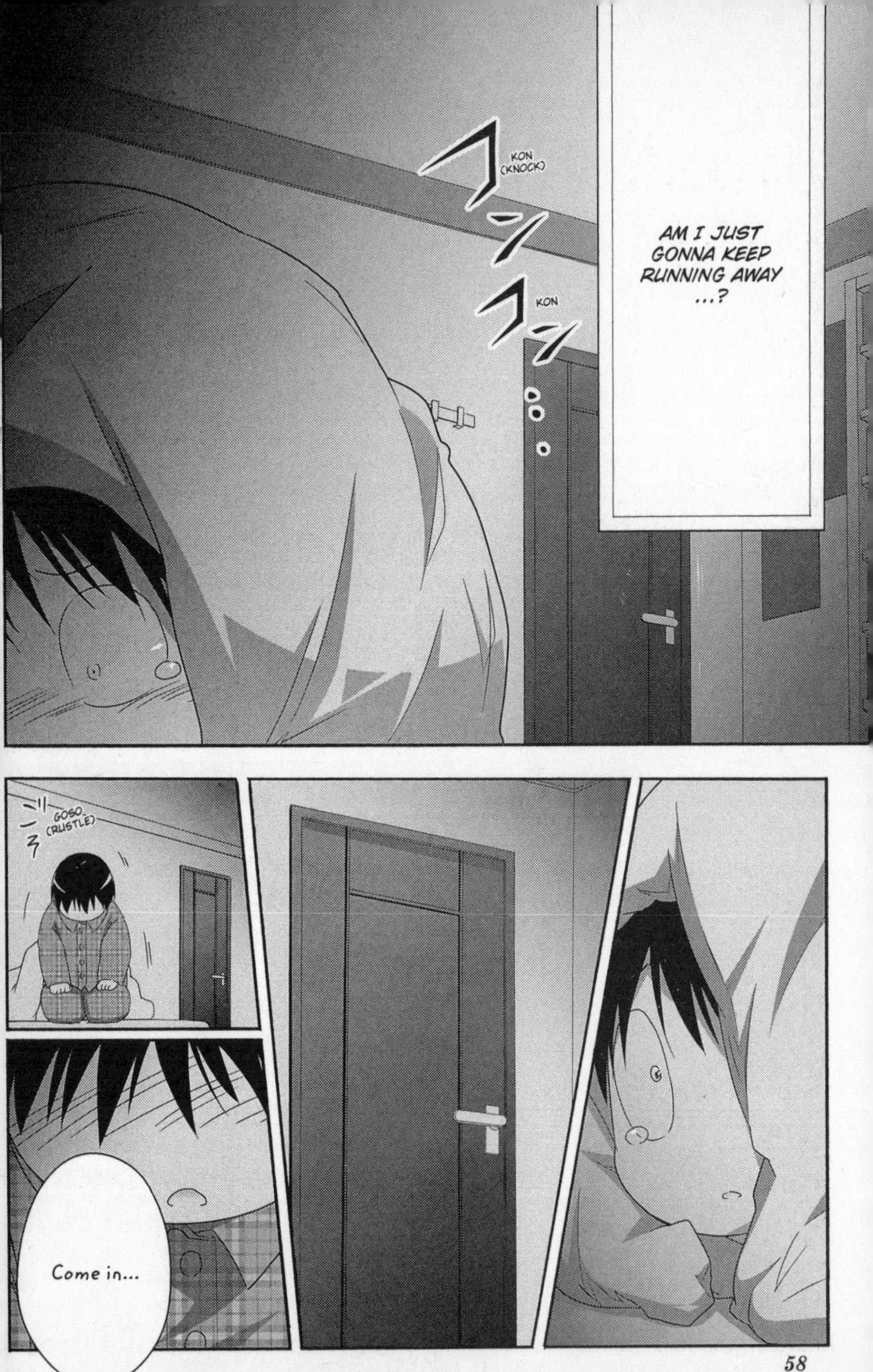
AM I JUST GONNA KEEP RUNNING AWAY ...?
KON (KNOCK)
KON
GOSO (RUSTLE)
Come in...

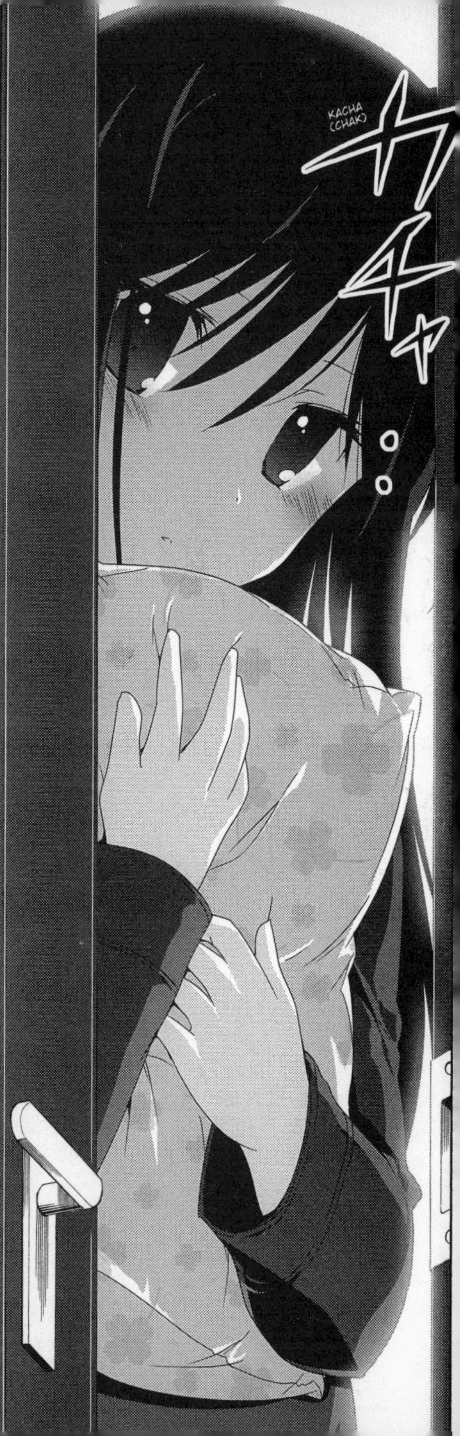
KACHA
(CHAK)

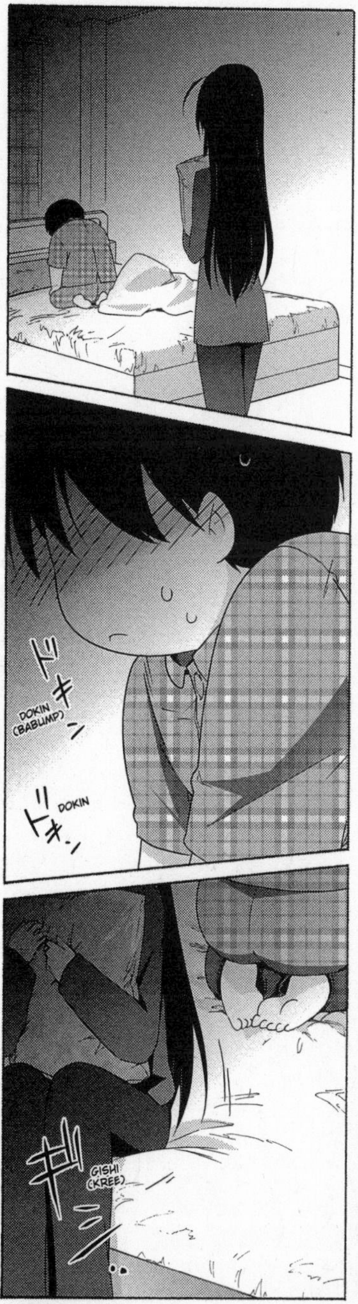
DOKIN
(BABUMP)
DOKIN
GISHI
(KREE)

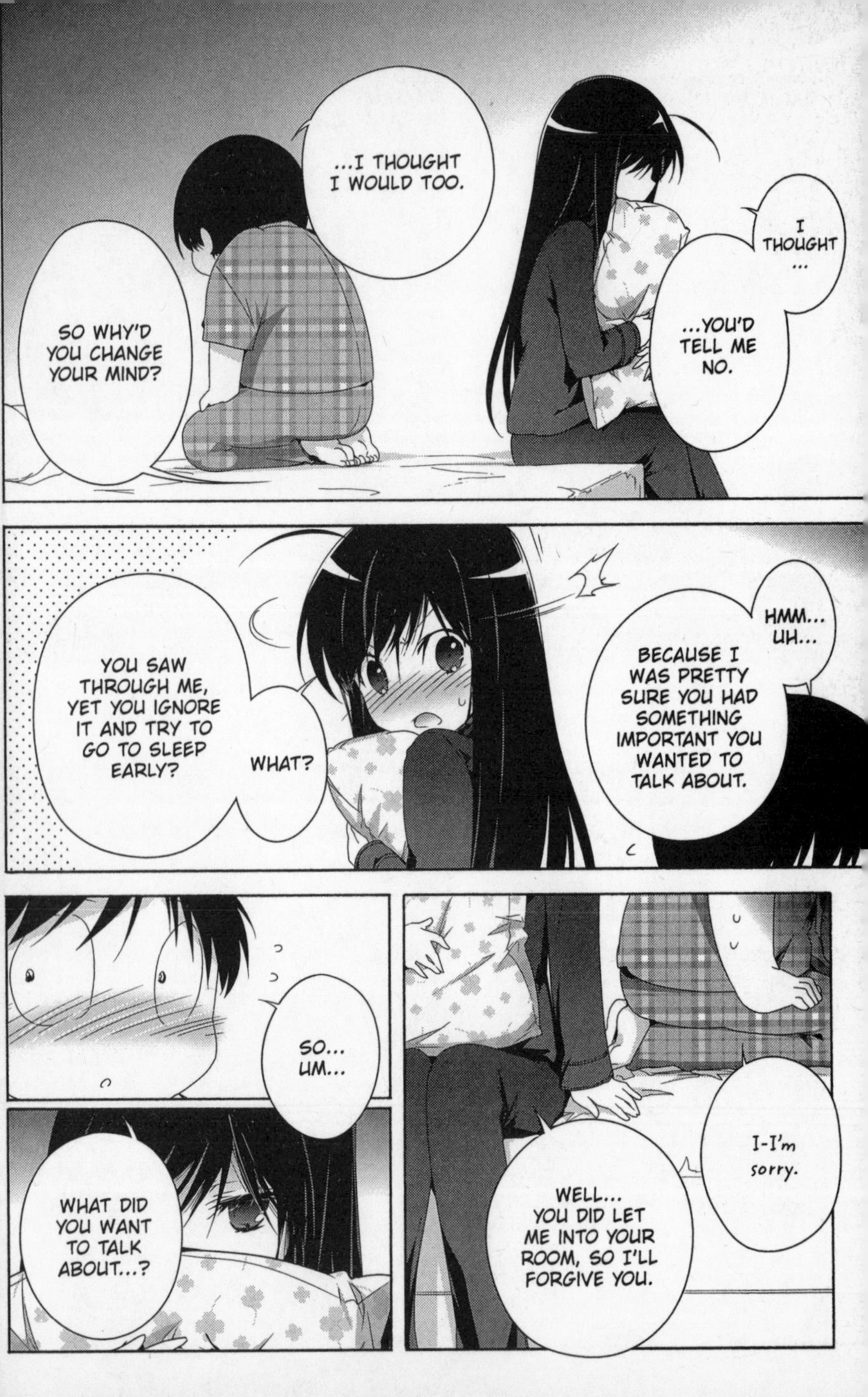
I THOUGHT ...
...YOU'D TELL ME NO.
...I THOUGHT I WOULD TOO.
SO WHY'D YOU CHANGE YOUR MIND?
HMM... UH...
BECAUSE I WAS PRETTY SURE YOU HAD SOMETHING IMPORTANT YOU WANTED TO TALK ABOUT.
WHAT?
YOU SAW THROUGH ME, YET YOU IGNORE IT AND TRY TO GO TO SLEEP EARLY?
I-I'm sorry.
WELL... YOU DID LET ME INTO YOUR ROOM, SO I'LL FORGIVE YOU.
SO... UM...
WHAT DID YOU WANT TO TALK ABOUT...?

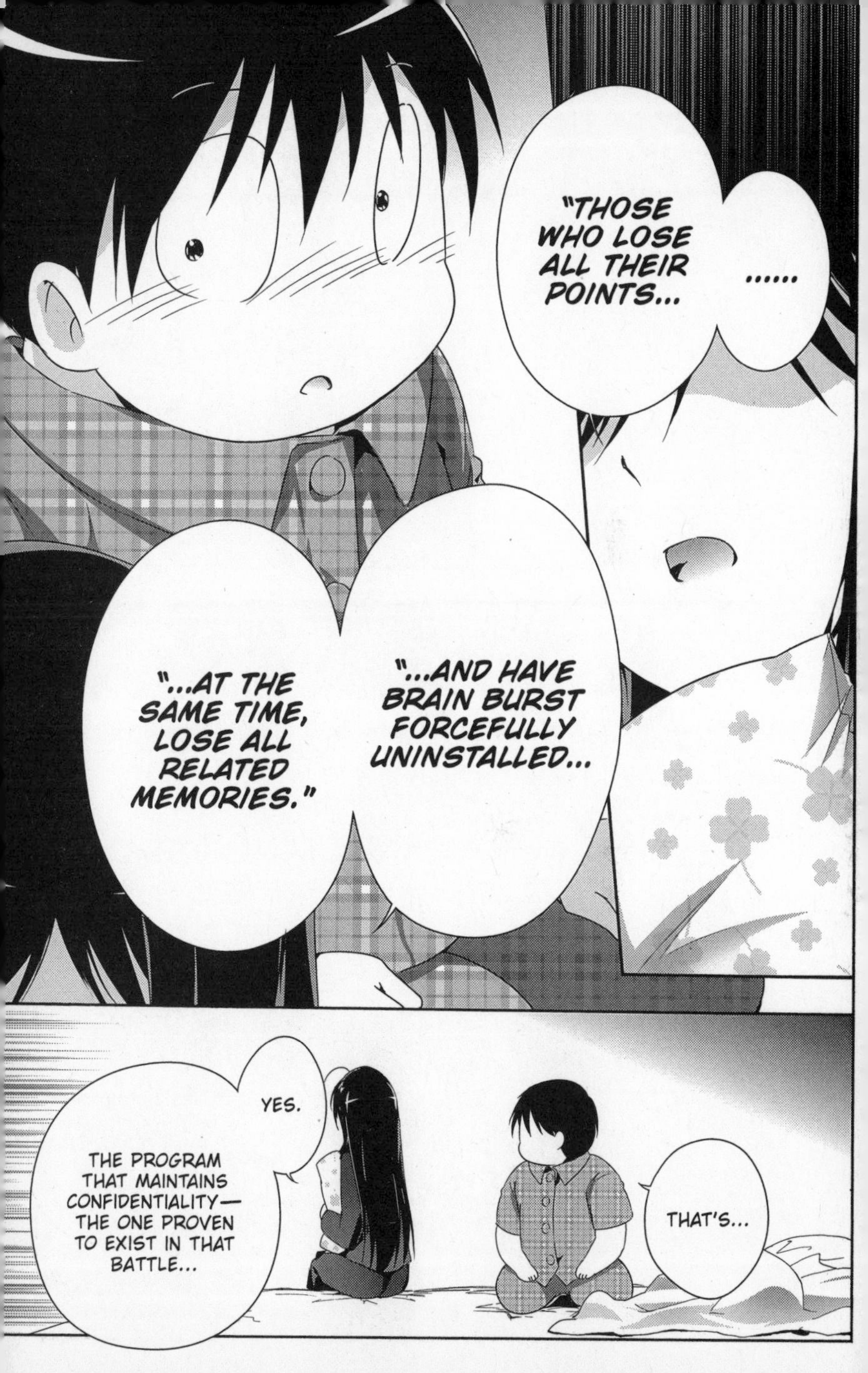
"THOSE WHO LOSE ALL THEIR POINTS...
......
"...AND HAVE BRAIN BURST FORCEFULLY UNINSTALLED...
"...AT THE SAME TIME, LOSE ALL RELATED MEMORIES."
THAT'S...
YES.
THE PROGRAM THAT MAINTAINS CONFIDENTIALITY—THE ONE PROVEN TO EXIST IN THAT BATTLE...

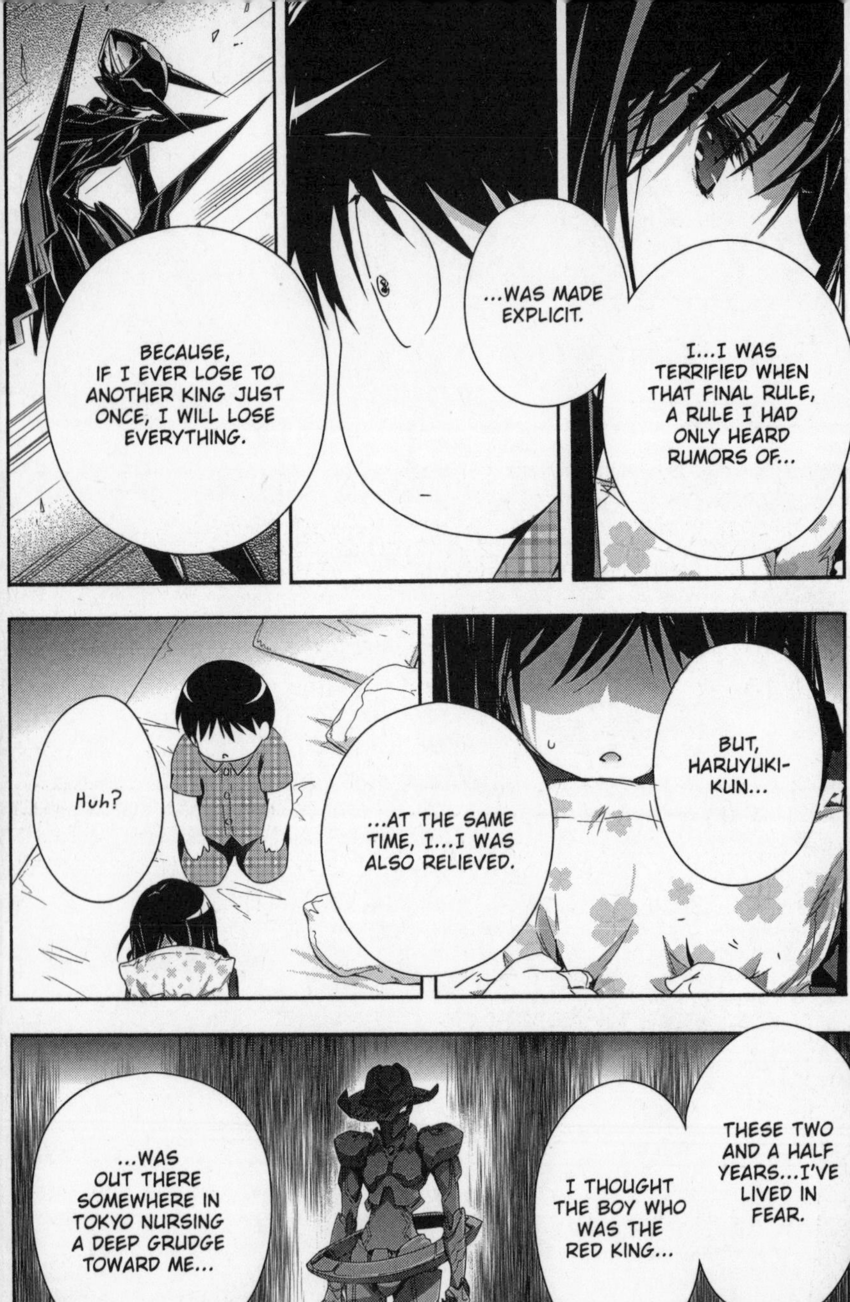
I...I WAS TERRIFIED WHEN THAT FINAL RULE, A RULE I HAD ONLY HEARD RUMORS OF...
...WAS MADE EXPLICIT.
BECAUSE, IF I EVER LOSE TO ANOTHER KING JUST ONCE, I WILL LOSE EVERYTHING.
BUT, HARUYUKI-KUN...
...AT THE SAME TIME, I...I WAS ALSO RELIEVED.
Huh?
THESE TWO AND A HALF YEARS...I'VE LIVED IN FEAR.
I THOUGHT THE BOY WHO WAS THE RED KING...
...WAS OUT THERE SOMEWHERE IN TOKYO NURSING A DEEP GRUDGE TOWARD ME...

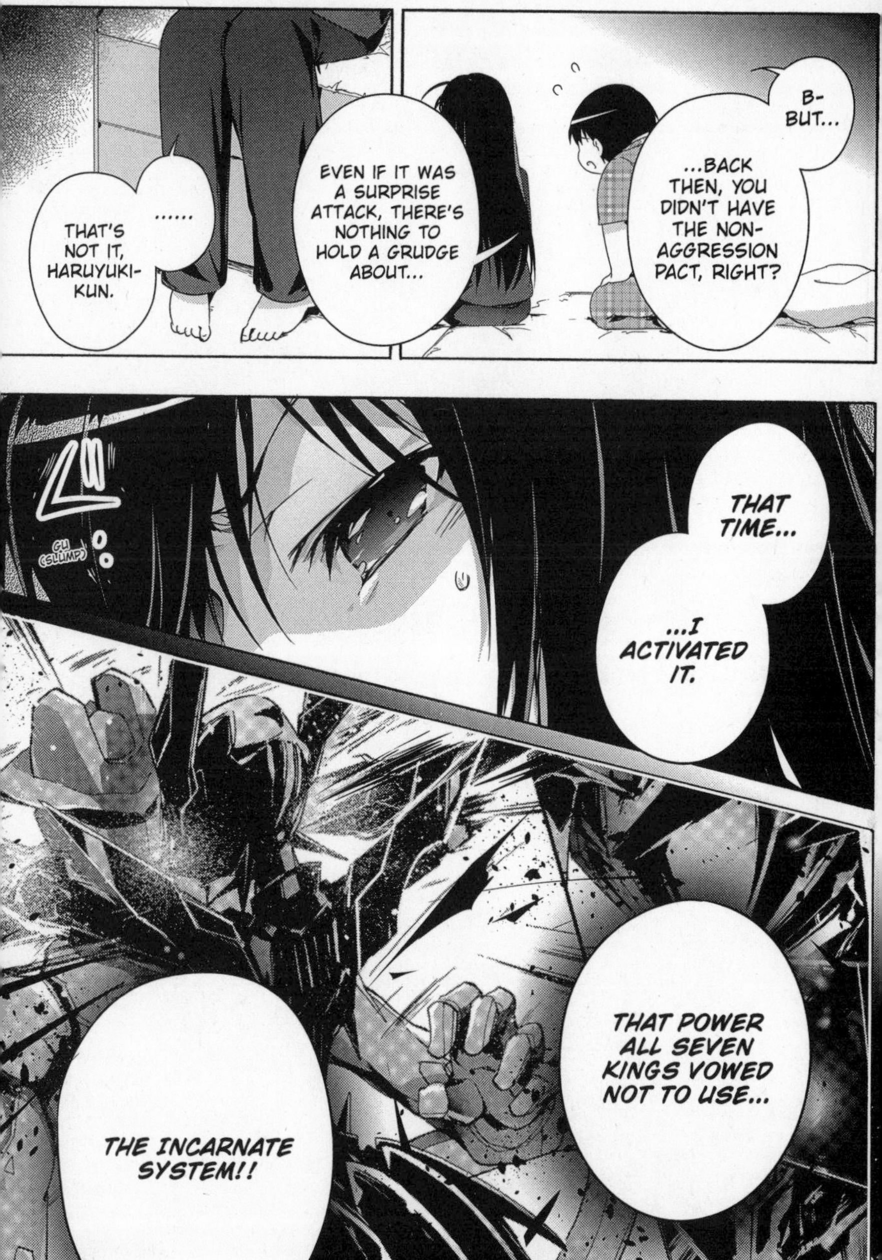
B-BUT...
...BACK THEN, YOU DIDN'T HAVE THE NON-AGGRESSION PACT, RIGHT?
EVEN IF IT WAS A SURPRISE ATTACK, THERE'S NOTHING TO HOLD A GRUDGE ABOUT...
......
THAT'S NOT IT, HARUYUKI-KUN.
THAT TIME...
...I ACTIVATED IT.
GU (SLUMP)
THAT POWER ALL SEVEN KINGS VOWED NOT TO USE...
THE INCARNATE SYSTEM!!

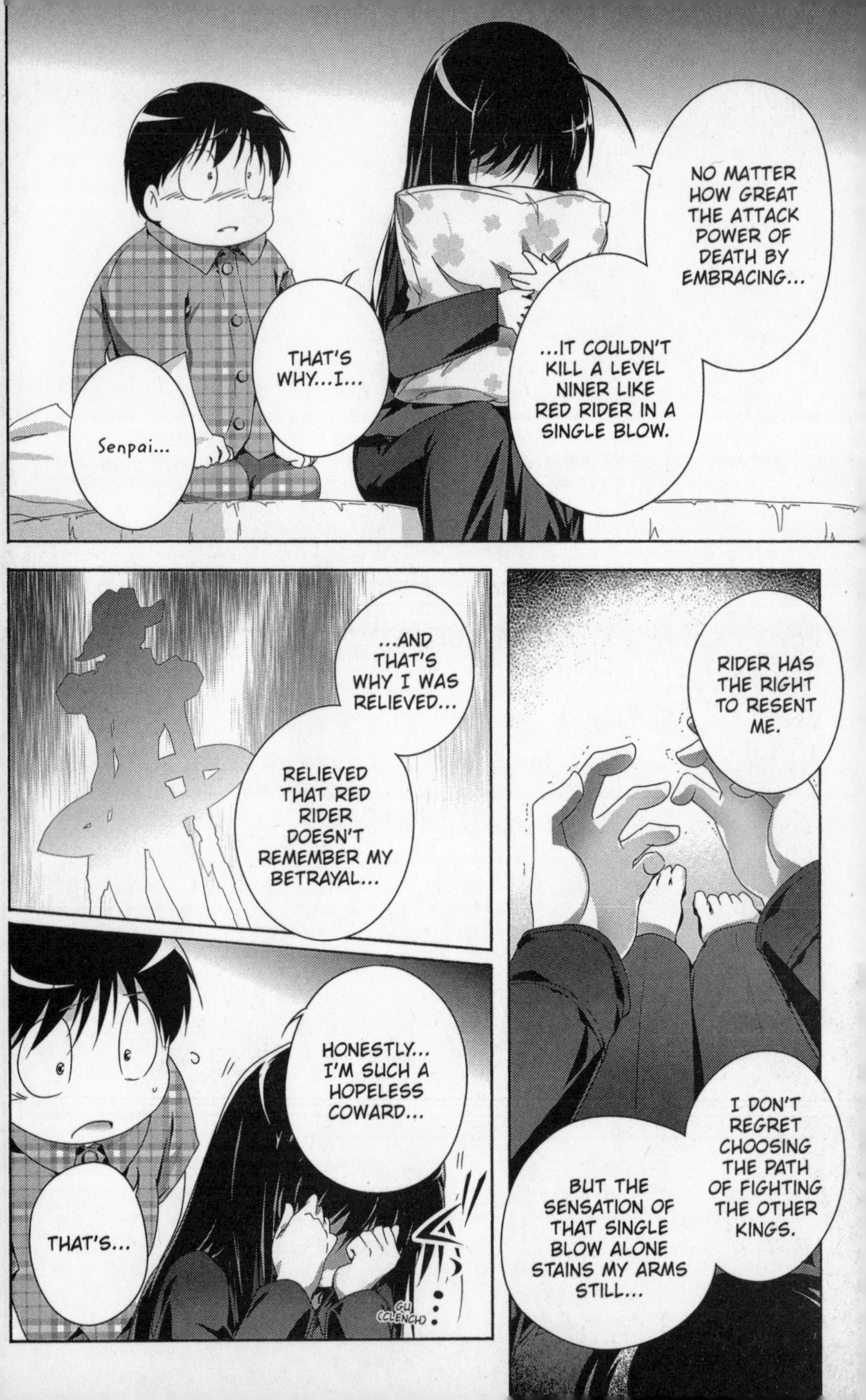
NO MATTER HOW GREAT THE ATTACK POWER OF DEATH BY EMBRACING...
...IT COULDN'T KILL A LEVEL NINER LIKE RED RIDER IN A SINGLE BLOW.
THAT'S WHY...I...
Senpai...
RIDER HAS THE RIGHT TO RESENT ME.
I DON'T REGRET CHOOSING THE PATH OF FIGHTING THE OTHER KINGS.
BUT THE SENSATION OF THAT SINGLE BLOW ALONE STAINS MY ARMS STILL...
...AND THAT'S WHY I WAS RELIEVED...
RELIEVED THAT RED RIDER DOESN'T REMEMBER MY BETRAYAL...
HONESTLY... I'M SUCH A HOPELESS COWARD...
THAT'S...
GU (CLENCH)

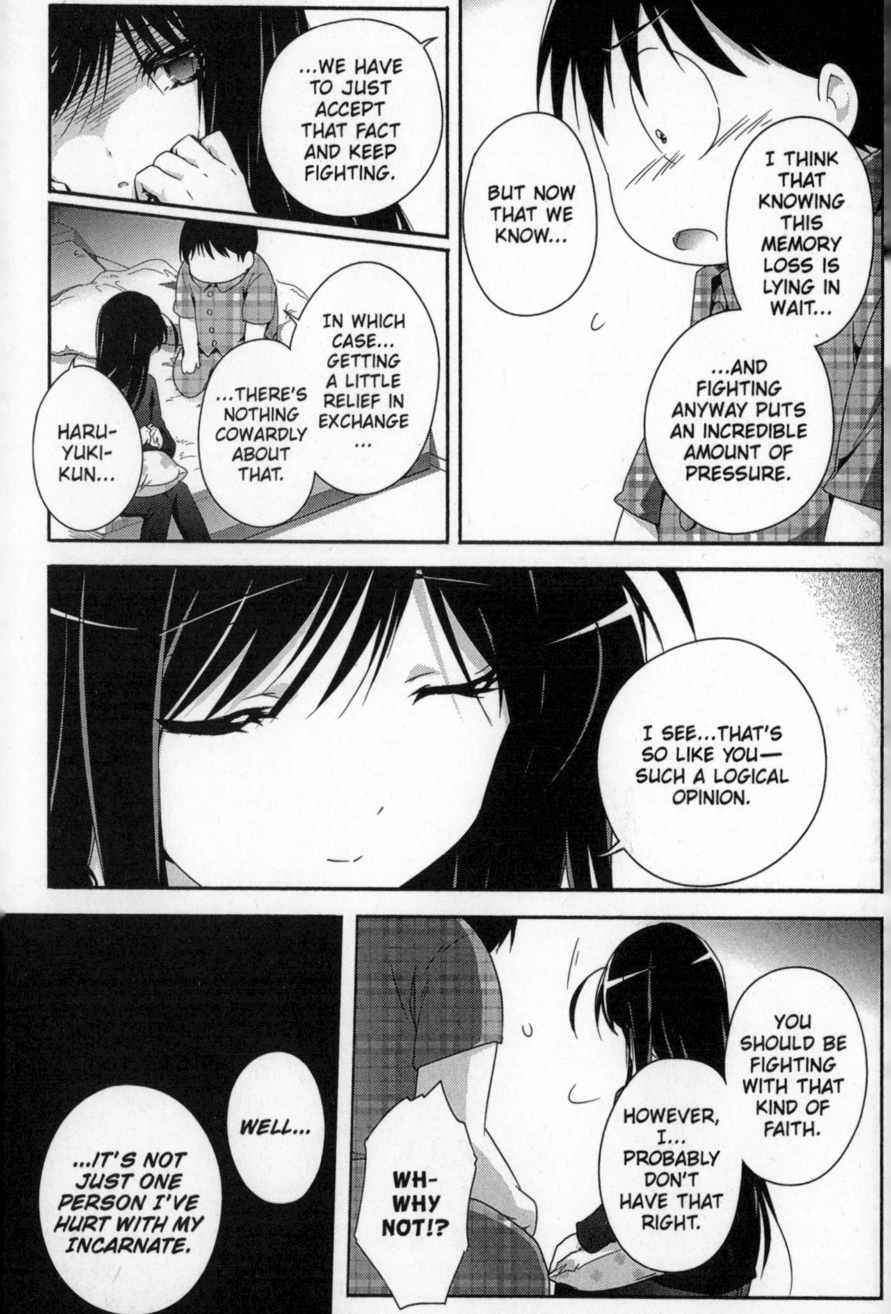
I THINK THAT KNOWING THIS MEMORY LOSS IS LYING IN WAIT...
...AND FIGHTING ANYWAY PUTS AN INCREDIBLE AMOUNT OF PRESSURE.
BUT NOW THAT WE KNOW...
...WE HAVE TO JUST ACCEPT THAT FACT AND KEEP FIGHTING.
IN WHICH CASE... GETTING A LITTLE RELIEF IN EXCHANGE...
...THERE'S NOTHING COWARDLY ABOUT THAT.
HARU-YUKI-KUN...
I SEE...THAT'S SO LIKE YOU—SUCH A LOGICAL OPINION.
YOU SHOULD BE FIGHTING WITH THAT KIND OF FAITH.
HOWEVER, I... PROBABLY DON'T HAVE THAT RIGHT.
WH-WHY NOT!?
WELL...
...IT'S NOT JUST ONE PERSON I'VE HURT WITH MY INCARNATE.

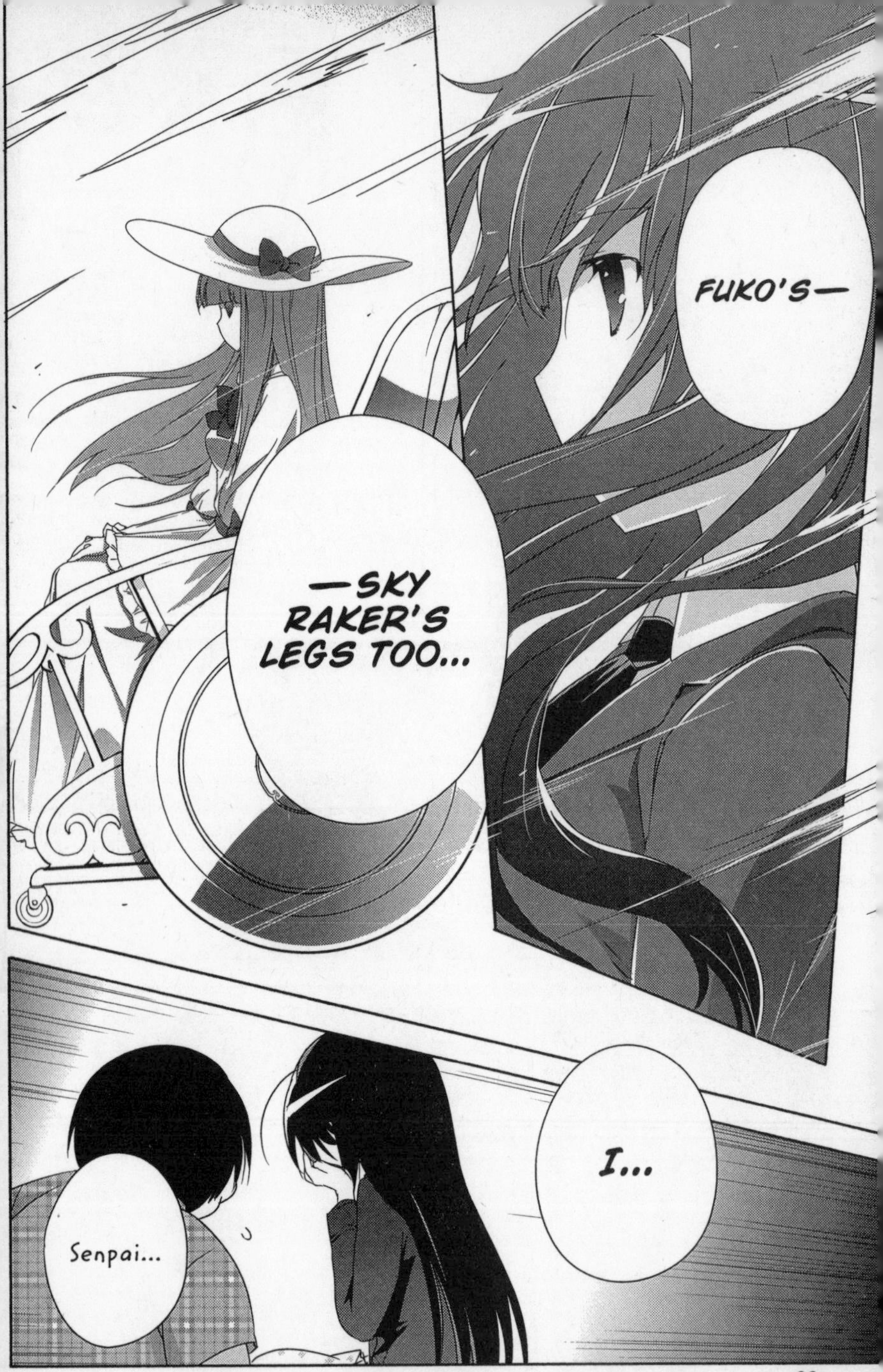
FUKO'S—
—SKY RAKER'S LEGS TOO...
I...
Senpai...

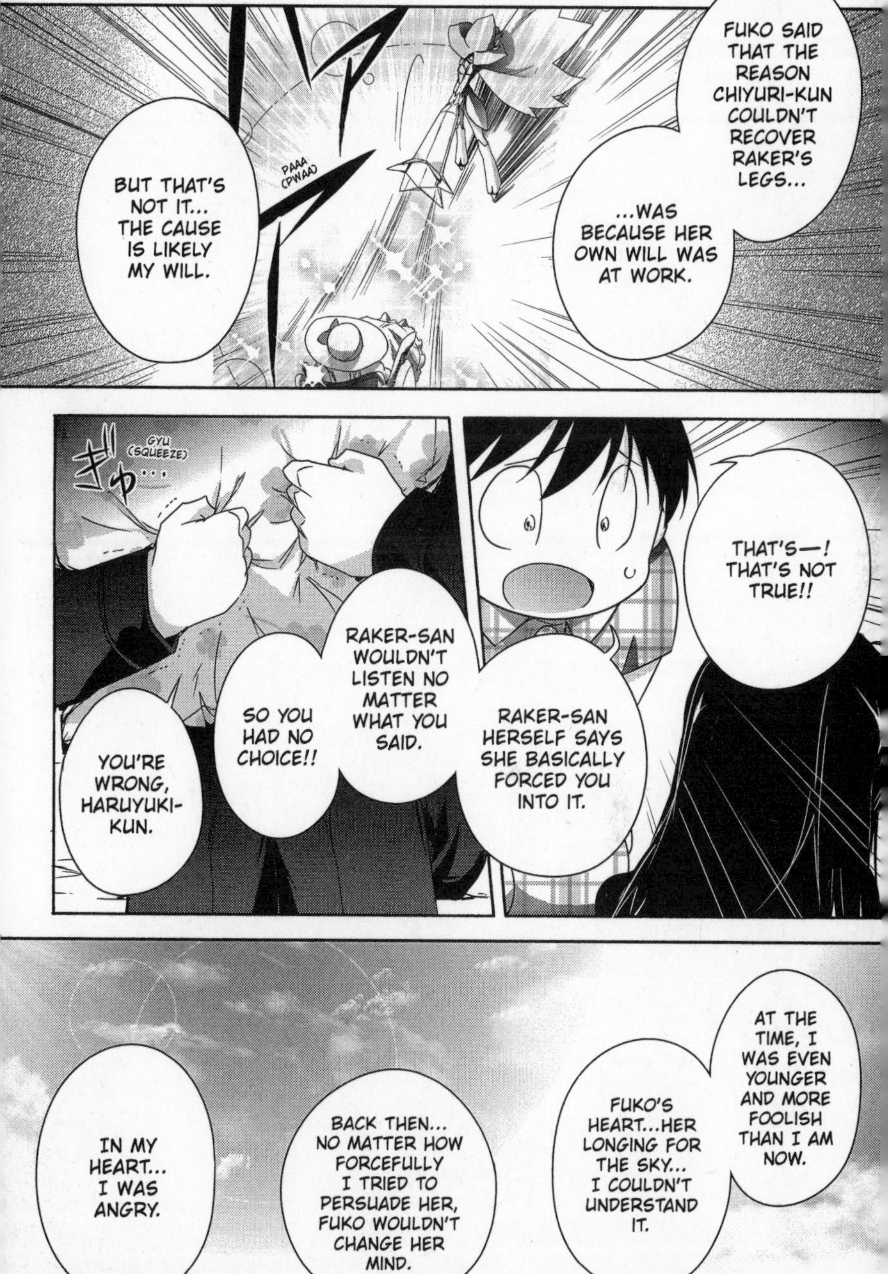
FUKO SAID THAT THE REASON CHIYURI-KUN COULDN'T RECOVER RAKER'S LEGS...
...WAS BECAUSE HER OWN WILL WAS AT WORK.
PAAA (PWAA)
BUT THAT'S NOT IT... THE CAUSE IS LIKELY MY WILL.
THAT'S—! THAT'S NOT TRUE!!
RAKER-SAN HERSELF SAYS SHE BASICALLY FORCED YOU INTO IT.
RAKER-SAN WOULDN'T LISTEN NO MATTER WHAT YOU SAID.
SO YOU HAD NO CHOICE!!
GYU (SQUEEZE)
YOU'RE WRONG, HARUYUKI-KUN.
AT THE TIME, I WAS EVEN YOUNGER AND MORE FOOLISH THAN I AM NOW.
FUKO'S HEART...HER LONGING FOR THE SKY... I COULDN'T UNDERSTAND IT.
BACK THEN... NO MATTER HOW FORCEFULLY I TRIED TO PERSUADE HER, FUKO WOULDN'T CHANGE HER MIND.
IN MY HEART... I WAS ANGRY.

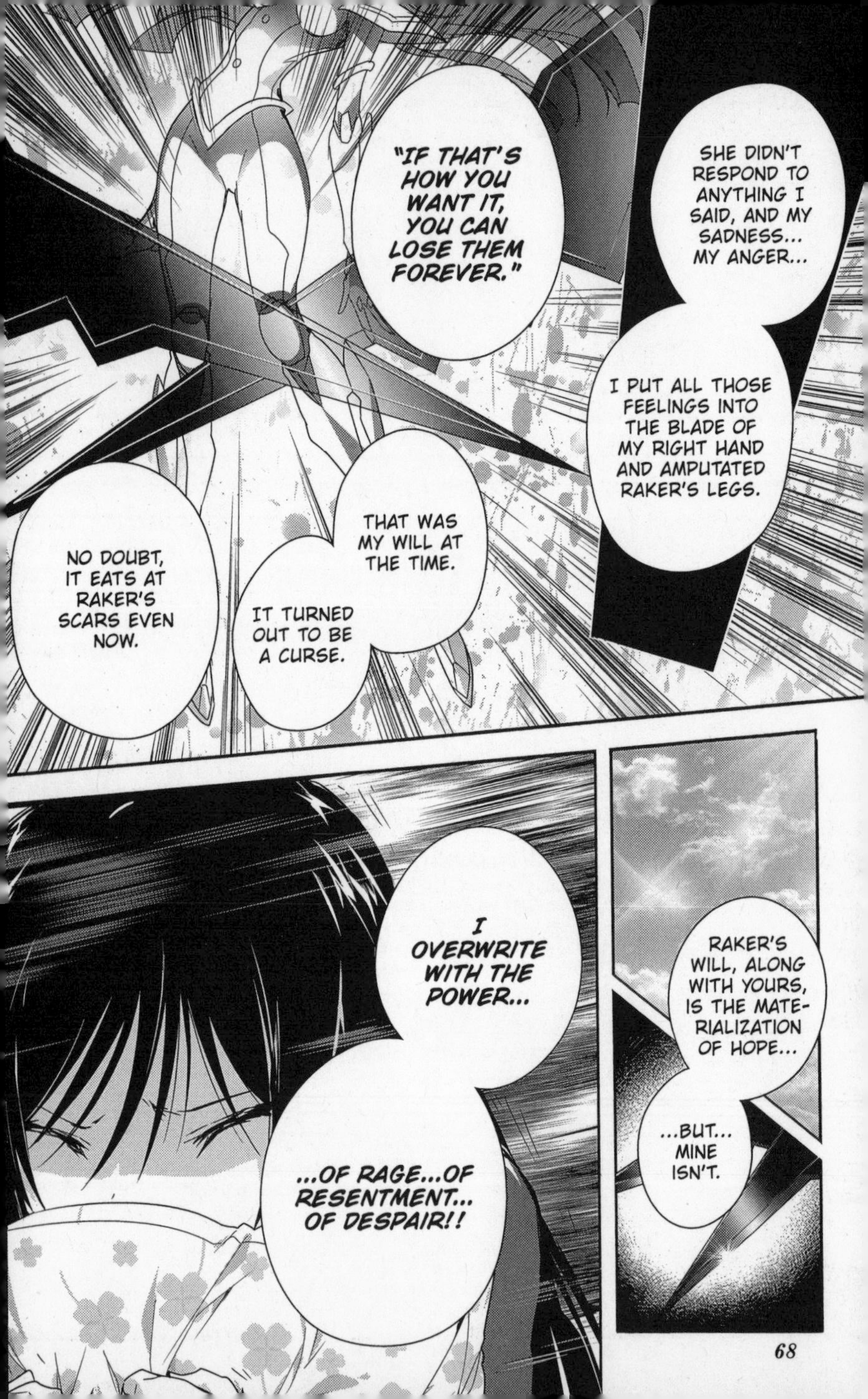
SHE DIDN'T RESPOND TO ANYTHING I SAID, AND MY SADNESS... MY ANGER...
"IF THAT'S HOW YOU WANT IT, YOU CAN LOSE THEM FOREVER."
I PUT ALL THOSE FEELINGS INTO THE BLADE OF MY RIGHT HAND AND AMPUTATED RAKER'S LEGS.
THAT WAS MY WILL AT THE TIME.
IT TURNED OUT TO BE A CURSE.
NO DOUBT, IT EATS AT RAKER'S SCARS EVEN NOW.
RAKER'S WILL, ALONG WITH YOURS, IS THE MATE-RIALIZATION OF HOPE...
...BUT... MINE ISN'T.
I OVERWRITE WITH THE POWER...
...OF RAGE...OF RESENTMENT... OF DESPAIR!!

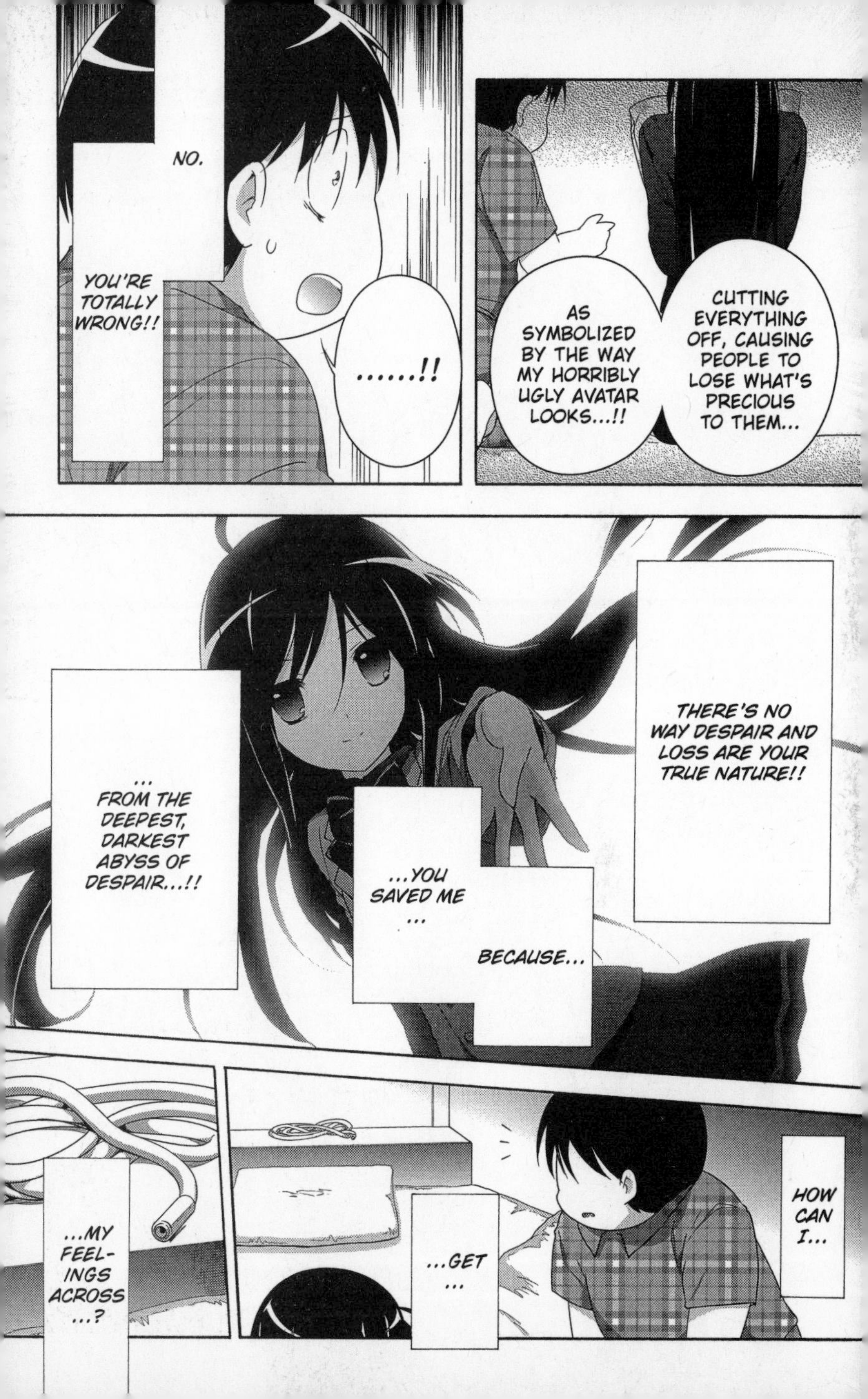
CUTTING EVERYTHING OFF, CAUSING PEOPLE TO LOSE WHAT'S PRECIOUS TO THEM...
AS SYMBOLIZED BY THE WAY MY HORRIBLY UGLY AVATAR LOOKS...!!
......!!
NO.
YOU'RE TOTALLY WRONG!!
THERE'S NO WAY DESPAIR AND LOSS ARE YOUR TRUE NATURE!!
...YOU SAVED ME ...
BECAUSE...
... FROM THE DEEPEST, DARKEST ABYSS OF DESPAIR...!!
HOW CAN I...
...GET ...
...MY FEEL-INGS ACROSS ...?

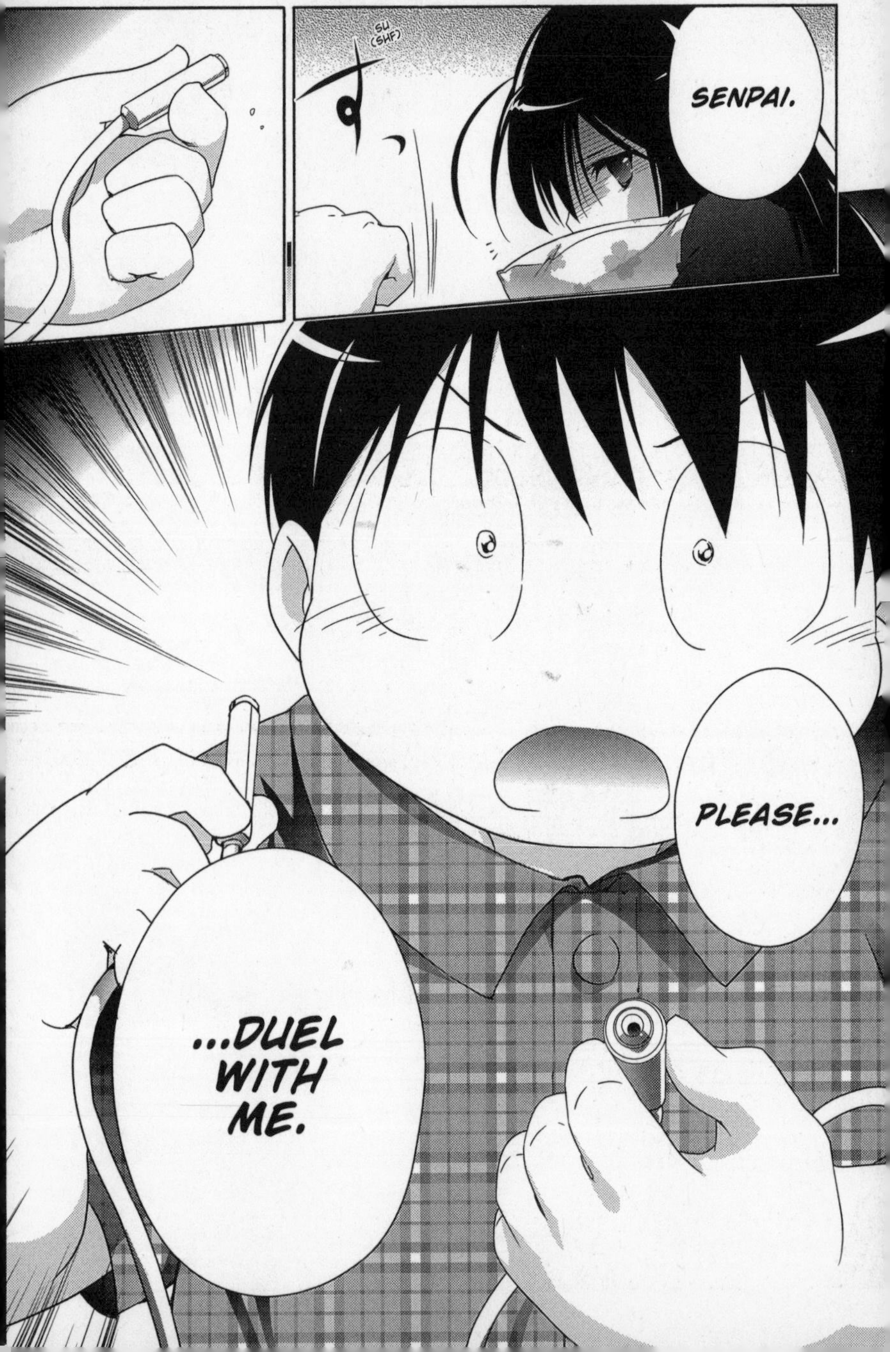
SU (SHF)
SENPAI.
PLEASE...
...DUEL WITH ME.

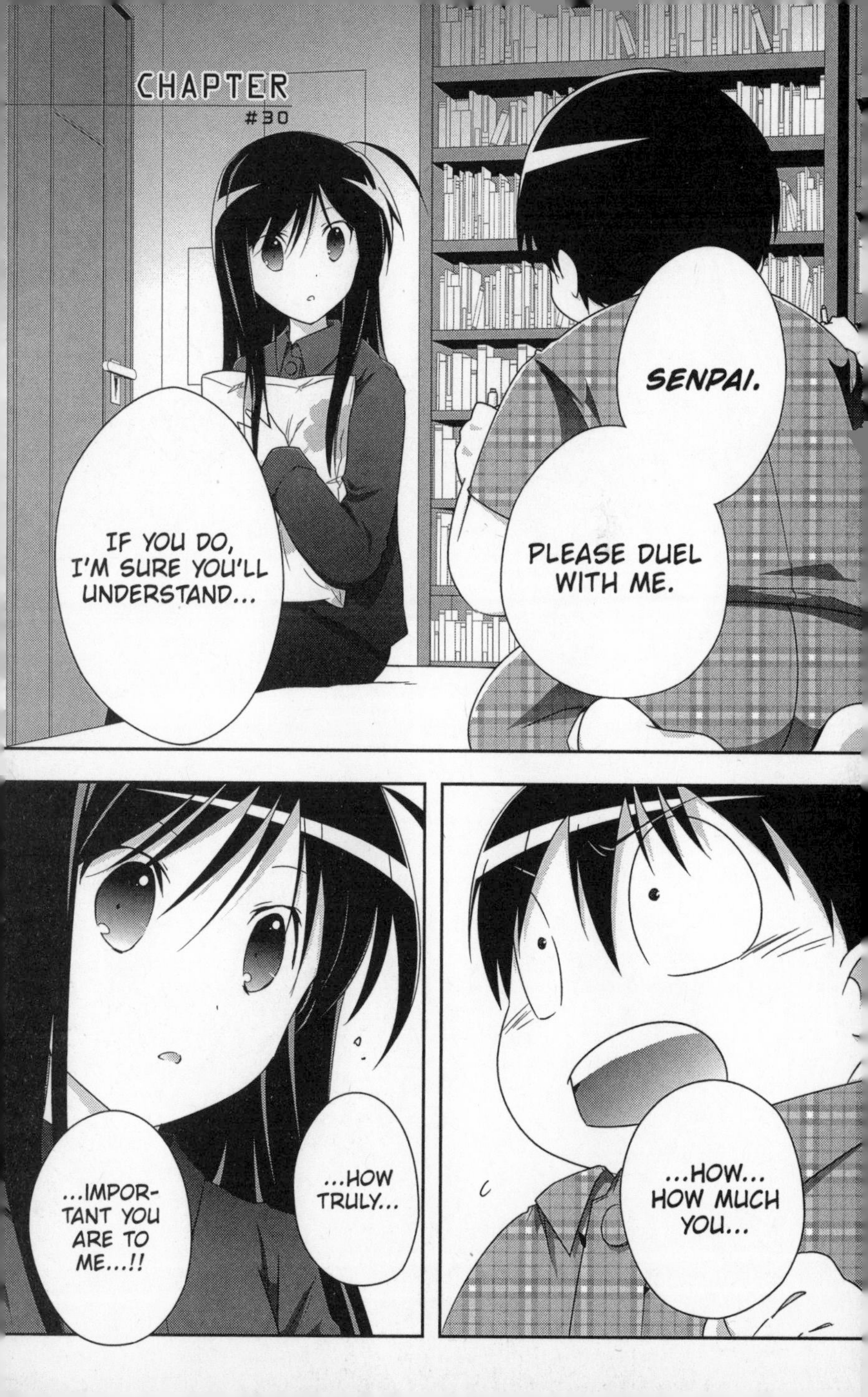
CHAPTER #30
SENPAI.
PLEASE DUEL WITH ME.
IF YOU DO, I'M SURE YOU'LL UNDERSTAND...
...HOW... HOW MUCH YOU...
...HOW TRULY...
...IMPOR-TANT YOU ARE TO ME...!!

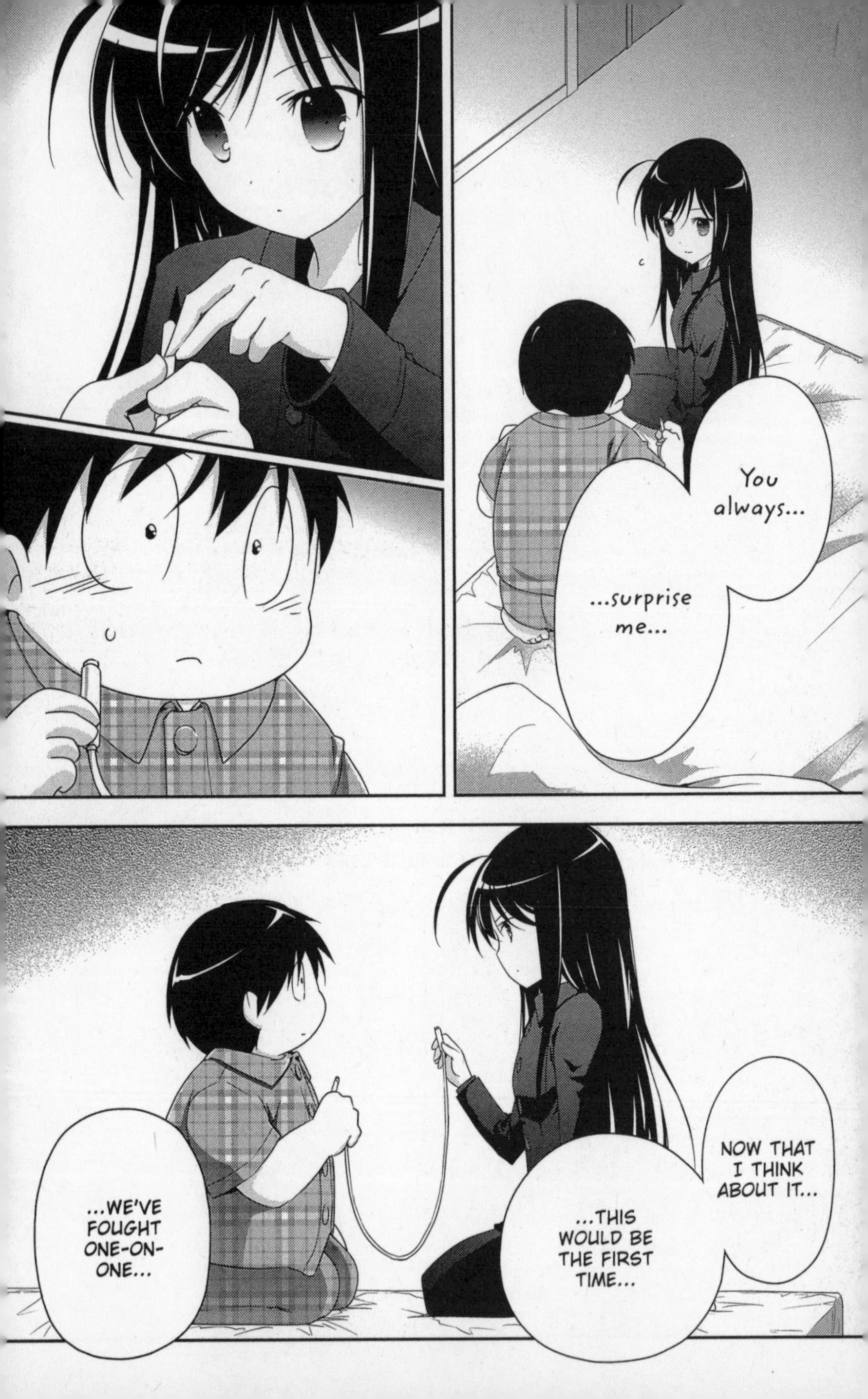
You always...
...surprise me...
NOW THAT I THINK ABOUT IT...
...THIS WOULD BE THE FIRST TIME...
...WE'VE FOUGHT ONE-ON-ONE...

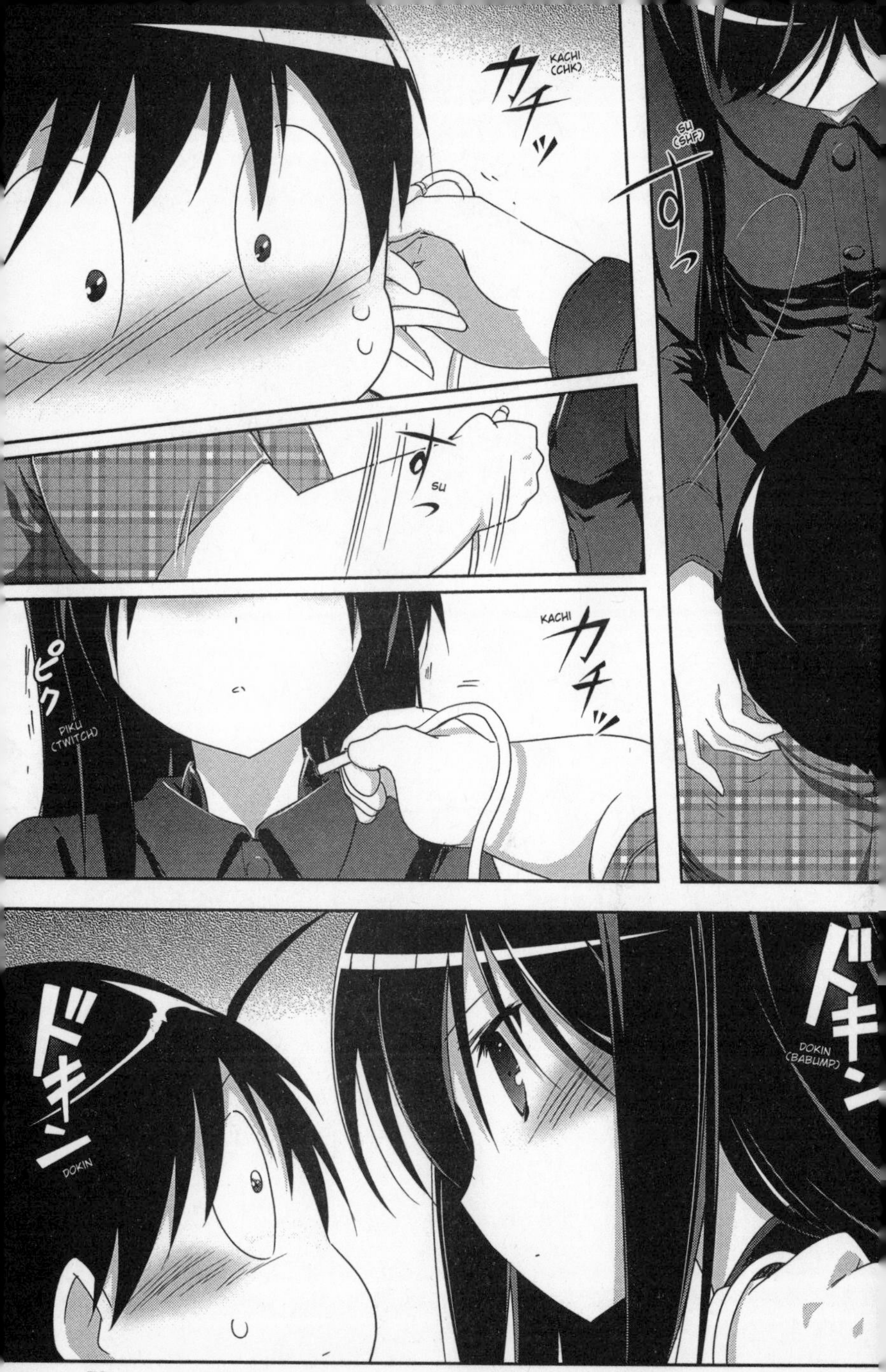
すっ
SU (SHF)
カチッ
KACHI (CHK)
すっ
SU
ピク
PIKU (TWITCH)
カチッ
KACHI
ドキン
DOKIN (BABUMP)
ドキン
DOKIN

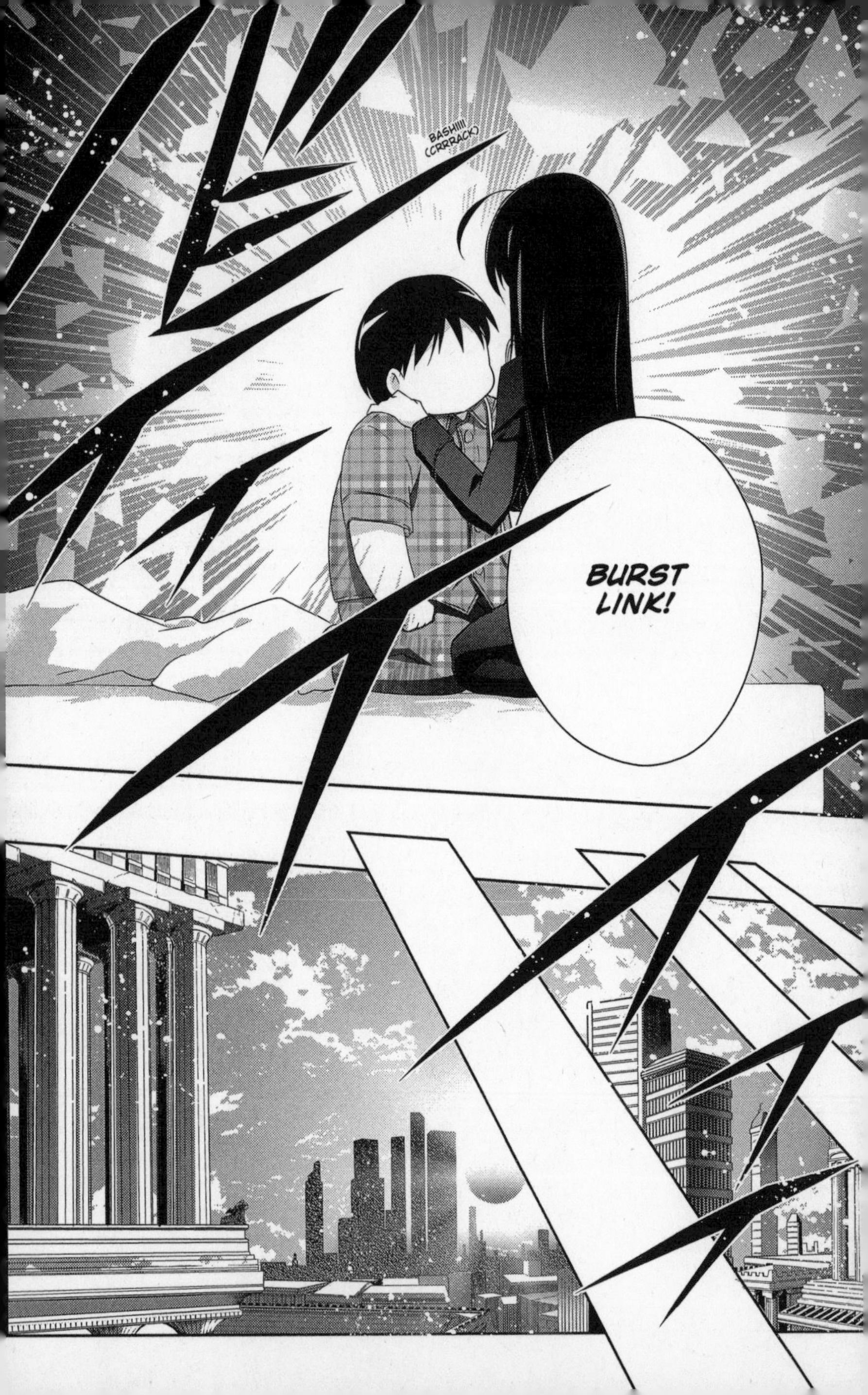
BASHIIIII
(CRRRACK)
BURST LINK!

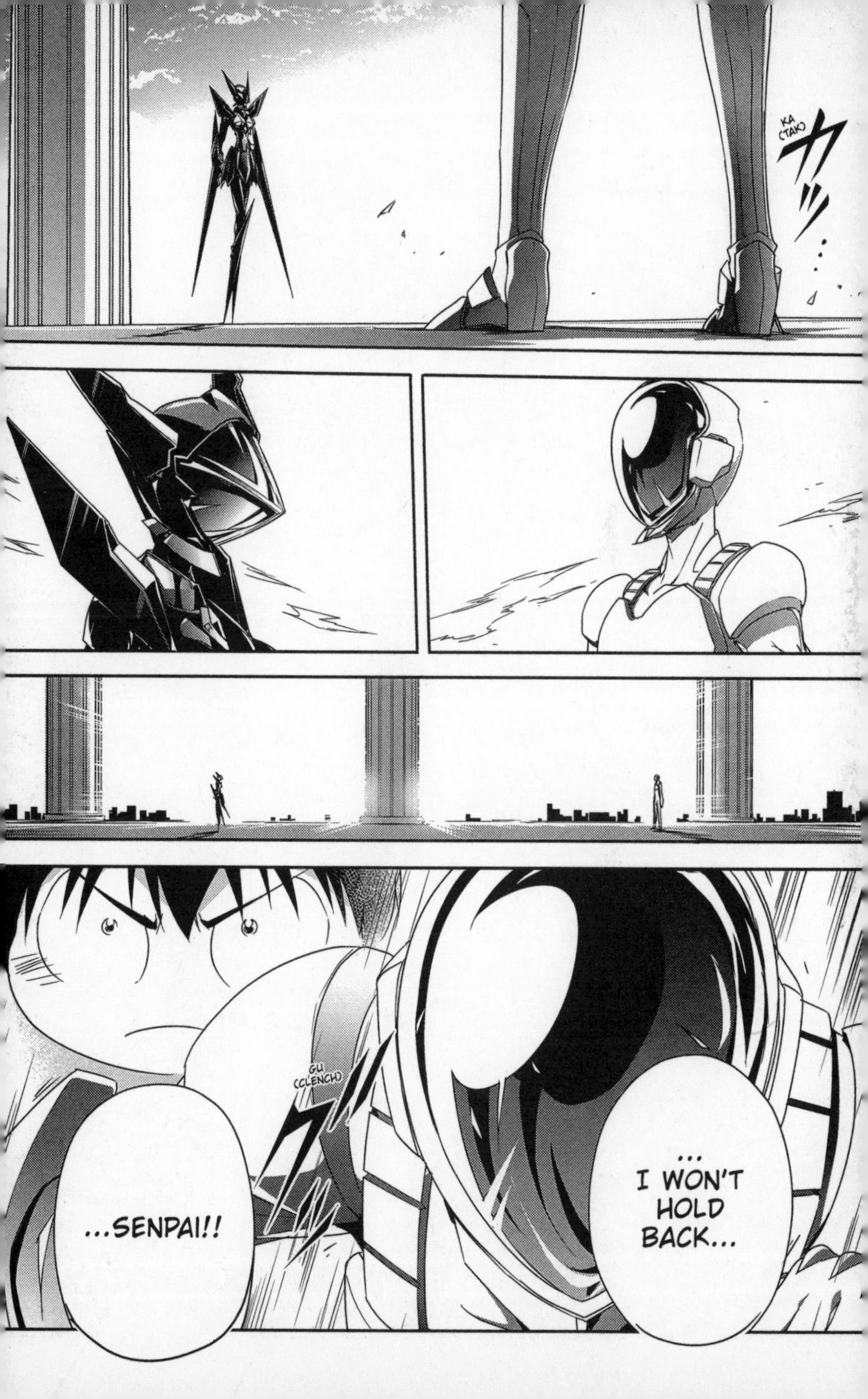
KA (TAK)
... I WON'T HOLD BACK...
GU (CLENCH)
...SENPAI!!

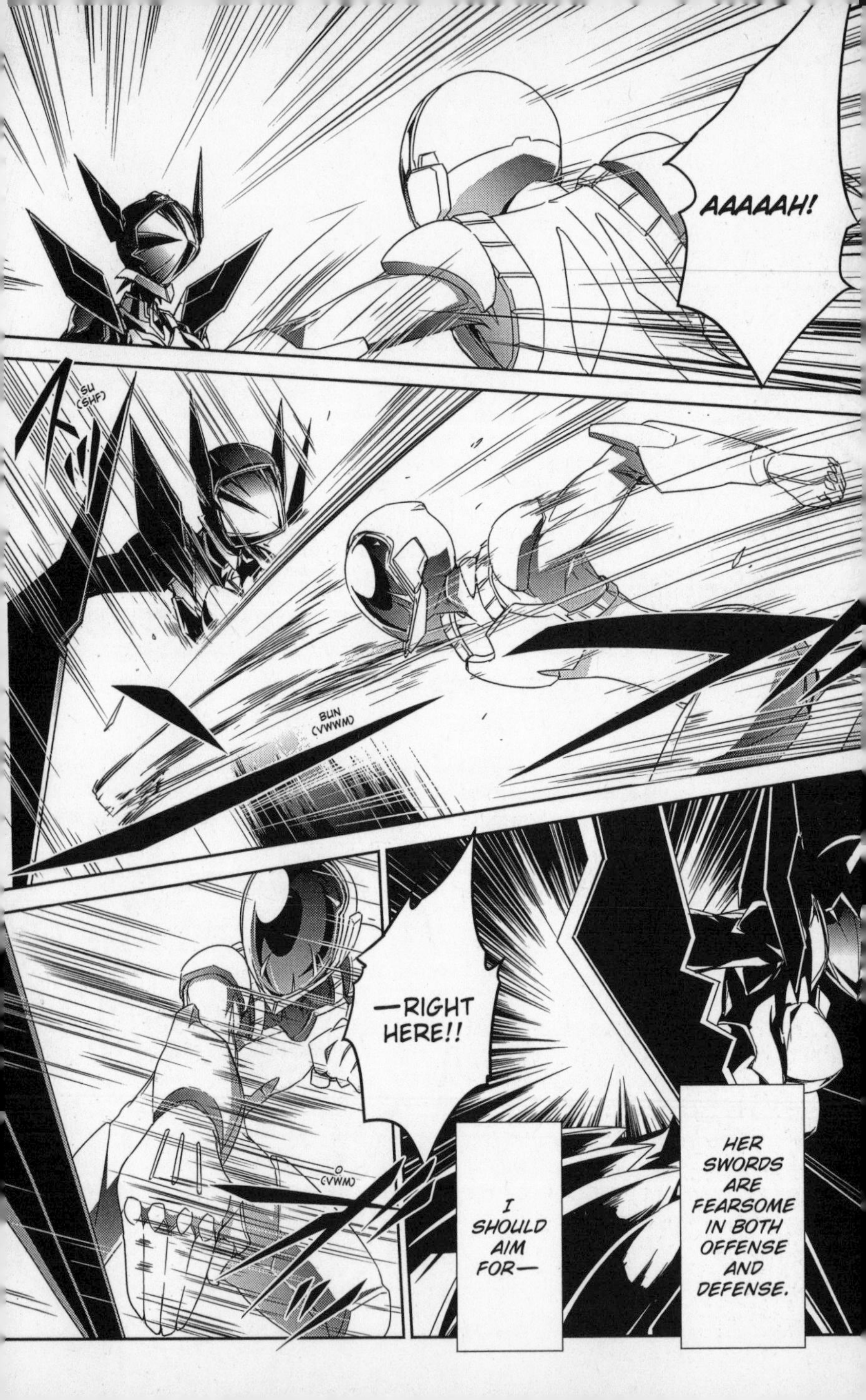
AAAAAH!
SU (SHF)
BUN (VWWM)
HER SWORDS ARE FEARSOME IN BOTH OFFENSE AND DEFENSE.
I SHOULD AIM FOR—
—RIGHT HERE!!
(VWM)

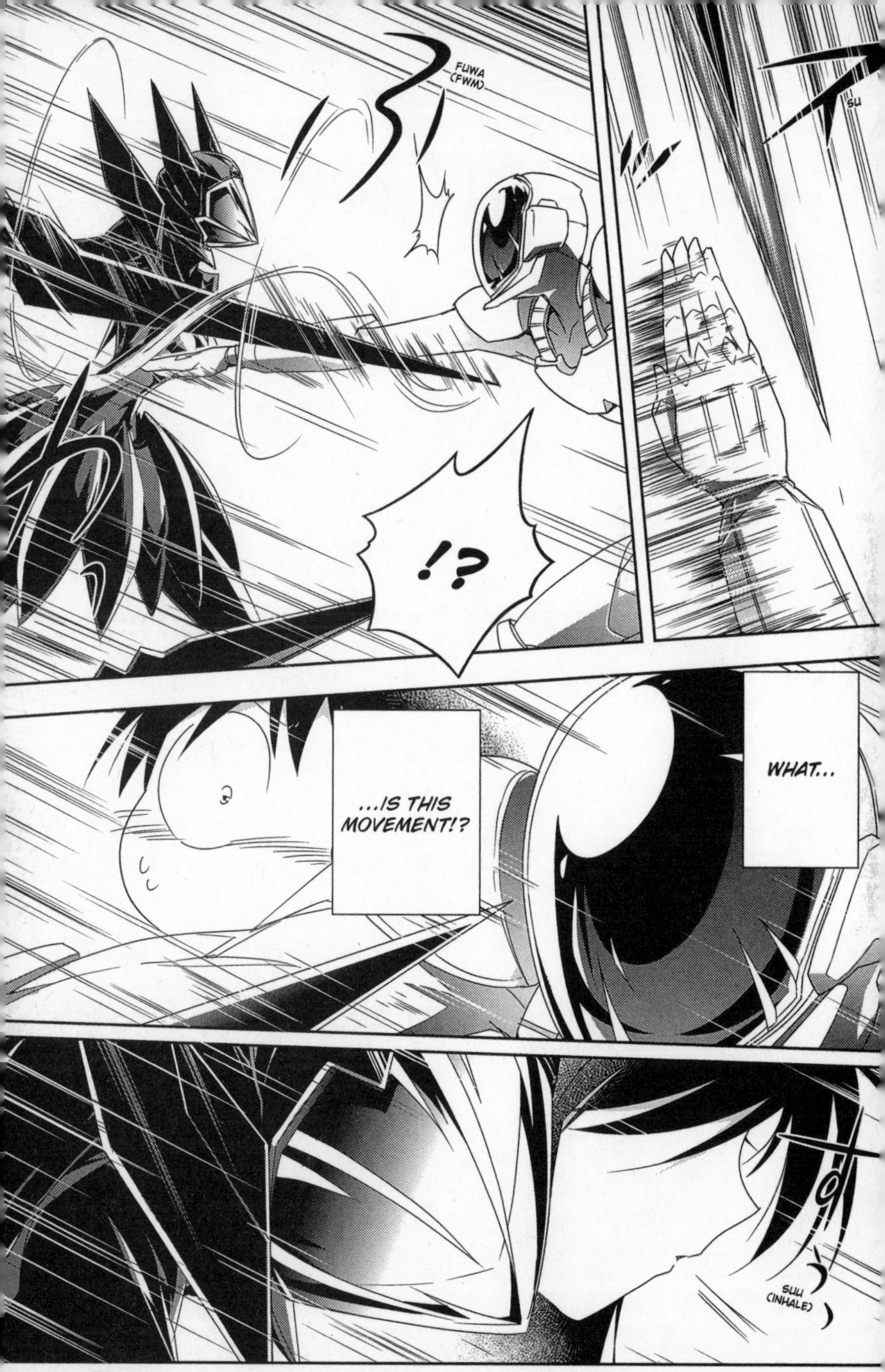
SU
FUWA (FWM)
!?
WHAT...
...IS THIS MOVEMENT!?
SUU (INHALE)

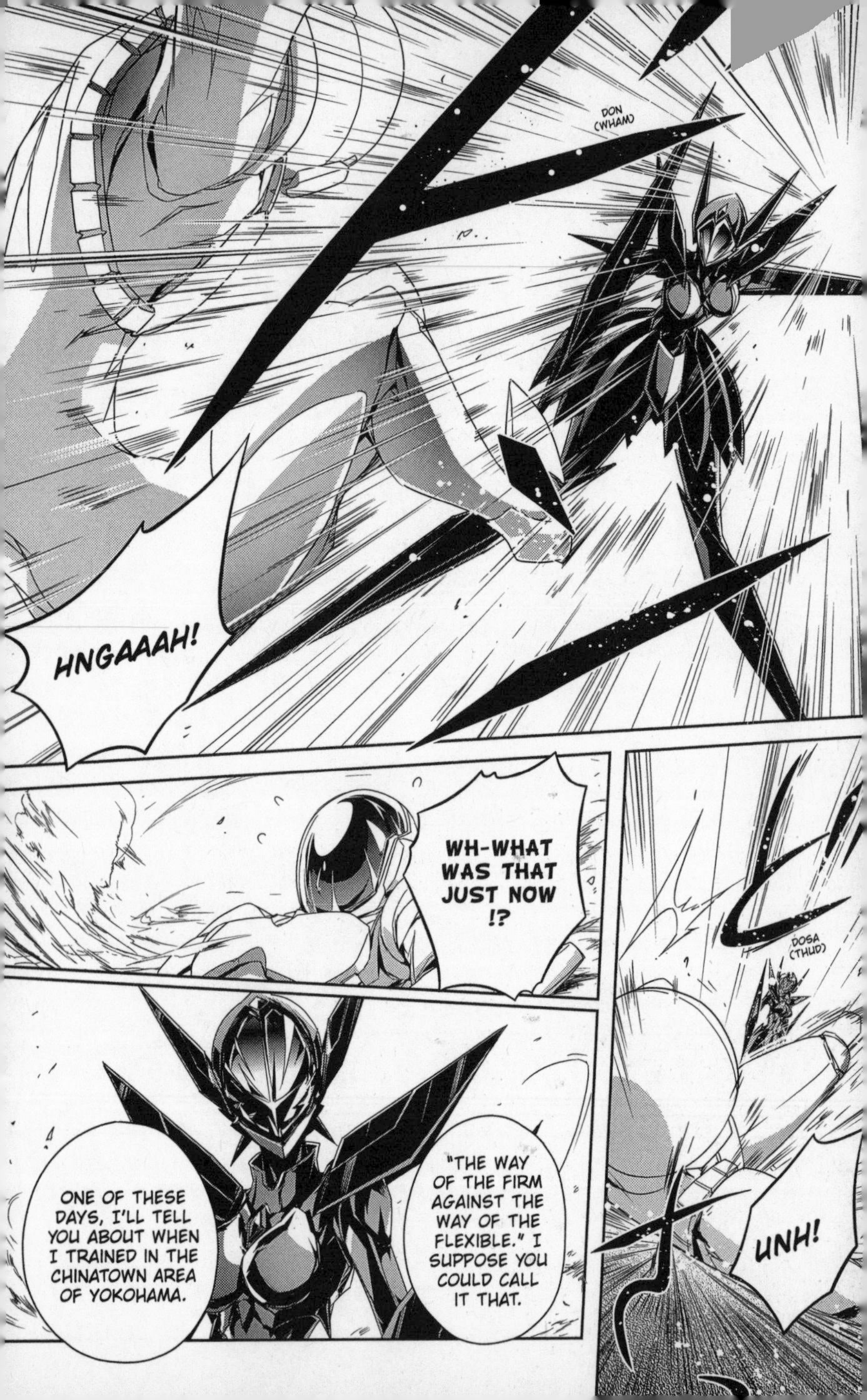
DON (WHAM)
HNGAAAH!
DOSA (THUD)
UNH!
WH-WHAT WAS THAT JUST NOW !?
"THE WAY OF THE FIRM AGAINST THE WAY OF THE FLEXIBLE." I SUPPOSE YOU COULD CALL IT THAT.
ONE OF THESE DAYS, I'LL TELL YOU ABOUT WHEN I TRAINED IN THE CHINATOWN AREA OF YOKOHAMA.

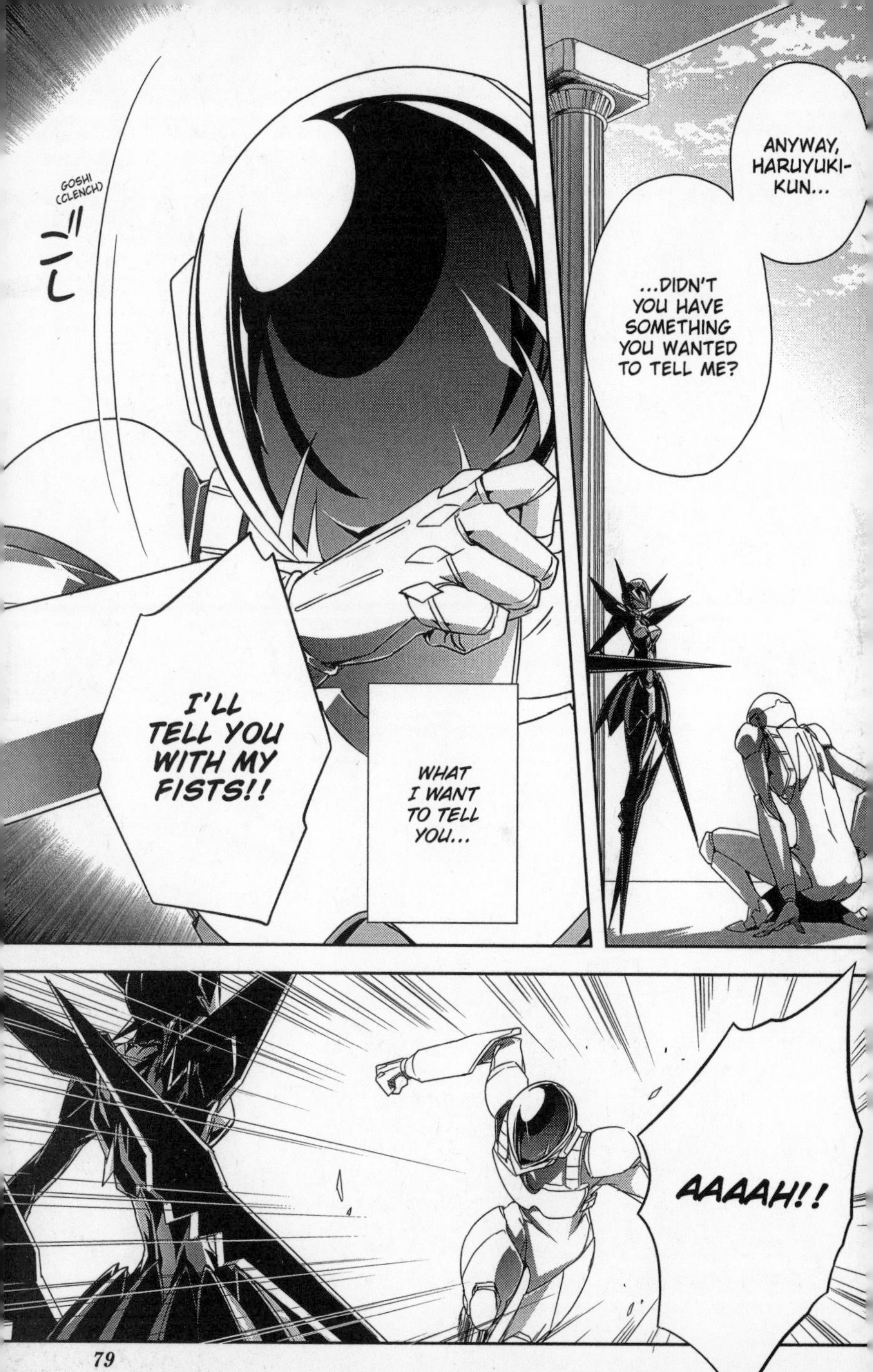
ANYWAY, HARUYUKI-KUN...
...DIDN'T YOU HAVE SOMETHING YOU WANTED TO TELL ME?
GOSHI (CLENCH)
WHAT I WANT TO TELL YOU...
I'LL TELL YOU WITH MY FISTS!!
AAAAH!!

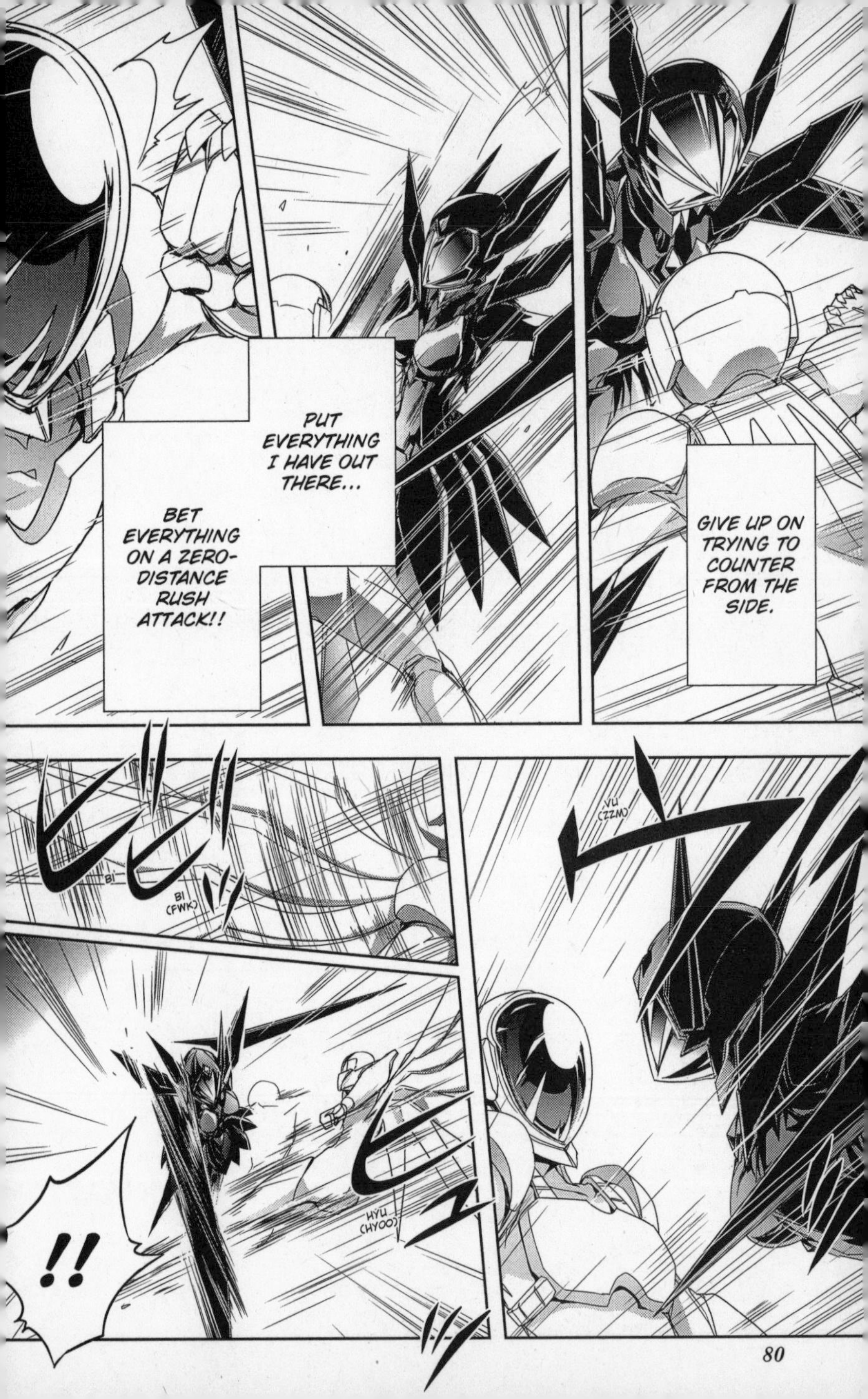
GIVE UP ON TRYING TO COUNTER FROM THE SIDE.
PUT EVERYTHING I HAVE OUT THERE...
BET EVERYTHING ON A ZERO-DISTANCE RUSH ATTACK!!
VU (ZZM)
BI
BI (FWK)
HYU (HYOO)
!!

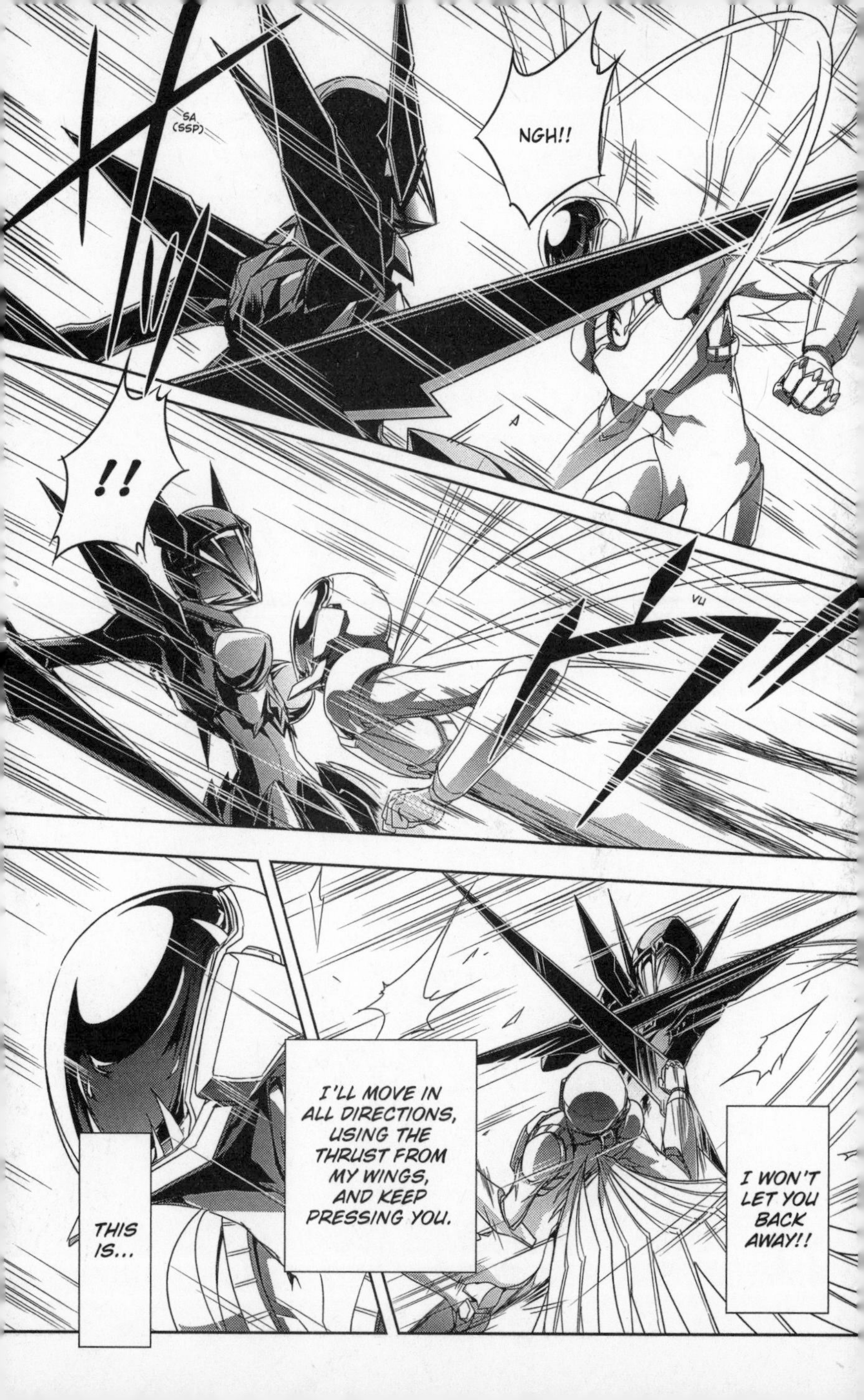
NGH!!
SA (SSP)
!!
VU
I WON'T LET YOU BACK AWAY!!
I'LL MOVE IN ALL DIRECTIONS, USING THE THRUST FROM MY WINGS, AND KEEP PRESSING YOU.
THIS IS...

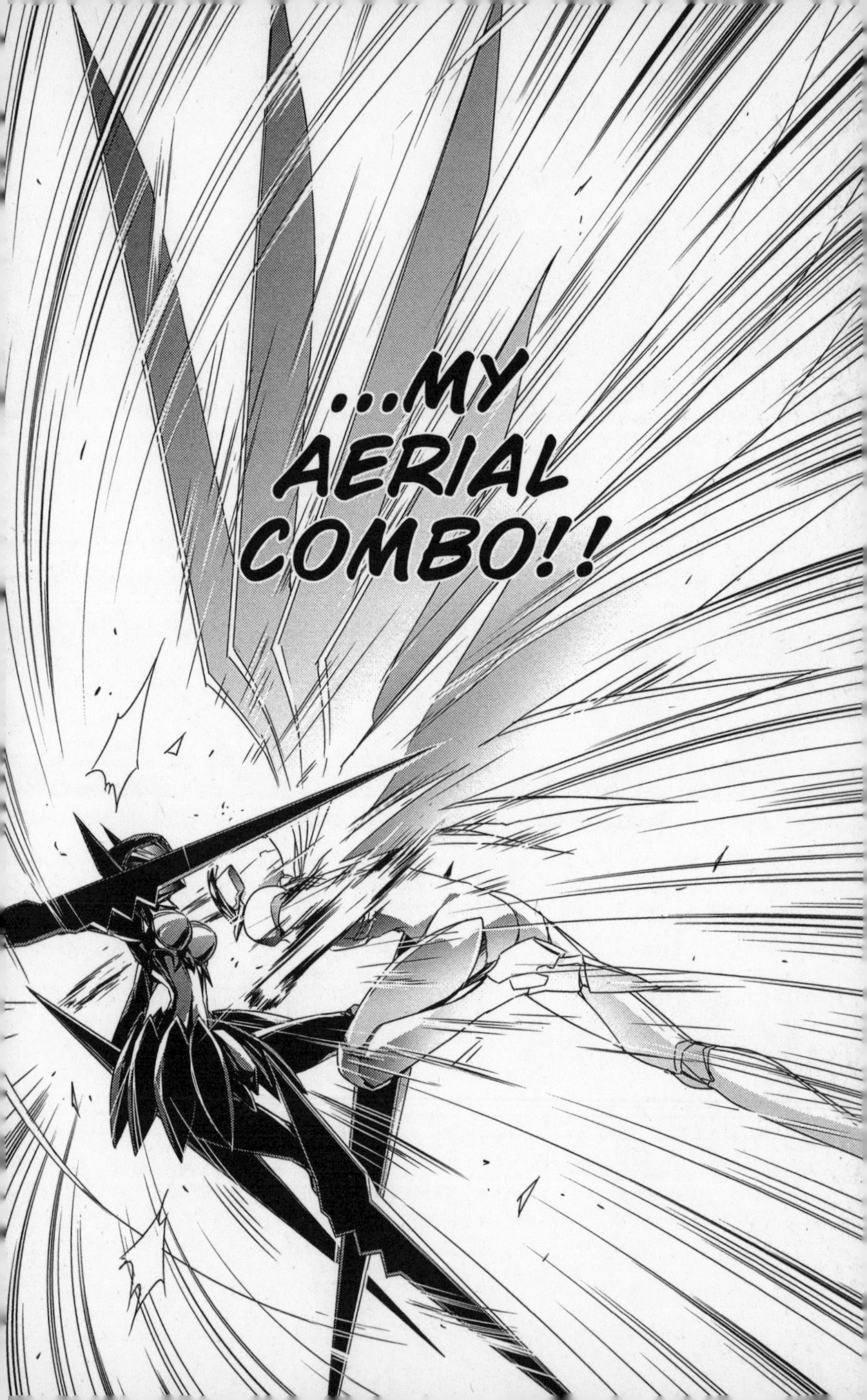
...MY AERIAL COMBO!!

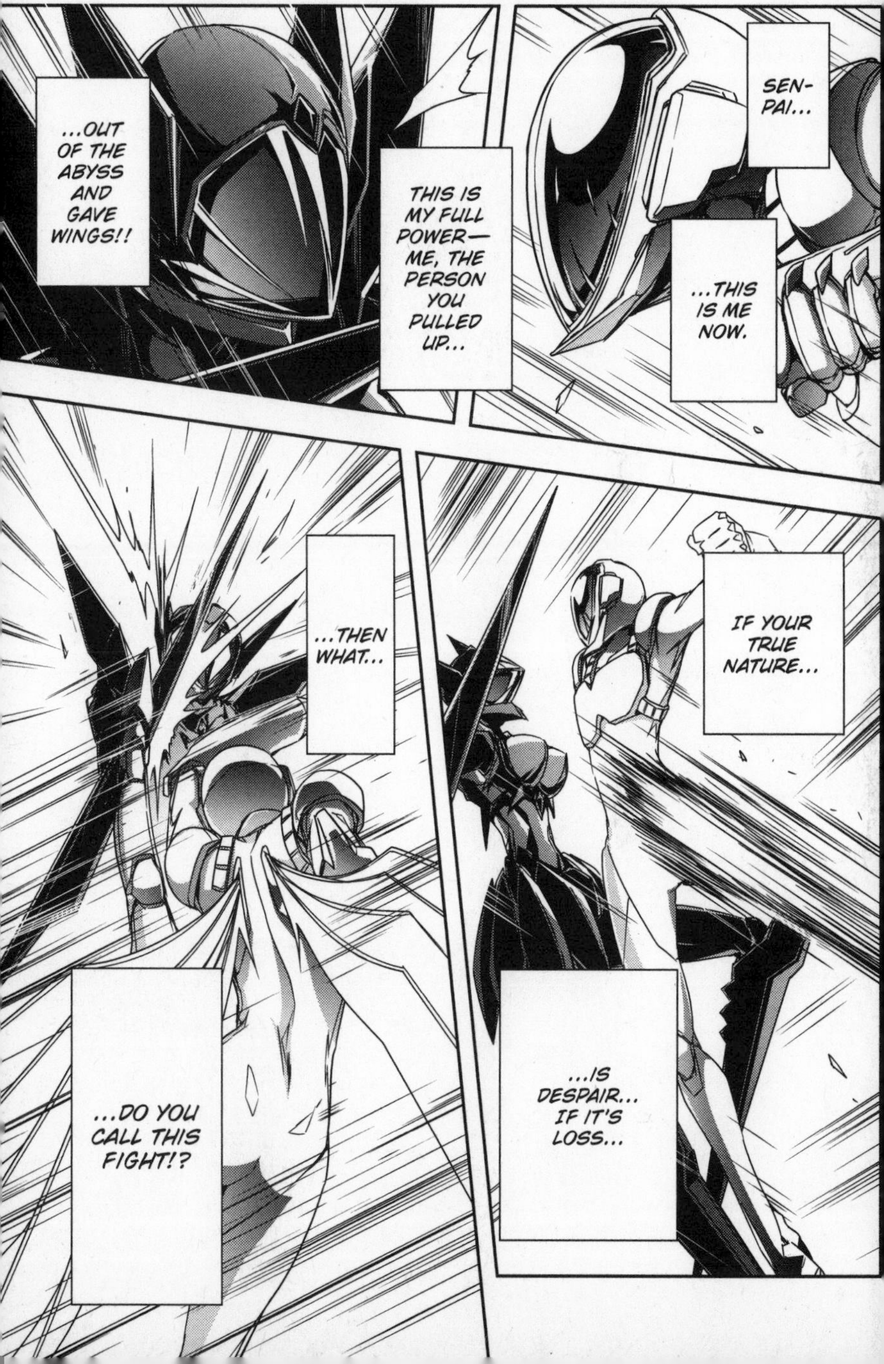
SEN-PAI...
...THIS IS ME NOW.
THIS IS MY FULL POWER—ME, THE PERSON YOU PULLED UP...
...OUT OF THE ABYSS AND GAVE WINGS!!
IF YOUR TRUE NATURE...
...IS DESPAIR... IF IT'S LOSS...
...THEN WHAT...
...DO YOU CALL THIS FIGHT!?

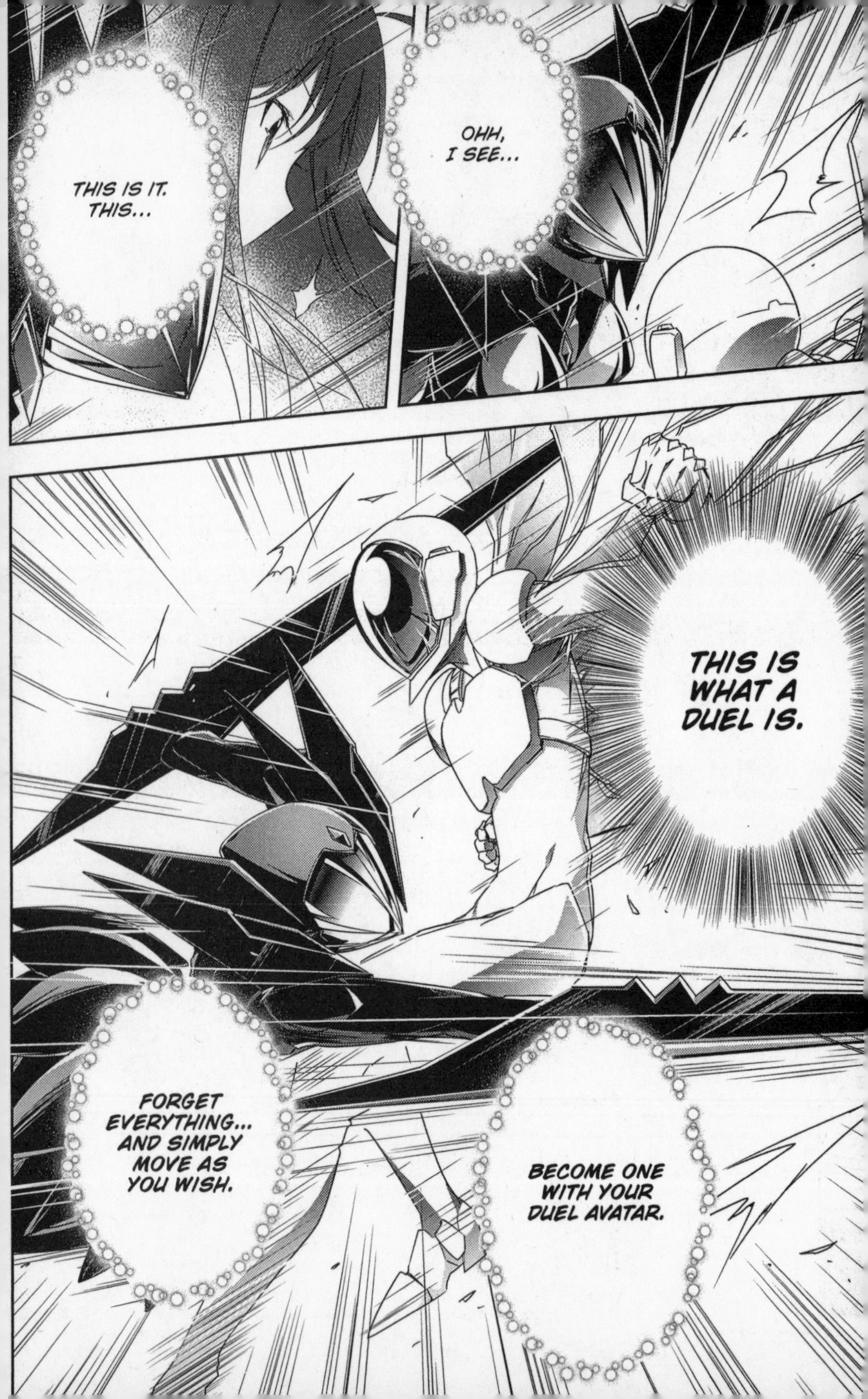
OHH, I SEE...
THIS IS IT. THIS...
THIS IS WHAT A DUEL IS.
BECOME ONE WITH YOUR DUEL AVATAR.
FORGET EVERYTHING... AND SIMPLY MOVE AS YOU WISH.

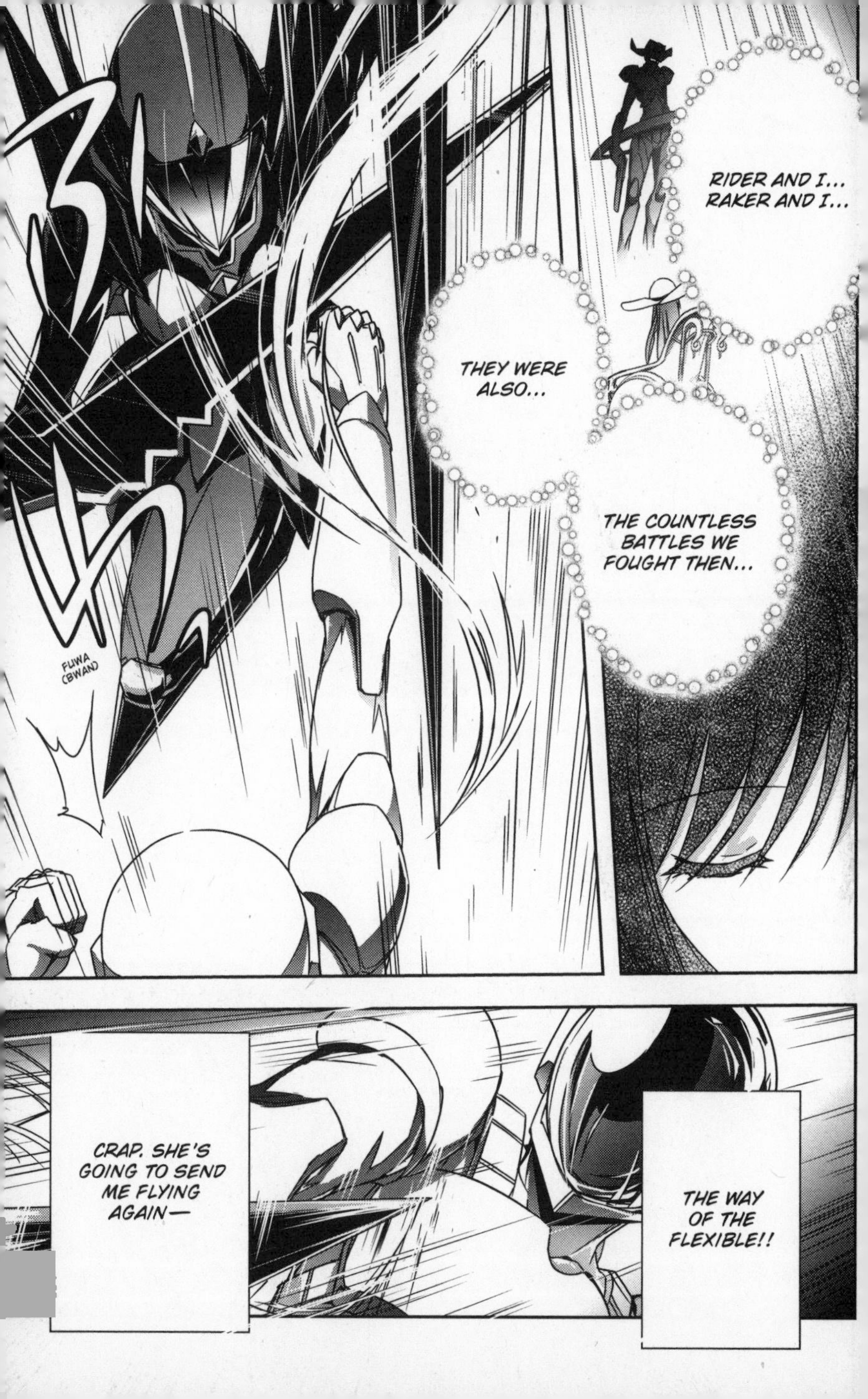
RIDER AND I...
RAKER AND I...
THEY WERE ALSO...
THE COUNTLESS BATTLES WE FOUGHT THEN...
FUWA (BWAN)
THE WAY OF THE FLEXIBLE!!
CRAP. SHE'S GOING TO SEND ME FLYING AGAIN—

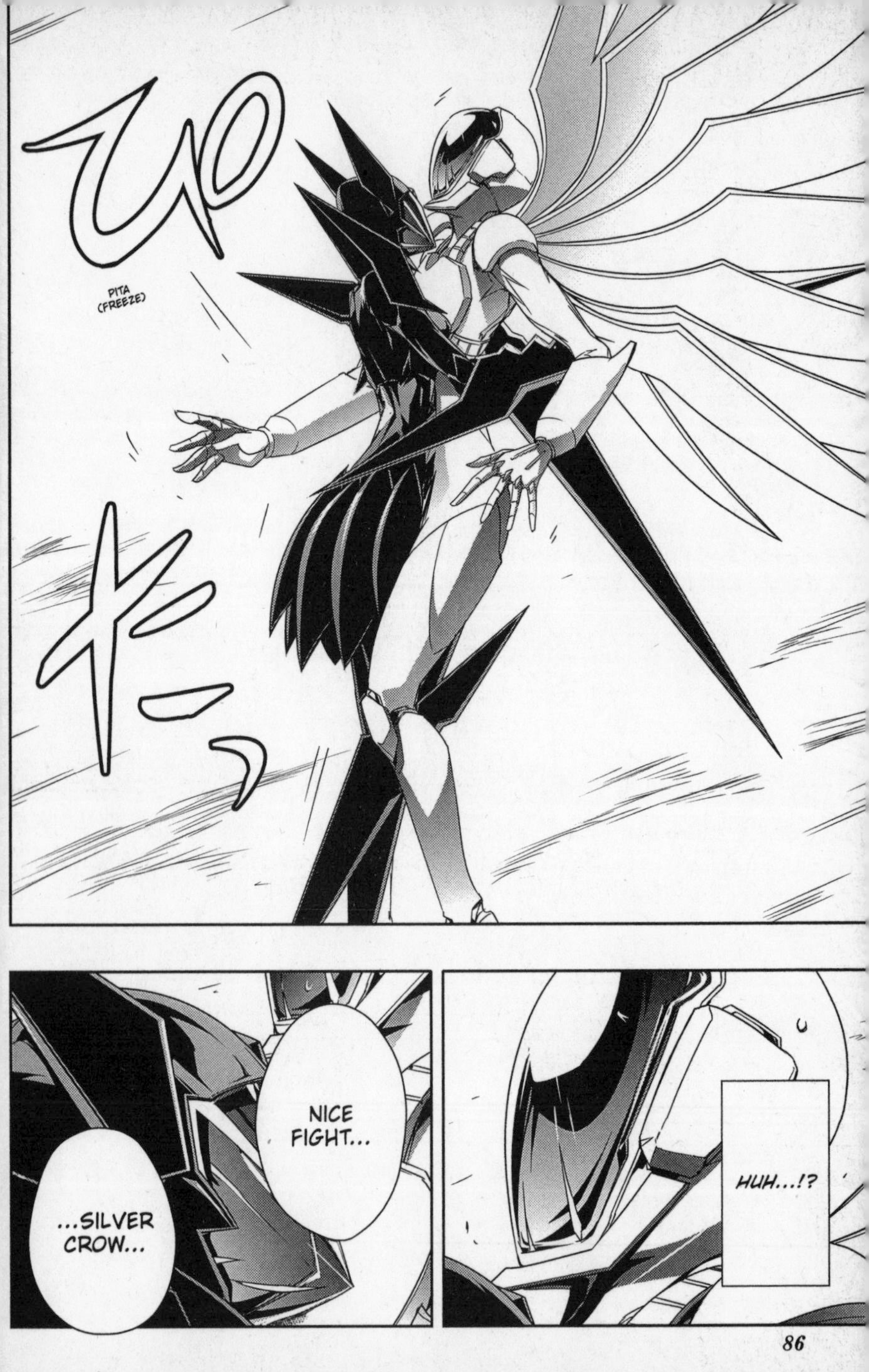
PITA
(FREEZE)
HUH...!?
NICE FIGHT...
...SILVER CROW...

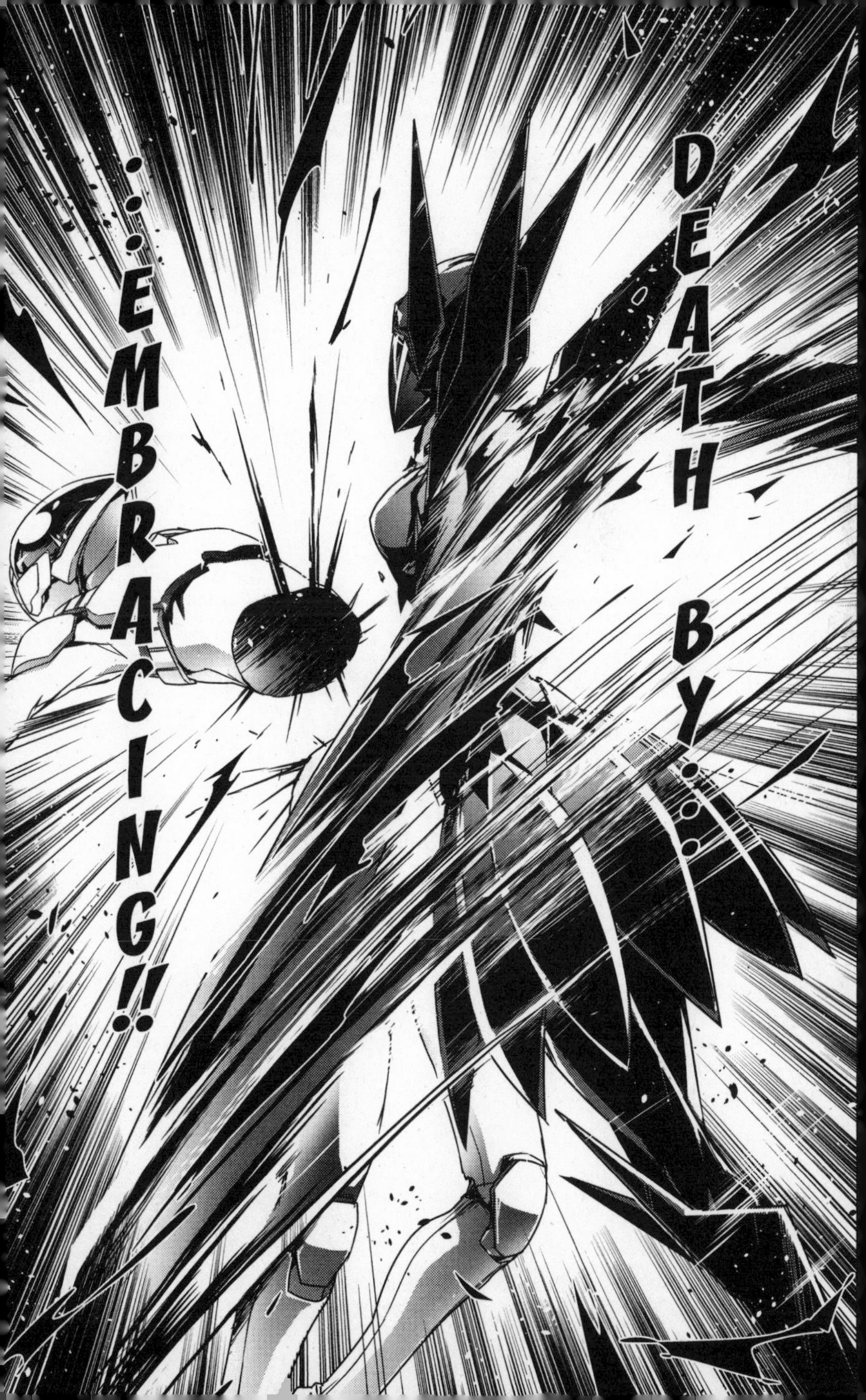
DEATH BY...
...EMBRACING!!

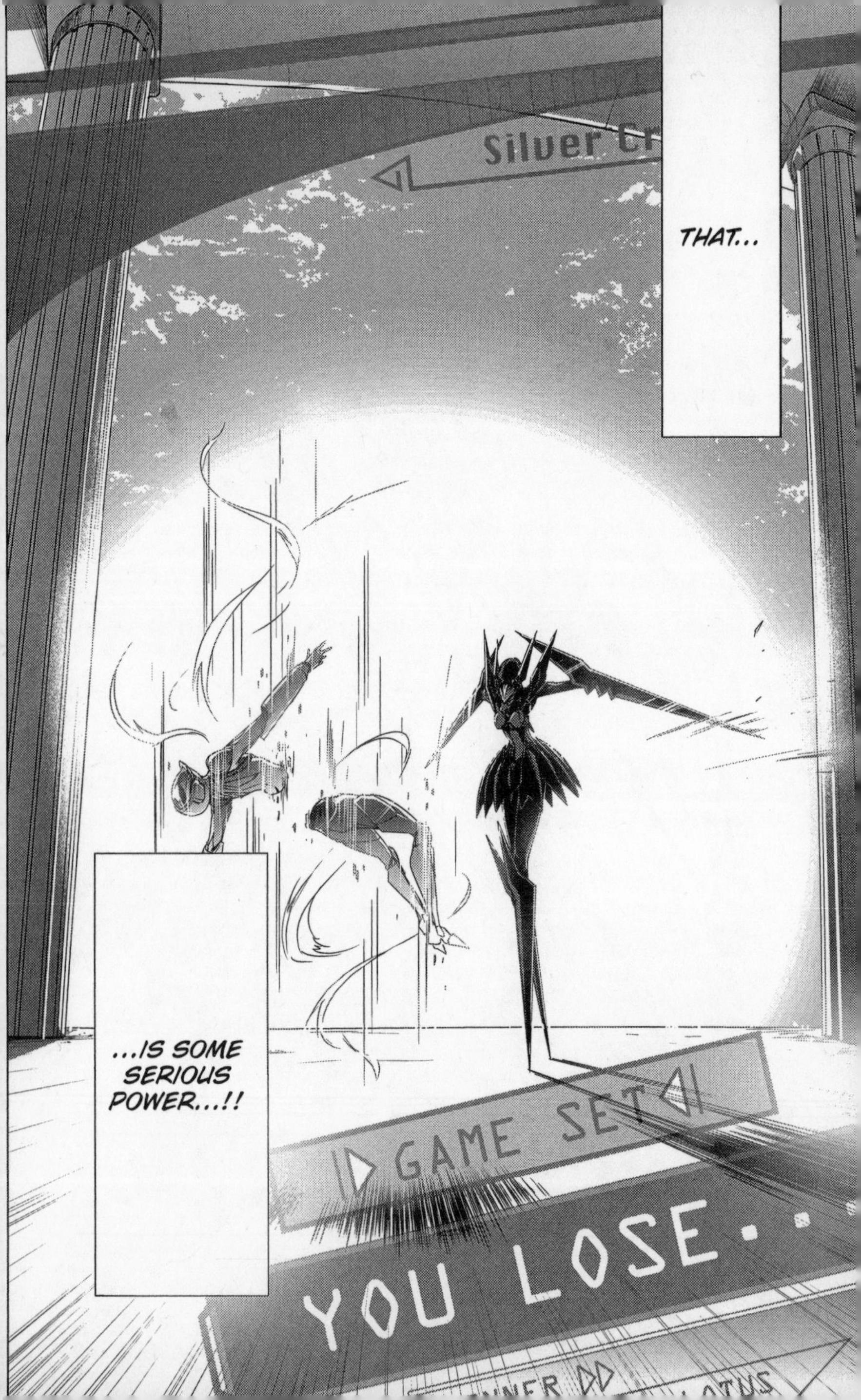

THAT...
Silver Cr
...IS SOME SERIOUS POWER...!!
GAME SET
YOU LOSE..

▶▶▶*ACCEL·WORLD*

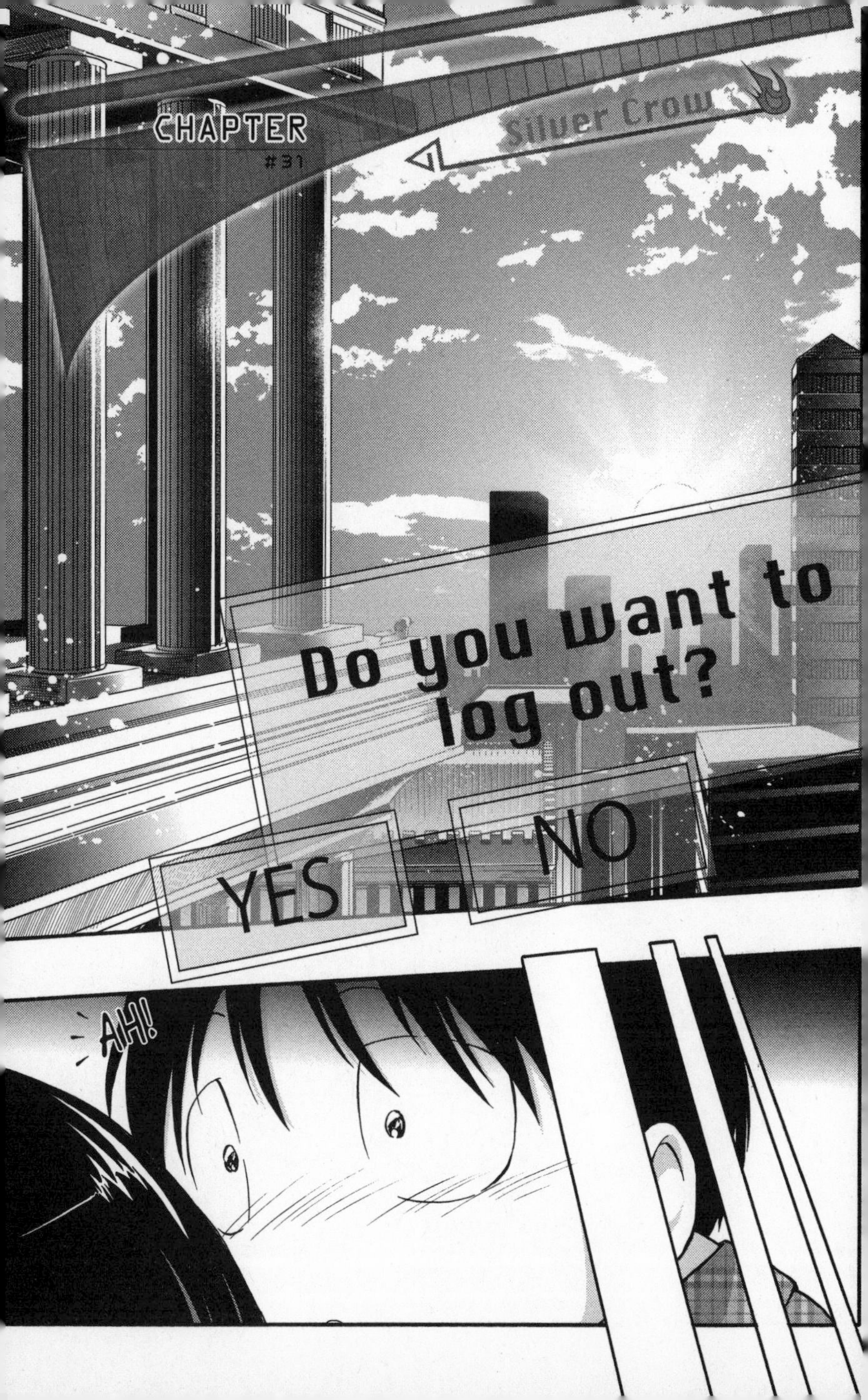
CHAPTER
#31
Silver Crow
Do you want to log out?
YES
NO
AH!

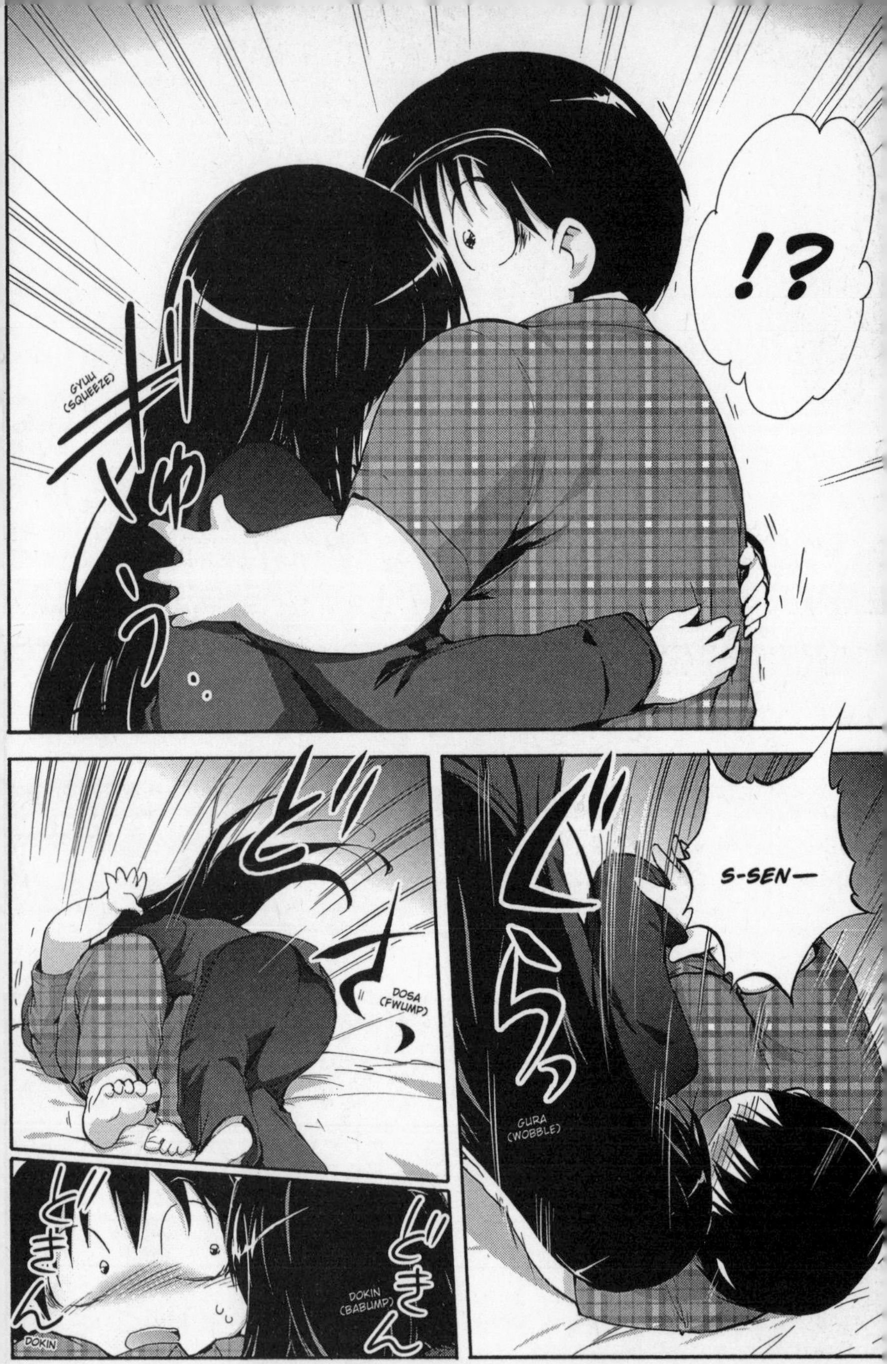
!?
GYUU (SQUEEZE)
S-SEN—
GURA (WOBBLE)
DOSA (FWUMP)
DOKIN (BABUMP)
DOKIN

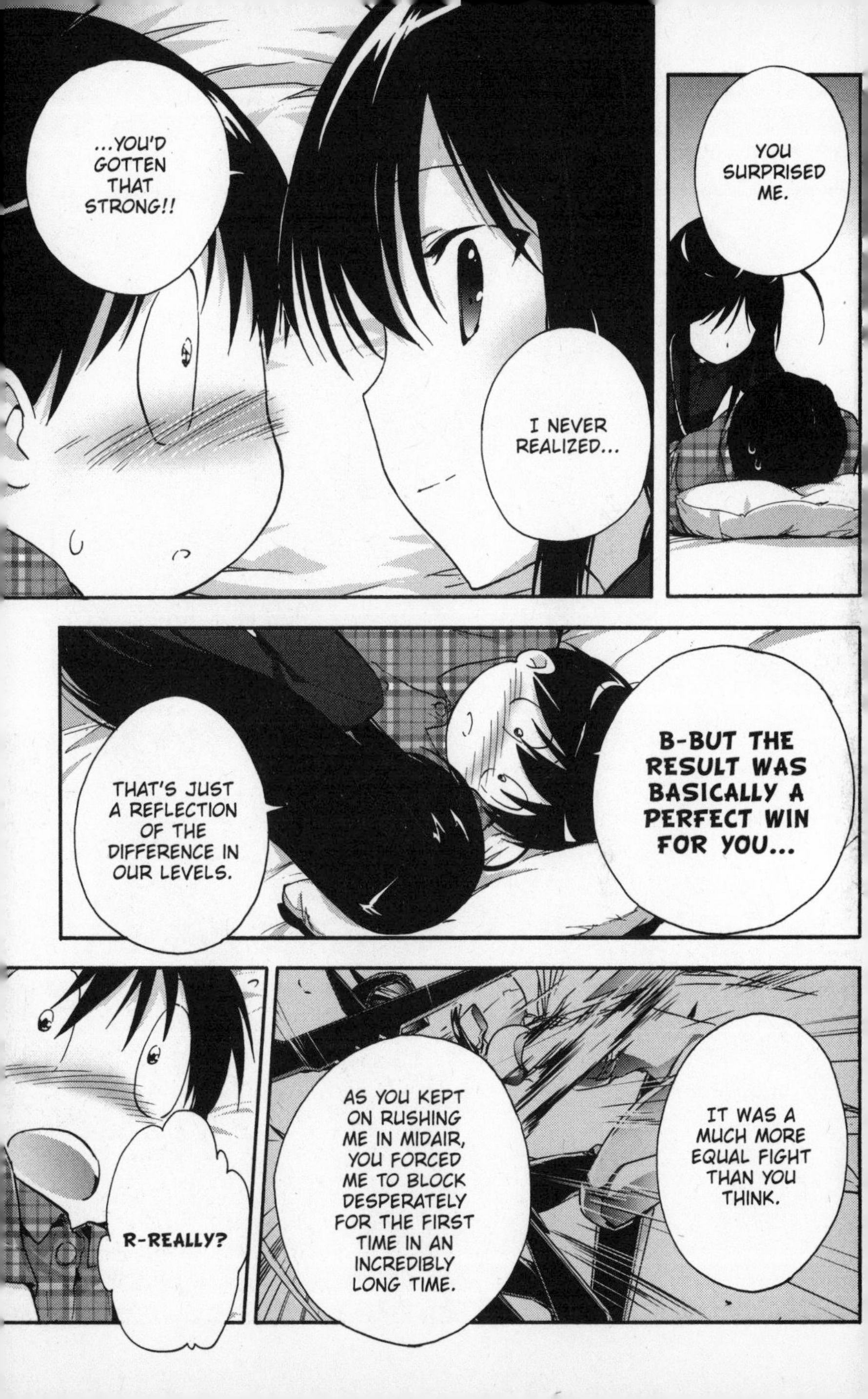
YOU SURPRISED ME.
I NEVER REALIZED...
...YOU'D GOTTEN THAT STRONG!!
B-BUT THE RESULT WAS BASICALLY A PERFECT WIN FOR YOU...
THAT'S JUST A REFLECTION OF THE DIFFERENCE IN OUR LEVELS.
IT WAS A MUCH MORE EQUAL FIGHT THAN YOU THINK.
AS YOU KEPT ON RUSHING ME IN MIDAIR, YOU FORCED ME TO BLOCK DESPERATELY FOR THE FIRST TIME IN AN INCREDIBLY LONG TIME.
R-REALLY?

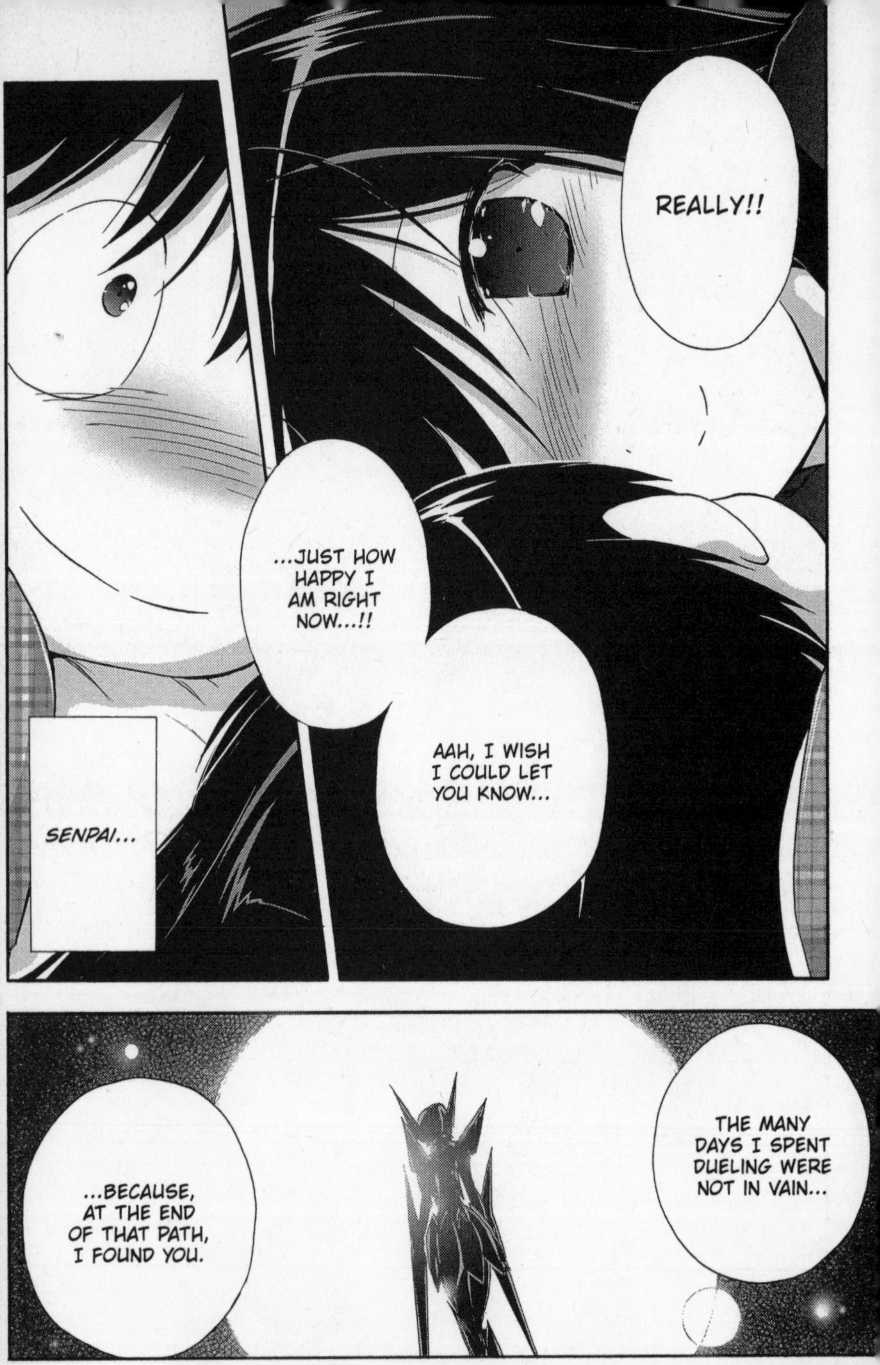
REALLY!!
...JUST HOW HAPPY I AM RIGHT NOW...!!
AAH, I WISH I COULD LET YOU KNOW...
SENPAI...
THE MANY DAYS I SPENT DUELING WERE NOT IN VAIN...
...BECAUSE, AT THE END OF THAT PATH, I FOUND YOU.

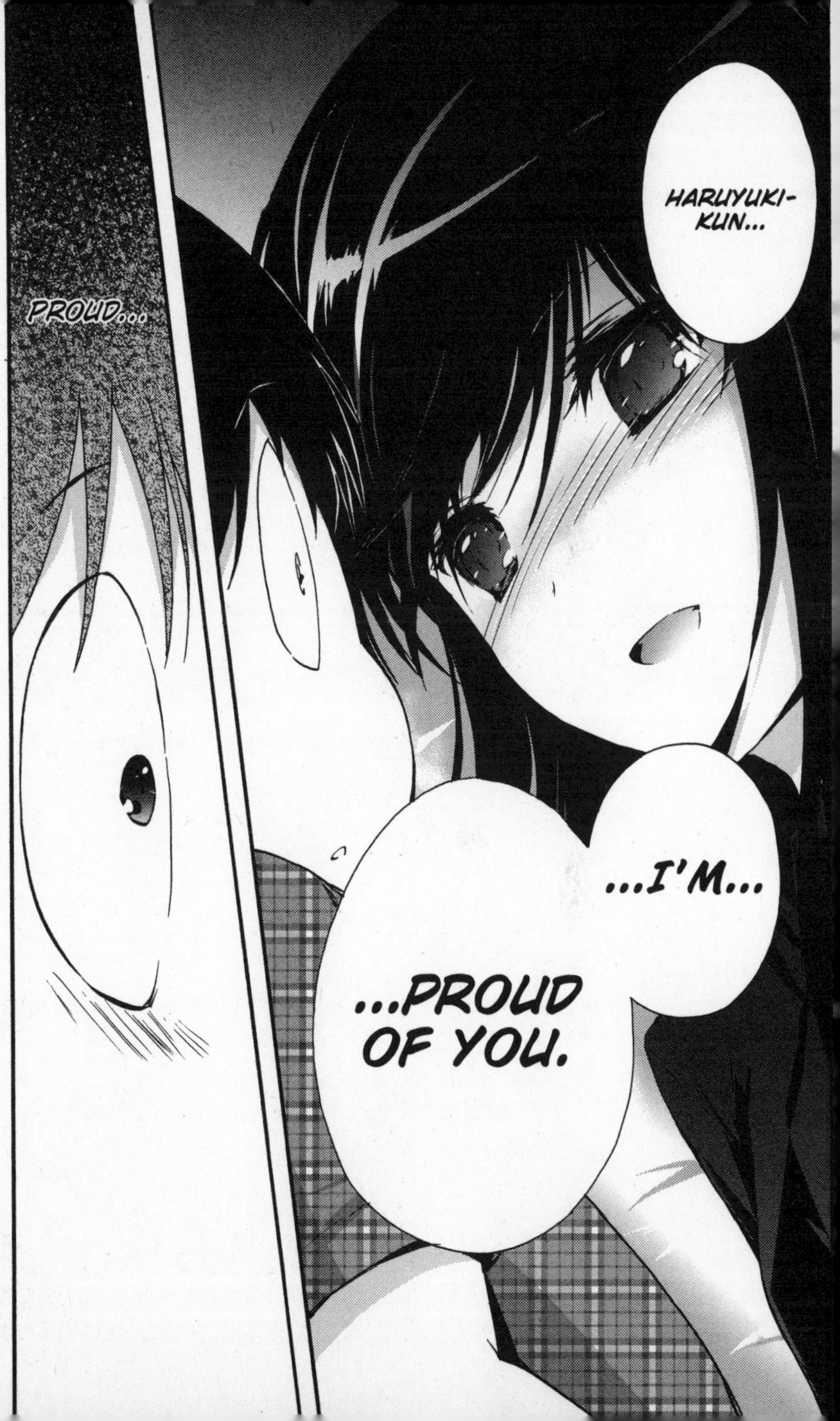
HARUYUKI-KUN...
PROUD...
...I'M...
...PROUD OF YOU.

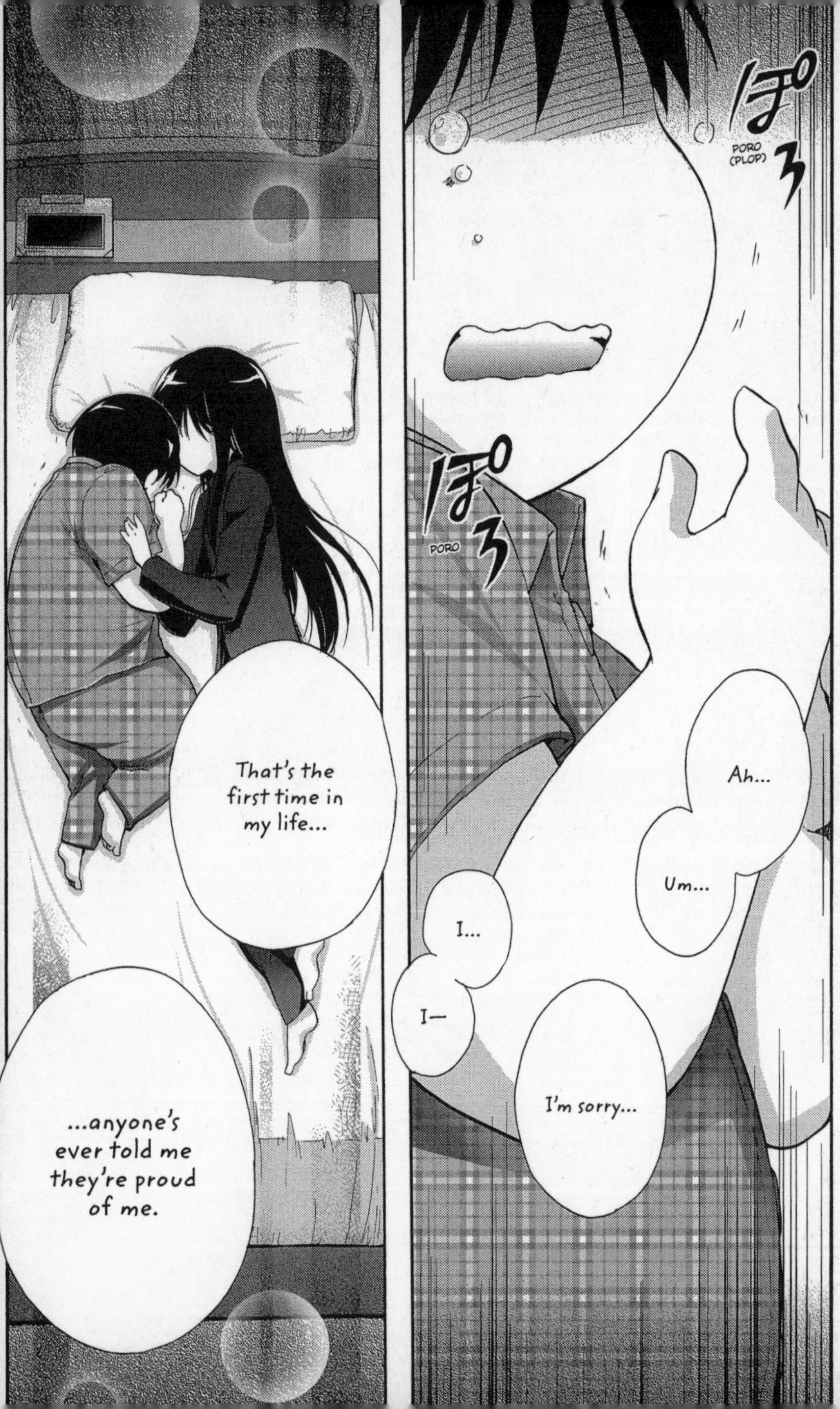

ぽろ
PORO (PLOP)
ぽろ
PORO
Ah...
Um...
I...
I—
I'm sorry...
That's the first time in my life...
...anyone's ever told me they're proud of me.

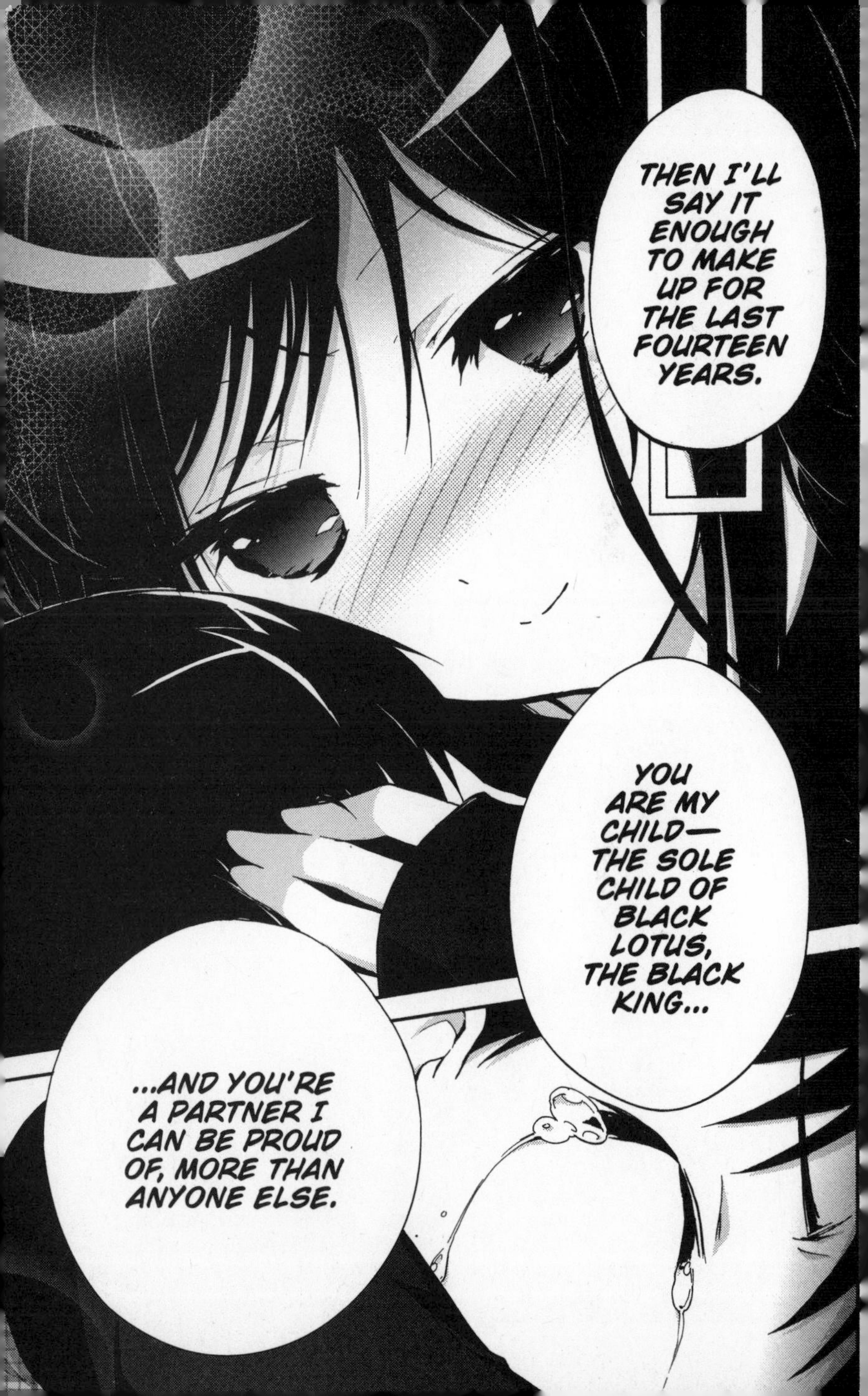
THEN I'LL SAY IT ENOUGH TO MAKE UP FOR THE LAST FOURTEEN YEARS.
YOU ARE MY CHILD—THE SOLE CHILD OF BLACK LOTUS, THE BLACK KING...
...AND YOU'RE A PARTNER I CAN BE PROUD OF, MORE THAN ANYONE ELSE.

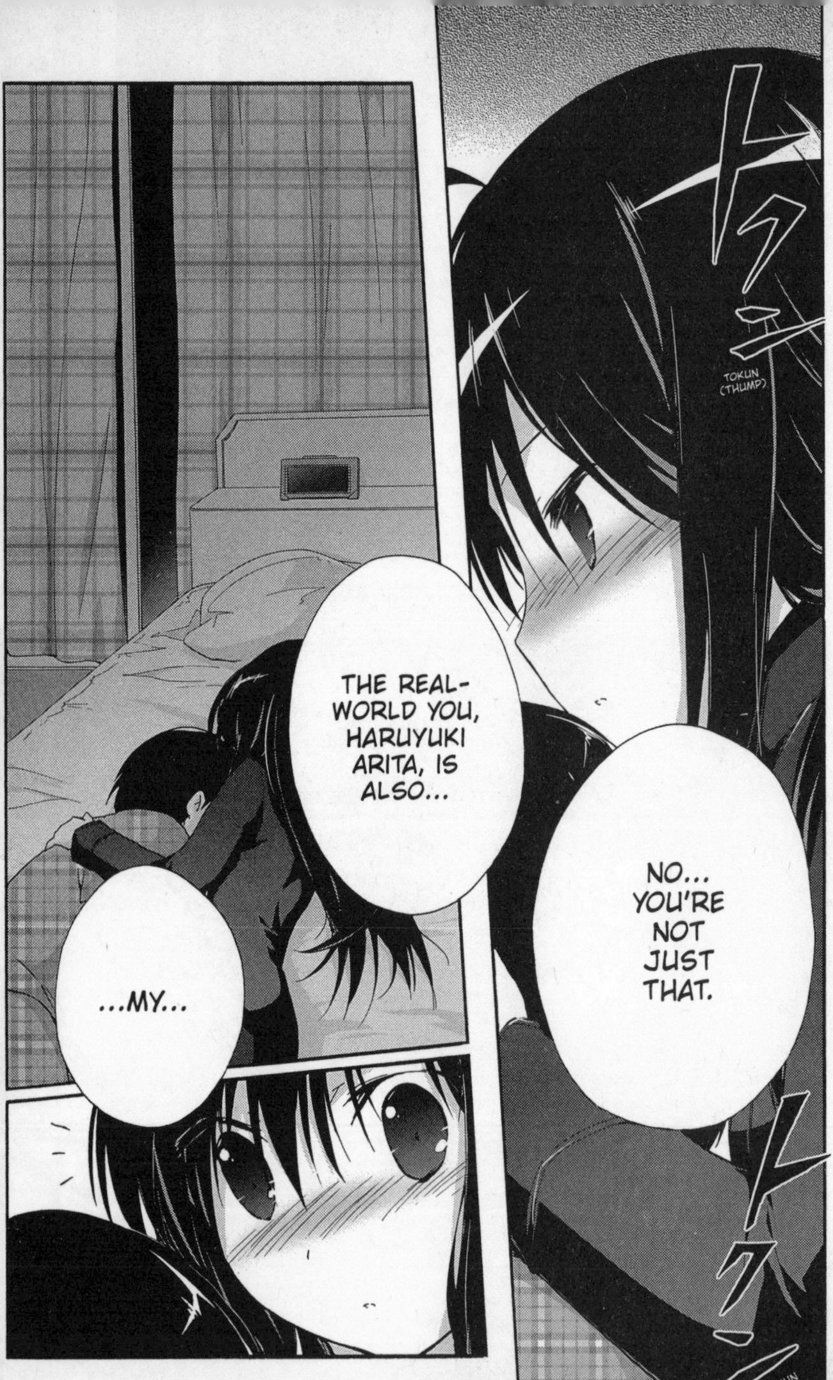
TOKUN (THUMP)
THE REAL-WORLD YOU, HARUYUKI ARITA, IS ALSO...
NO... YOU'RE NOT JUST THAT.
...MY...
TOKUN

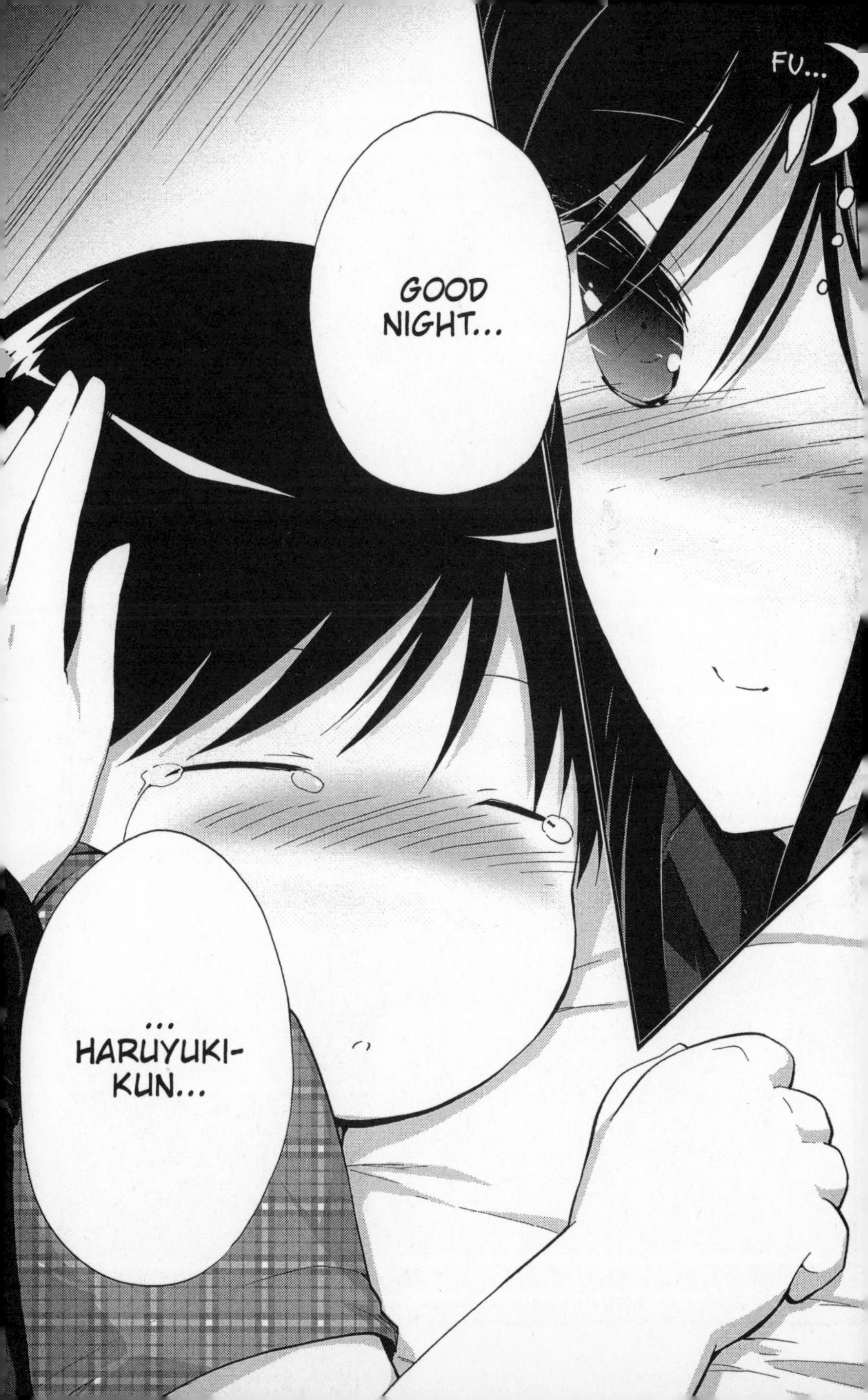
FU...
GOOD NIGHT...
... HARUYUKI-KUN...

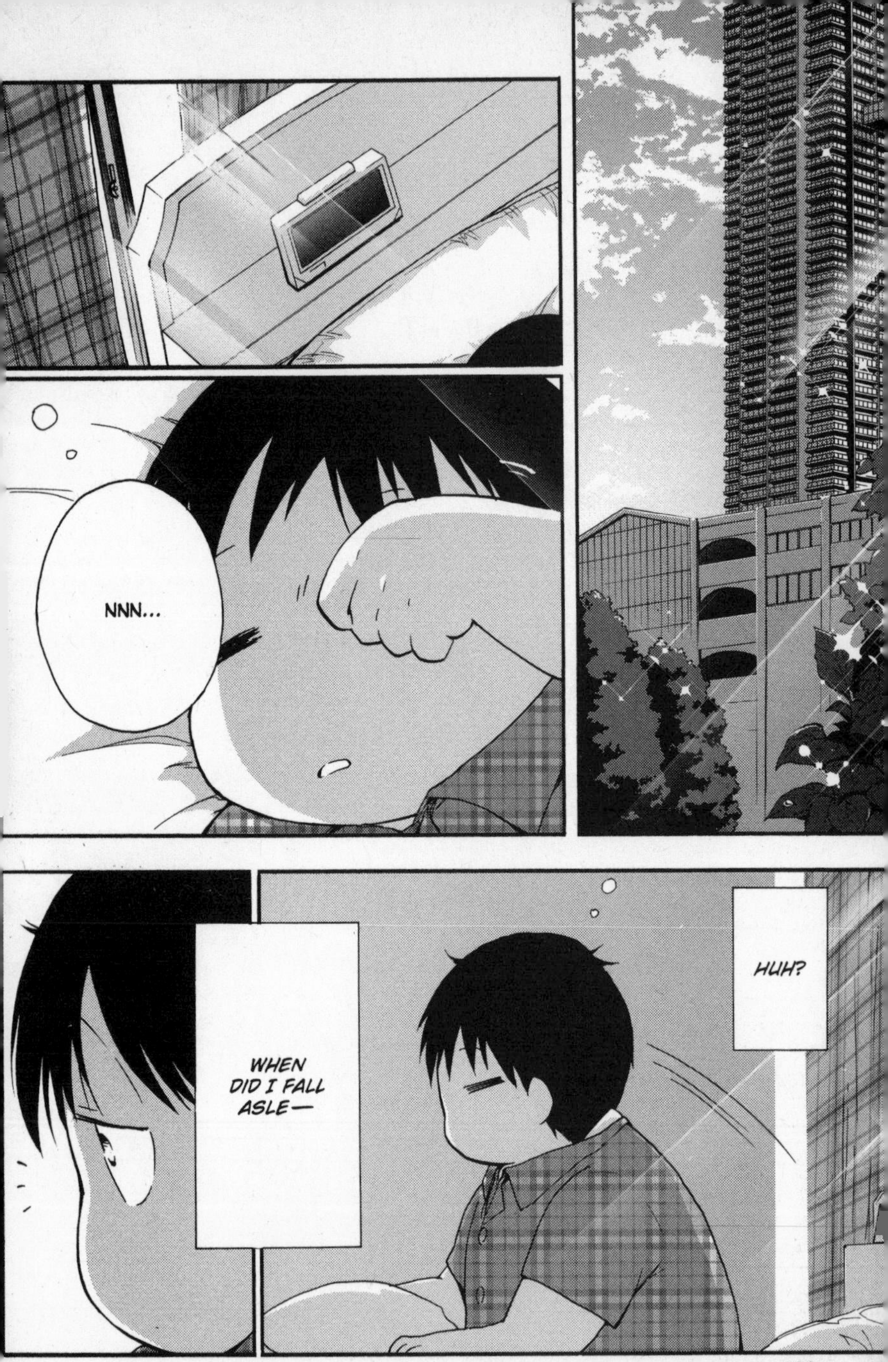
NNN...
HUH?
WHEN DID I FALL ASLE—

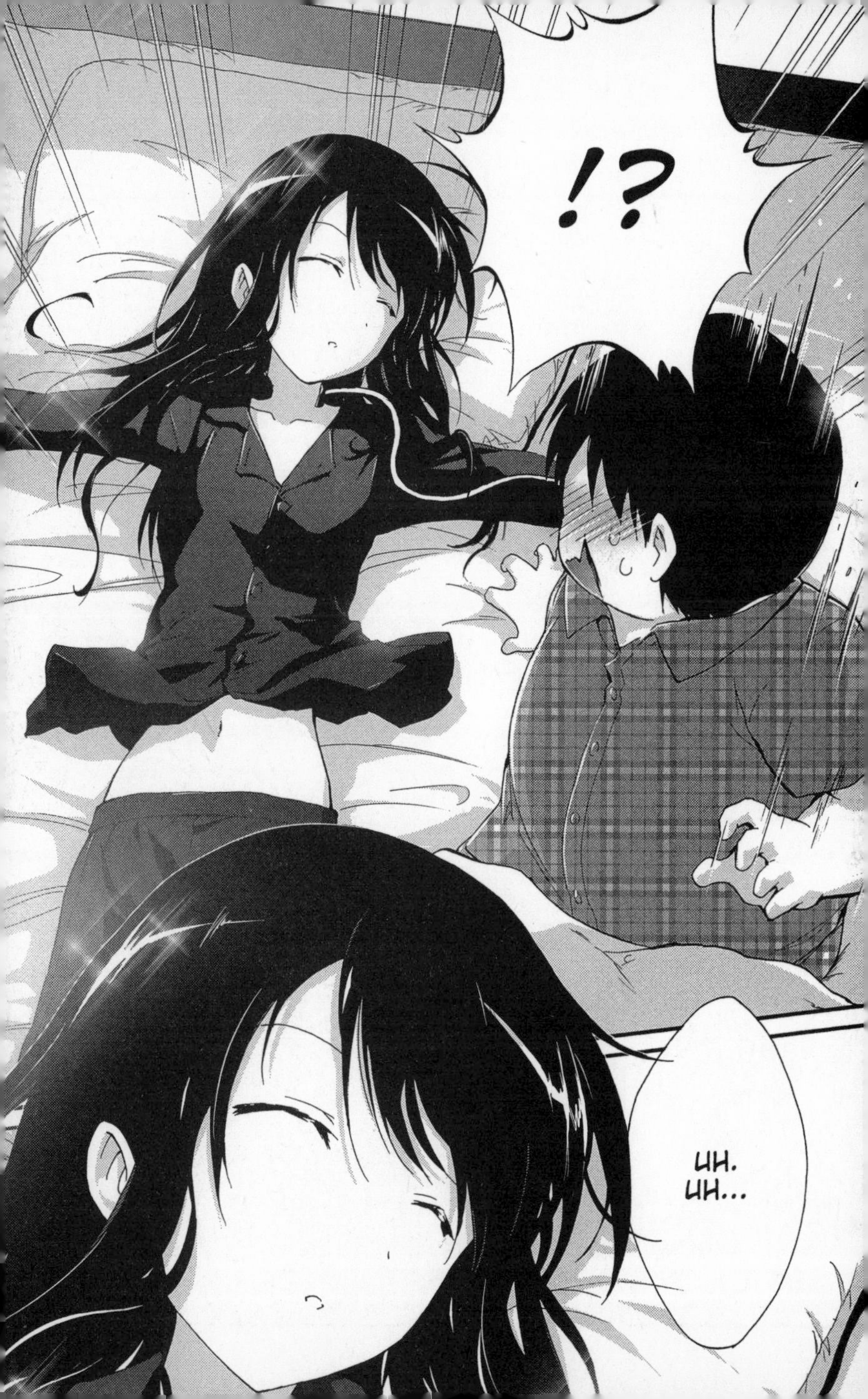
!?
UH.
UH...

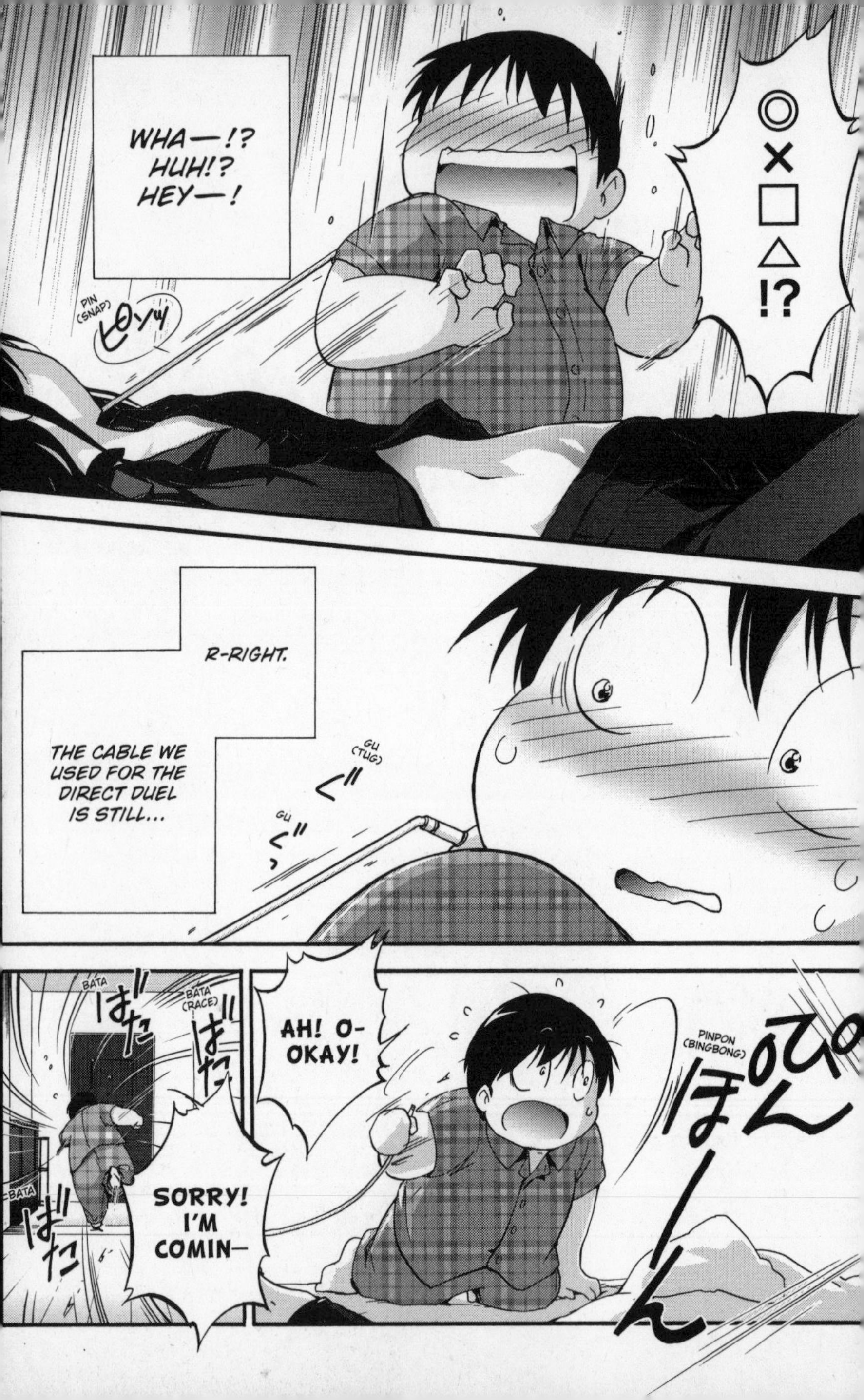

◎×□△!?
WHA—!? HUH!? HEY—!
PIN (SNAP)
ピンッ
R-RIGHT.
THE CABLE WE USED FOR THE DIRECT DUEL IS STILL...
GU (TUG)
ぐ
GU
ぐっ
PINPON (BINGBONG)
ぴんぽ〜ん
AH! O-OKAY!
BATA (RACE)
ばた
BATA
ばた
SORRY! I'M COMIN—
BATA
ばた

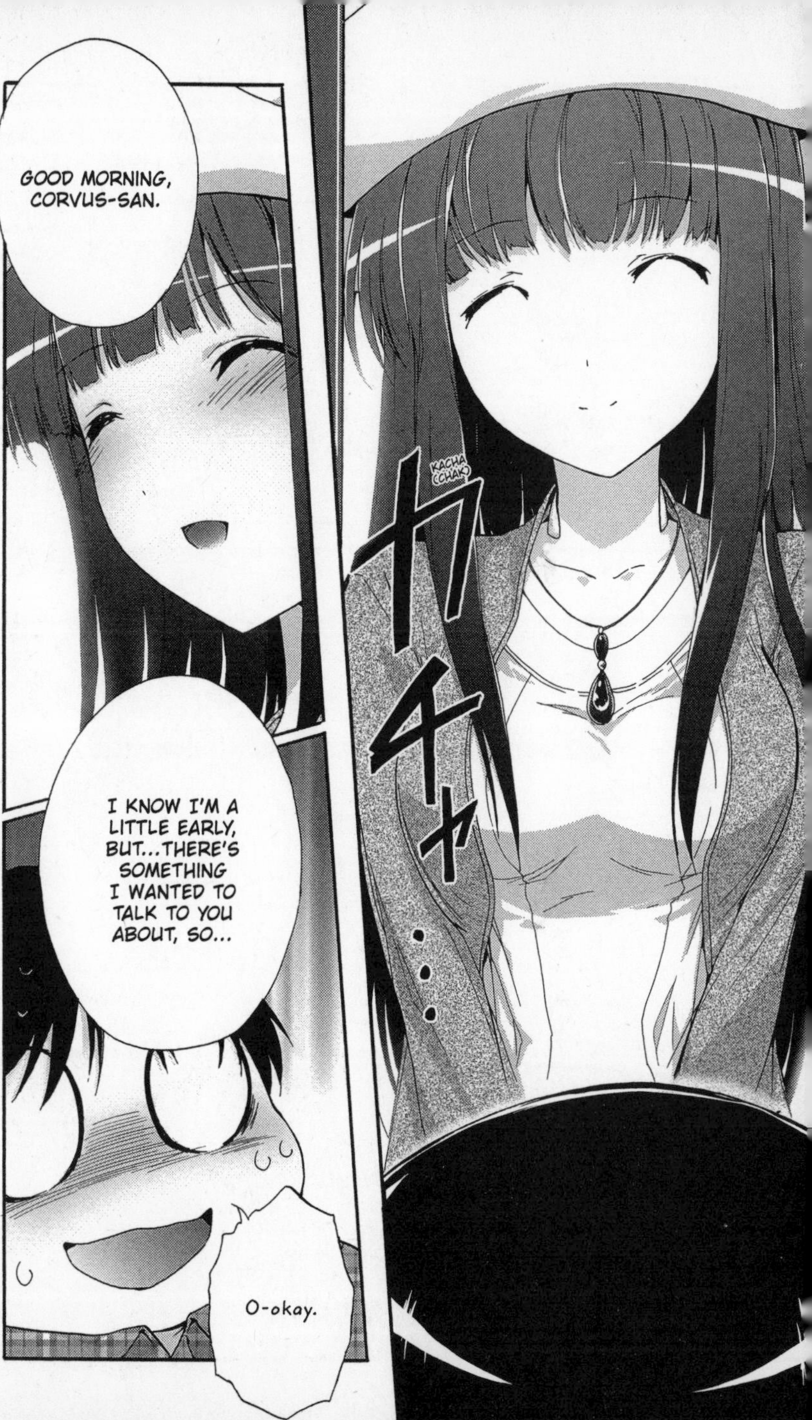
KACHA (CHAK)
...
GOOD MORNING, CORVUS-SAN.
I KNOW I'M A LITTLE EARLY, BUT...THERE'S SOMETHING I WANTED TO TALK TO YOU ABOUT, SO...
O-okay.

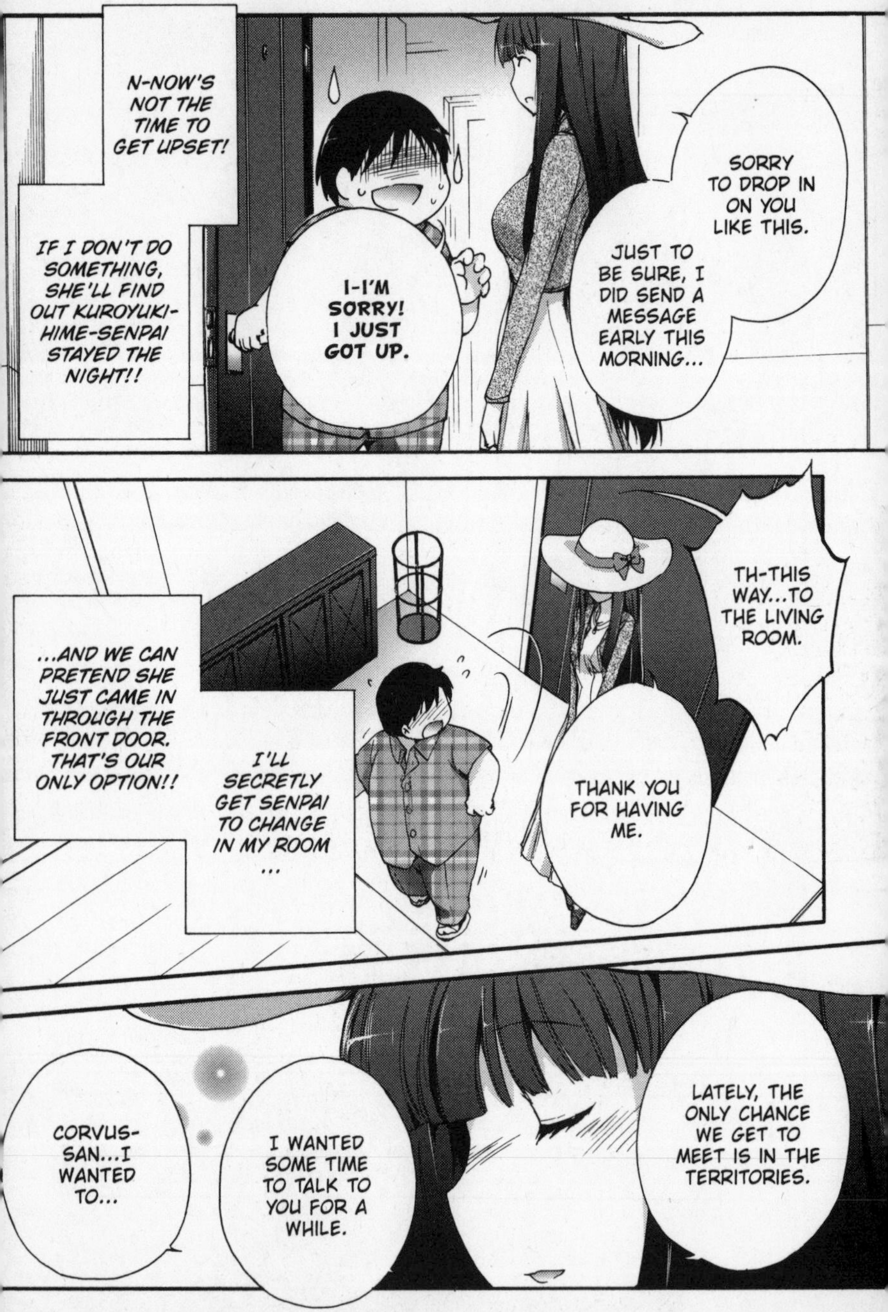
SORRY TO DROP IN ON YOU LIKE THIS.
JUST TO BE SURE, I DID SEND A MESSAGE EARLY THIS MORNING...
I-I'M SORRY! I JUST GOT UP.
N-NOW'S NOT THE TIME TO GET UPSET!
IF I DON'T DO SOMETHING, SHE'LL FIND OUT KUROYUKI-HIME-SENPAI STAYED THE NIGHT!!
TH-THIS WAY...TO THE LIVING ROOM.
THANK YOU FOR HAVING ME.
I'LL SECRETLY GET SENPAI TO CHANGE IN MY ROOM...
...AND WE CAN PRETEND SHE JUST CAME IN THROUGH THE FRONT DOOR. THAT'S OUR ONLY OPTION!!
LATELY, THE ONLY CHANCE WE GET TO MEET IS IN THE TERRITORIES.
I WANTED SOME TIME TO TALK TO YOU FOR A WHILE.
CORVUS-SAN...I WANTED TO...

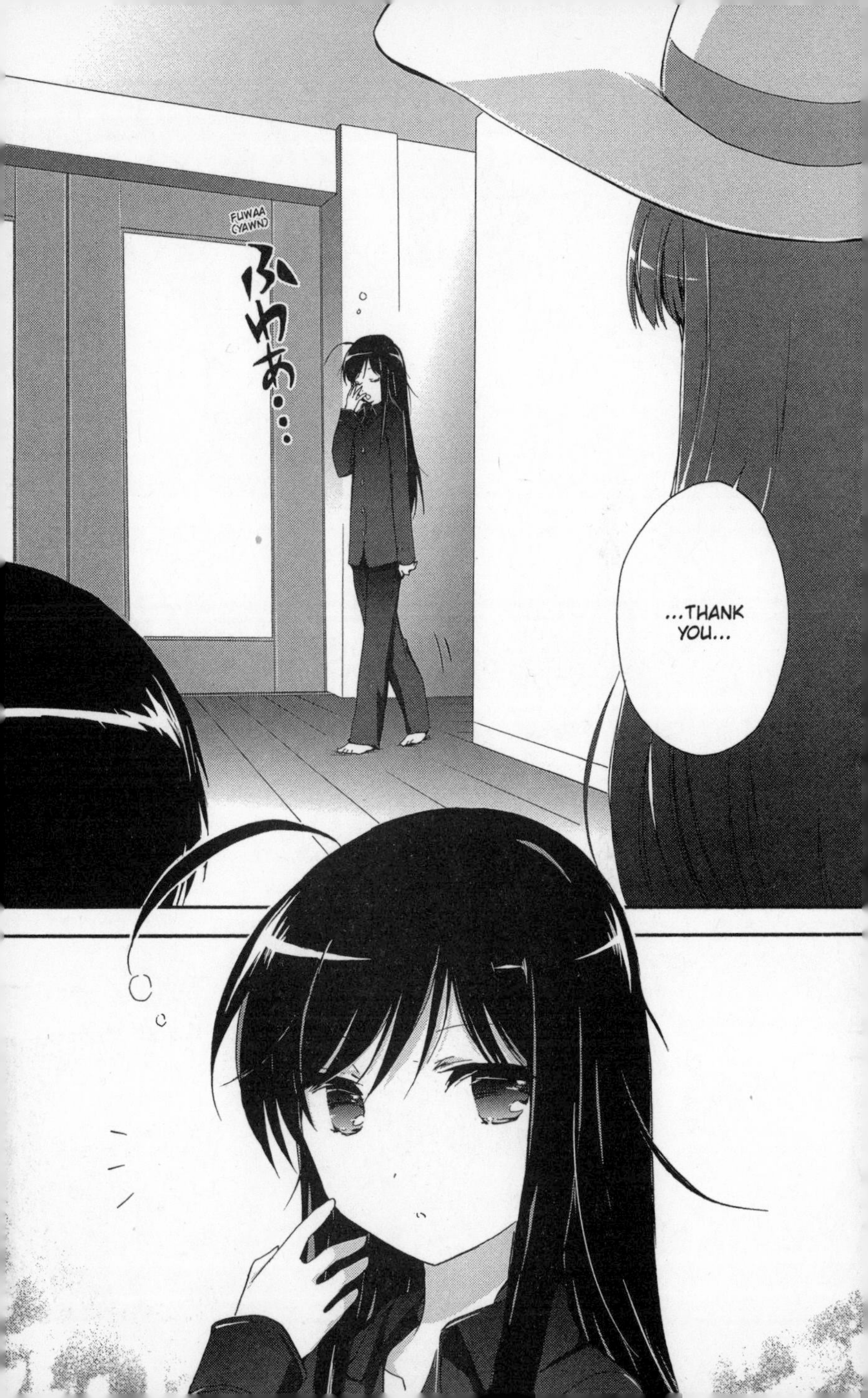
...THANK YOU...
FUWAA (YAWN)
ふわあ…

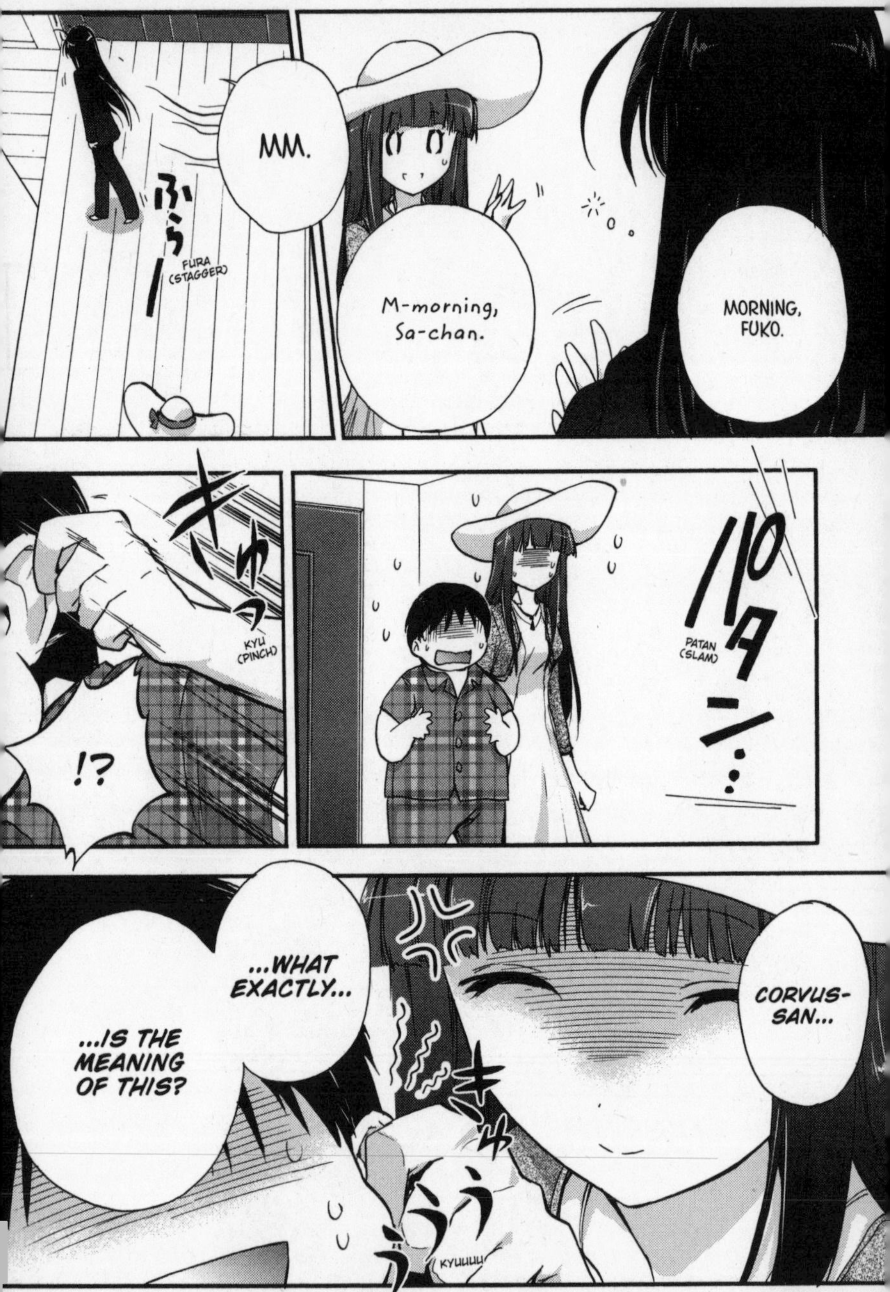
MORNING, FUKO.
M-morning, Sa-chan.
MM.
ふらー
FURA (STAGGER)
パタンー
PATAN (SLAM)
キュッ
KYU (PINCH)
!?
CORVUS-SAN...
...WHAT EXACTLY...
...IS THE MEANING OF THIS?
ギュうう
KYUUUU

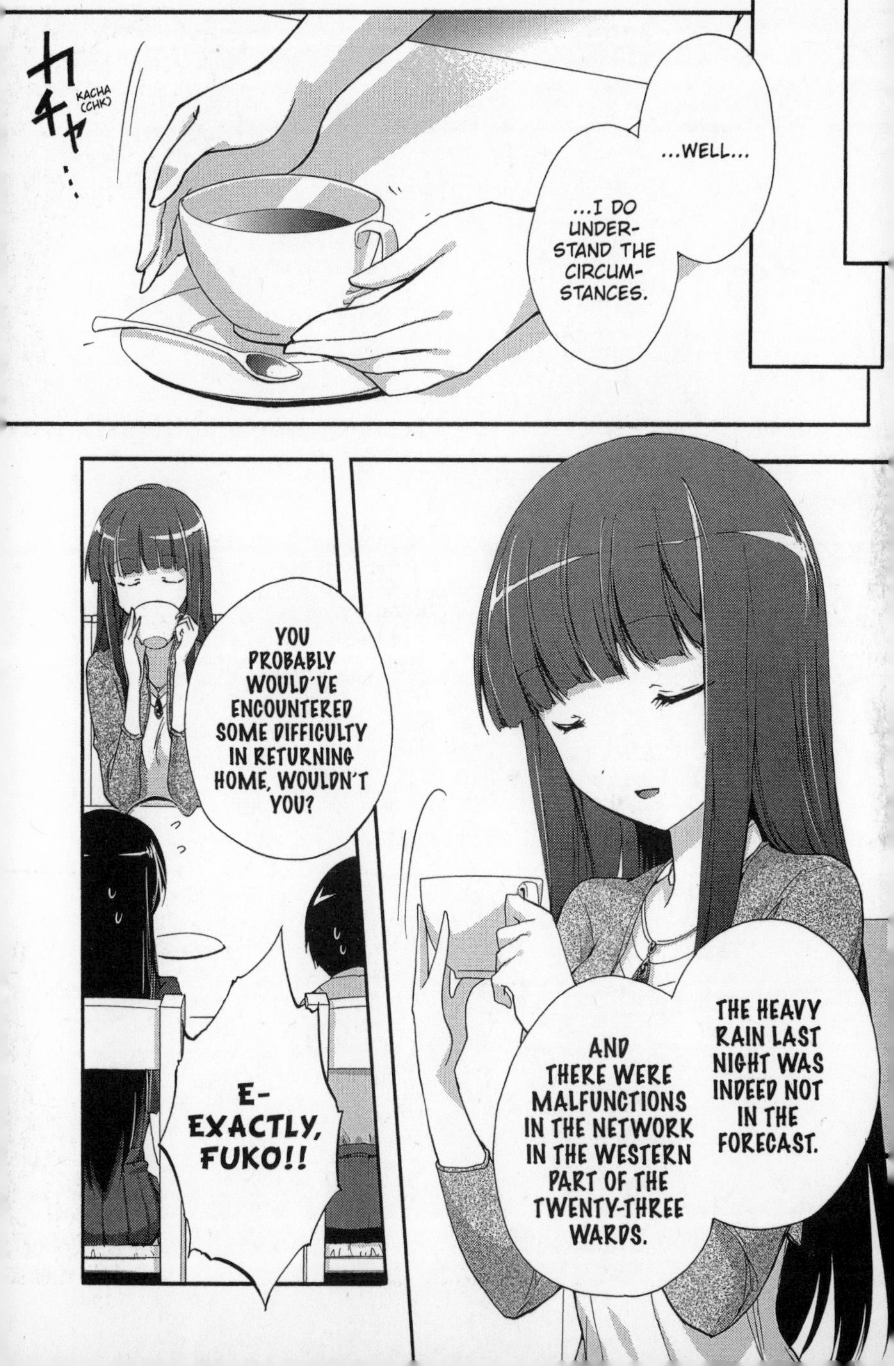
カチャ…
KACHA (CHK)
...WELL...
...I DO UNDER-STAND THE CIRCUM-STANCES.
THE HEAVY RAIN LAST NIGHT WAS INDEED NOT IN THE FORECAST.
AND THERE WERE MALFUNCTIONS IN THE NETWORK IN THE WESTERN PART OF THE TWENTY-THREE WARDS.
YOU PROBABLY WOULD'VE ENCOUNTERED SOME DIFFICULTY IN RETURNING HOME, WOULDN'T YOU?
E-EXACTLY, FUKO!!

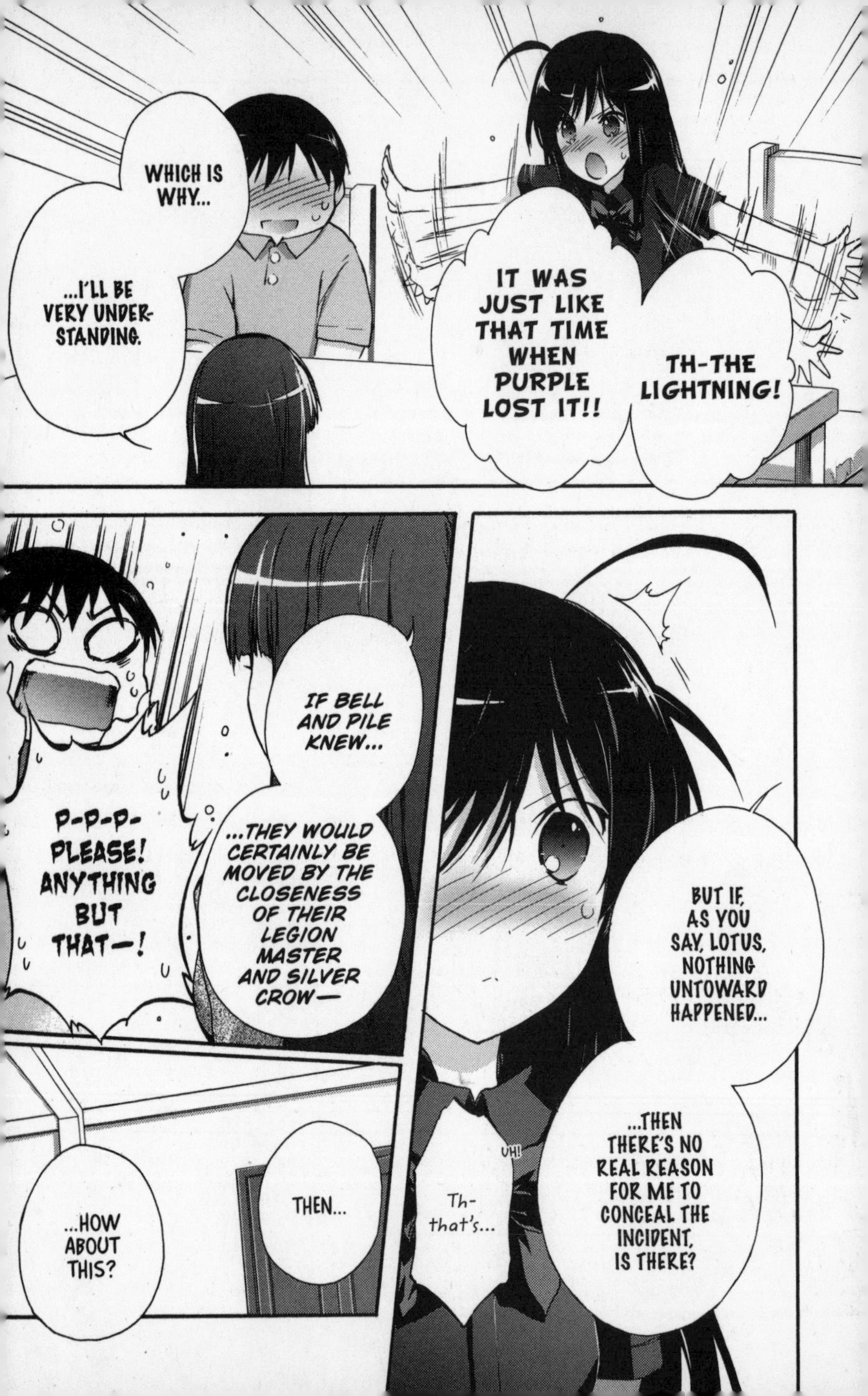
TH-THE LIGHTNING!
IT WAS JUST LIKE THAT TIME WHEN PURPLE LOST IT!!
WHICH IS WHY...
...I'LL BE VERY UNDER-STANDING.
BUT IF, AS YOU SAY, LOTUS, NOTHING UNTOWARD HAPPENED...
...THEN THERE'S NO REAL REASON FOR ME TO CONCEAL THE INCIDENT, IS THERE?
UH!
Th-that's...
IF BELL AND PILE KNEW...
...THEY WOULD CERTAINLY BE MOVED BY THE CLOSENESS OF THEIR LEGION MASTER AND SILVER CROW—
P-P-P-PLEASE! ANYTHING BUT THAT—!
THEN...
...HOW ABOUT THIS?

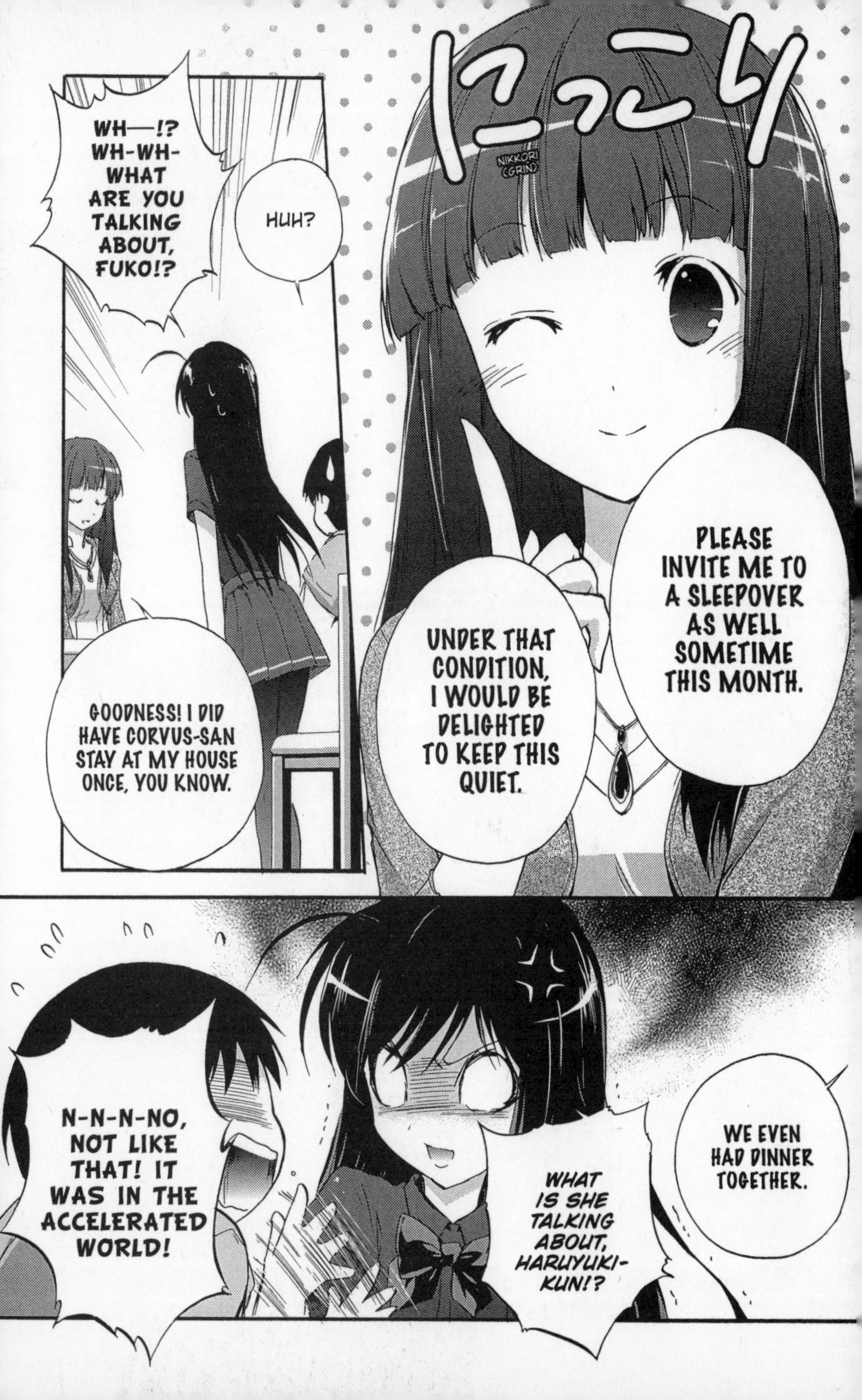
にっこり
NIKKORI (GRIN)
PLEASE INVITE ME TO A SLEEPOVER AS WELL SOMETIME THIS MONTH.
UNDER THAT CONDITION, I WOULD BE DELIGHTED TO KEEP THIS QUIET.
WH—!? WH-WH-WHAT ARE YOU TALKING ABOUT, FUKO!?
HUH?
GOODNESS! I DID HAVE CORVUS-SAN STAY AT MY HOUSE ONCE, YOU KNOW.
WE EVEN HAD DINNER TOGETHER.
WHAT IS SHE TALKING ABOUT, HARUYUKI-KUN!?
N-N-N-NO, NOT LIKE THAT! IT WAS IN THE ACCELERATED WORLD!

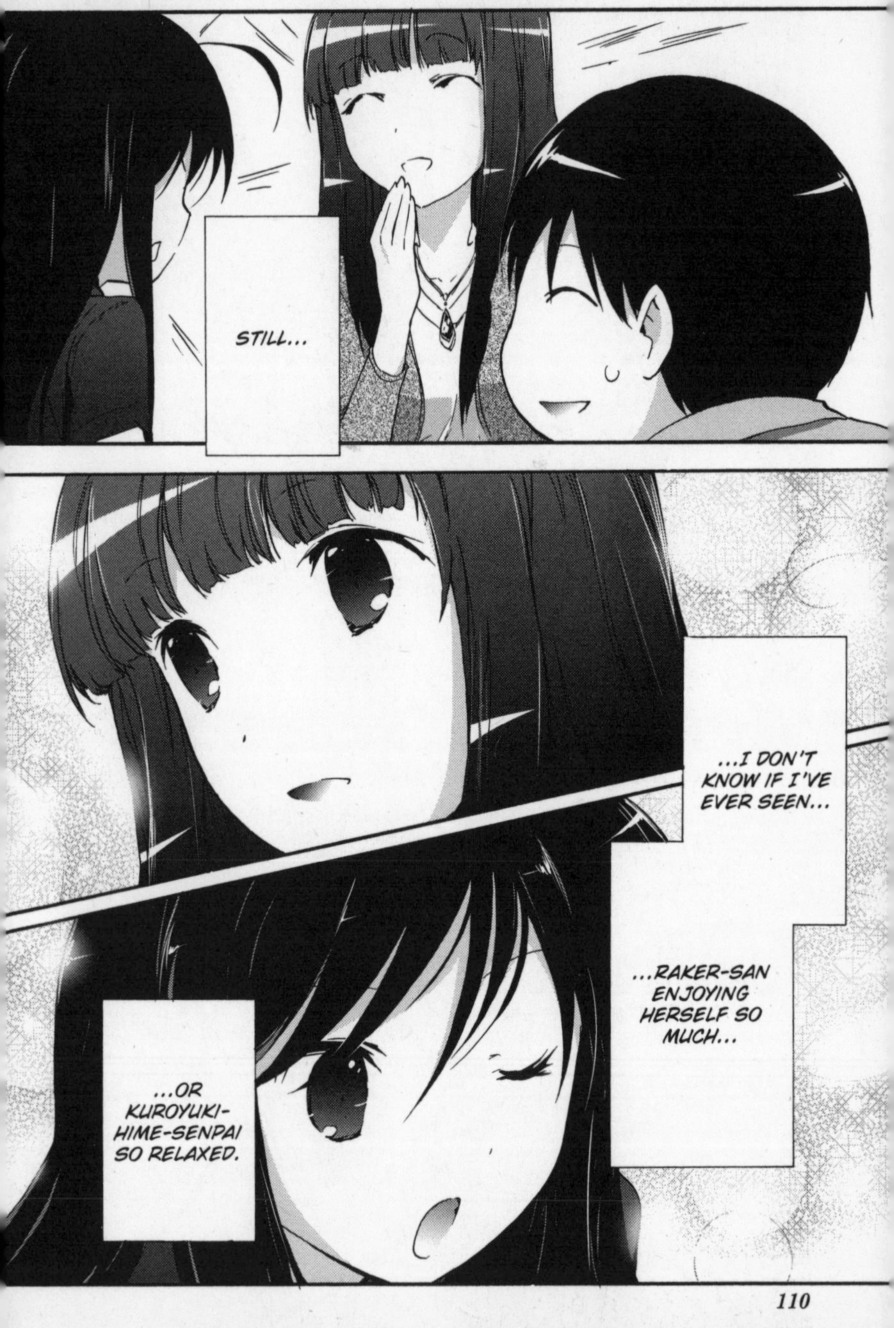
STILL...
...I DON'T KNOW IF I'VE EVER SEEN...
...RAKER-SAN ENJOYING HERSELF SO MUCH...
...OR KUROYUKI-HIME-SENPAI SO RELAXED.

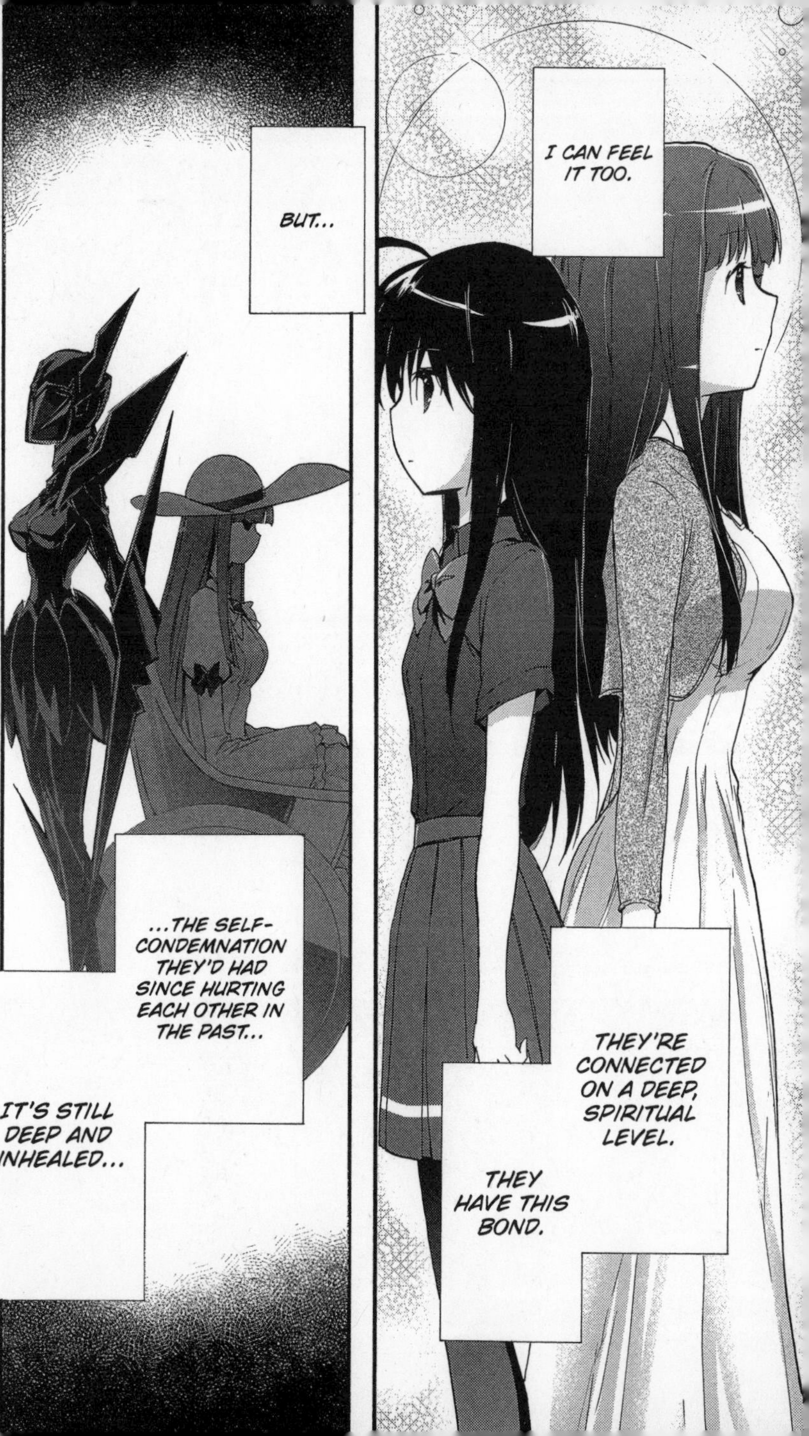
I CAN FEEL IT TOO.
THEY'RE CONNECTED ON A DEEP, SPIRITUAL LEVEL.
THEY HAVE THIS BOND.
BUT...
...THE SELF-CONDEMNATION THEY'D HAD SINCE HURTING EACH OTHER IN THE PAST...
IT'S STILL DEEP AND UNHEALED...

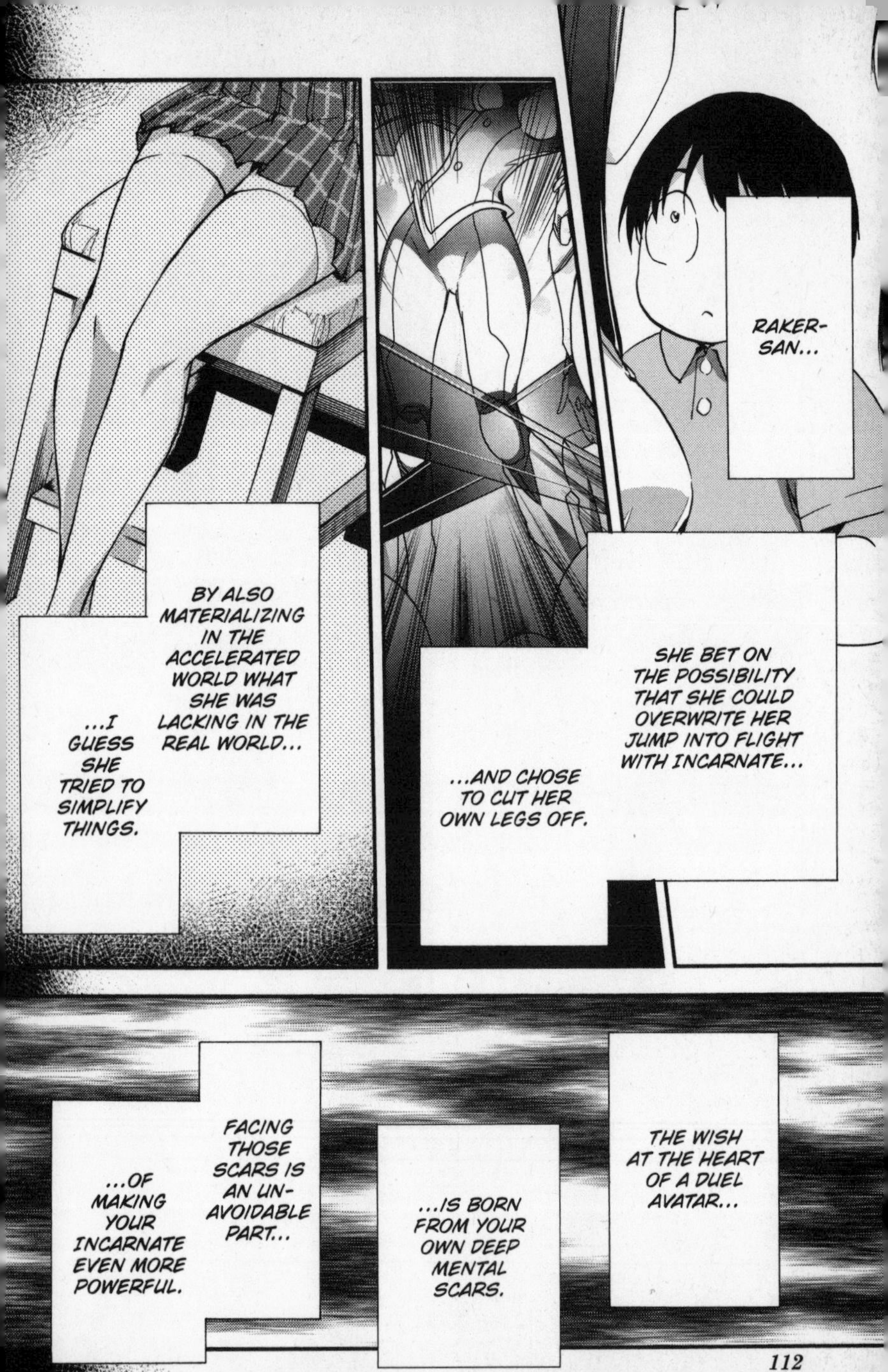
RAKER-SAN...
SHE BET ON THE POSSIBILITY THAT SHE COULD OVERWRITE HER JUMP INTO FLIGHT WITH INCARNATE...
...AND CHOSE TO CUT HER OWN LEGS OFF.
BY ALSO MATERIALIZING IN THE ACCELERATED WORLD WHAT SHE WAS LACKING IN THE REAL WORLD...
...I GUESS SHE TRIED TO SIMPLIFY THINGS.
THE WISH AT THE HEART OF A DUEL AVATAR...
...IS BORN FROM YOUR OWN DEEP MENTAL SCARS.
FACING THOSE SCARS IS AN UN-AVOIDABLE PART...
...OF MAKING YOUR INCARNATE EVEN MORE POWERFUL.

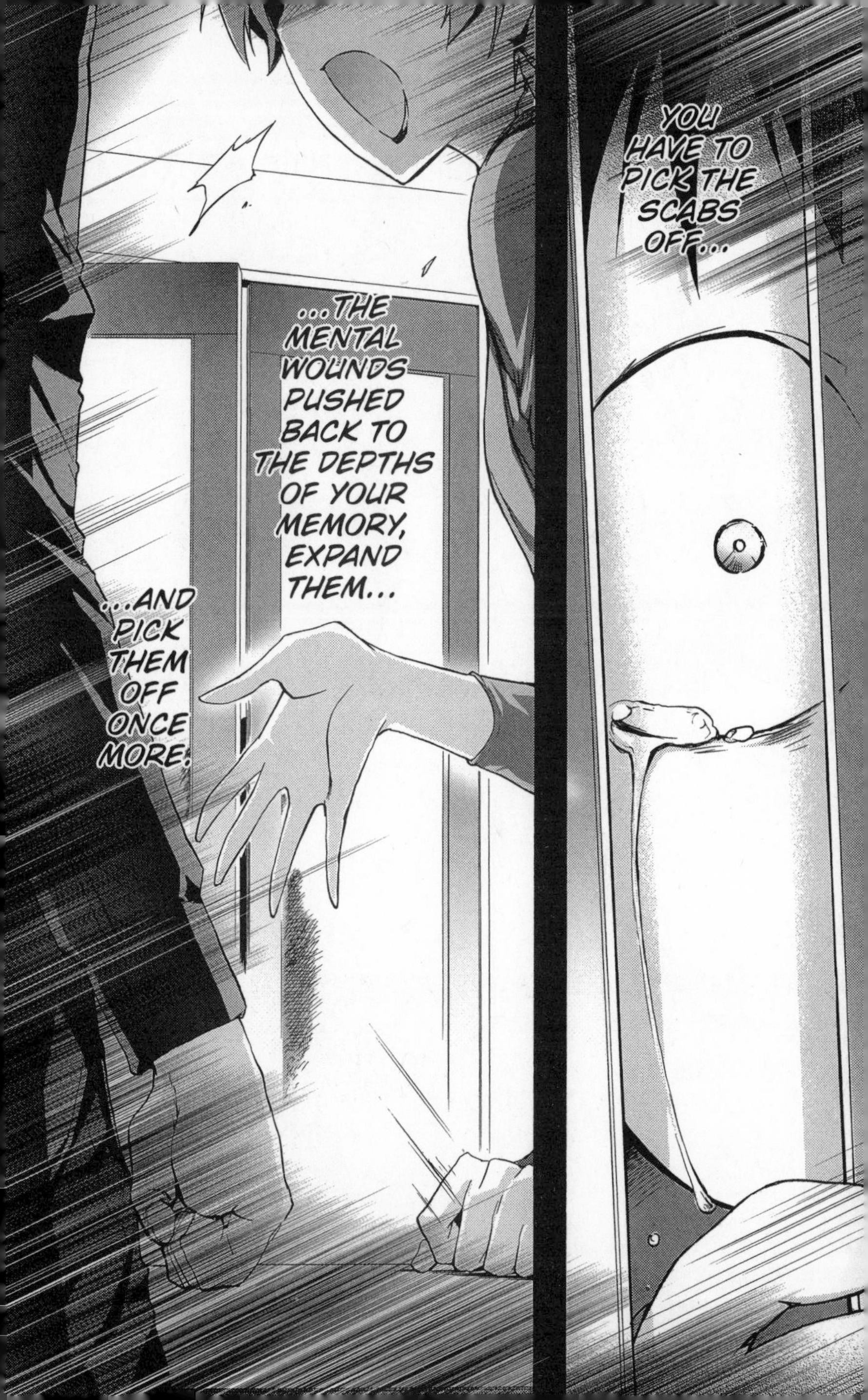
YOU HAVE TO PICK THE SCABS OFF...
...THE MENTAL WOUNDS PUSHED BACK TO THE DEPTHS OF YOUR MEMORY, EXPAND THEM...
...AND PICK THEM OFF ONCE MORE!

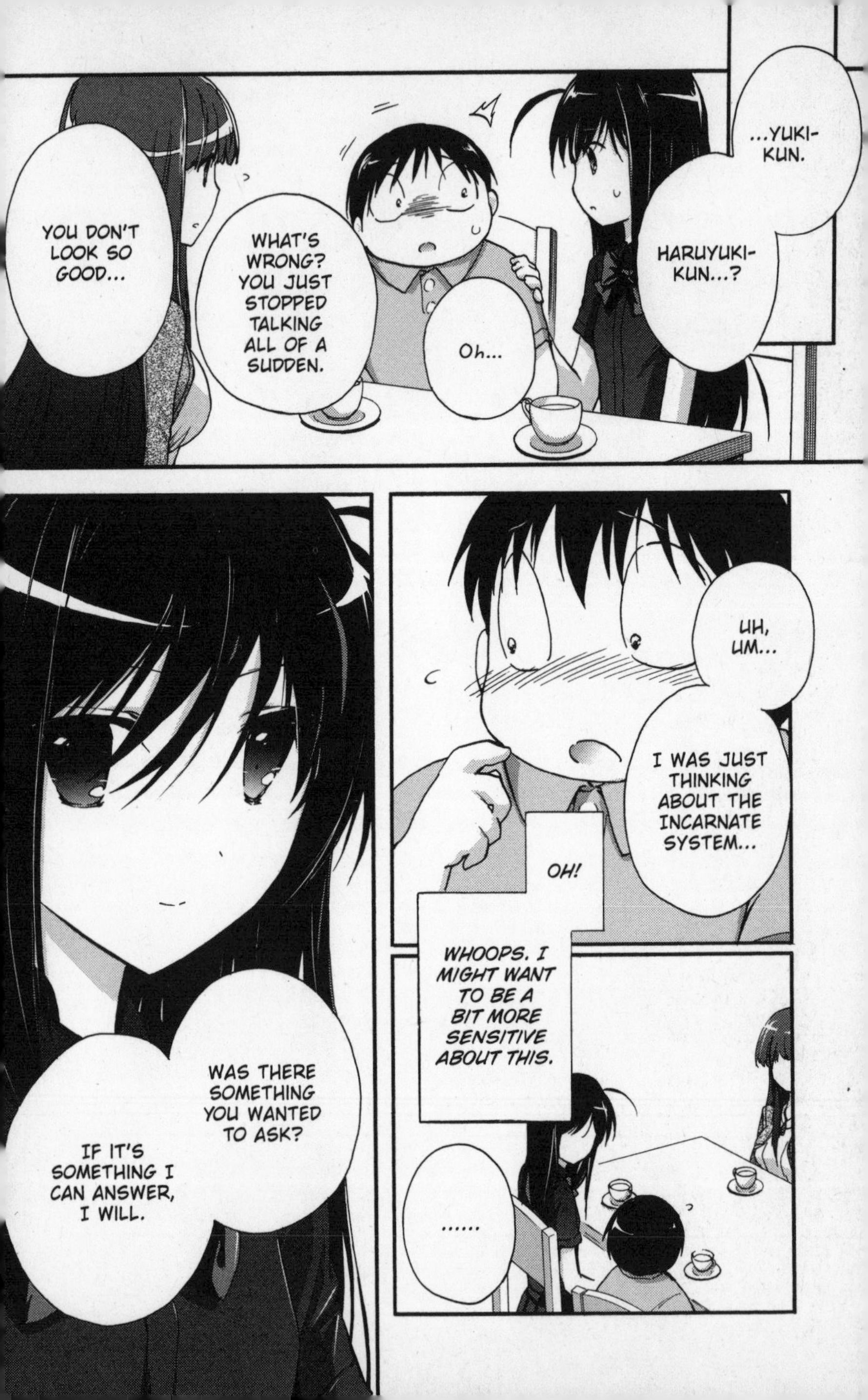
...YUKI-KUN.
HARUYUKI-KUN...?
Oh...
WHAT'S WRONG? YOU JUST STOPPED TALKING ALL OF A SUDDEN.
YOU DON'T LOOK SO GOOD...
UH, UM...
I WAS JUST THINKING ABOUT THE INCARNATE SYSTEM...
OH!
WHOOPS. I MIGHT WANT TO BE A BIT MORE SENSITIVE ABOUT THIS.
......
WAS THERE SOMETHING YOU WANTED TO ASK?
IF IT'S SOMETHING I CAN ANSWER, I WILL.

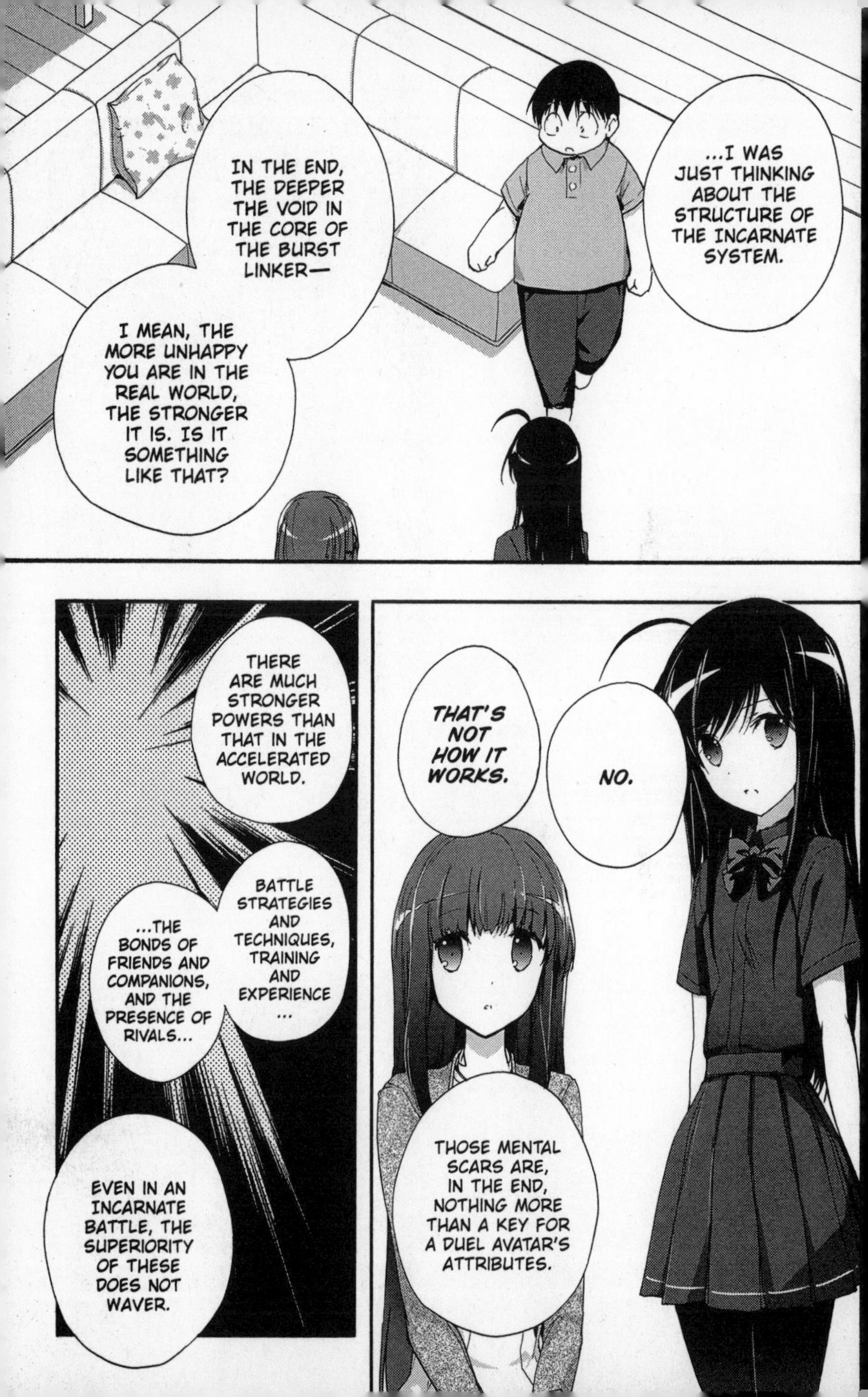
...I WAS JUST THINKING ABOUT THE STRUCTURE OF THE INCARNATE SYSTEM.
IN THE END, THE DEEPER THE VOID IN THE CORE OF THE BURST LINKER—
I MEAN, THE MORE UNHAPPY YOU ARE IN THE REAL WORLD, THE STRONGER IT IS. IS IT SOMETHING LIKE THAT?
NO.
THAT'S NOT HOW IT WORKS.
THOSE MENTAL SCARS ARE, IN THE END, NOTHING MORE THAN A KEY FOR A DUEL AVATAR'S ATTRIBUTES.
THERE ARE MUCH STRONGER POWERS THAN THAT IN THE ACCELERATED WORLD.
BATTLE STRATEGIES AND TECHNIQUES, TRAINING AND EXPERIENCE...
...THE BONDS OF FRIENDS AND COMPANIONS, AND THE PRESENCE OF RIVALS...
EVEN IN AN INCARNATE BATTLE, THE SUPERIORITY OF THESE DOES NOT WAVER.

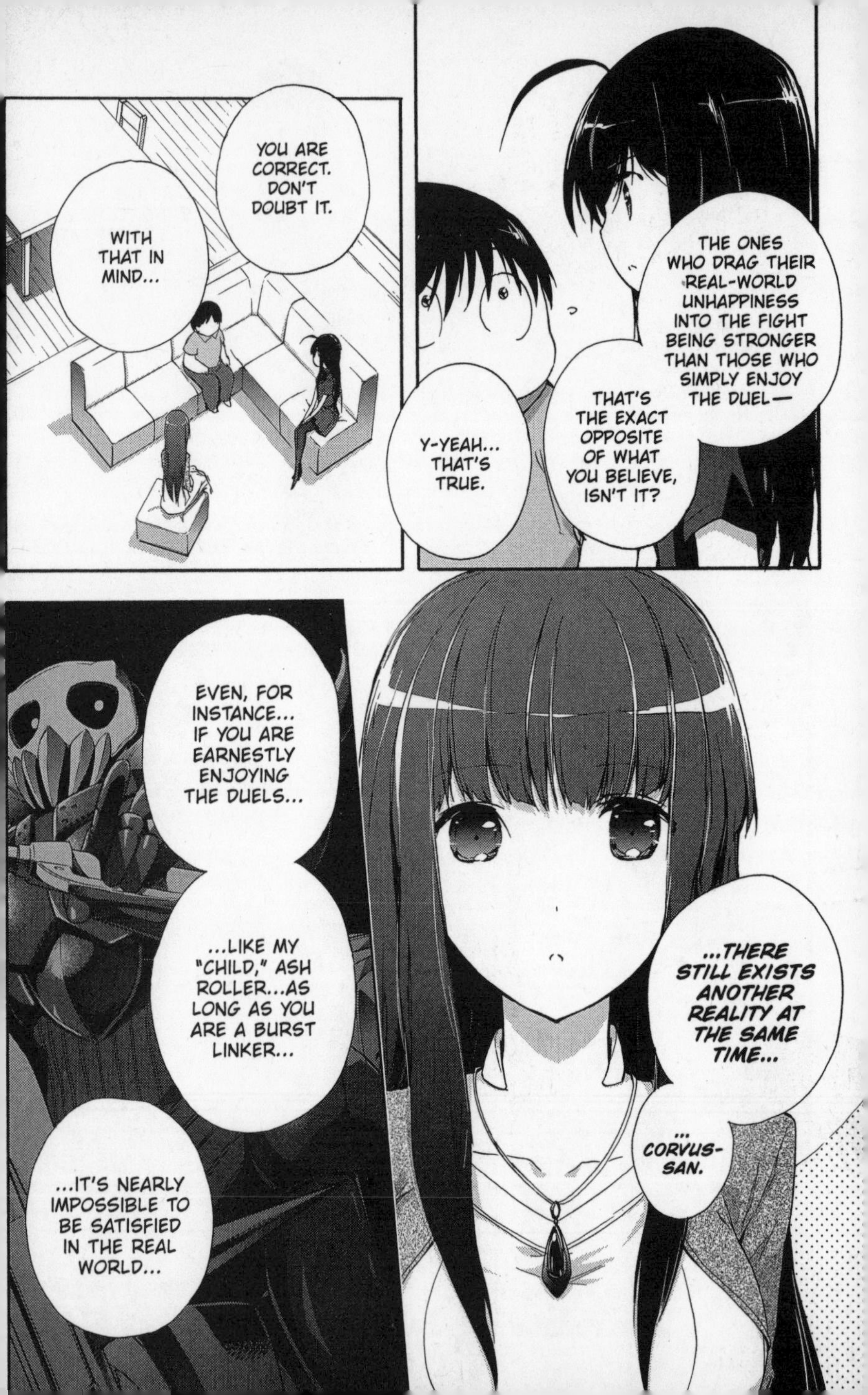
THE ONES WHO DRAG THEIR REAL-WORLD UNHAPPINESS INTO THE FIGHT BEING STRONGER THAN THOSE WHO SIMPLY ENJOY THE DUEL—
THAT'S THE EXACT OPPOSITE OF WHAT YOU BELIEVE, ISN'T IT?
Y-YEAH... THAT'S TRUE.
YOU ARE CORRECT. DON'T DOUBT IT.
WITH THAT IN MIND...
EVEN, FOR INSTANCE... IF YOU ARE EARNESTLY ENJOYING THE DUELS...
...LIKE MY "CHILD," ASH ROLLER...AS LONG AS YOU ARE A BURST LINKER...
...IT'S NEARLY IMPOSSIBLE TO BE SATISFIED IN THE REAL WORLD...
...THERE STILL EXISTS ANOTHER REALITY AT THE SAME TIME...
... CORVUS-SAN.

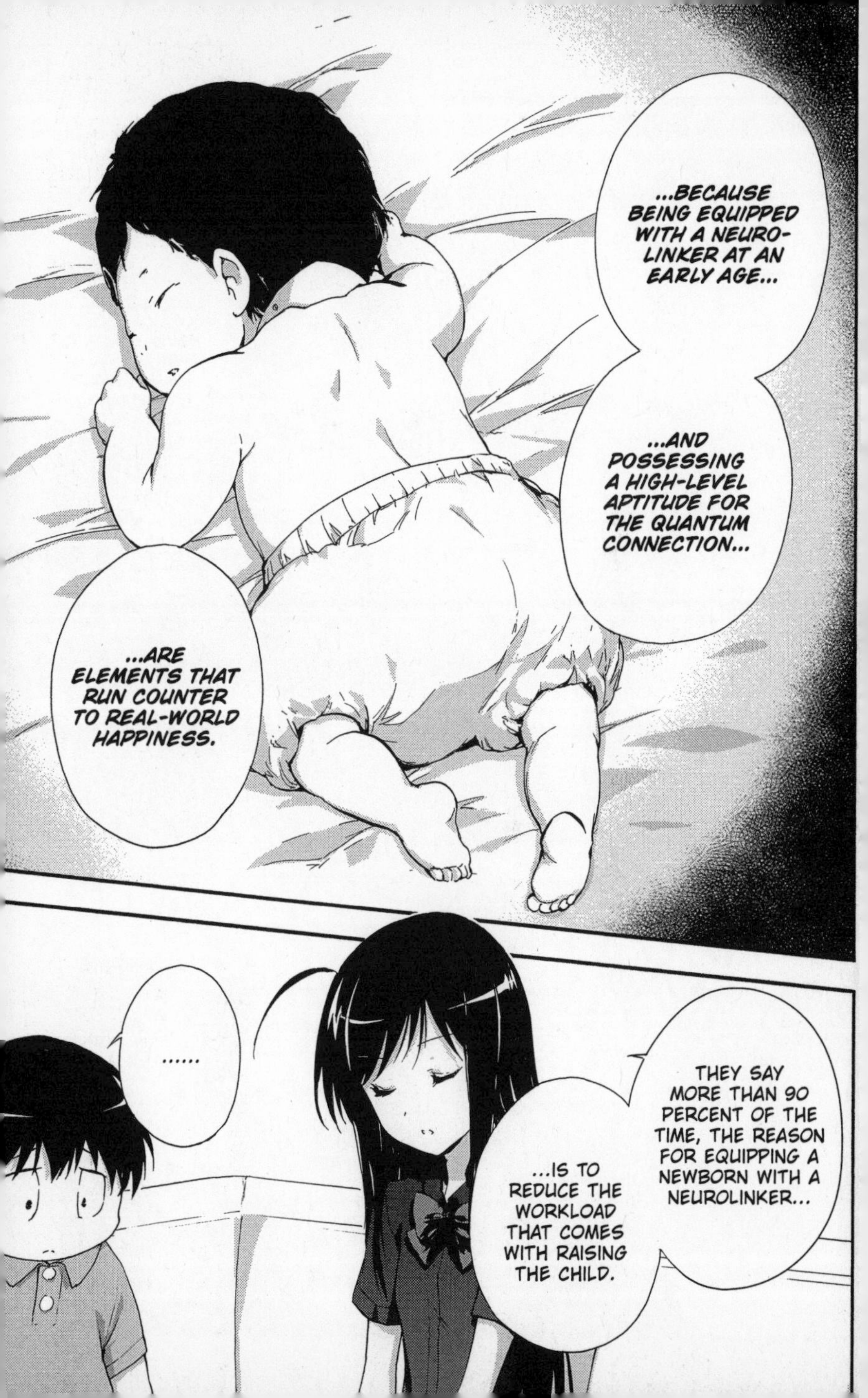
...BECAUSE BEING EQUIPPED WITH A NEURO-LINKER AT AN EARLY AGE...
...AND POSSESSING A HIGH-LEVEL APTITUDE FOR THE QUANTUM CONNECTION...
...ARE ELEMENTS THAT RUN COUNTER TO REAL-WORLD HAPPINESS.
THEY SAY MORE THAN 90 PERCENT OF THE TIME, THE REASON FOR EQUIPPING A NEWBORN WITH A NEUROLINKER...
...IS TO REDUCE THE WORKLOAD THAT COMES WITH RAISING THE CHILD.
......

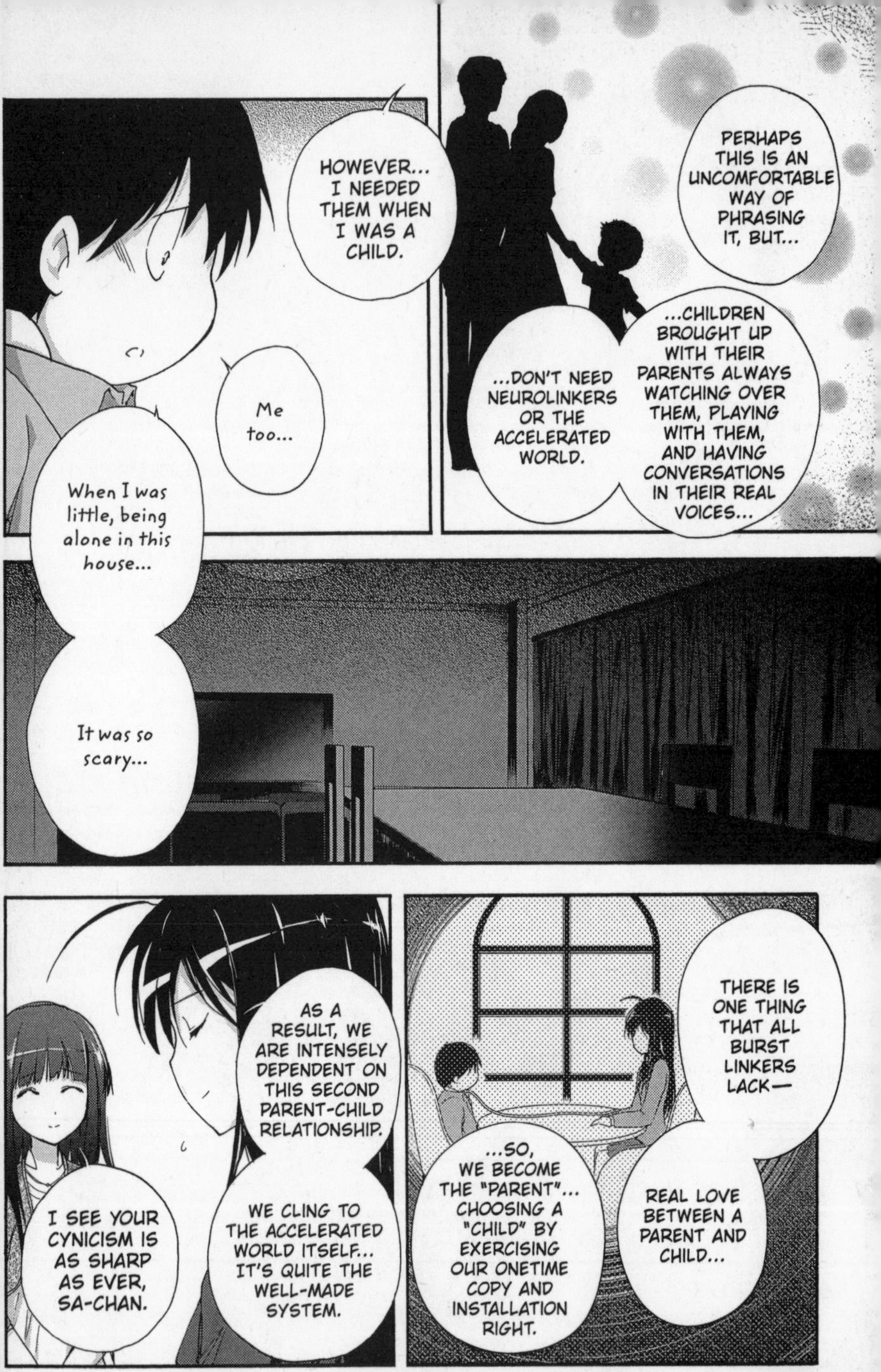
PERHAPS THIS IS AN UNCOMFORTABLE WAY OF PHRASING IT, BUT...
...CHILDREN BROUGHT UP WITH THEIR PARENTS ALWAYS WATCHING OVER THEM, PLAYING WITH THEM, AND HAVING CONVERSATIONS IN THEIR REAL VOICES...
...DON'T NEED NEUROLINKERS OR THE ACCELERATED WORLD.
HOWEVER... I NEEDED THEM WHEN I WAS A CHILD.
Me too...
When I was little, being alone in this house...
It was so scary...
THERE IS ONE THING THAT ALL BURST LINKERS LACK—
REAL LOVE BETWEEN A PARENT AND CHILD...
...SO, WE BECOME THE "PARENT"... CHOOSING A "CHILD" BY EXERCISING OUR ONETIME COPY AND INSTALLATION RIGHT.
AS A RESULT, WE ARE INTENSELY DEPENDENT ON THIS SECOND PARENT-CHILD RELATIONSHIP.
WE CLING TO THE ACCELERATED WORLD ITSELF... IT'S QUITE THE WELL-MADE SYSTEM.
I SEE YOUR CYNICISM IS AS SHARP AS EVER, SA-CHAN.

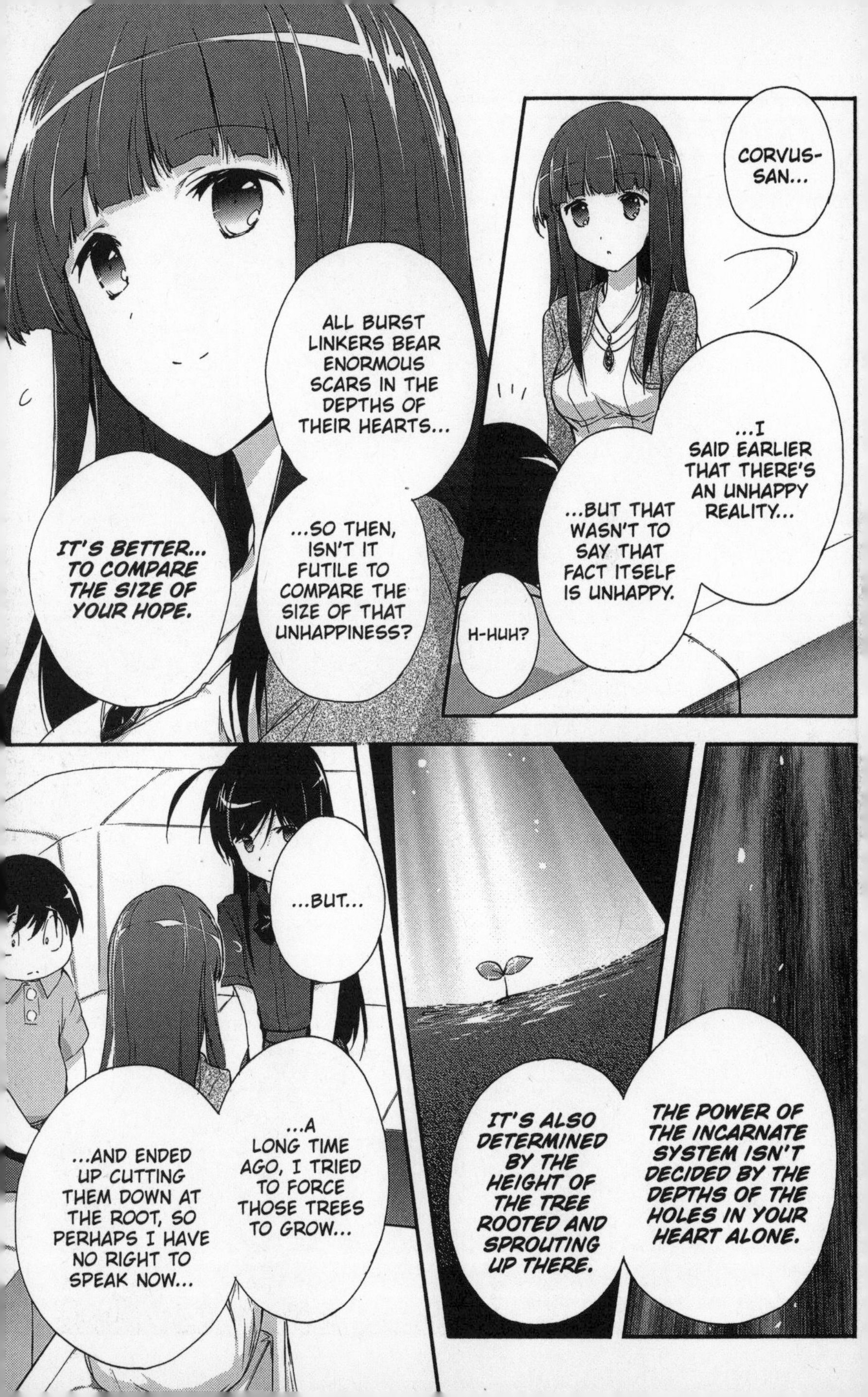
CORVUS-SAN...
...I SAID EARLIER THAT THERE'S AN UNHAPPY REALITY...
...BUT THAT WASN'T TO SAY THAT FACT ITSELF IS UNHAPPY.
H-HUH?
ALL BURST LINKERS BEAR ENORMOUS SCARS IN THE DEPTHS OF THEIR HEARTS...
...SO THEN, ISN'T IT FUTILE TO COMPARE THE SIZE OF THAT UNHAPPINESS?
IT'S BETTER... TO COMPARE THE SIZE OF YOUR HOPE.
THE POWER OF THE INCARNATE SYSTEM ISN'T DECIDED BY THE DEPTHS OF THE HOLES IN YOUR HEART ALONE.
IT'S ALSO DETERMINED BY THE HEIGHT OF THE TREE ROOTED AND SPROUTING UP THERE.
...BUT...
...A LONG TIME AGO, I TRIED TO FORCE THOSE TREES TO GROW...
...AND ENDED UP CUTTING THEM DOWN AT THE ROOT, SO PERHAPS I HAVE NO RIGHT TO SPEAK NOW...

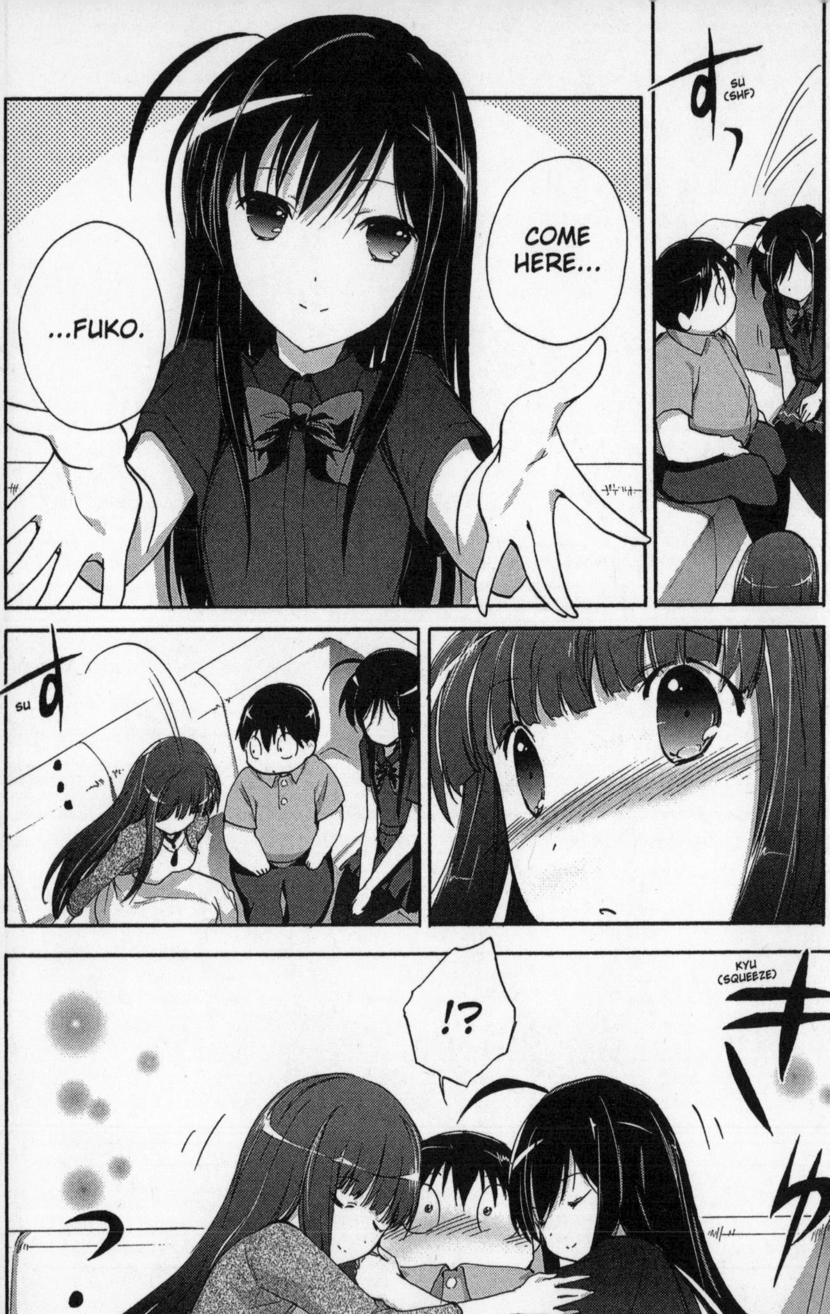
SU (SHF)
COME HERE...
...FUKO.
SU
KYU (SQUEEZE)
!?

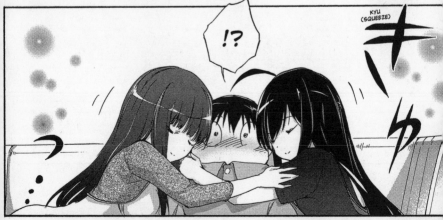

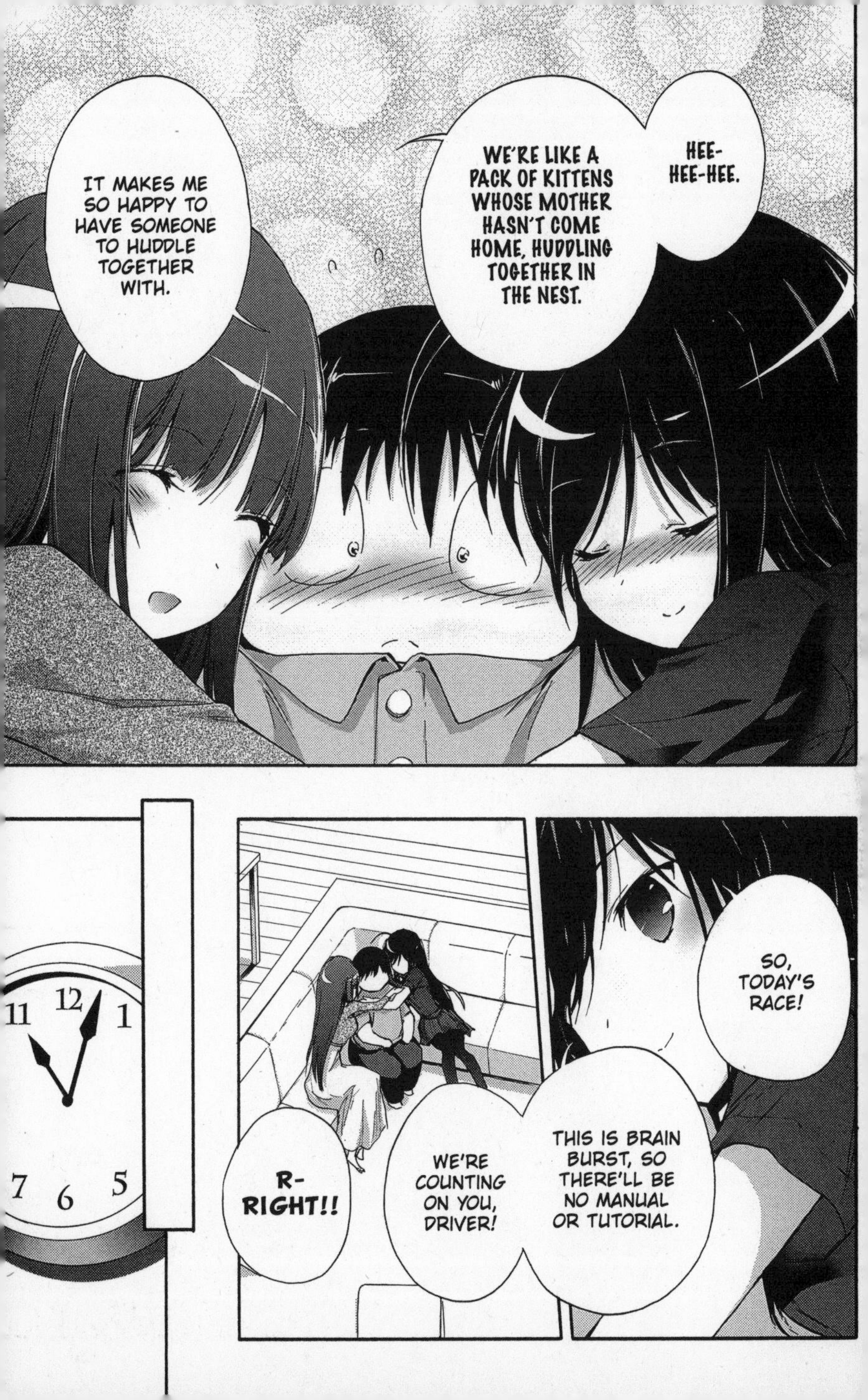
HEE-HEE-HEE.
WE'RE LIKE A PACK OF KITTENS WHOSE MOTHER HASN'T COME HOME, HUDDLING TOGETHER IN THE NEST.
IT MAKES ME SO HAPPY TO HAVE SOMEONE TO HUDDLE TOGETHER WITH.
SO, TODAY'S RACE!
THIS IS BRAIN BURST, SO THERE'LL BE NO MANUAL OR TUTORIAL.
WE'RE COUNTING ON YOU, DRIVER!
R-RIGHT!!

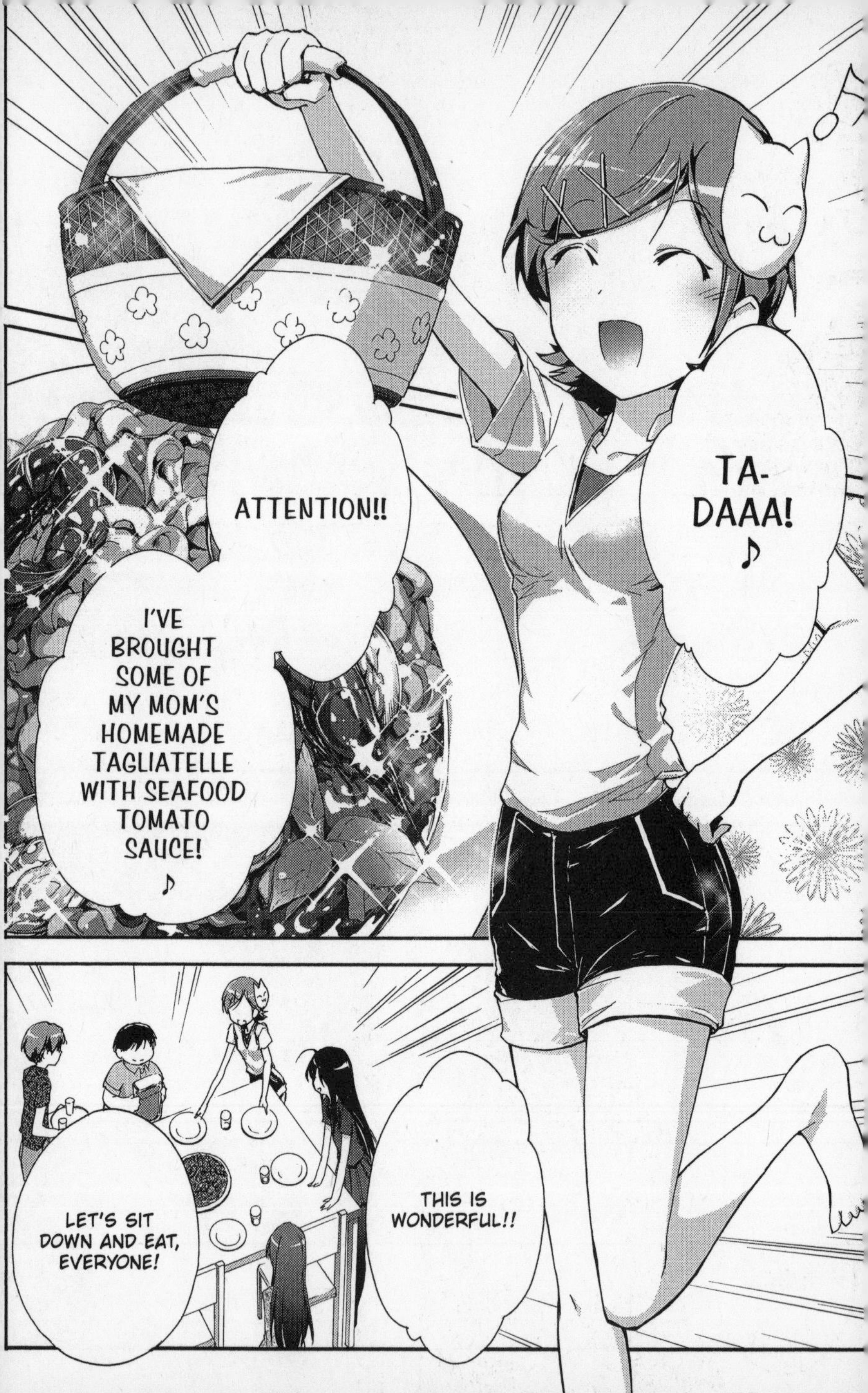
TA-DAAA! ♪
ATTENTION!!
I'VE BROUGHT SOME OF MY MOM'S HOMEMADE TAGLIATELLE WITH SEAFOOD TOMATO SAUCE! ♪
THIS IS WONDERFUL!!
LET'S SIT DOWN AND EAT, EVERYONE!

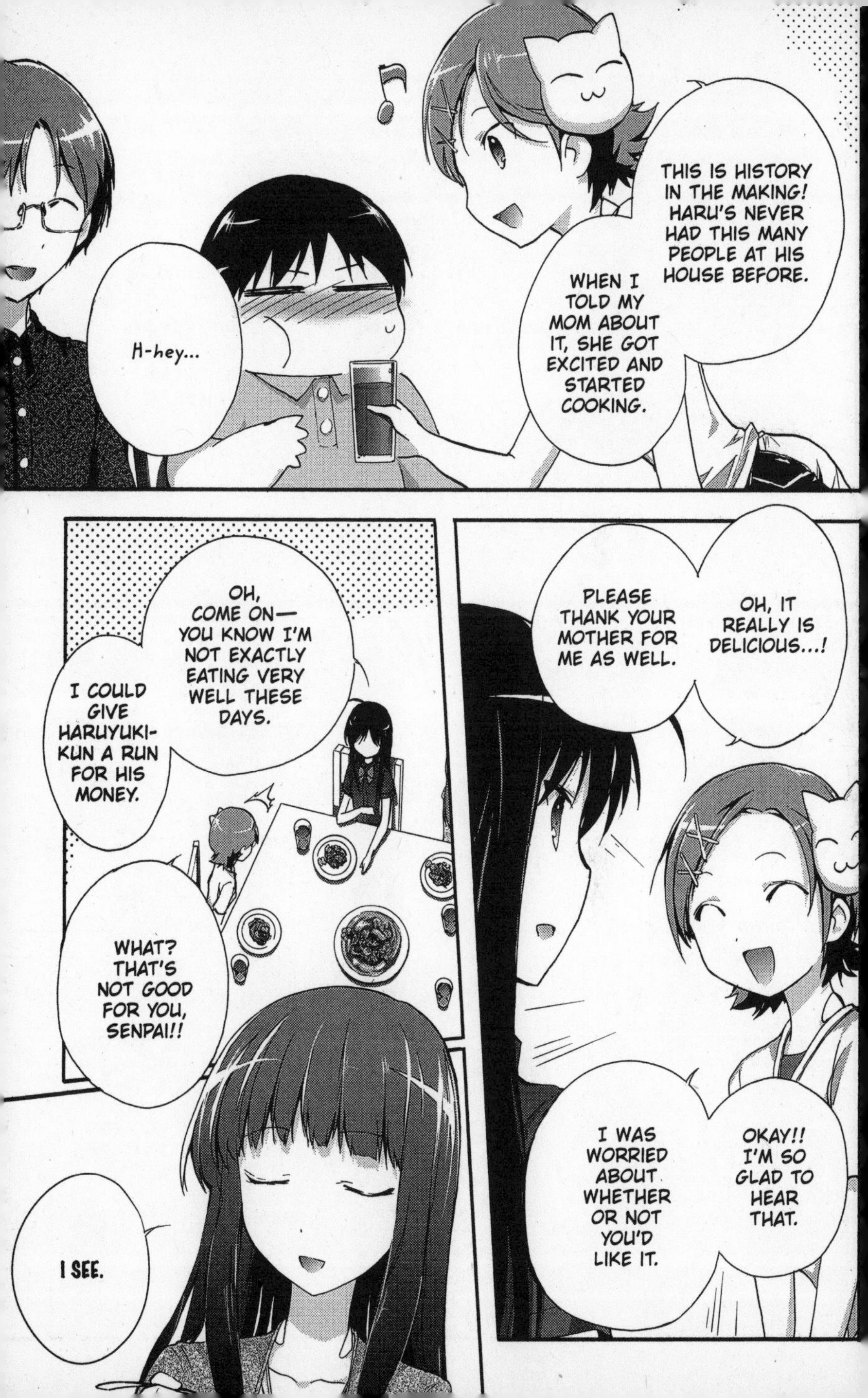
THIS IS HISTORY IN THE MAKING! HARU'S NEVER HAD THIS MANY PEOPLE AT HIS HOUSE BEFORE.
WHEN I TOLD MY MOM ABOUT IT, SHE GOT EXCITED AND STARTED COOKING.
H-hey...
OH, IT REALLY IS DELICIOUS...!
PLEASE THANK YOUR MOTHER FOR ME AS WELL.
OKAY!! I'M SO GLAD TO HEAR THAT.
I WAS WORRIED ABOUT WHETHER OR NOT YOU'D LIKE IT.
OH, COME ON—YOU KNOW I'M NOT EXACTLY EATING VERY WELL THESE DAYS.
I COULD GIVE HARUYUKI-KUN A RUN FOR HIS MONEY.
WHAT? THAT'S NOT GOOD FOR YOU, SENPAI!!
I SEE.

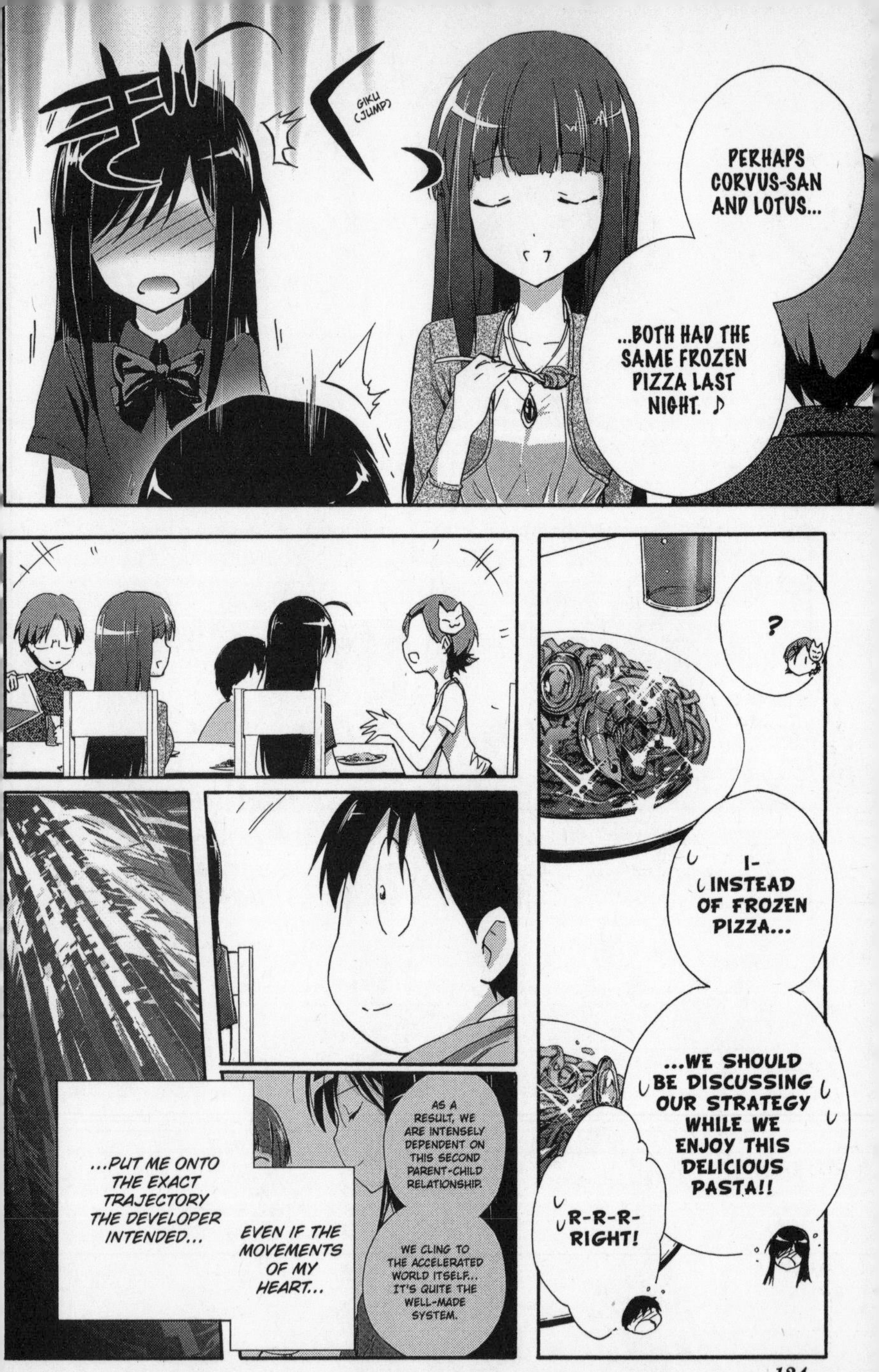
PERHAPS CORVUS-SAN AND LOTUS...
...BOTH HAD THE SAME FROZEN PIZZA LAST NIGHT. ♪
GIKU (JUMP)
?
I- INSTEAD OF FROZEN PIZZA...
...WE SHOULD BE DISCUSSING OUR STRATEGY WHILE WE ENJOY THIS DELICIOUS PASTA!!
R-R-R-RIGHT!
AS A RESULT, WE ARE INTENSELY DEPENDENT ON THIS SECOND PARENT-CHILD RELATIONSHIP.
WE CLING TO THE ACCELERATED WORLD ITSELF... IT'S QUITE THE WELL-MADE SYSTEM.
EVEN IF THE MOVEMENTS OF MY HEART...
...PUT ME ONTO THE EXACT TRAJECTORY THE DEVELOPER INTENDED...

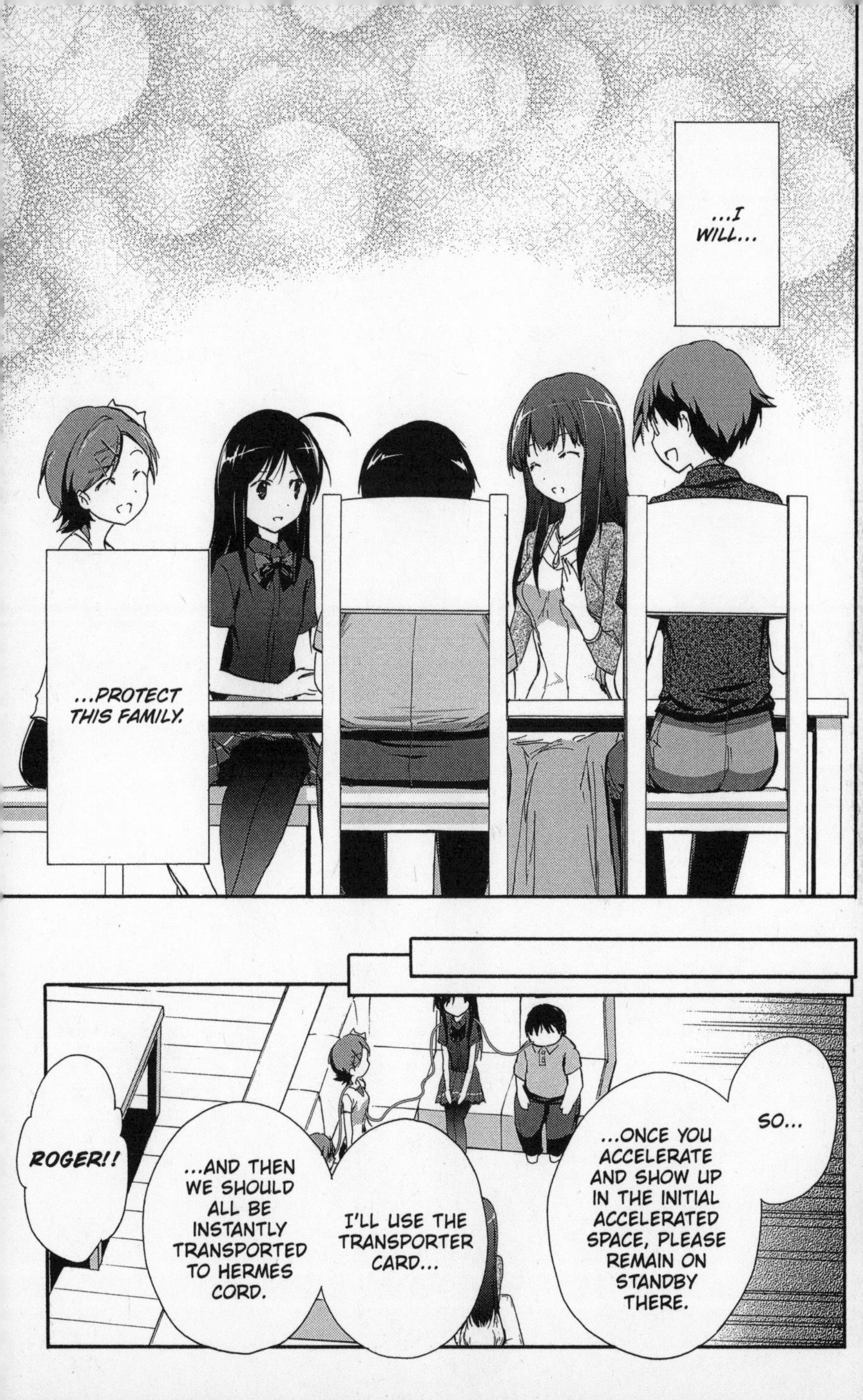
...I WILL...
...PROTECT THIS FAMILY.
SO...
...ONCE YOU ACCELERATE AND SHOW UP IN THE INITIAL ACCELERATED SPACE, PLEASE REMAIN ON STANDBY THERE.
I'LL USE THE TRANSPORTER CARD...
...AND THEN WE SHOULD ALL BE INSTANTLY TRANSPORTED TO HERMES CORD.
ROGER!!

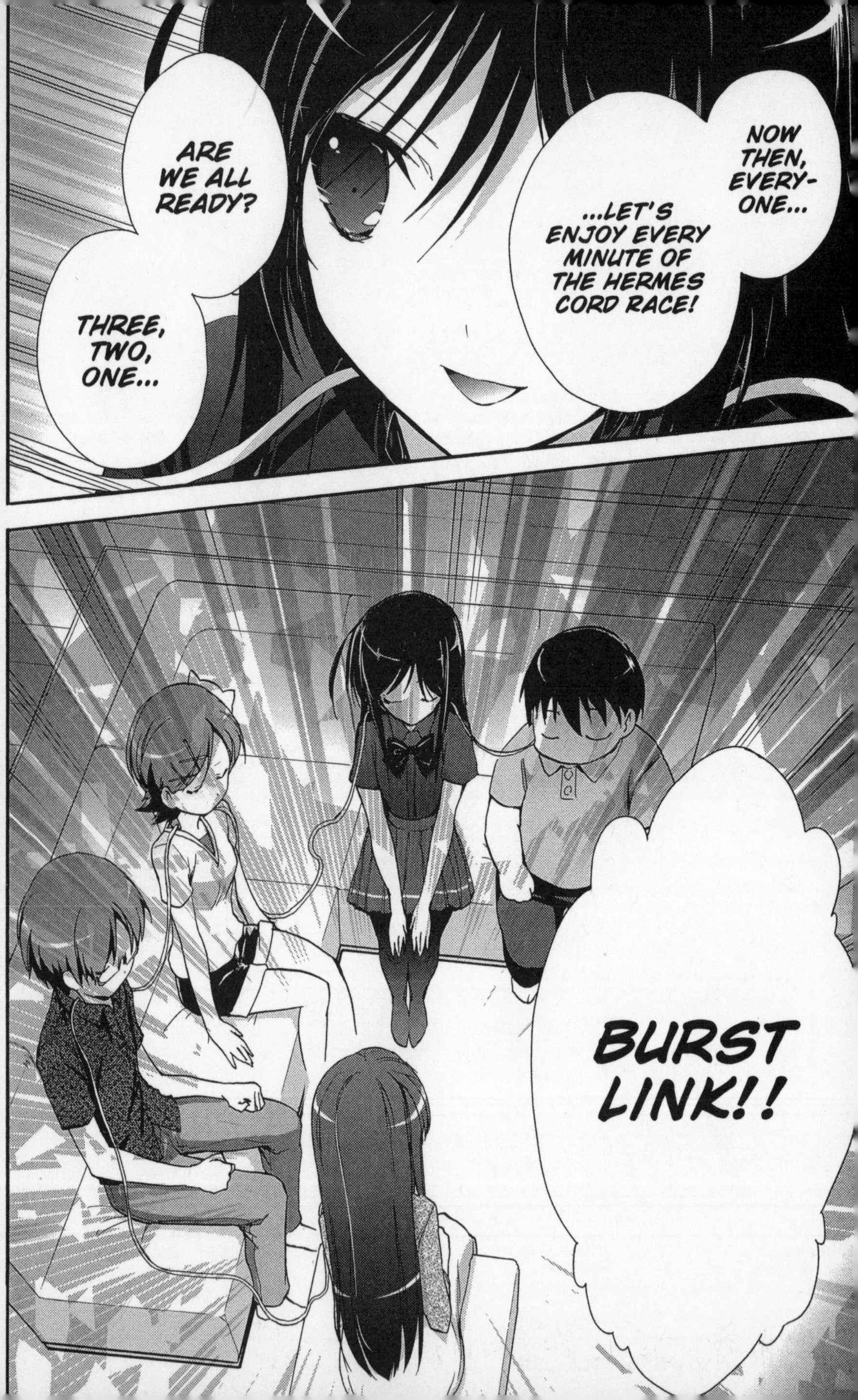
NOW THEN, EVERY-ONE...
...LET'S ENJOY EVERY MINUTE OF THE HERMES CORD RACE!
ARE WE ALL READY?
THREE, TWO, ONE...
BURST LINK!!

▶▶▶*ACCEL·WORLD*

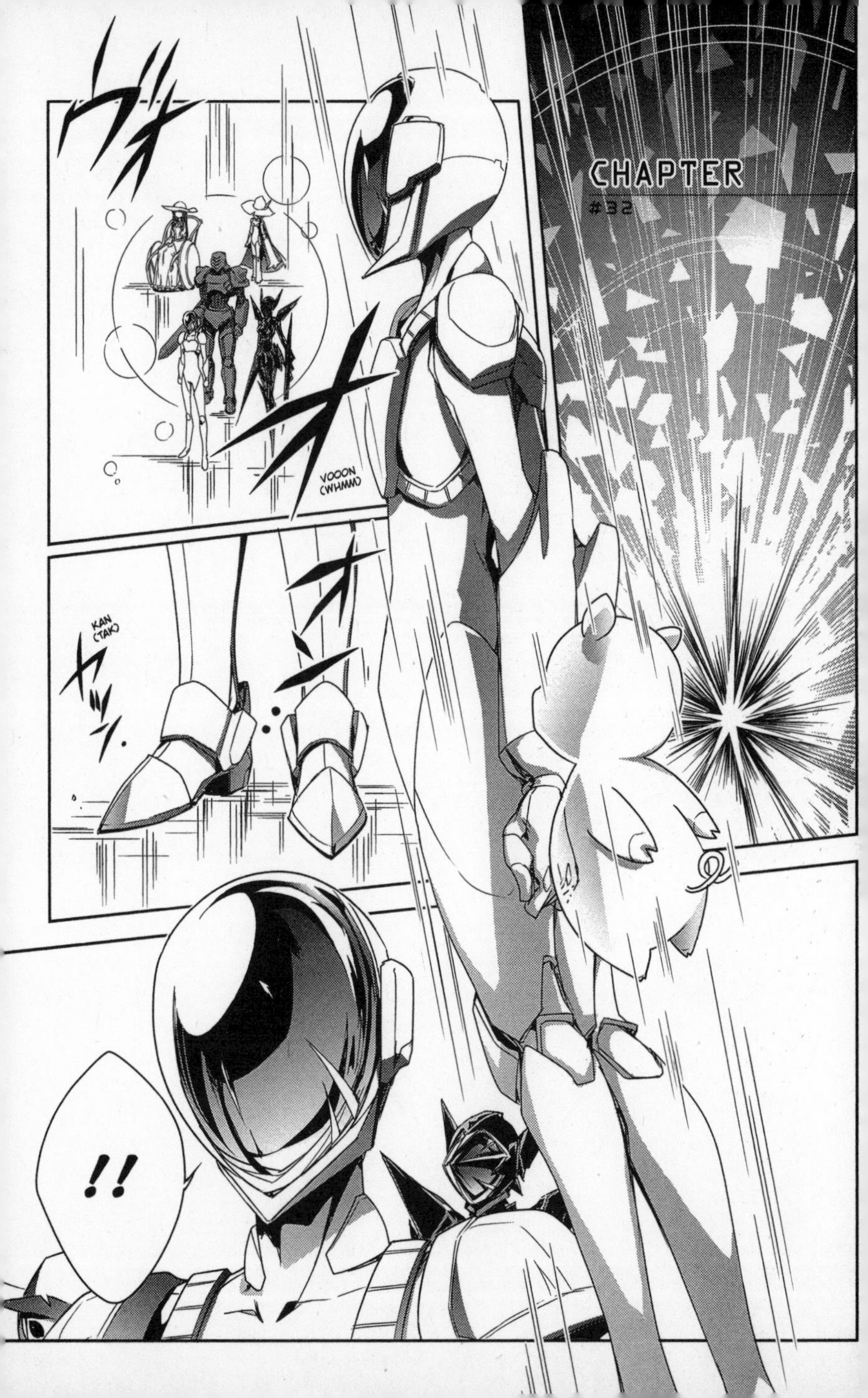
CHAPTER
#32
VOOON
(WHMM)
KAN
(TAK)
!!

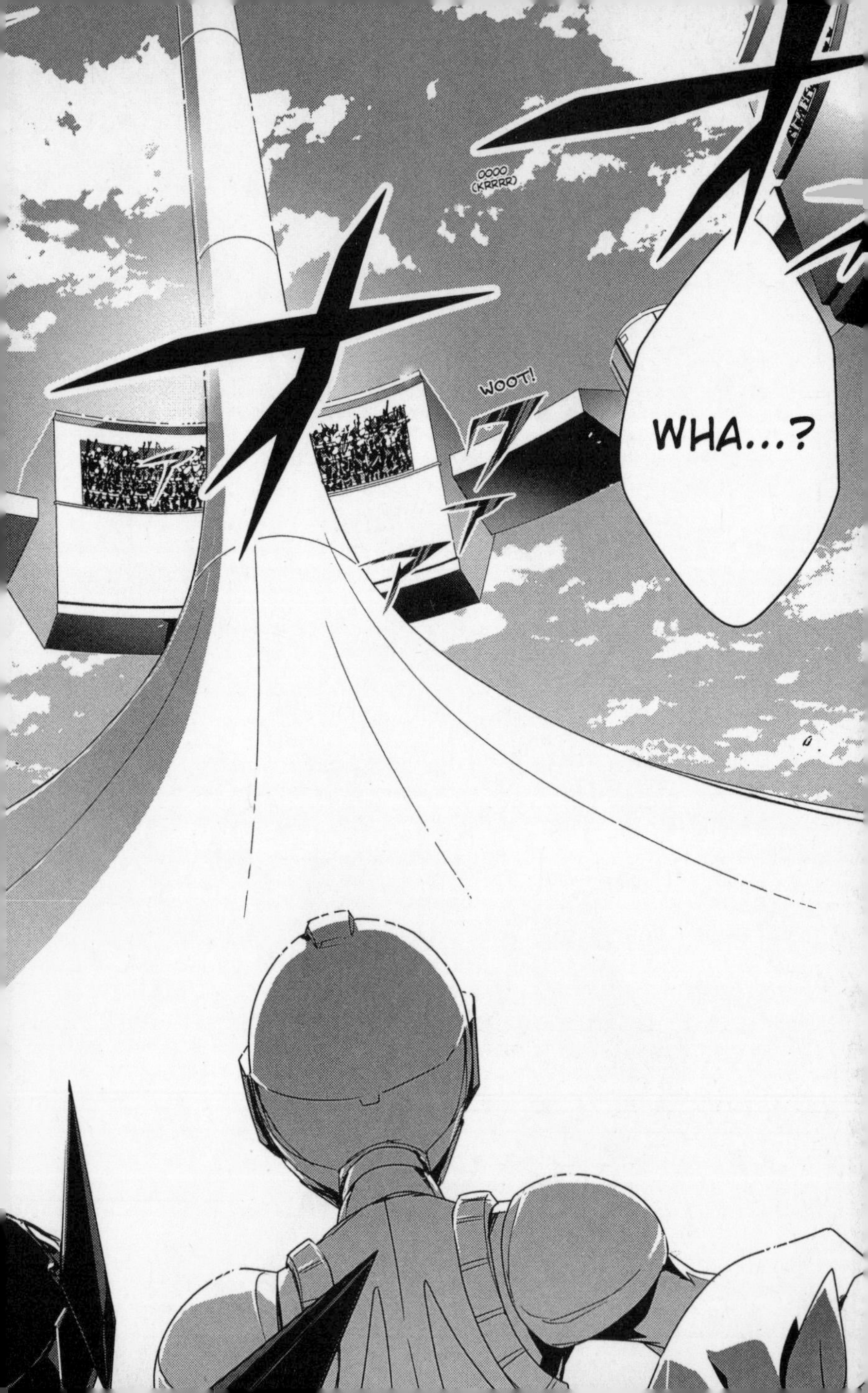
WHA...?
OOOO (KRRRR)
WOOT!

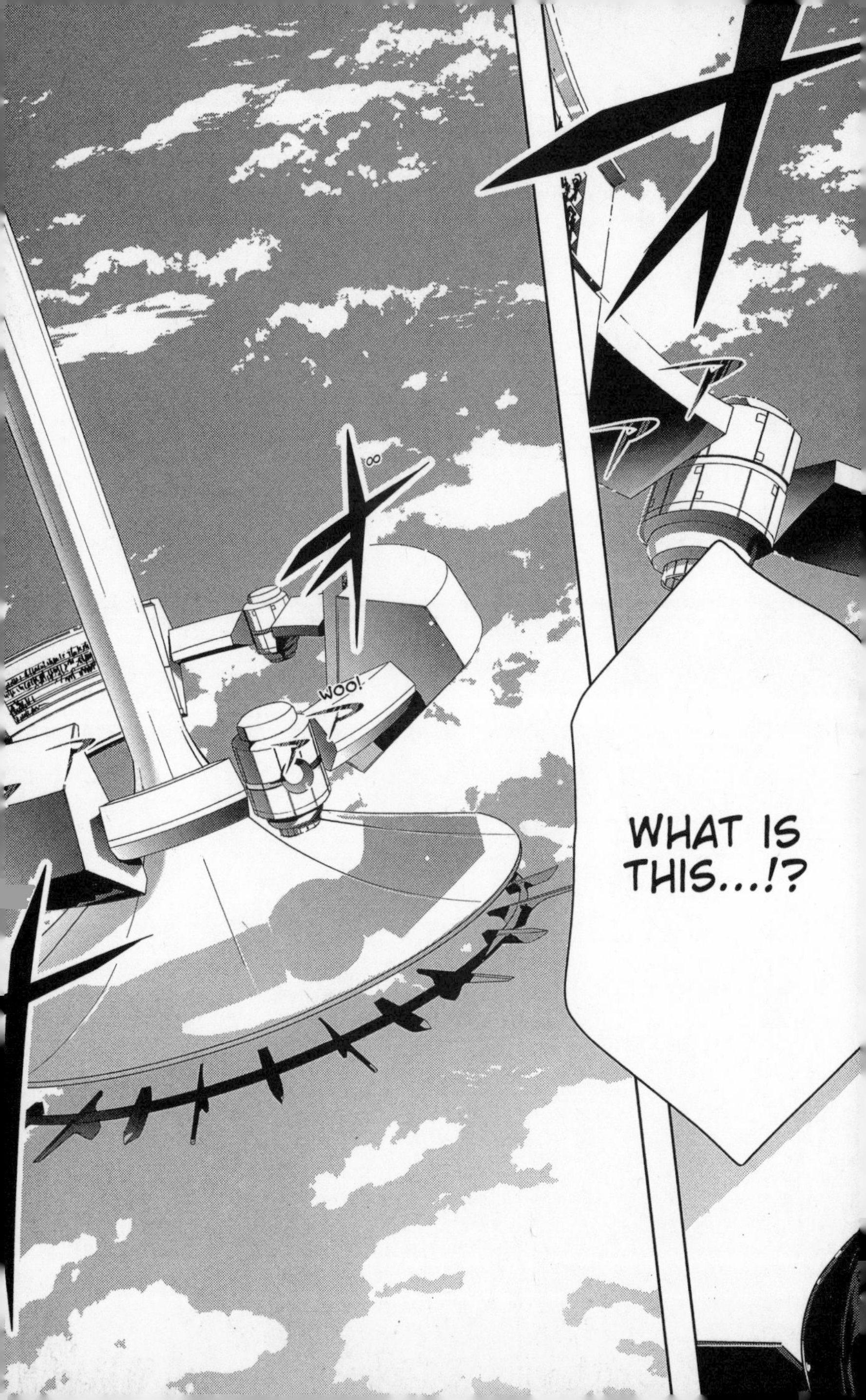
WHAT IS THIS...!?
WOO!

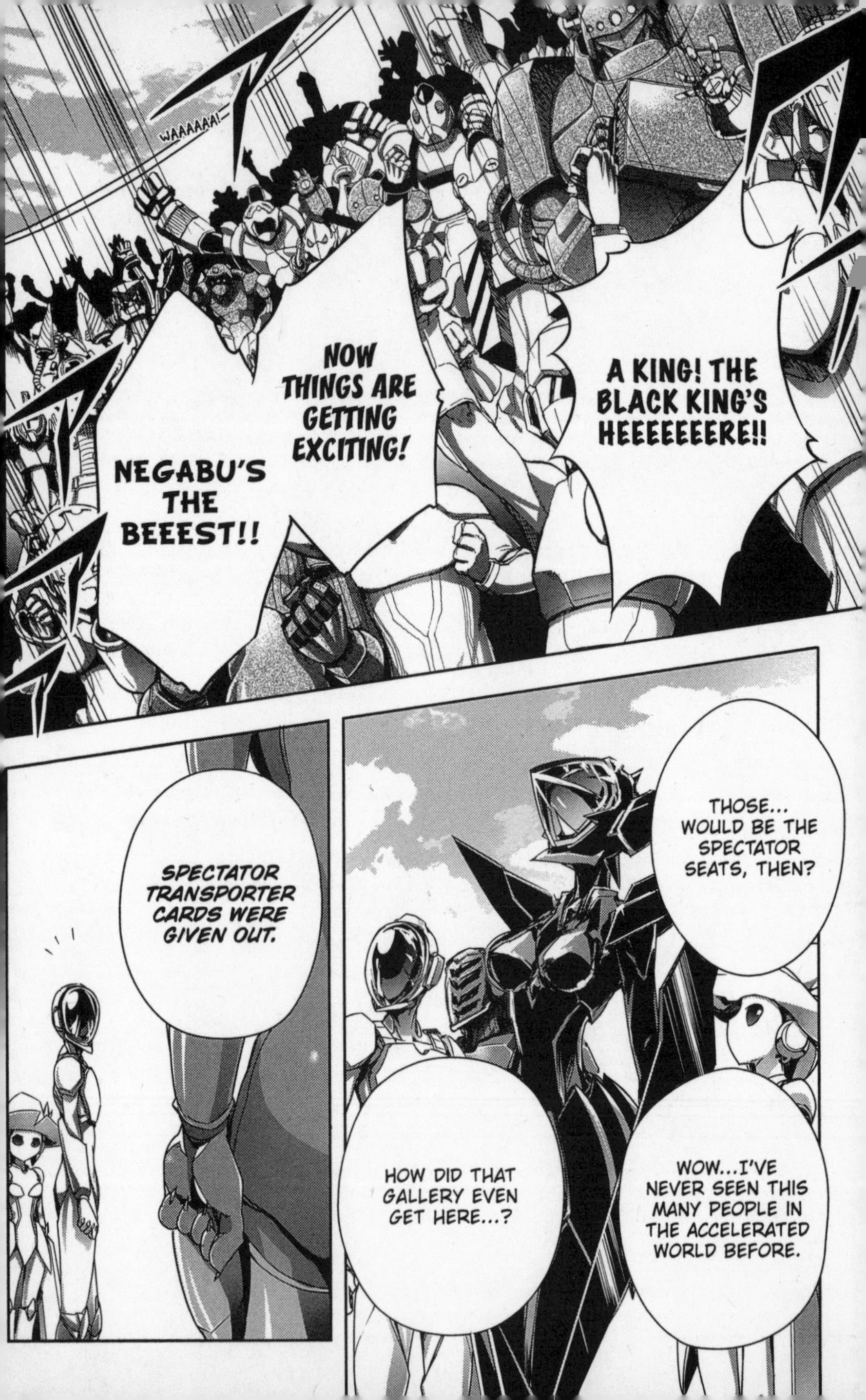
WAAAAAA!
A KING! THE BLACK KING'S HEEEEEEEERE!!
NOW THINGS ARE GETTING EXCITING!
NEGABU'S THE BEEEST!!
THOSE... WOULD BE THE SPECTATOR SEATS, THEN?
WOW...I'VE NEVER SEEN THIS MANY PEOPLE IN THE ACCELERATED WORLD BEFORE.
HOW DID THAT GALLERY EVEN GET HERE...?
SPECTATOR TRANSPORTER CARDS WERE GIVEN OUT.

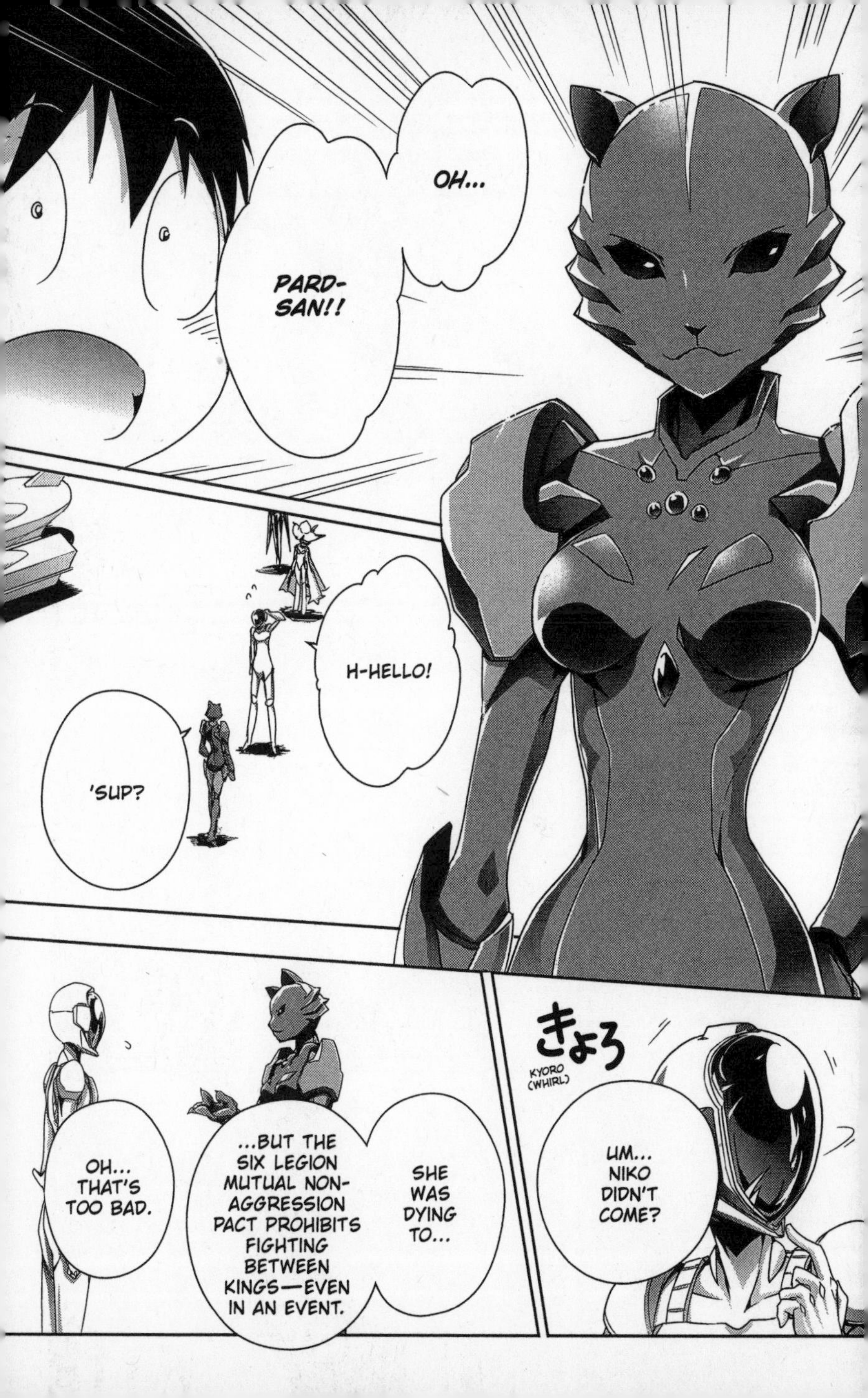
OH...
PARD-SAN!!
H-HELLO!
'SUP?
きょろ
KYORO (WHIRL)
UM... NIKO DIDN'T COME?
SHE WAS DYING TO...
...BUT THE SIX LEGION MUTUAL NON-AGGRESSION PACT PROHIBITS FIGHTING BETWEEN KINGS—EVEN IN AN EVENT.
OH... THAT'S TOO BAD.

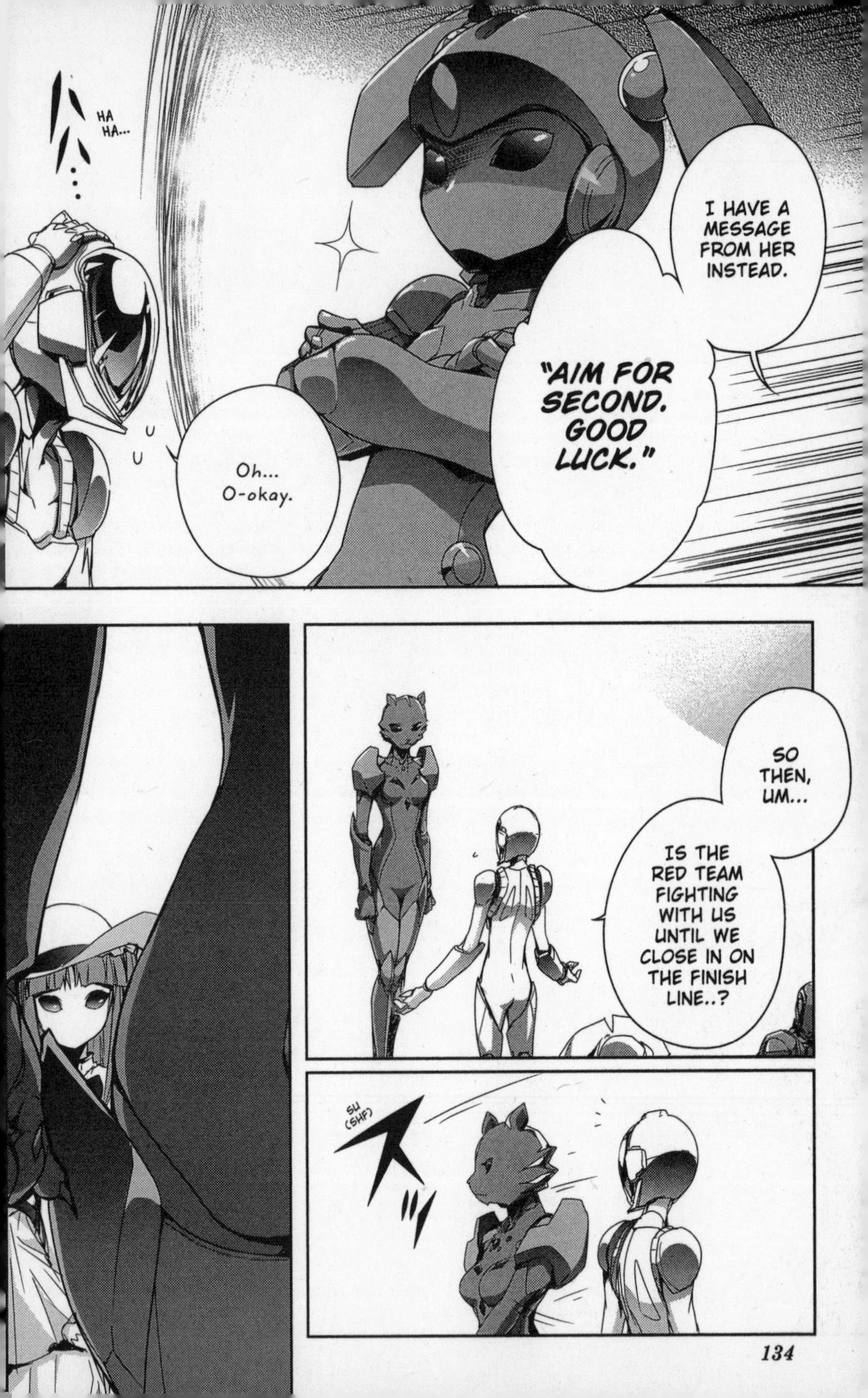
I HAVE A MESSAGE FROM HER INSTEAD.
"AIM FOR SECOND. GOOD LUCK."
Oh... O-okay.
HA HA...
SO THEN, UM...
IS THE RED TEAM FIGHTING WITH US UNTIL WE CLOSE IN ON THE FINISH LINE..?
SU (SHF)

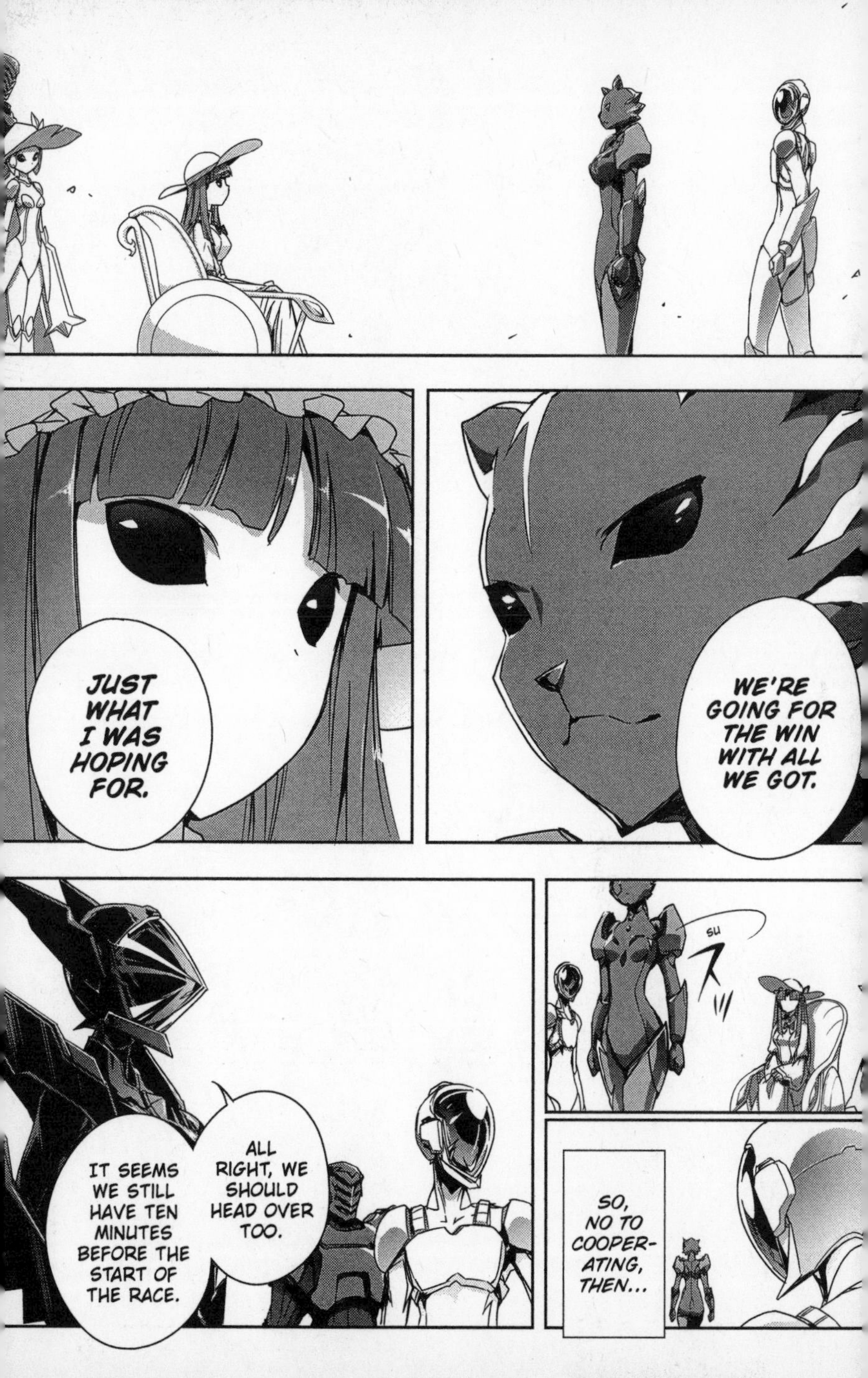
WE'RE GOING FOR THE WIN WITH ALL WE GOT.
JUST WHAT I WAS HOPING FOR.
SU
SO, NO TO COOPER-ATING, THEN...
ALL RIGHT, WE SHOULD HEAD OVER TOO.
IT SEEMS WE STILL HAVE TEN MINUTES BEFORE THE START OF THE RACE.

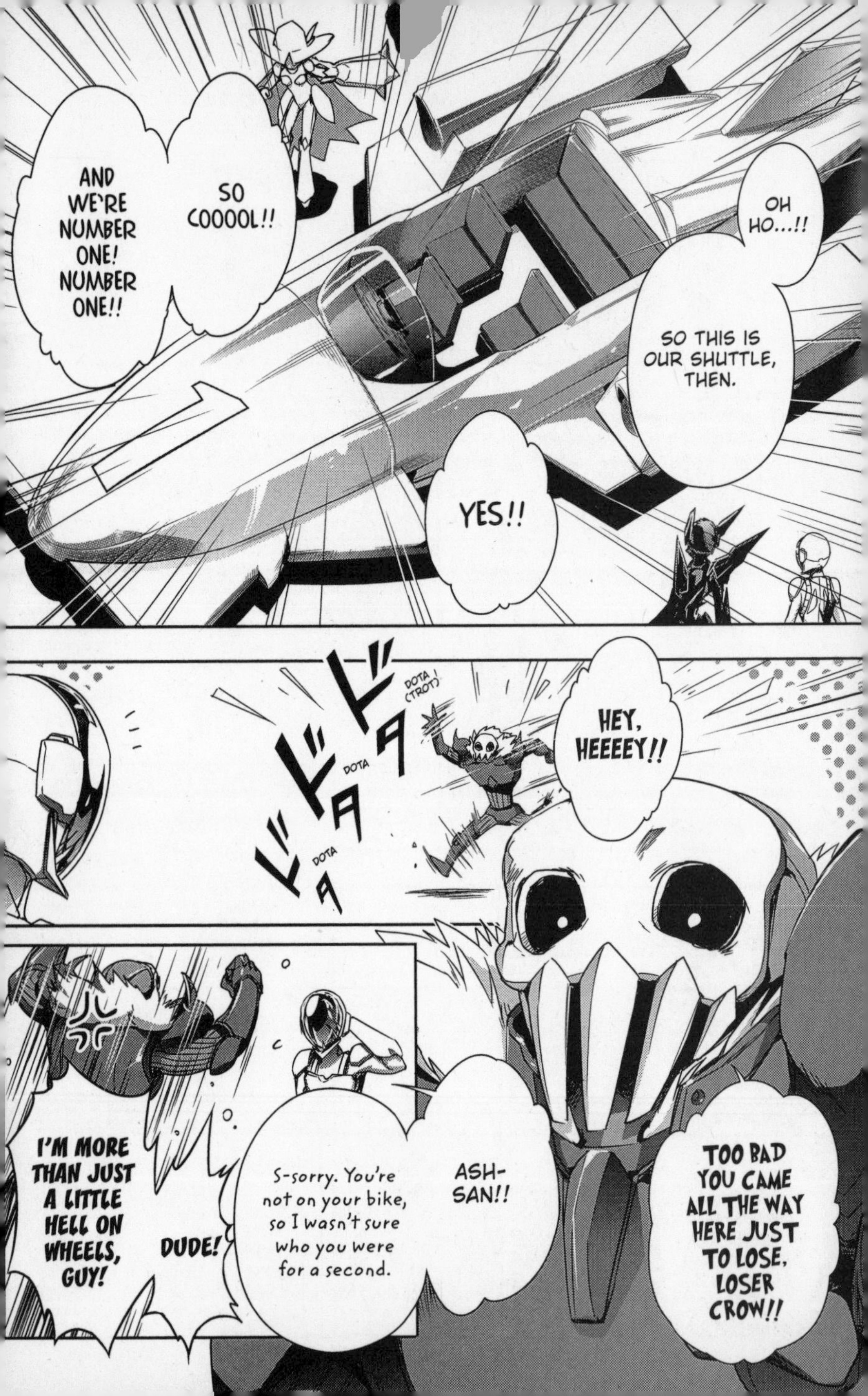
OH HO...!!
SO THIS IS OUR SHUTTLE, THEN.
YES!!
SO COOOOL!!
AND WE'RE NUMBER ONE! NUMBER ONE!!
HEY, HEEEEY!!
ドタ
DOTA (TROT)
ドタ
DOTA
ドタ
DOTA
TOO BAD YOU CAME ALL THE WAY HERE JUST TO LOSE, LOSER CROW!!
ASH-SAN!!
S-sorry. You're not on your bike, so I wasn't sure who you were for a second.
DUDE!
I'M MORE THAN JUST A LITTLE HELL ON WHEELS, GUY!

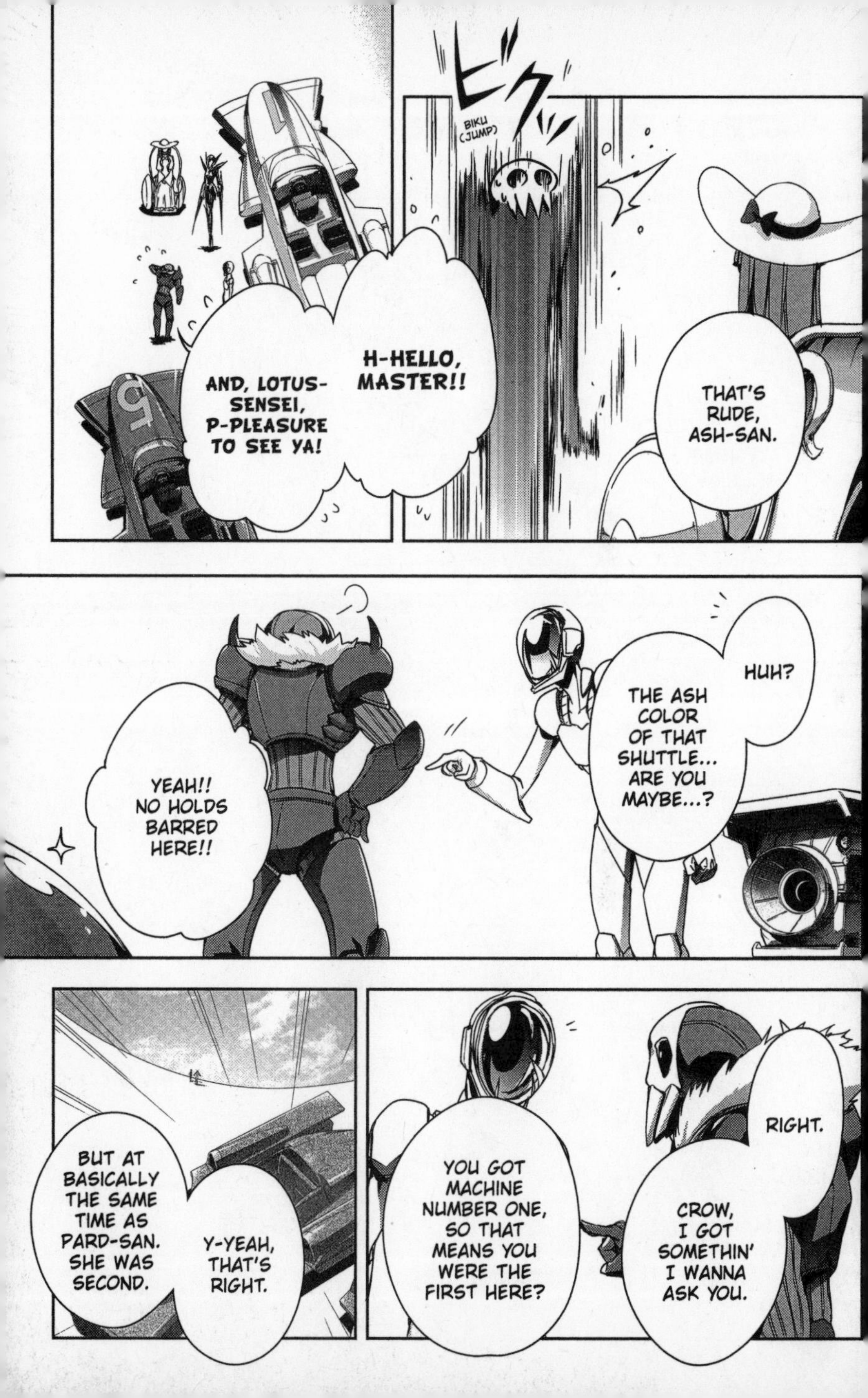
ビク
BIKU (JUMP)
THAT'S RUDE, ASH-SAN.
H-HELLO, MASTER!!
AND, LOTUS-SENSEI, P-PLEASURE TO SEE YA!
HUH?
THE ASH COLOR OF THAT SHUTTLE... ARE YOU MAYBE...?
YEAH!! NO HOLDS BARRED HERE!!
CROW, I GOT SOMETHIN' I WANNA ASK YOU.
RIGHT.
YOU GOT MACHINE NUMBER ONE, SO THAT MEANS YOU WERE THE FIRST HERE?
Y-YEAH, THAT'S RIGHT.
BUT AT BASICALLY THE SAME TIME AS PARD-SAN. SHE WAS SECOND.

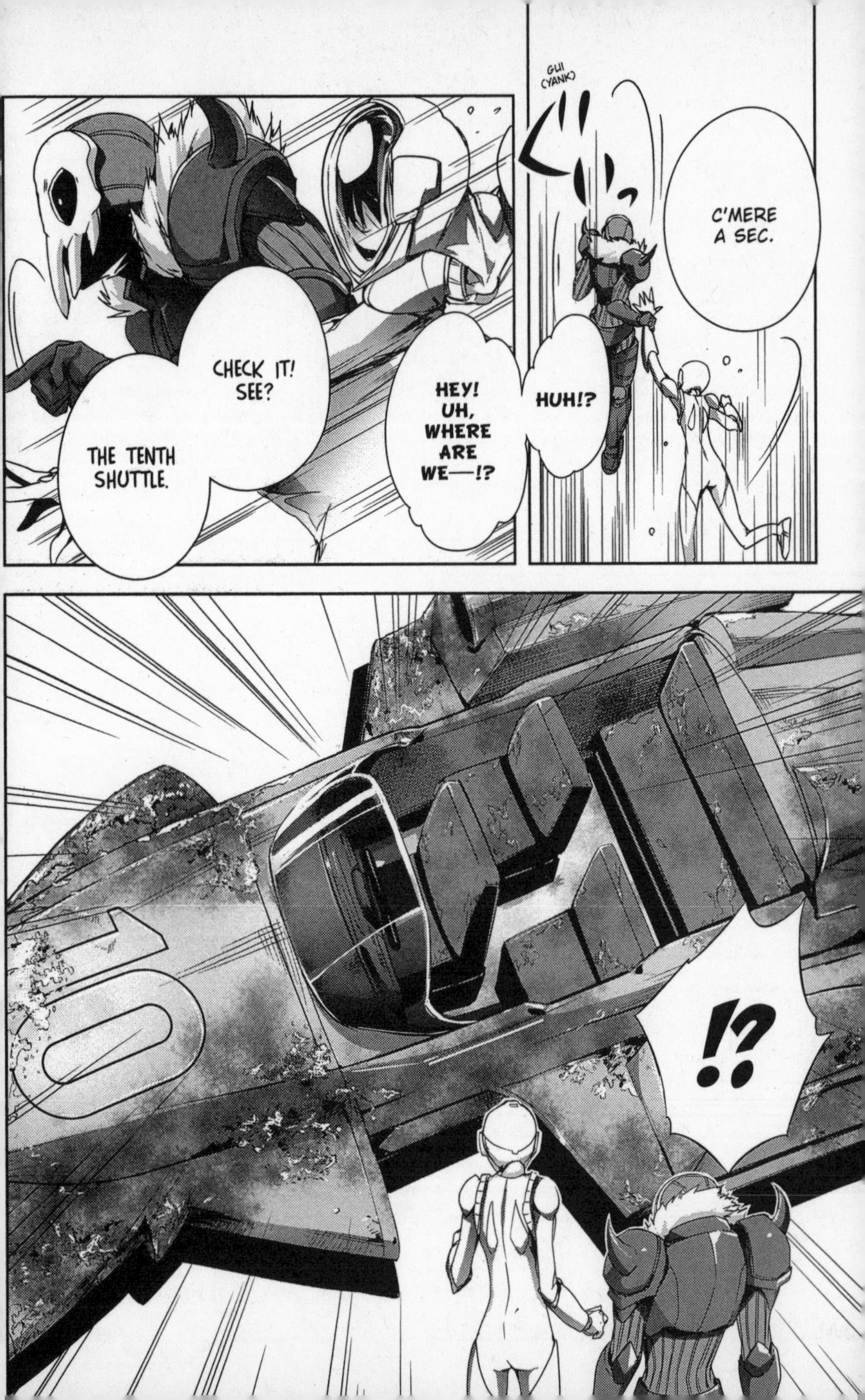
GUI (YANK)
C'MERE A SEC.
HUH!?
HEY! UH, WHERE ARE WE—!?
CHECK IT! SEE?
THE TENTH SHUTTLE.
!?

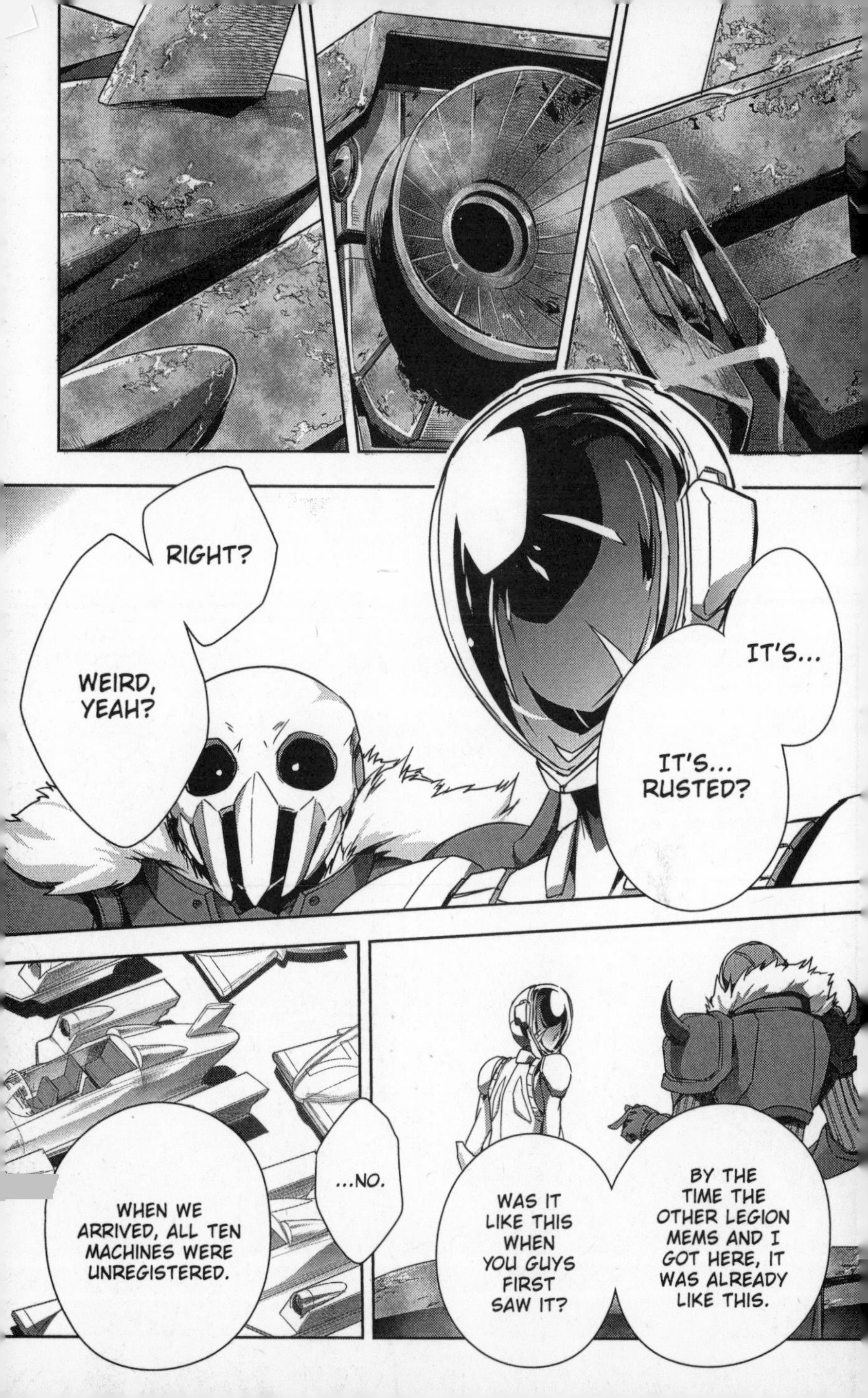
IT'S...
IT'S... RUSTED?
RIGHT?
WEIRD, YEAH?
BY THE TIME THE OTHER LEGION MEMS AND I GOT HERE, IT WAS ALREADY LIKE THIS.
WAS IT LIKE THIS WHEN YOU GUYS FIRST SAW IT?
...NO.
WHEN WE ARRIVED, ALL TEN MACHINES WERE UNREGISTERED.

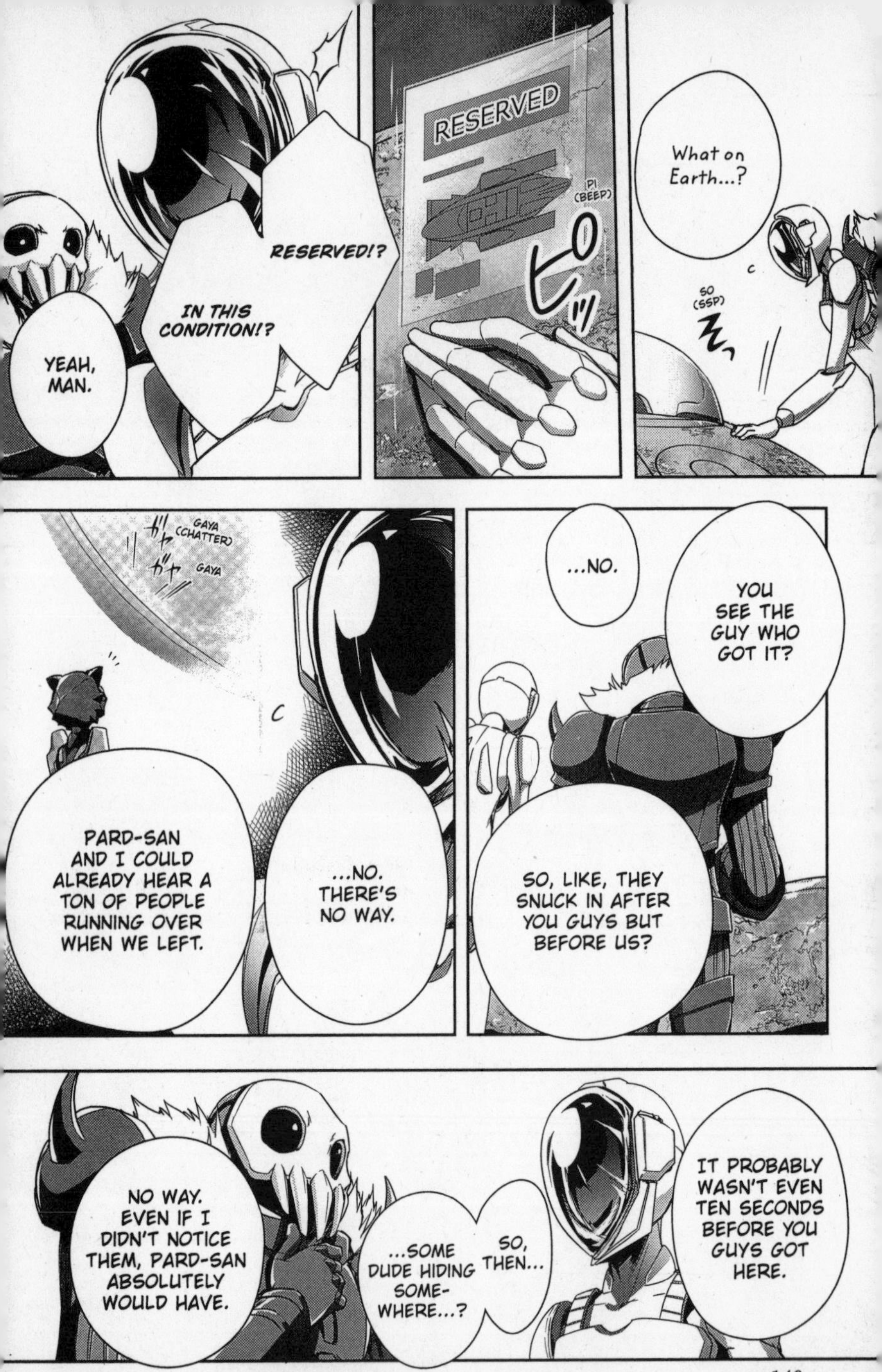
What on Earth...?
SO (SSP)
RESERVED
PI (BEEP)
RESERVED!?
IN THIS CONDITION!?
YEAH, MAN.
YOU SEE THE GUY WHO GOT IT?
...NO.
SO, LIKE, THEY SNUCK IN AFTER YOU GUYS BUT BEFORE US?
GAYA (CHATTER)
GAYA
...NO. THERE'S NO WAY.
PARD-SAN AND I COULD ALREADY HEAR A TON OF PEOPLE RUNNING OVER WHEN WE LEFT.
IT PROBABLY WASN'T EVEN TEN SECONDS BEFORE YOU GUYS GOT HERE.
SO, THEN...
...SOME DUDE HIDING SOME-WHERE...?
NO WAY. EVEN IF I DIDN'T NOTICE THEM, PARD-SAN ABSOLUTELY WOULD HAVE.

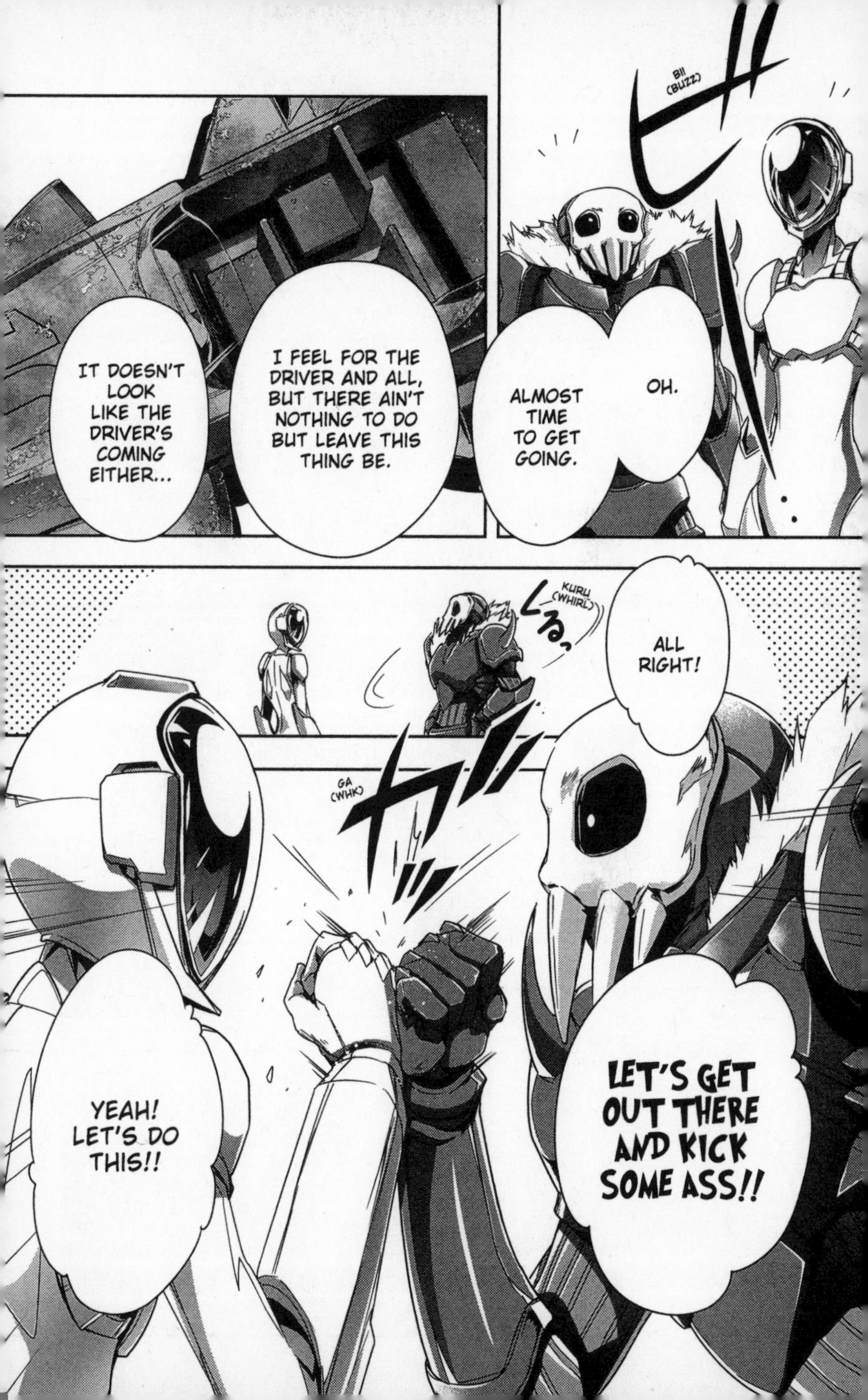
BII (BUZZ)
OH.
ALMOST TIME TO GET GOING.
I FEEL FOR THE DRIVER AND ALL, BUT THERE AIN'T NOTHING TO DO BUT LEAVE THIS THING BE.
IT DOESN'T LOOK LIKE THE DRIVER'S COMING EITHER...
KURU (WHIRL)
ALL RIGHT!
GA (WHK)
LET'S GET OUT THERE AND KICK SOME ASS!!
YEAH! LET'S DO THIS!!

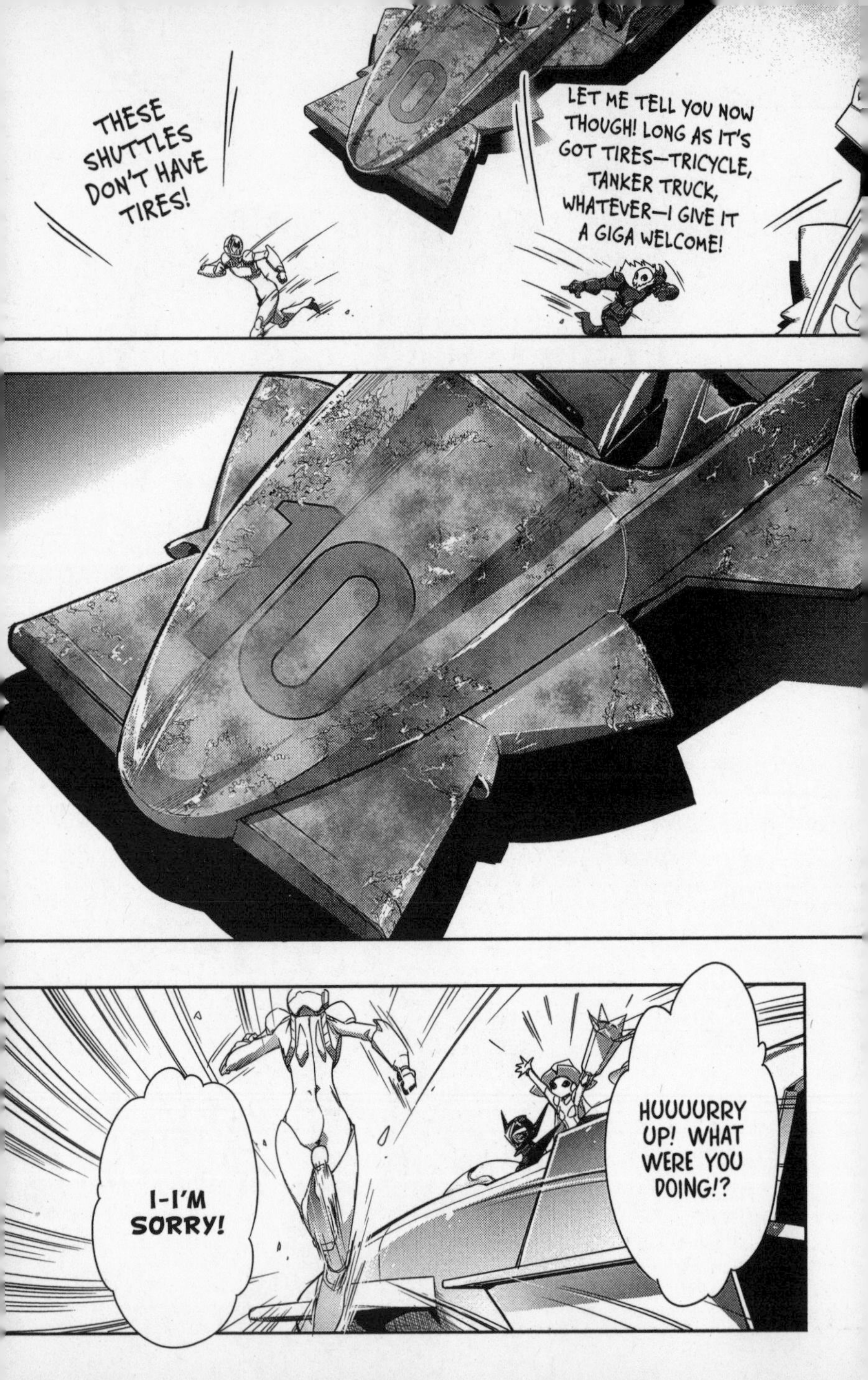
LET ME TELL YOU NOW THOUGH! LONG AS IT'S GOT TIRES—TRICYCLE, TANKER TRUCK, WHATEVER—I GIVE IT A GIGA WELCOME!
THESE SHUTTLES DON'T HAVE TIRES!
HUUUURRY UP! WHAT WERE YOU DOING!?
I-I'M SORRY!

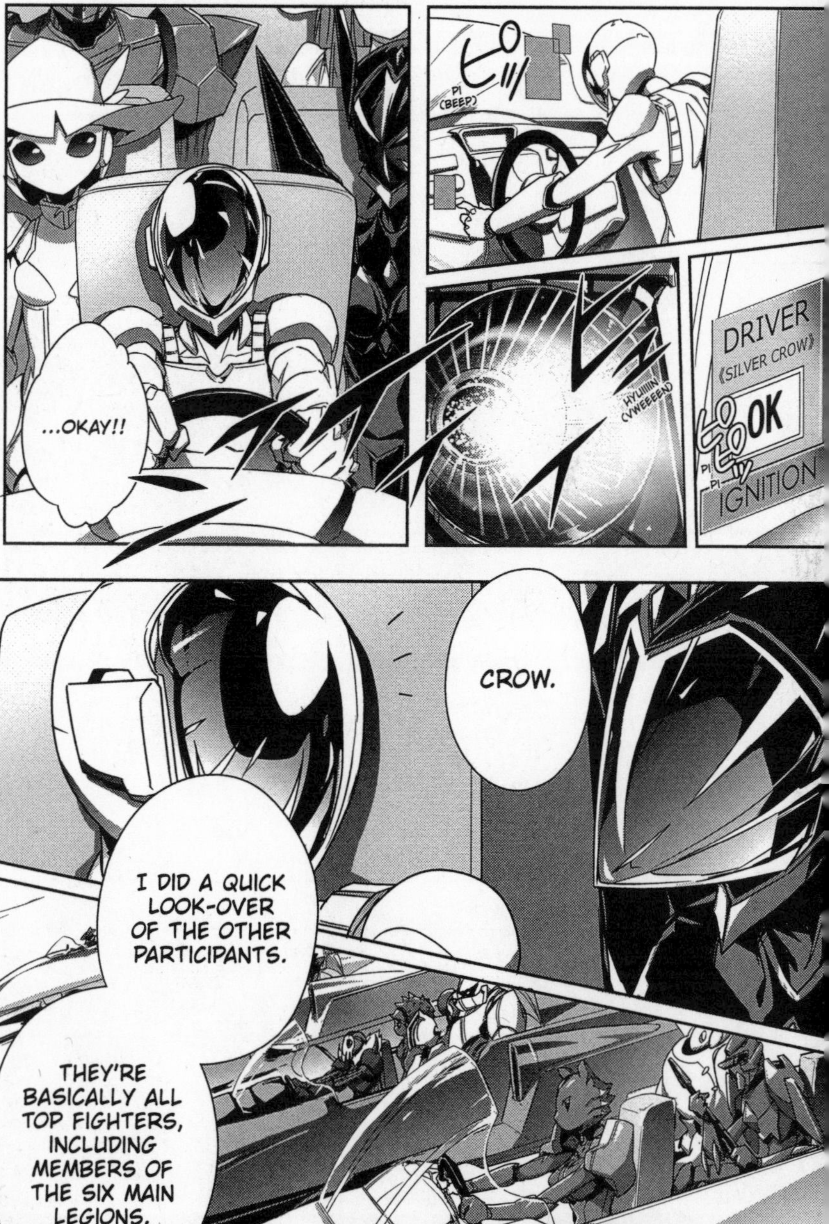
PI (BEEP)
DRIVER
《SILVER CROW》
OK
PI PI
IGNITION
HYUIIIN (VWEEEEN)
...OKAY!!
CROW.
I DID A QUICK LOOK-OVER OF THE OTHER PARTICIPANTS.
THEY'RE BASICALLY ALL TOP FIGHTERS, INCLUDING MEMBERS OF THE SIX MAIN LEGIONS.

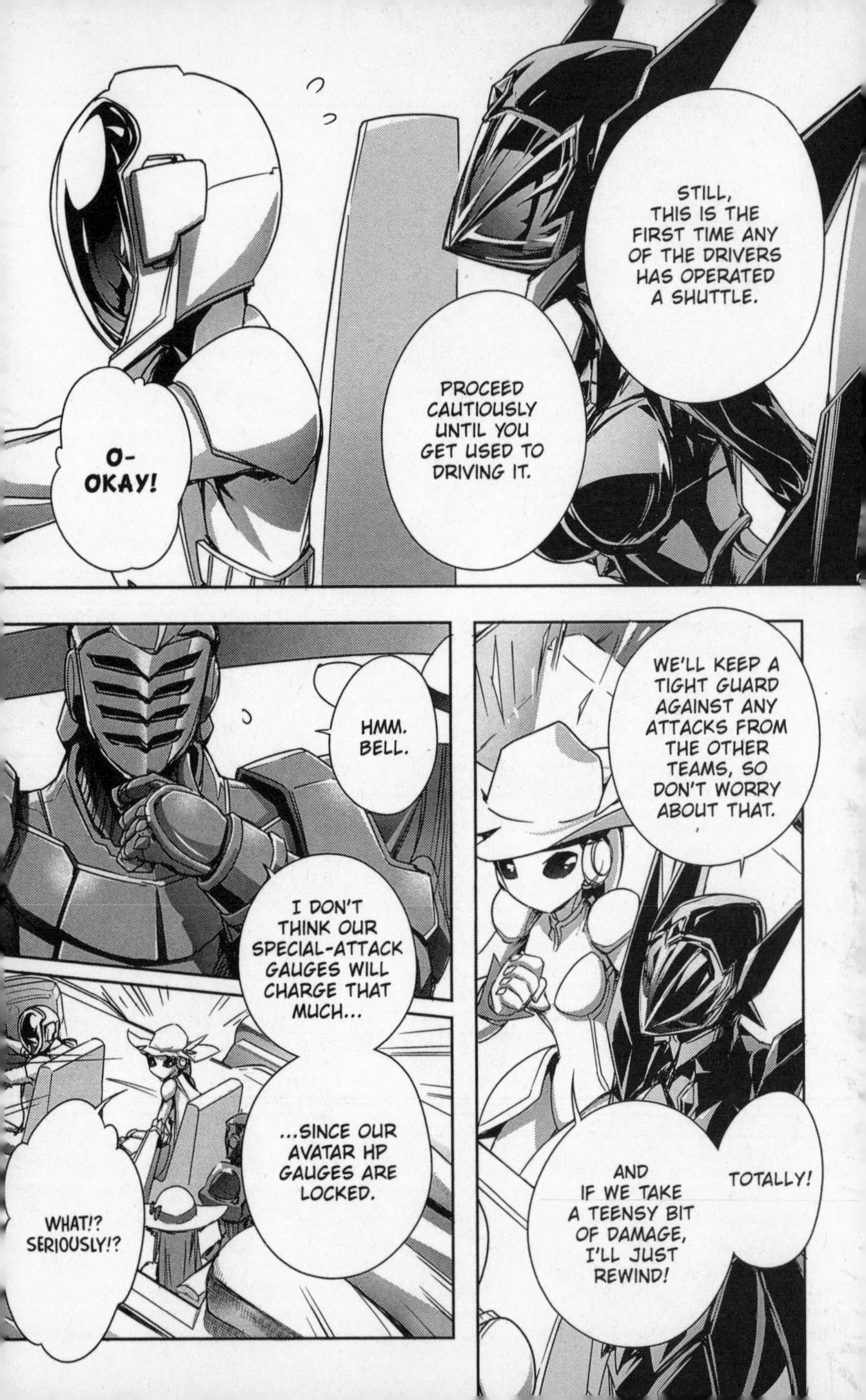
STILL, THIS IS THE FIRST TIME ANY OF THE DRIVERS HAS OPERATED A SHUTTLE.
PROCEED CAUTIOUSLY UNTIL YOU GET USED TO DRIVING IT.
O-OKAY!
WE'LL KEEP A TIGHT GUARD AGAINST ANY ATTACKS FROM THE OTHER TEAMS, SO DON'T WORRY ABOUT THAT.
TOTALLY!
AND IF WE TAKE A TEENSY BIT OF DAMAGE, I'LL JUST REWIND!
HMM. BELL.
I DON'T THINK OUR SPECIAL-ATTACK GAUGES WILL CHARGE THAT MUCH...
...SINCE OUR AVATAR HP GAUGES ARE LOCKED.
WHAT!? SERIOUSLY!?

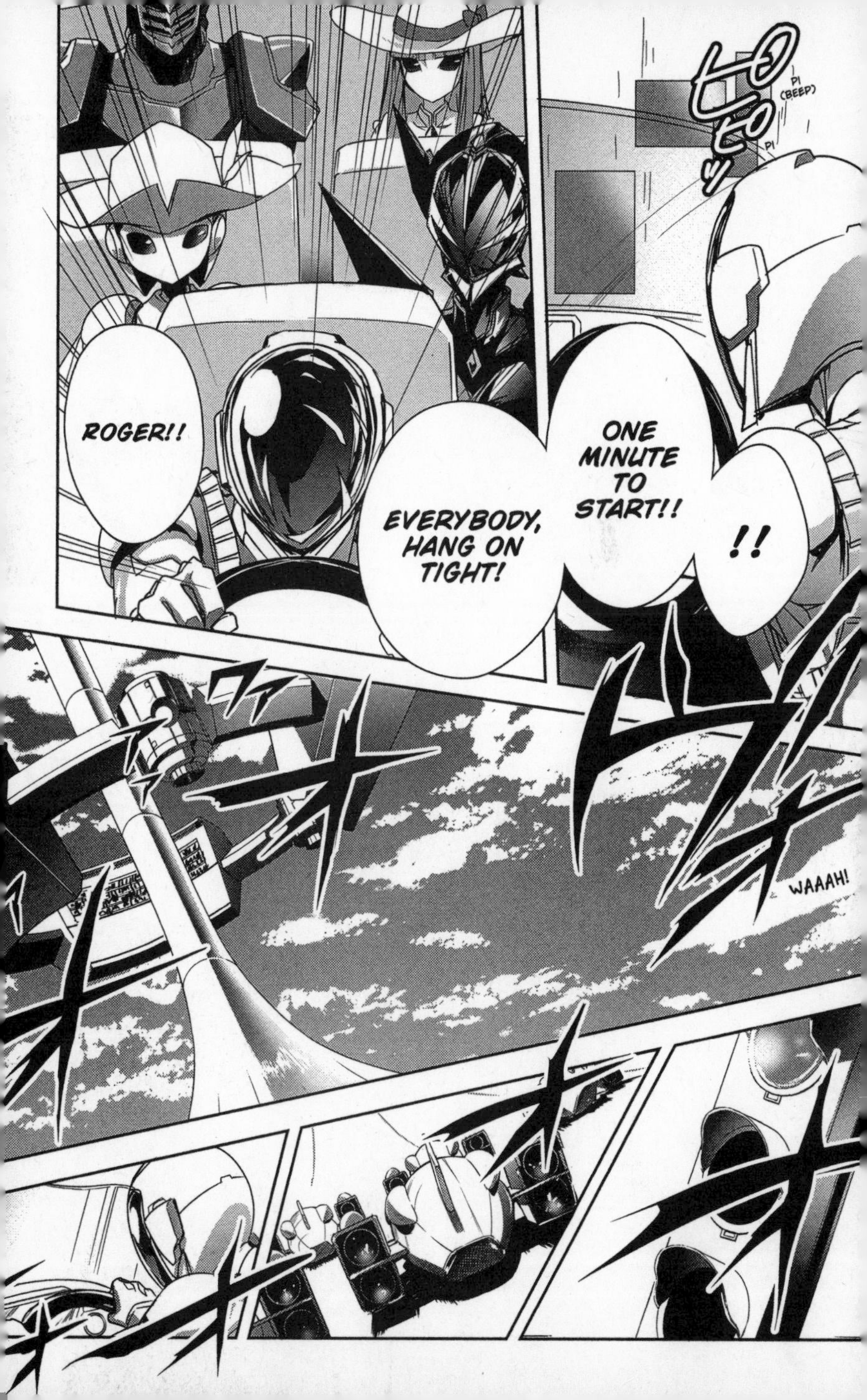
PI (BEEP)
PI
ONE MINUTE TO START!!
!!
EVERYBODY, HANG ON TIGHT!
ROGER!!
WAAAH!

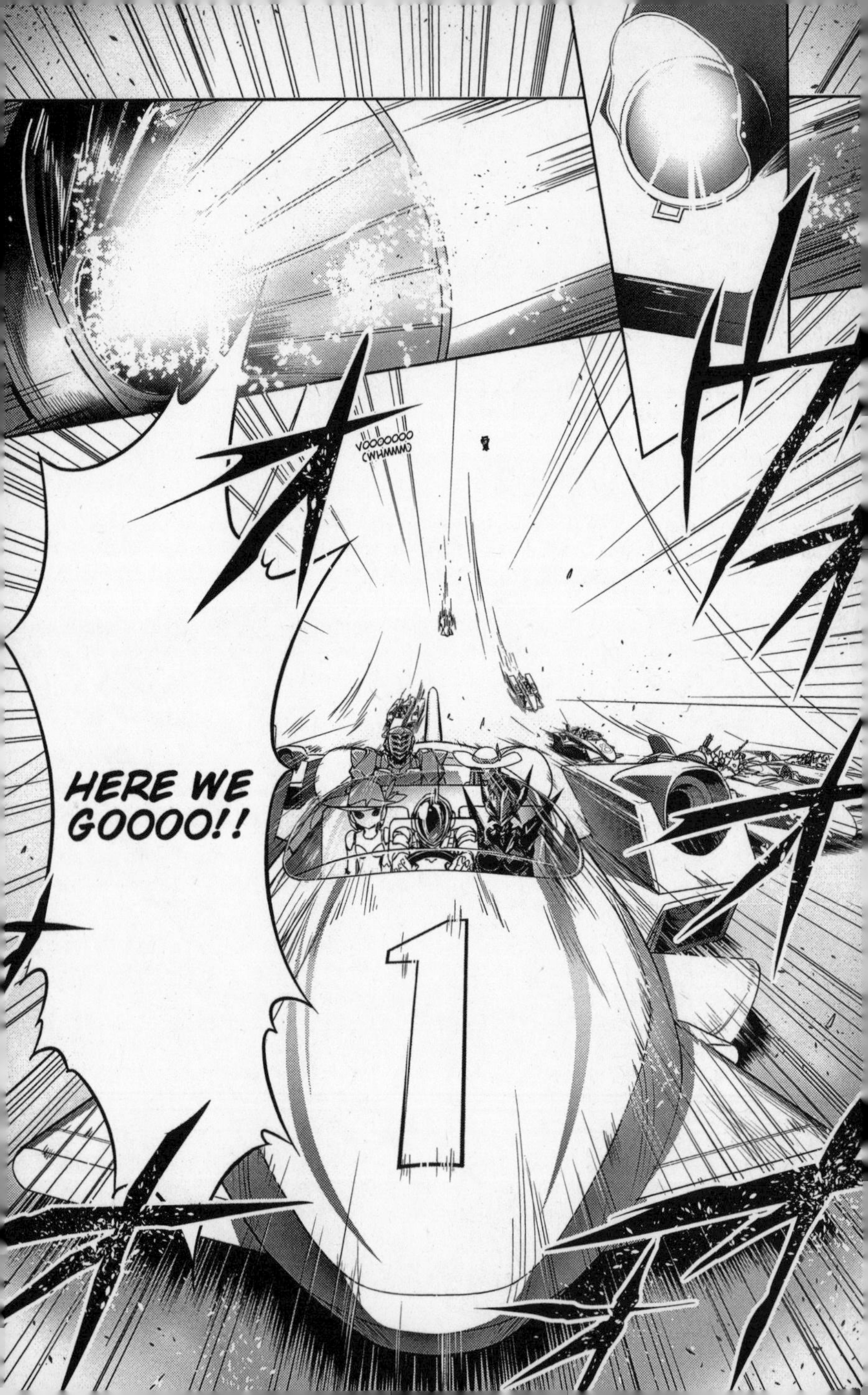
VOOOOOOO (WHMMM)
HERE WE GOOOO!!

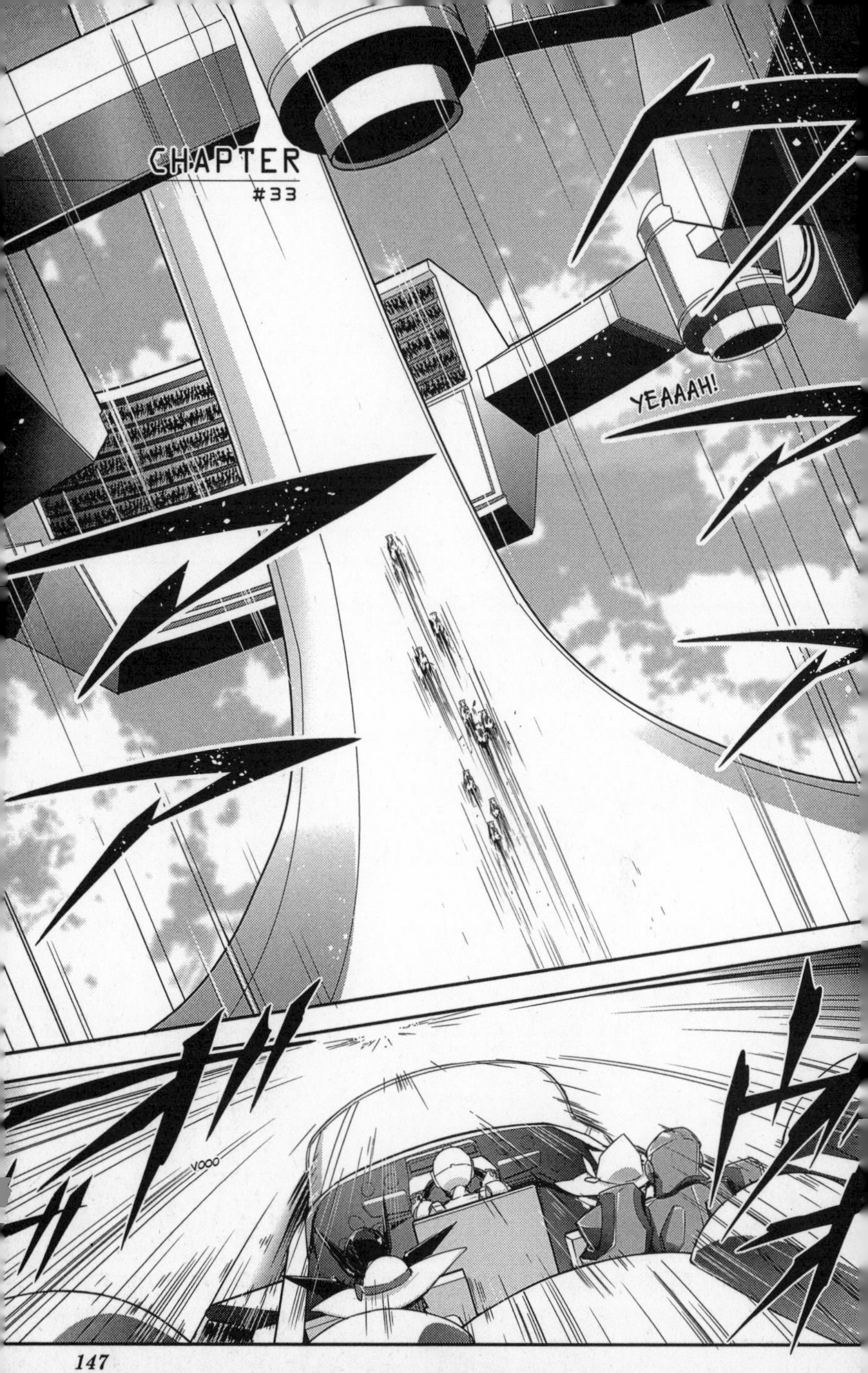
CHAPTER
#33
YEAAAH!
VOOO

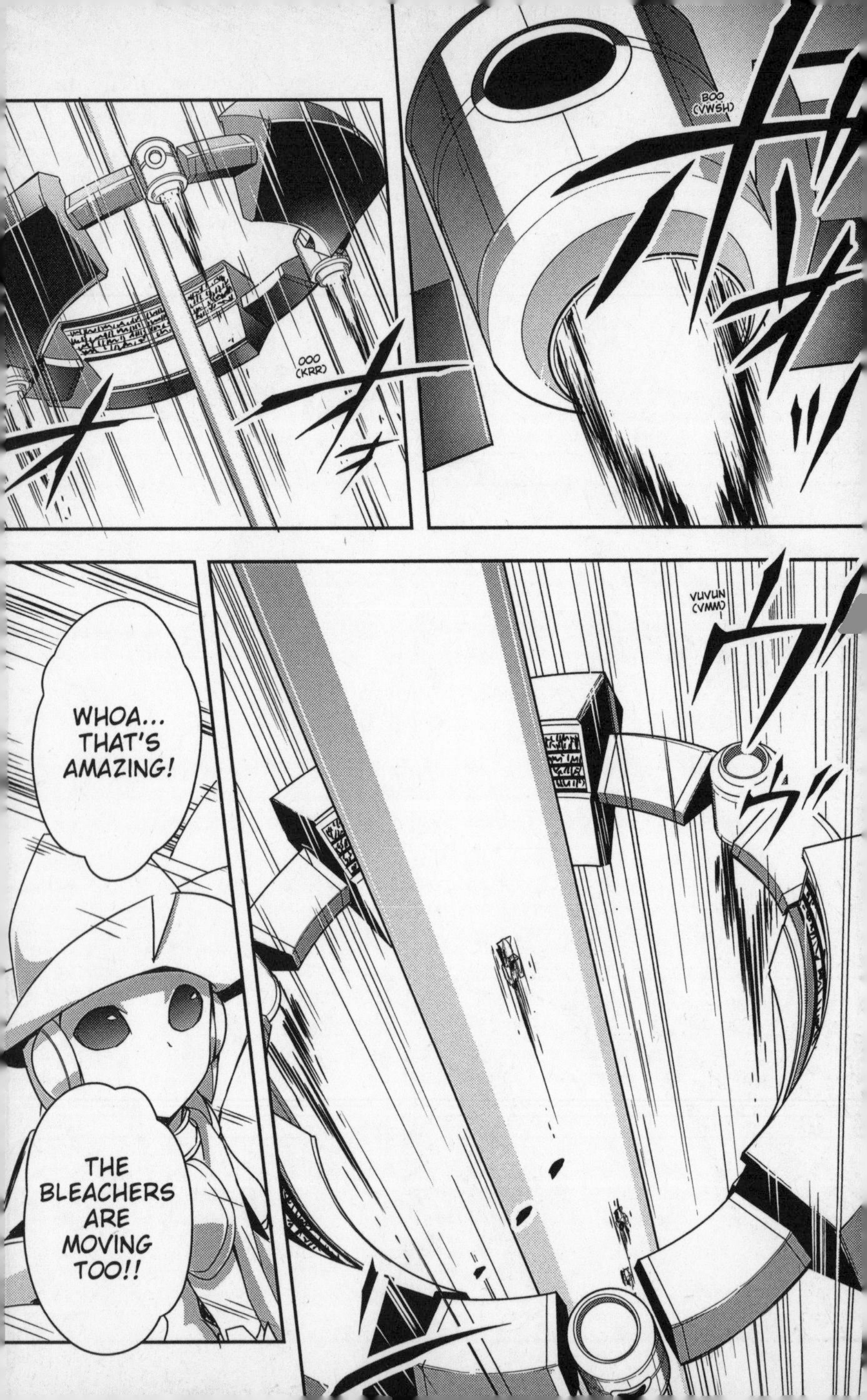
BOO (VWSH)
OOO (KRR)
VUVUN (VMM)
WHOA... THAT'S AMAZING!
THE BLEACHERS ARE MOVING TOO!!

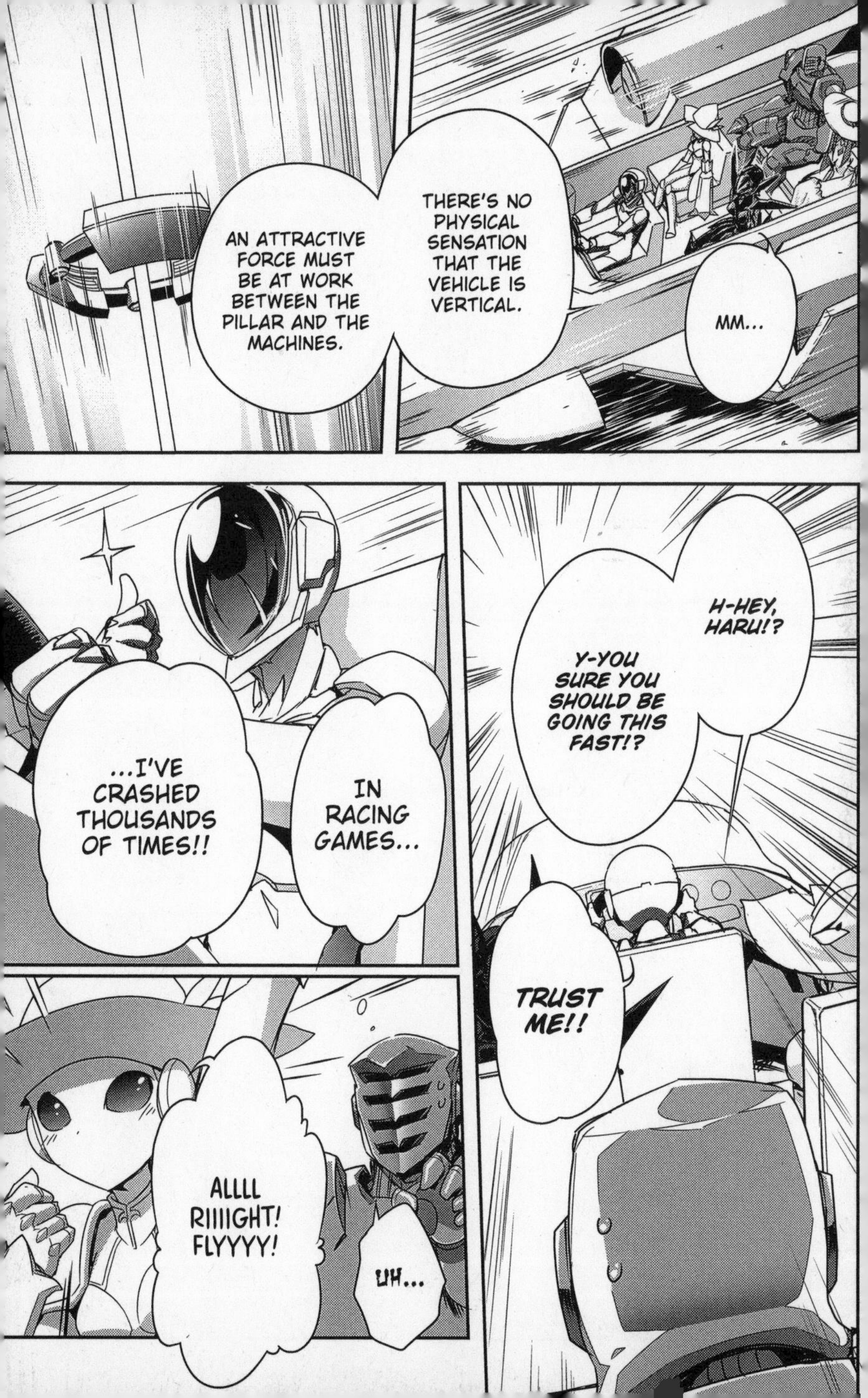
MM...
THERE'S NO PHYSICAL SENSATION THAT THE VEHICLE IS VERTICAL.
AN ATTRACTIVE FORCE MUST BE AT WORK BETWEEN THE PILLAR AND THE MACHINES.
H-HEY, HARU!?
Y-YOU SURE YOU SHOULD BE GOING THIS FAST!?
TRUST ME!!
IN RACING GAMES...
...I'VE CRASHED THOUSANDS OF TIMES!!
ALLLL RIIIGHT! FLYYYY!
UH...

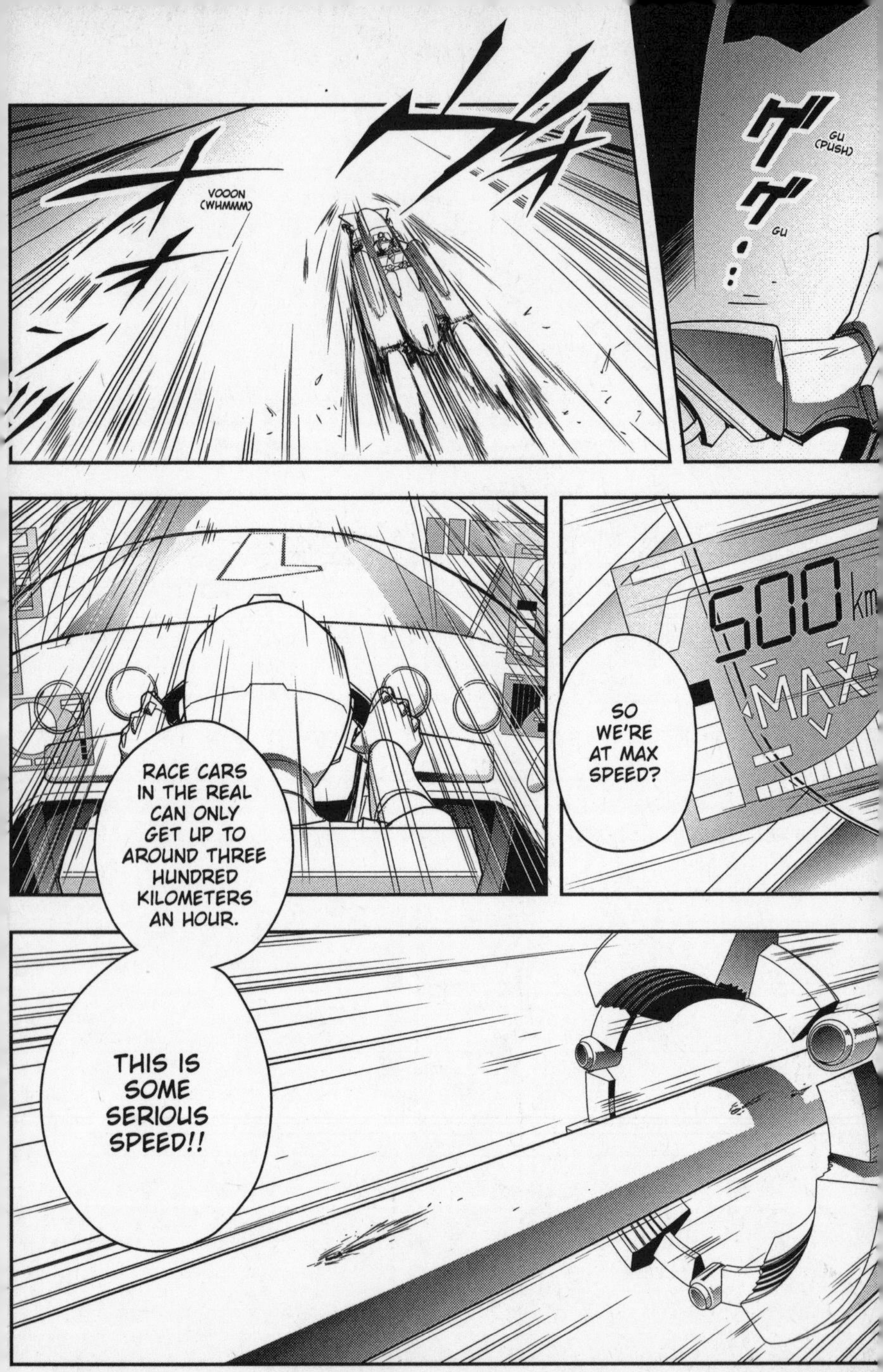
GU (PUSH)
GU
VOOON (WHMMM)
500 km
MAX
SO WE'RE AT MAX SPEED?
RACE CARS IN THE REAL CAN ONLY GET UP TO AROUND THREE HUNDRED KILOMETERS AN HOUR.
THIS IS SOME SERIOUS SPEED!!

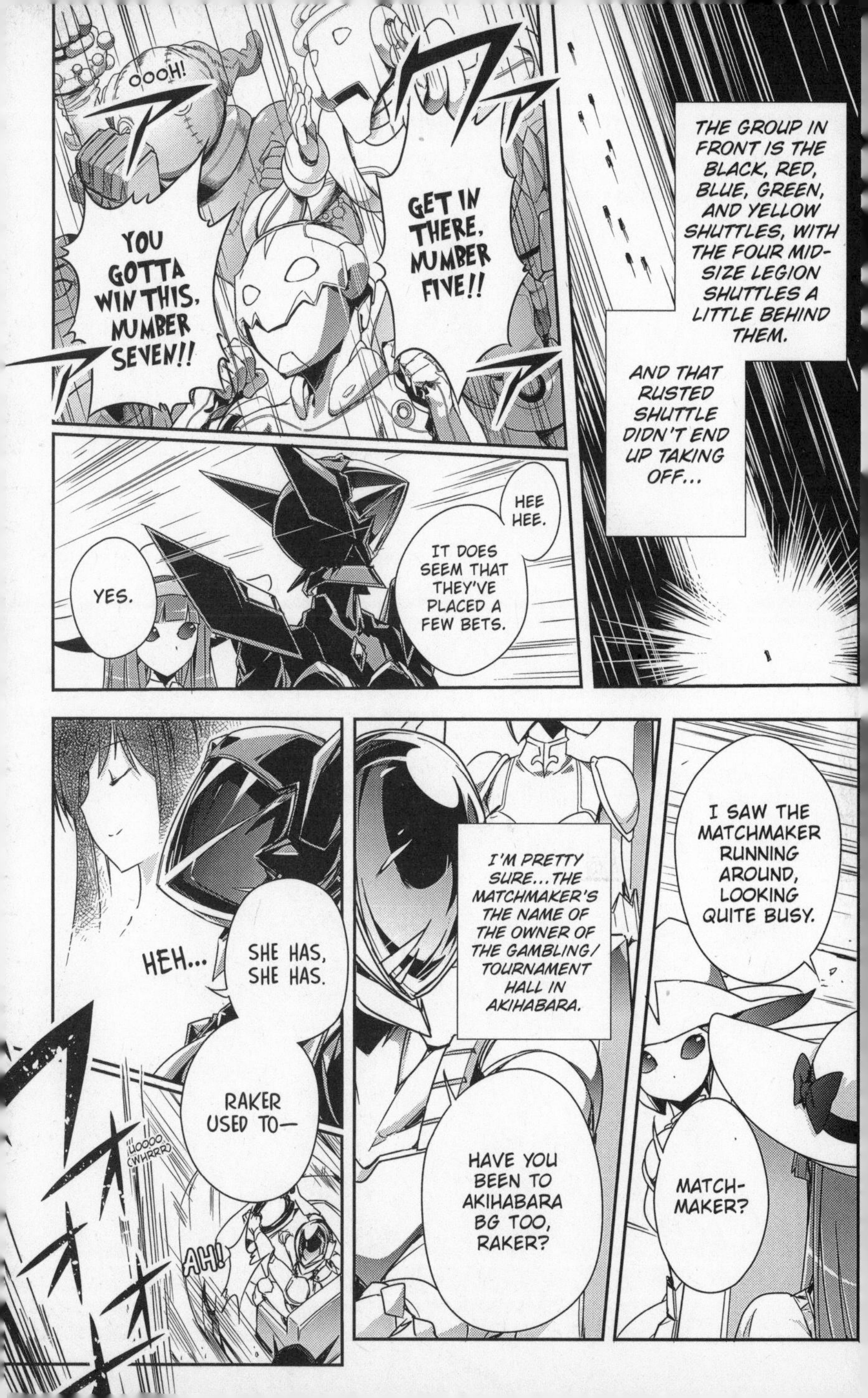
THE GROUP IN FRONT IS THE BLACK, RED, BLUE, GREEN, AND YELLOW SHUTTLES, WITH THE FOUR MID-SIZE LEGION SHUTTLES A LITTLE BEHIND THEM.
AND THAT RUSTED SHUTTLE DIDN'T END UP TAKING OFF...
GET IN THERE, NUMBER FIVE!!
OOOH!
YOU GOTTA WIN THIS, NUMBER SEVEN!!
HEE HEE.
IT DOES SEEM THAT THEY'VE PLACED A FEW BETS.
YES.
I SAW THE MATCHMAKER RUNNING AROUND, LOOKING QUITE BUSY.
MATCH-MAKER?
I'M PRETTY SURE...THE MATCHMAKER'S THE NAME OF THE OWNER OF THE GAMBLING/TOURNAMENT HALL IN AKIHABARA.
HAVE YOU BEEN TO AKIHABARA BG TOO, RAKER?
SHE HAS, SHE HAS.
HEH...
RAKER USED TO—
UOOOO (WHRRR)
AH!

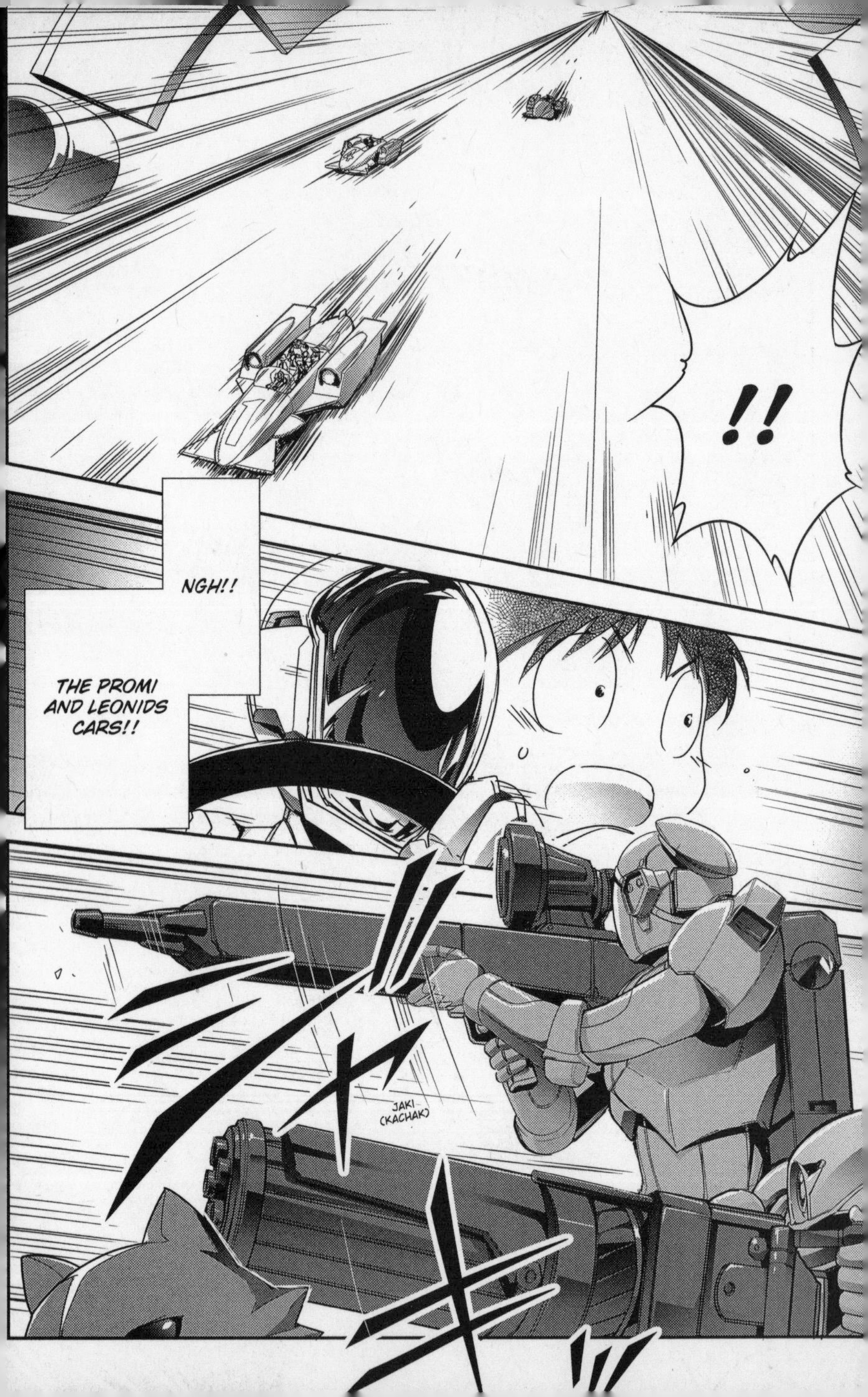
!!
NGH!!
THE PROMI AND LEONIDS CARS!!
JAKI (KACHAK)

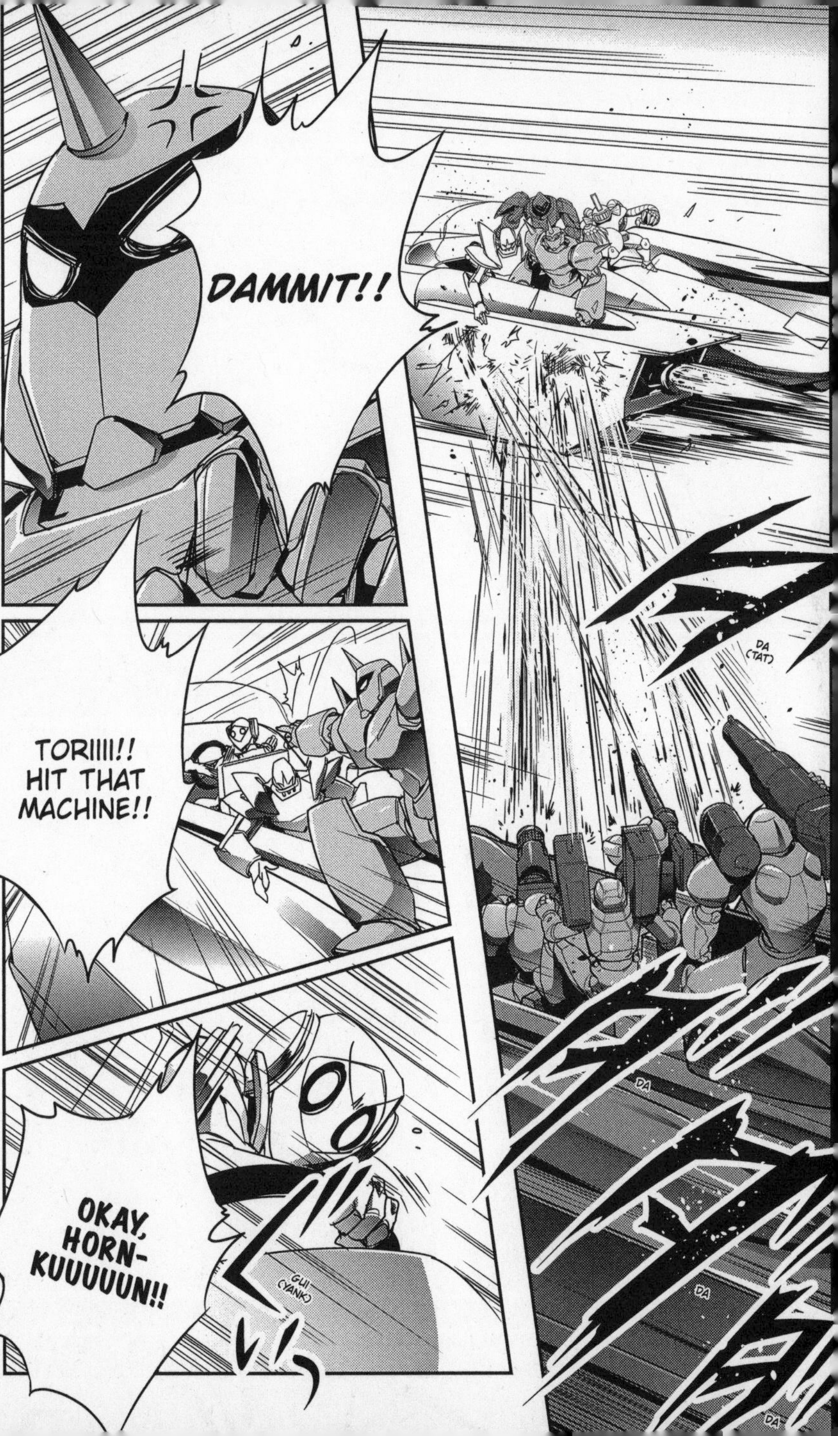
DA (TAT)
DA
DA
DA
DAMMIT!!
TORIIIII!! HIT THAT MACHINE!!
OKAY, HORN-KUUUUUN!!
GUI (YANK)

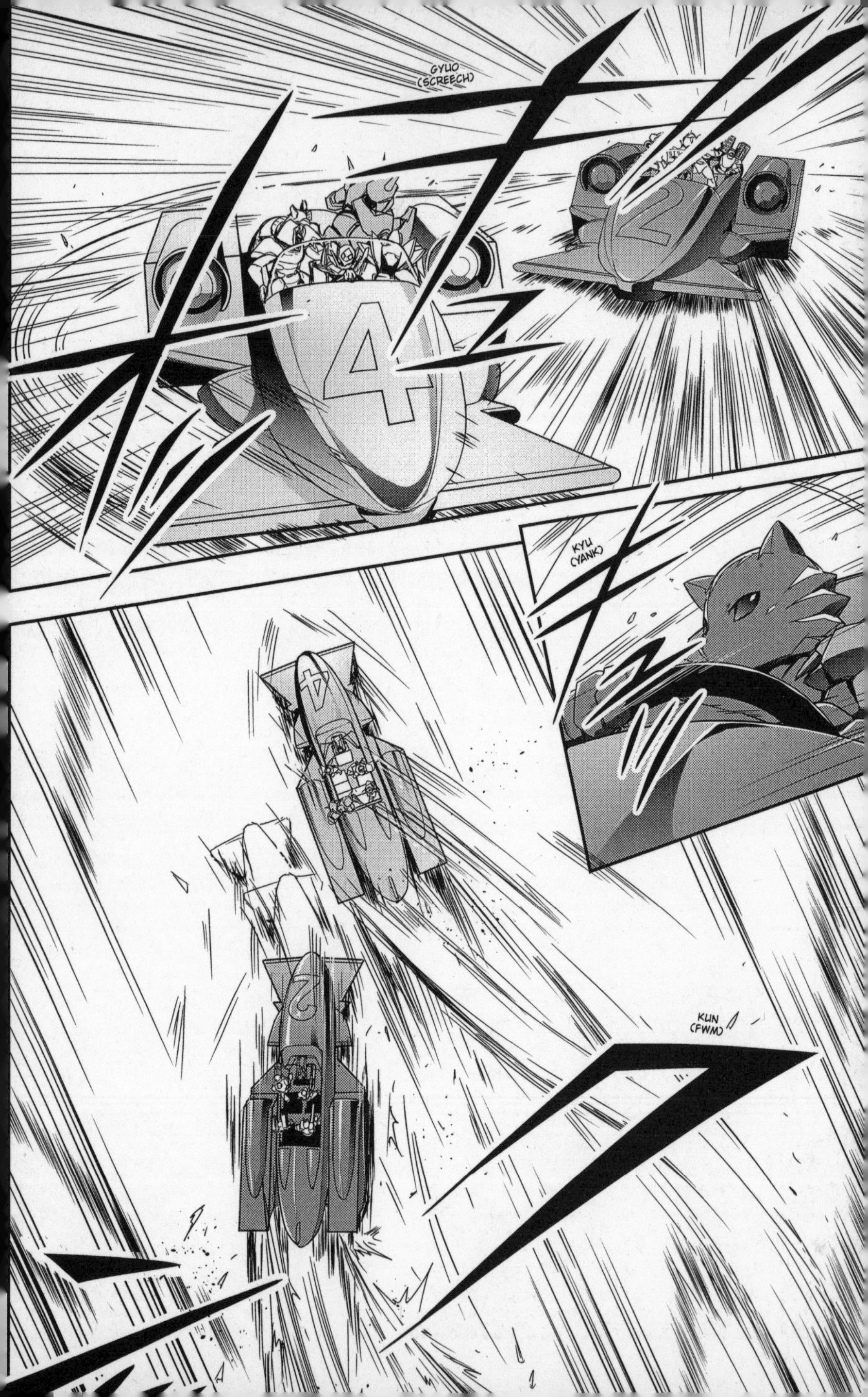
GYUO (SCREECH)
KYU (YANK)
KUN (FWM)

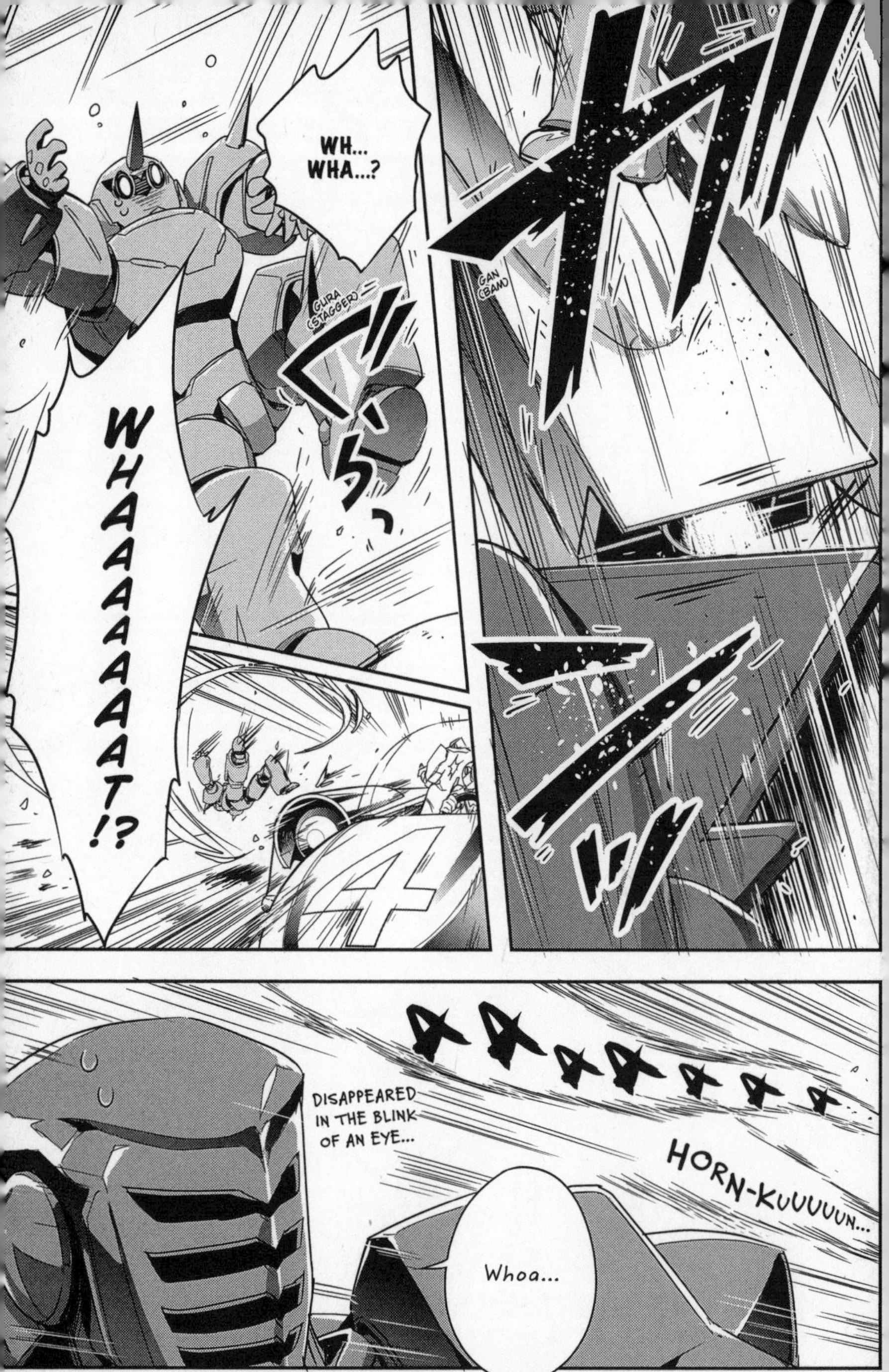
GAN (BAM)
WH... WHA...?
GURA (STAGGER)
WHAAAAAAAT!?
HORN-KUUUUUN...
DISAPPEARED IN THE BLINK OF AN EYE...
Whoa...

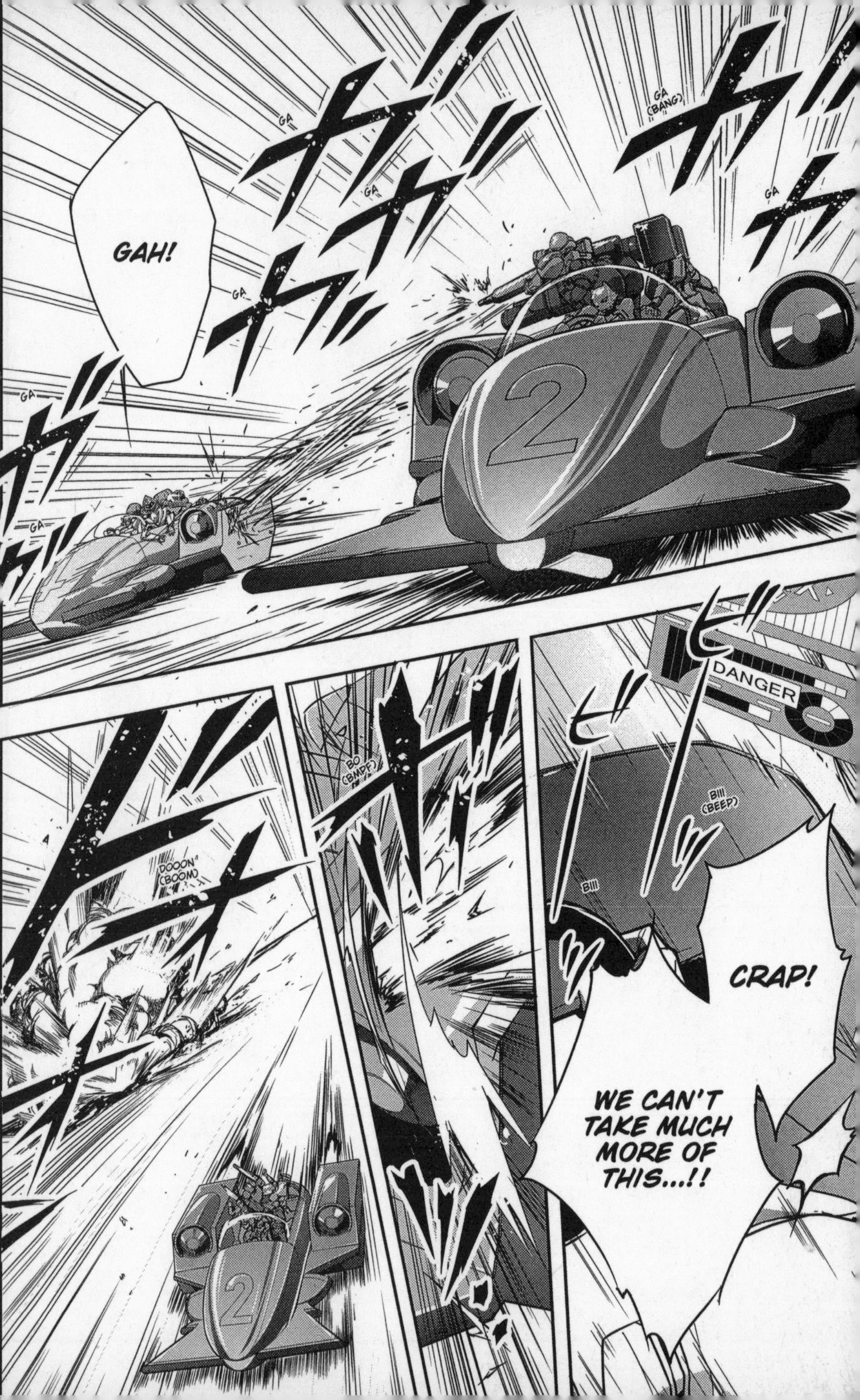
GA (BANG)
GA
GA
GA
GAH!
GA
GA
GA
DANGER
BIII (BEEP)
BIII
CRAP!
WE CAN'T TAKE MUCH MORE OF THIS...!!
BO (BMPF)
DOOON (BOOM)

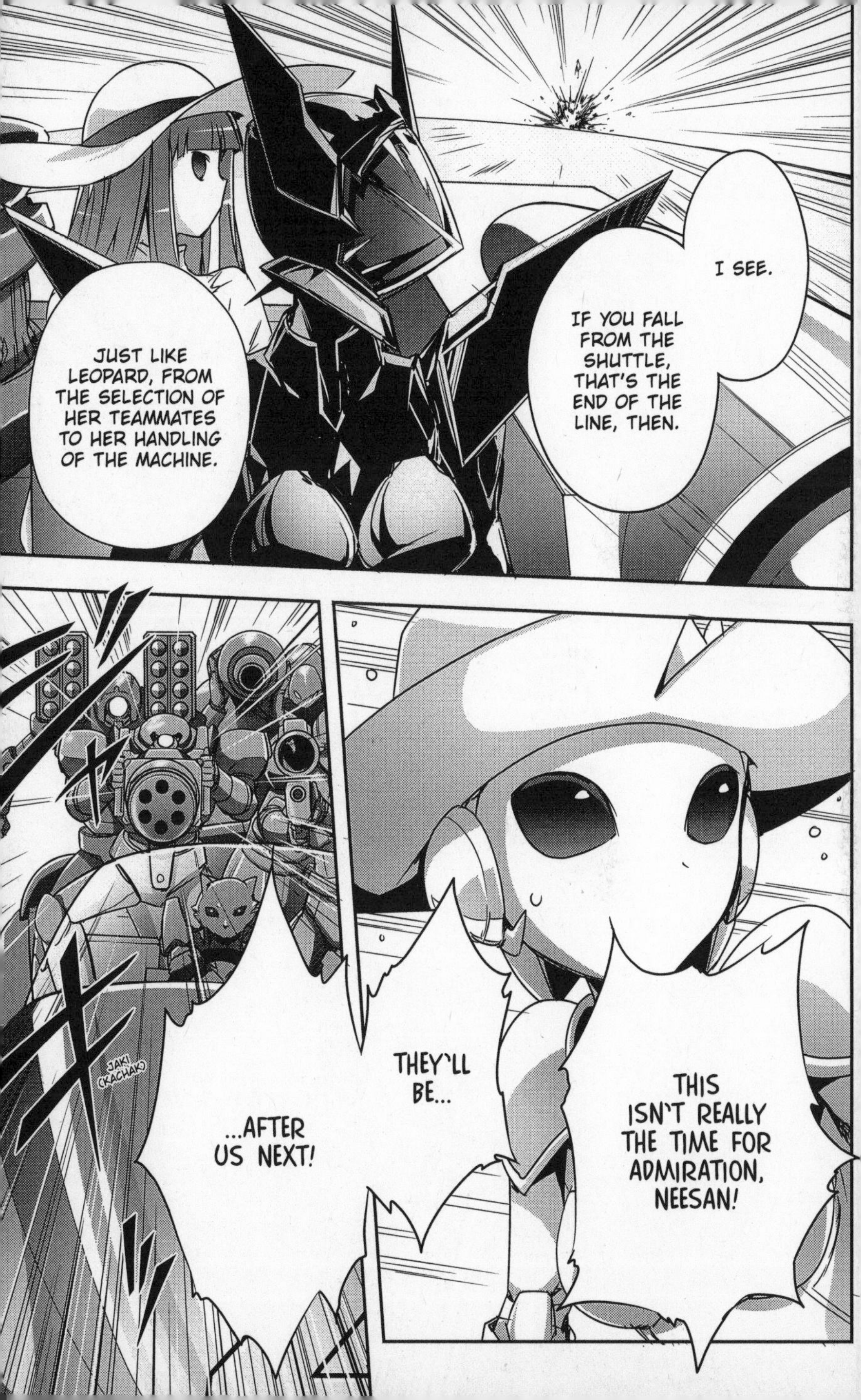
I SEE.
IF YOU FALL FROM THE SHUTTLE, THAT'S THE END OF THE LINE, THEN.
JUST LIKE LEOPARD, FROM THE SELECTION OF HER TEAMMATES TO HER HANDLING OF THE MACHINE.
THIS ISN'T REALLY THE TIME FOR ADMIRATION, NEESAN!
THEY'LL BE...
...AFTER US NEXT!
JAKI (KACHAK)

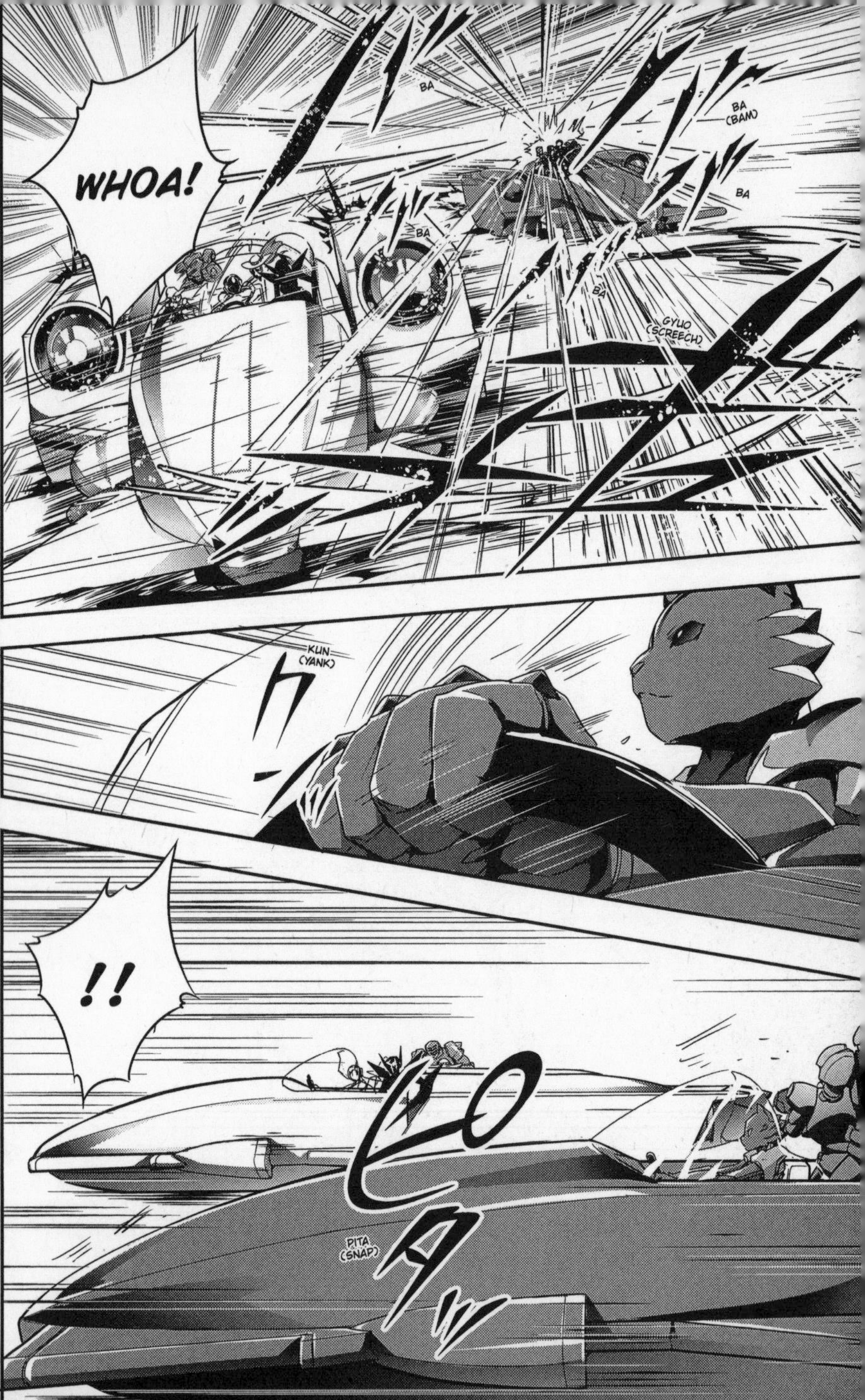
BA
(BAM)
BA
BA
BA
BA
GYUO
(SCREECH)
WHOA!
KUN
(YANK)
!!
PITA
(SNAP)

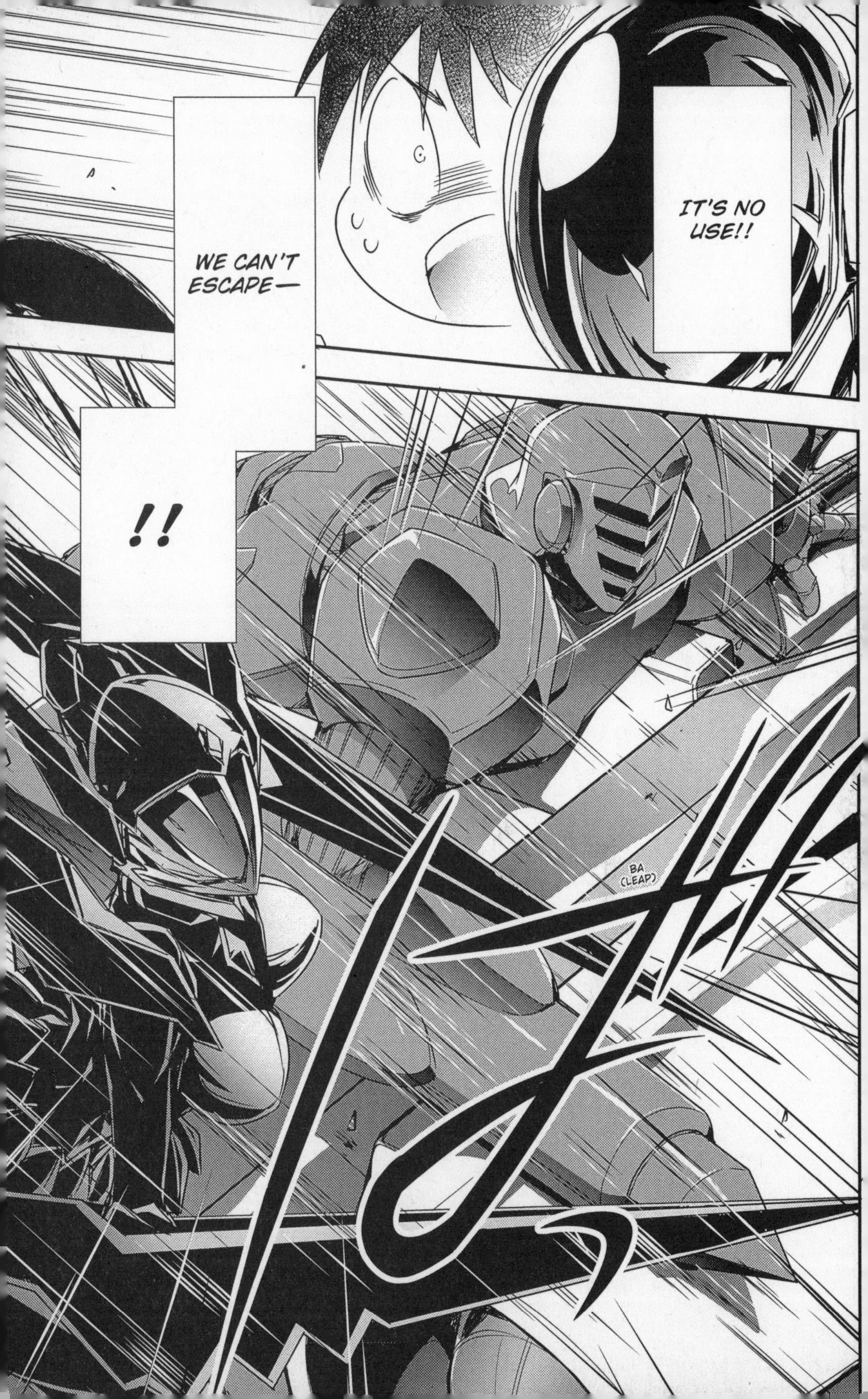
IT'S NO USE!!
WE CAN'T ESCAPE—
!!
BA (LEAP)

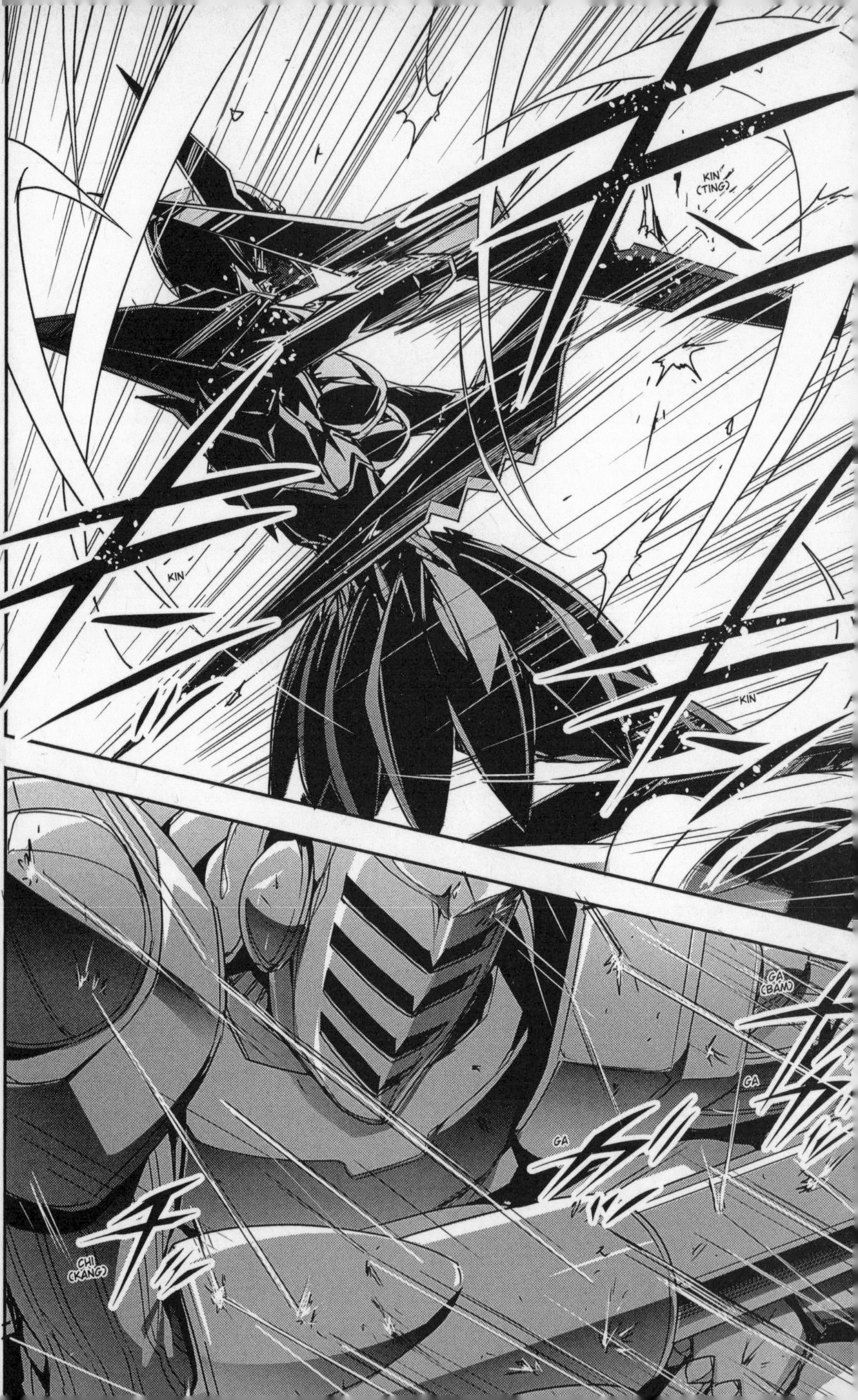
KIN (TING)
KIN
KIN
GA (BAM)
GA
GA
CHI (KANG)

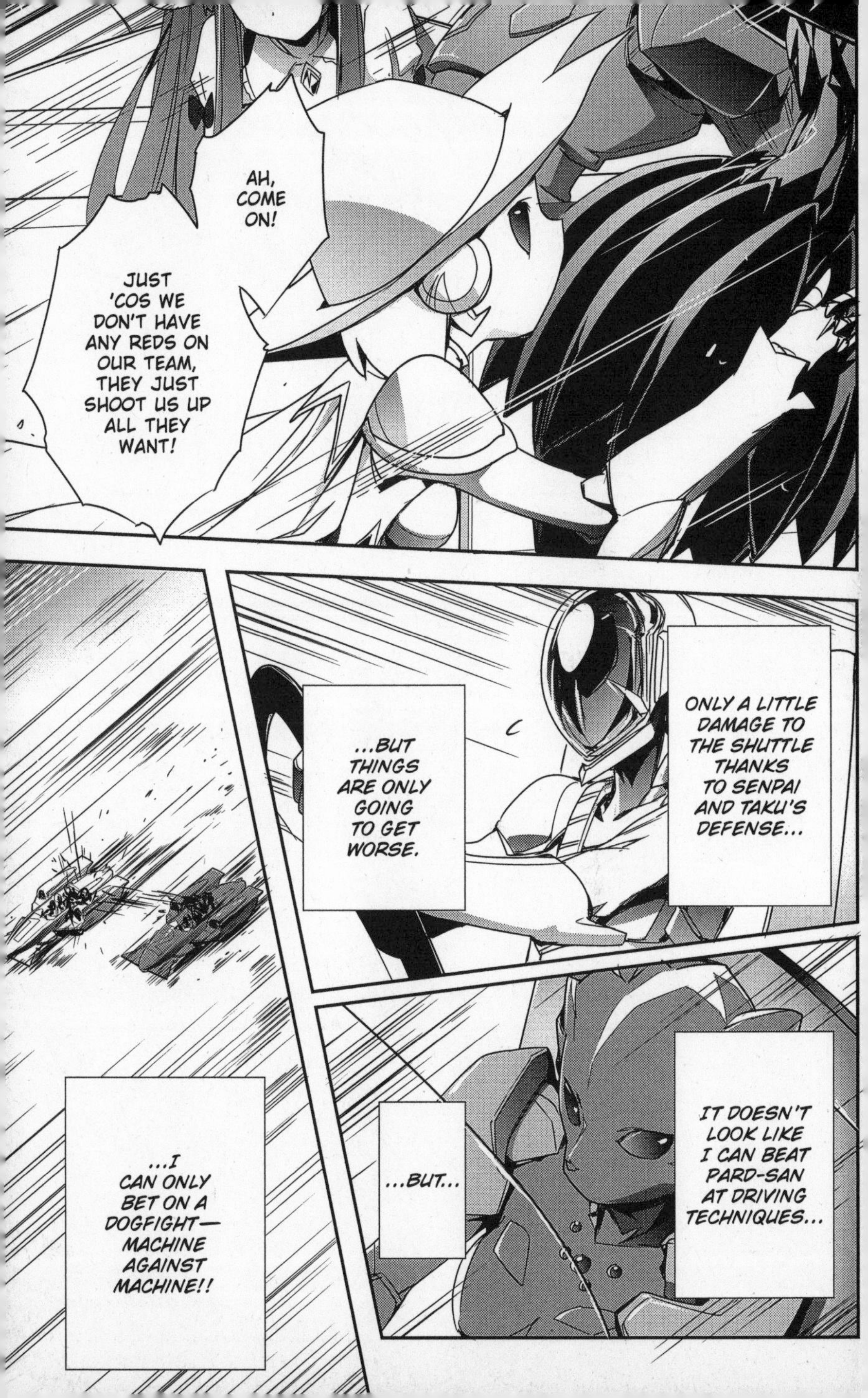
AH, COME ON!
JUST 'COS WE DON'T HAVE ANY REDS ON OUR TEAM, THEY JUST SHOOT US UP ALL THEY WANT!
ONLY A LITTLE DAMAGE TO THE SHUTTLE THANKS TO SENPAI AND TAKU'S DEFENSE...
...BUT THINGS ARE ONLY GOING TO GET WORSE.
IT DOESN'T LOOK LIKE I CAN BEAT PARD-SAN AT DRIVING TECHNIQUES...
...BUT...
...I CAN ONLY BET ON A DOGFIGHT—MACHINE AGAINST MACHINE!!

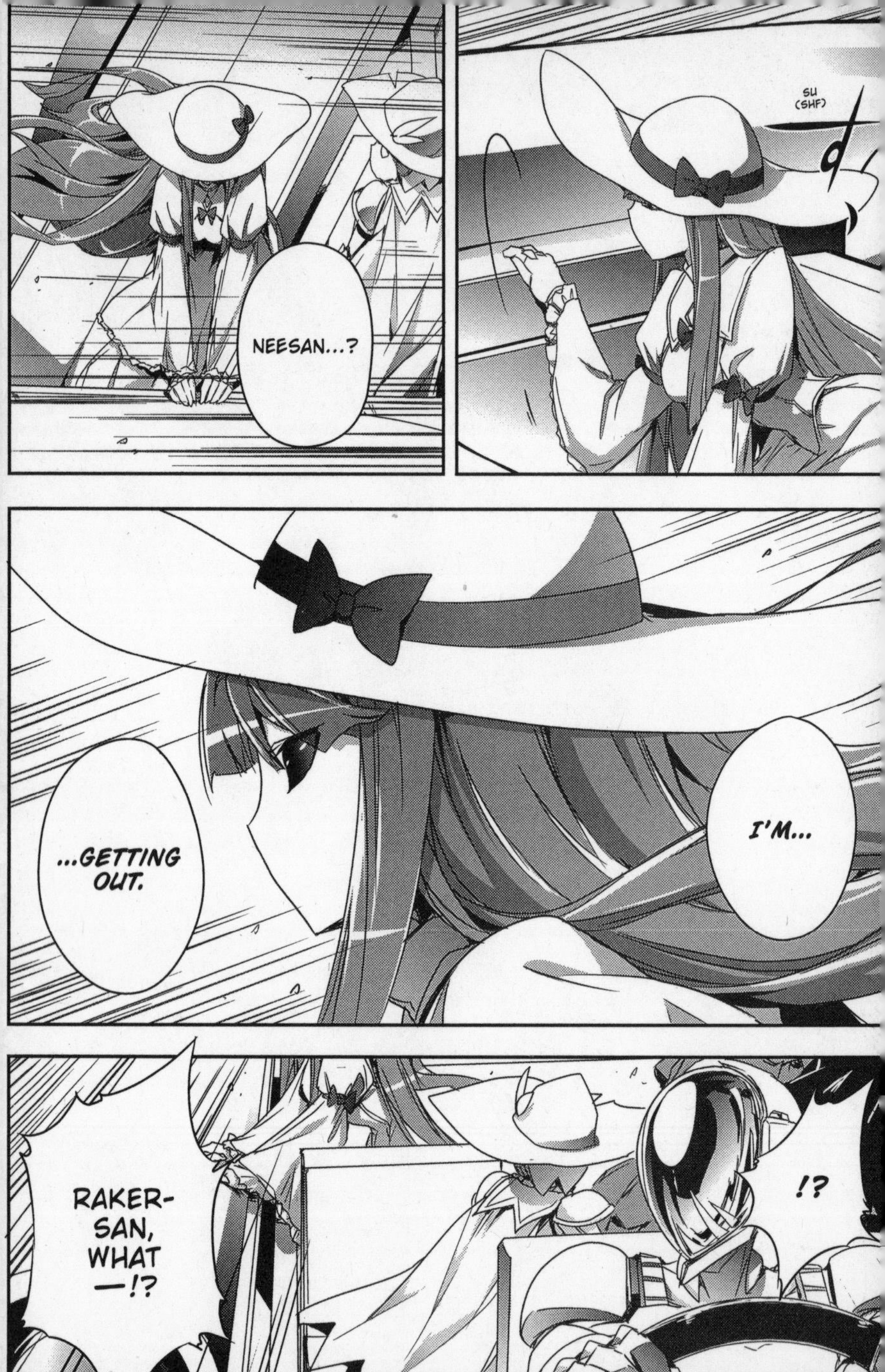
SU (SHF)
NEESAN...?
I'M...
...GETTING OUT.
!?
RAKER-SAN, WHAT—!?

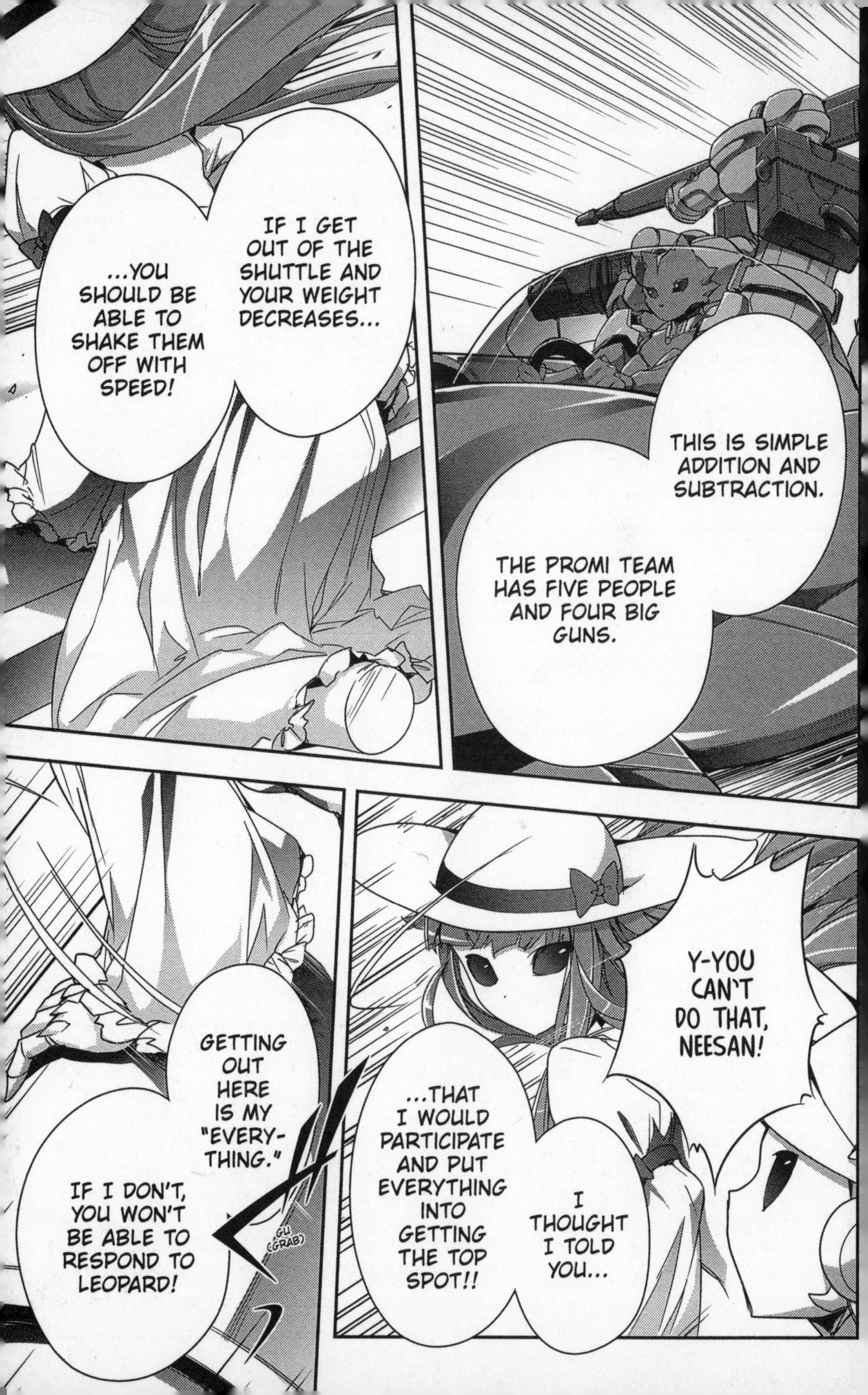
THIS IS SIMPLE ADDITION AND SUBTRACTION.
THE PROMI TEAM HAS FIVE PEOPLE AND FOUR BIG GUNS.
IF I GET OUT OF THE SHUTTLE AND YOUR WEIGHT DECREASES...
...YOU SHOULD BE ABLE TO SHAKE THEM OFF WITH SPEED!
Y-YOU CAN'T DO THAT, NEESAN!
I THOUGHT I TOLD YOU...
...THAT I WOULD PARTICIPATE AND PUT EVERYTHING INTO GETTING THE TOP SPOT!!
GETTING OUT HERE IS MY "EVERYTHING."
GU (GRAB)
IF I DON'T, YOU WON'T BE ABLE TO RESPOND TO LEOPARD!

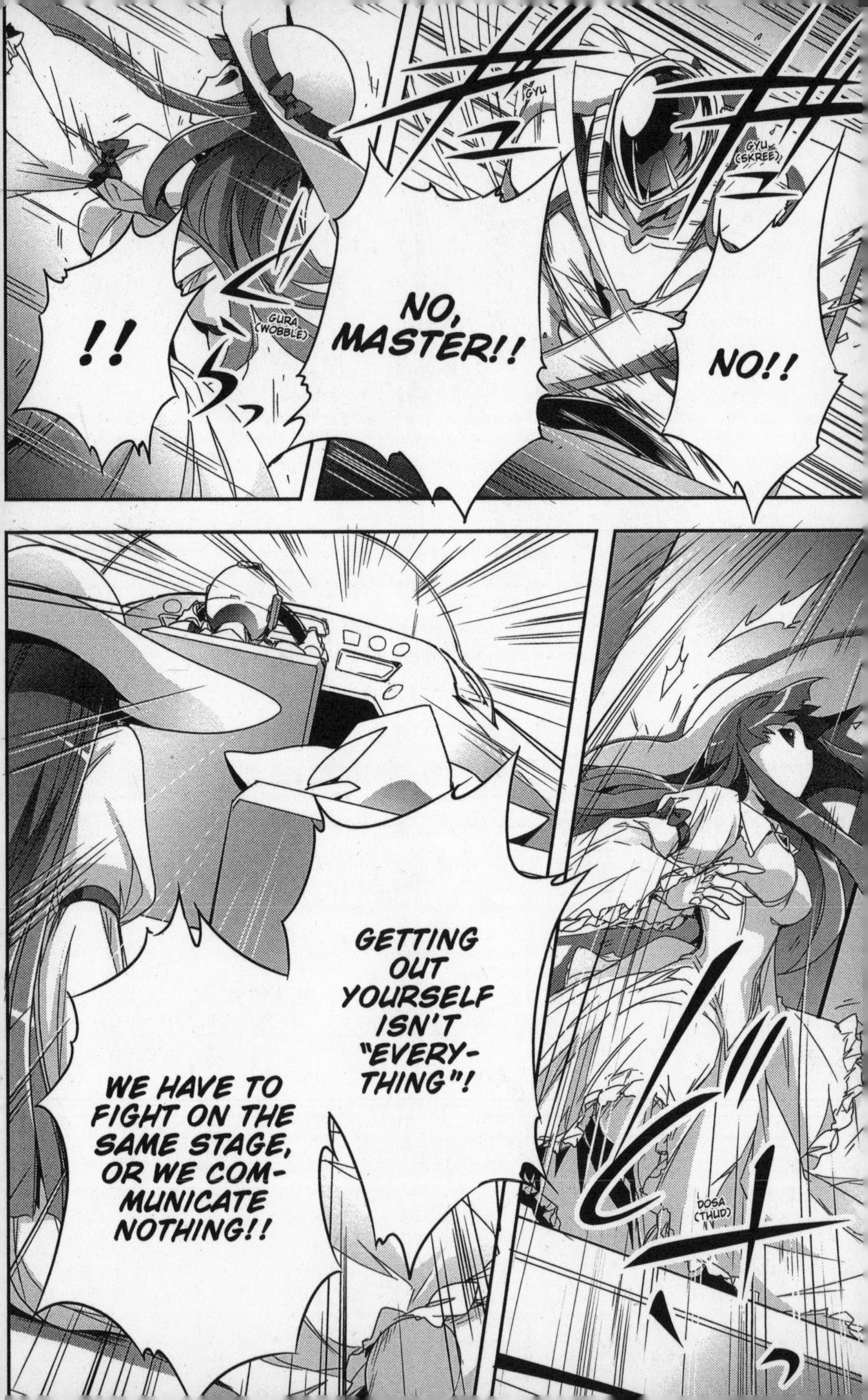
GYU (SKREE)
GYU
NO!!
NO, MASTER!!
GURA (WOBBLE)
!!
DOSA (THUD)
GETTING OUT YOURSELF ISN'T "EVERYTHING"!
WE HAVE TO FIGHT ON THE SAME STAGE, OR WE COM-MUNICATE NOTHING!!

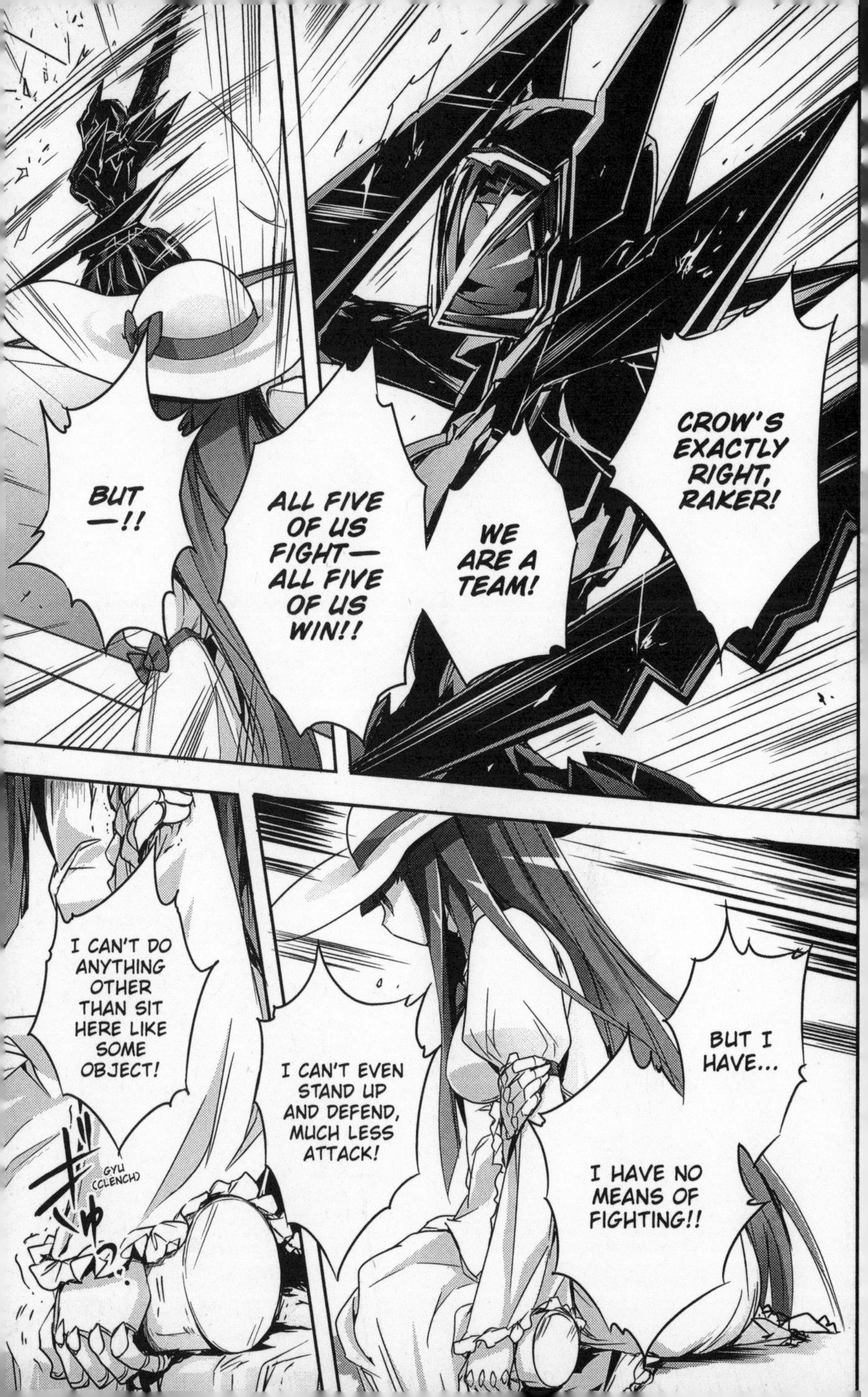
CROW'S EXACTLY RIGHT, RAKER!
WE ARE A TEAM!
ALL FIVE OF US FIGHT—ALL FIVE OF US WIN!!
BUT—!!
BUT I HAVE...
I HAVE NO MEANS OF FIGHTING!!
I CAN'T EVEN STAND UP AND DEFEND, MUCH LESS ATTACK!
I CAN'T DO ANYTHING OTHER THAN SIT HERE LIKE SOME OBJECT!
GYU (CLENCH)

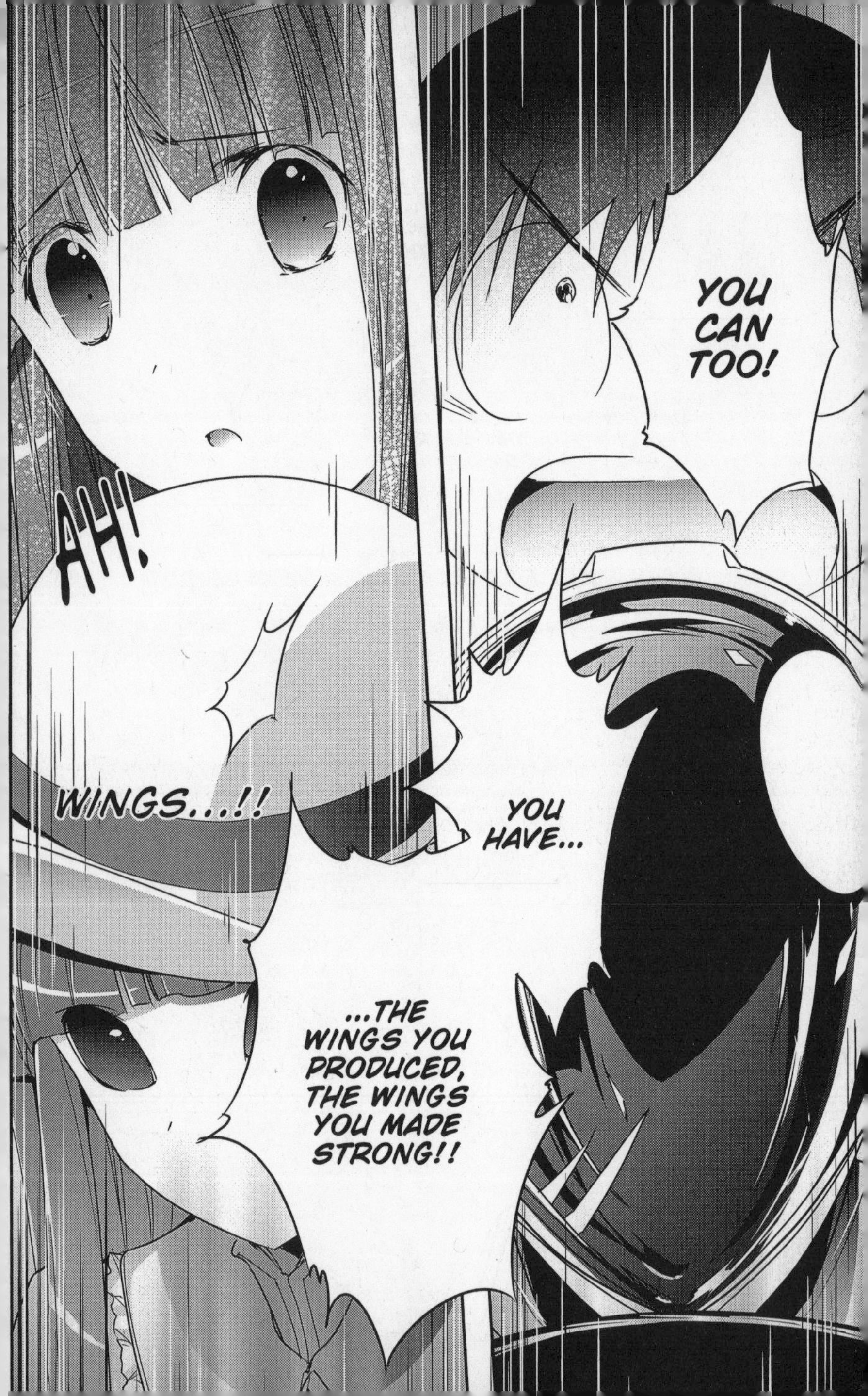
YOU CAN TOO!
YOU HAVE...
...THE WINGS YOU PRODUCED, THE WINGS YOU MADE STRONG!!
AH!
WINGS...!!

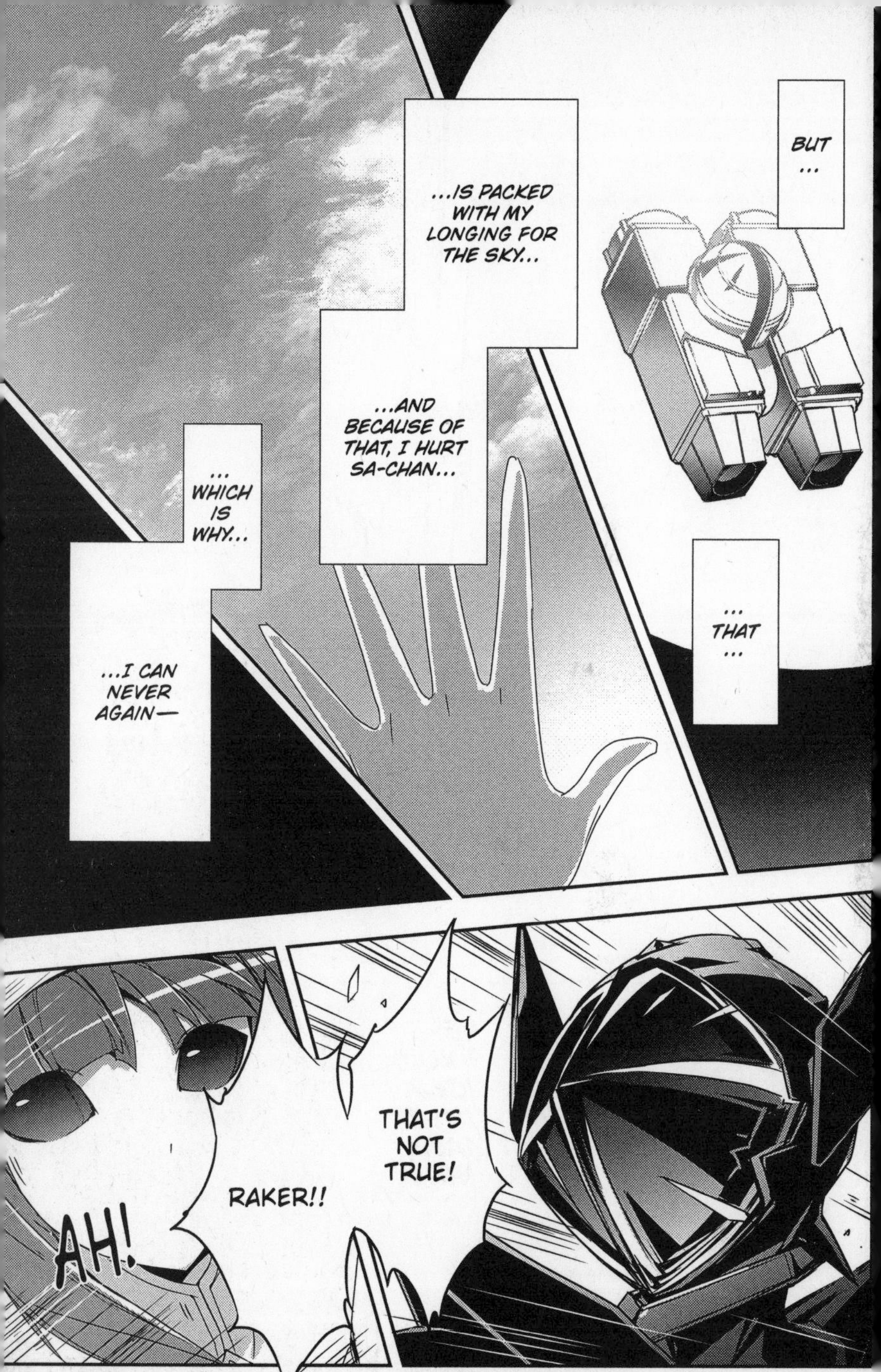
BUT ...
... THAT ...
...IS PACKED WITH MY LONGING FOR THE SKY...
...AND BECAUSE OF THAT, I HURT SA-CHAN...
... WHICH IS WHY...
...I CAN NEVER AGAIN—
THAT'S NOT TRUE!
RAKER!!
AH!

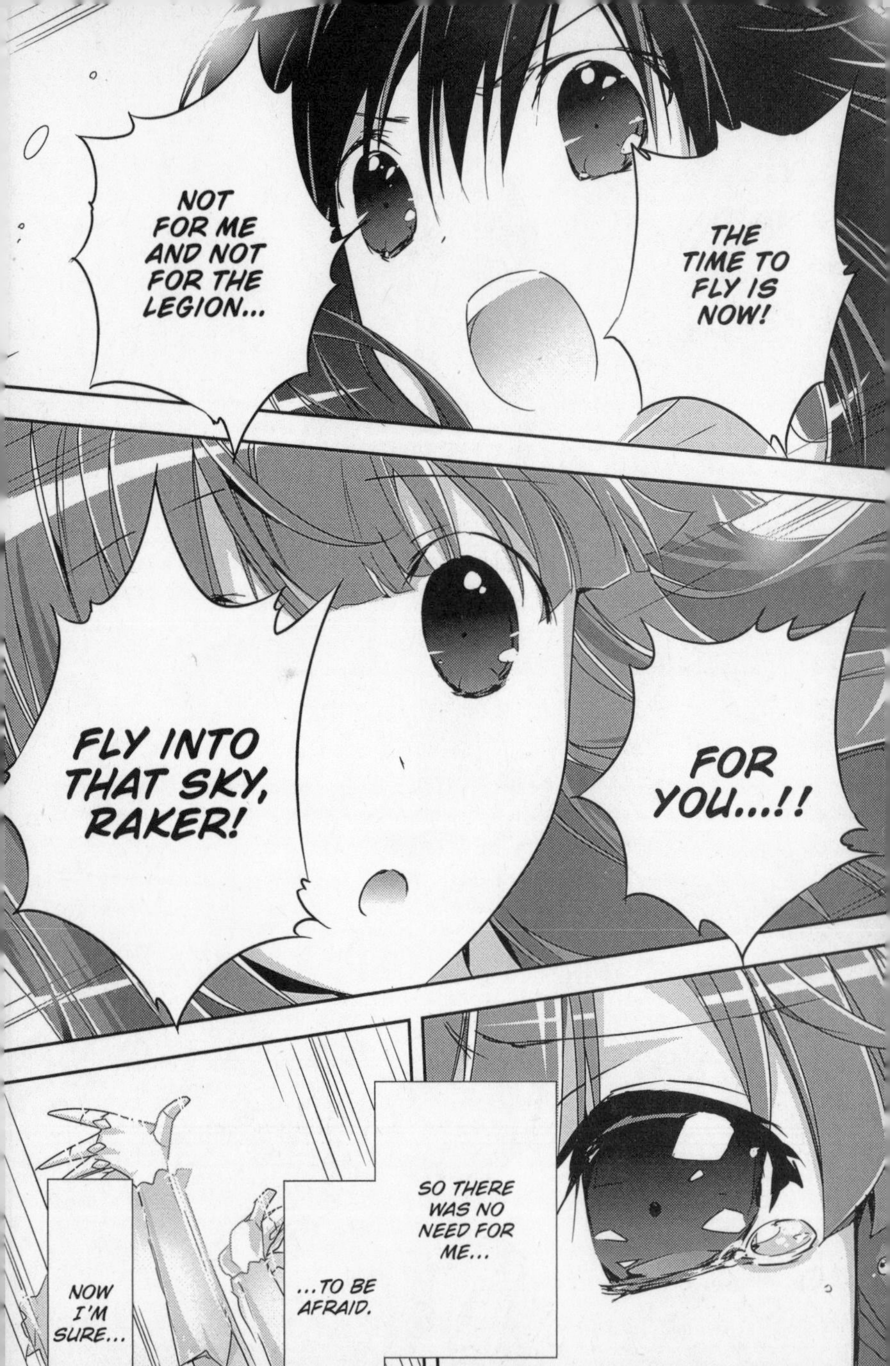
THE TIME TO FLY IS NOW!
NOT FOR ME AND NOT FOR THE LEGION...
FOR YOU...!!
FLY INTO THAT SKY, RAKER!
SO THERE WAS NO NEED FOR ME...
...TO BE AFRAID.
NOW I'M SURE...

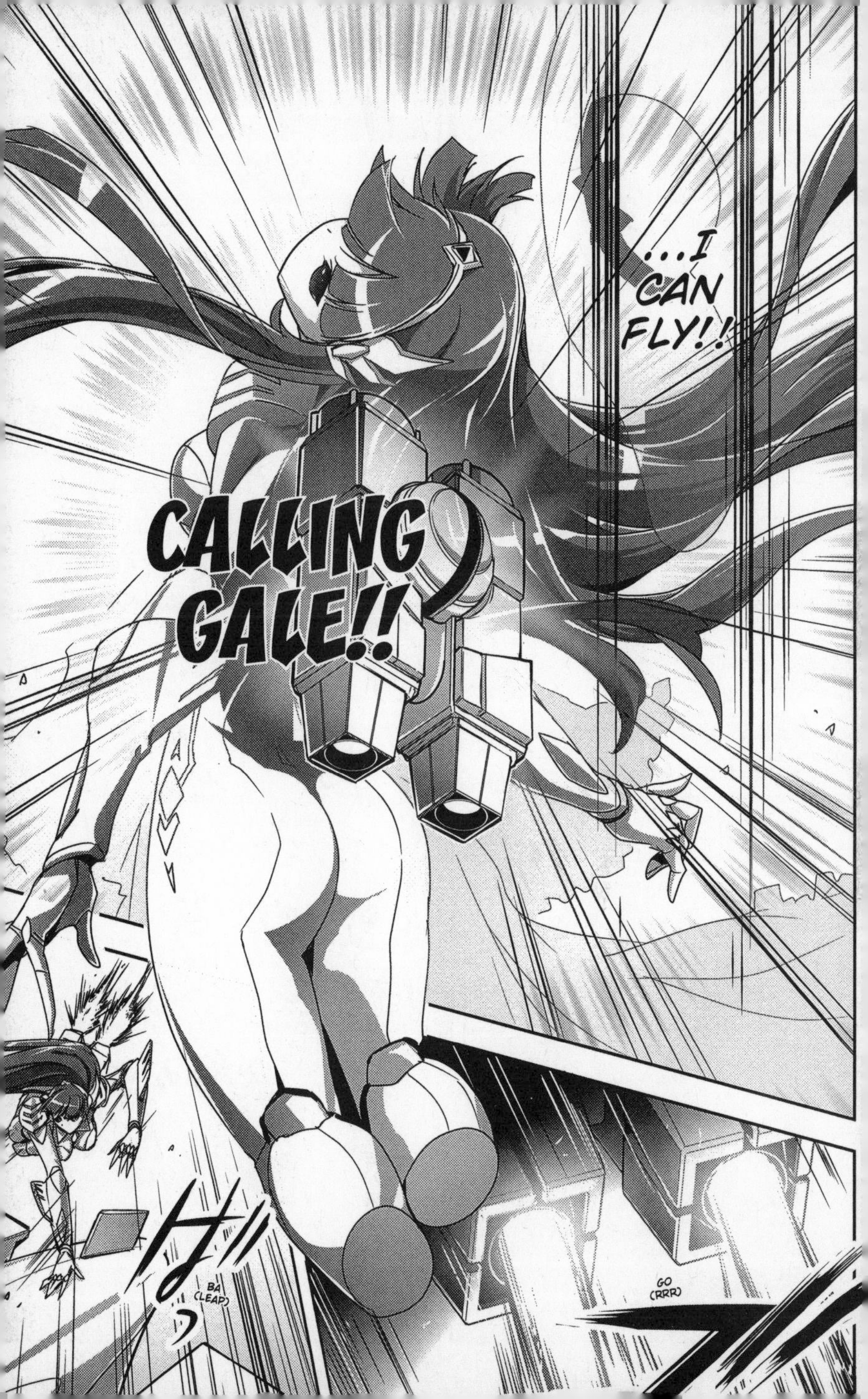
...I CAN FLY!!
CALLING GALE!!
BA (LEAP)
GO (RRR)

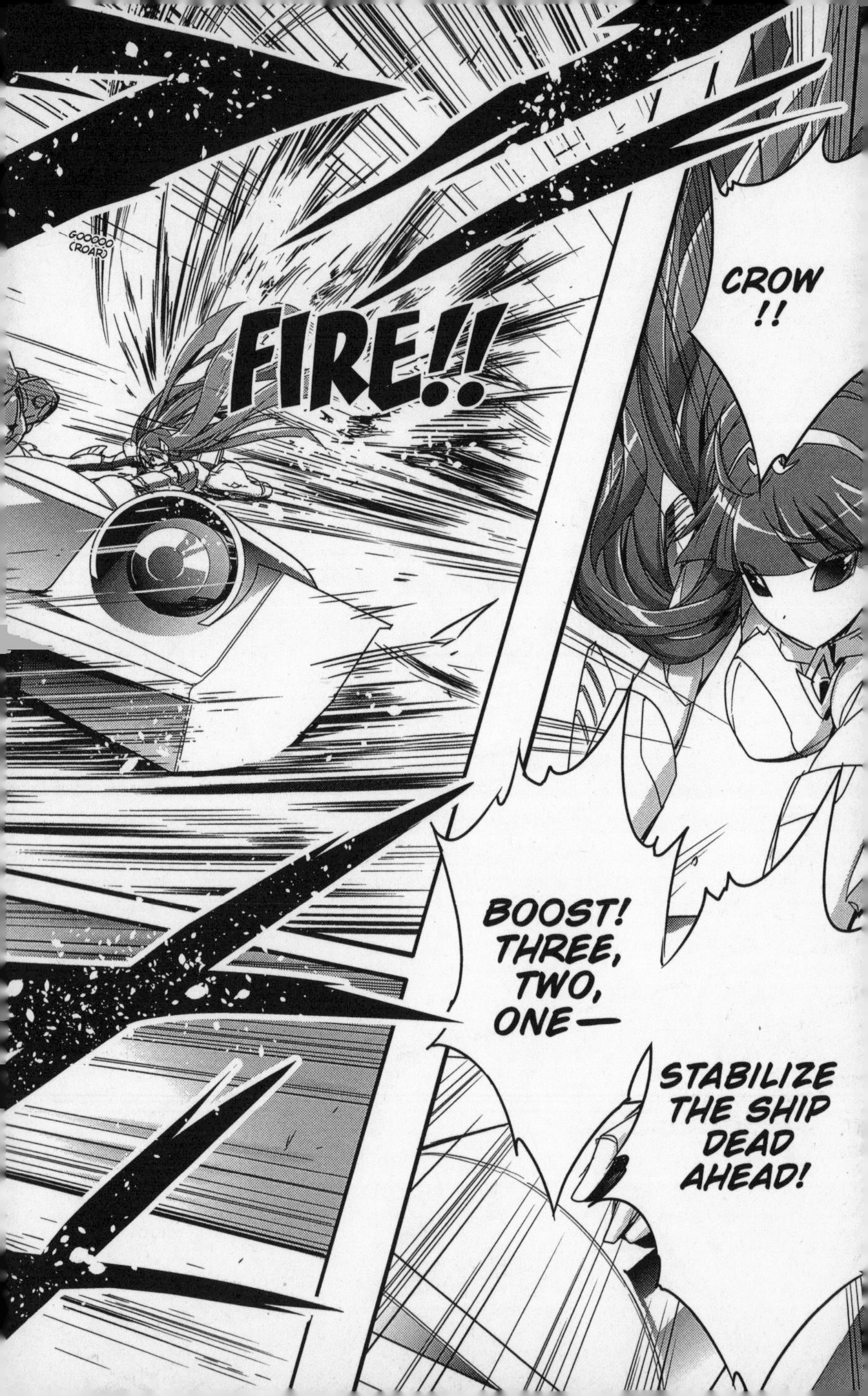
CROW!!
GOOOOO (ROAR)
FIRE!!
BOOST! THREE, TWO, ONE—
STABILIZE THE SHIP DEAD AHEAD!

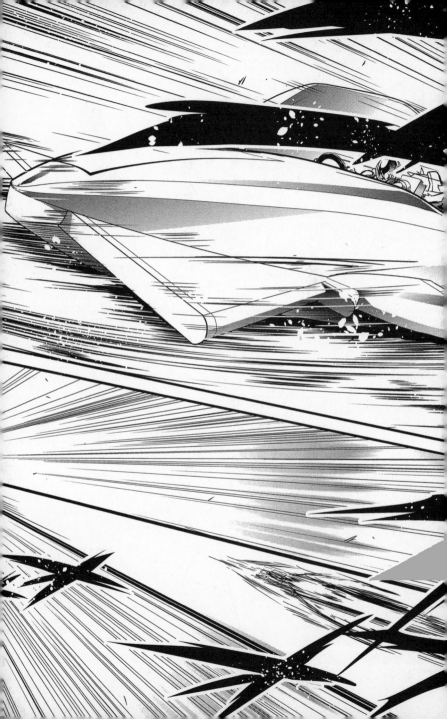

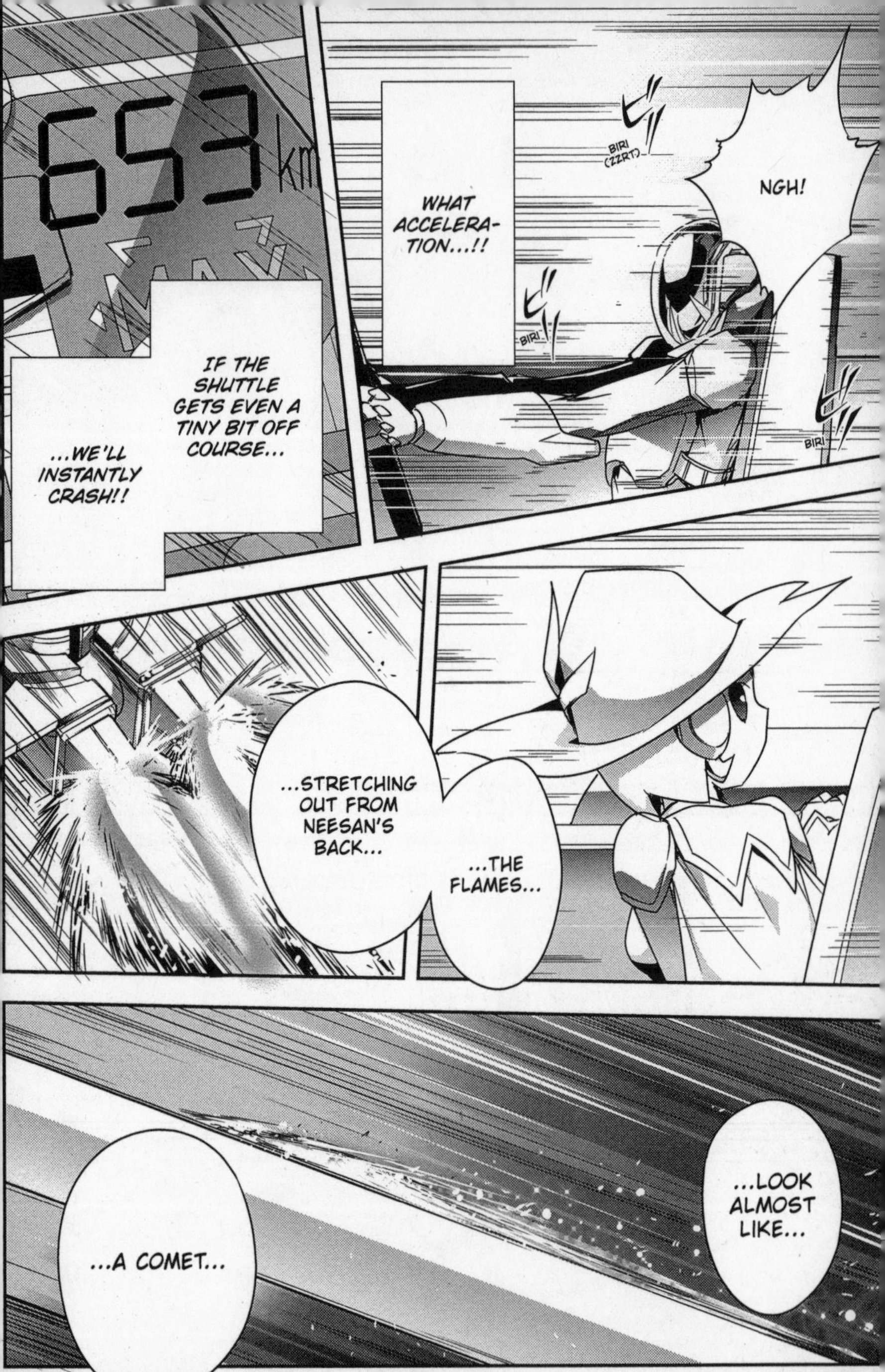

BIRI (ZZRT)
NGH!
WHAT ACCELERA-TION...!!
BIRI
BIRI
653 km
IF THE SHUTTLE GETS EVEN A TINY BIT OFF COURSE...
...WE'LL INSTANTLY CRASH!!
...STRETCHING OUT FROM NEESAN'S BACK...
...THE FLAMES...
...LOOK ALMOST LIKE...
...A COMET...

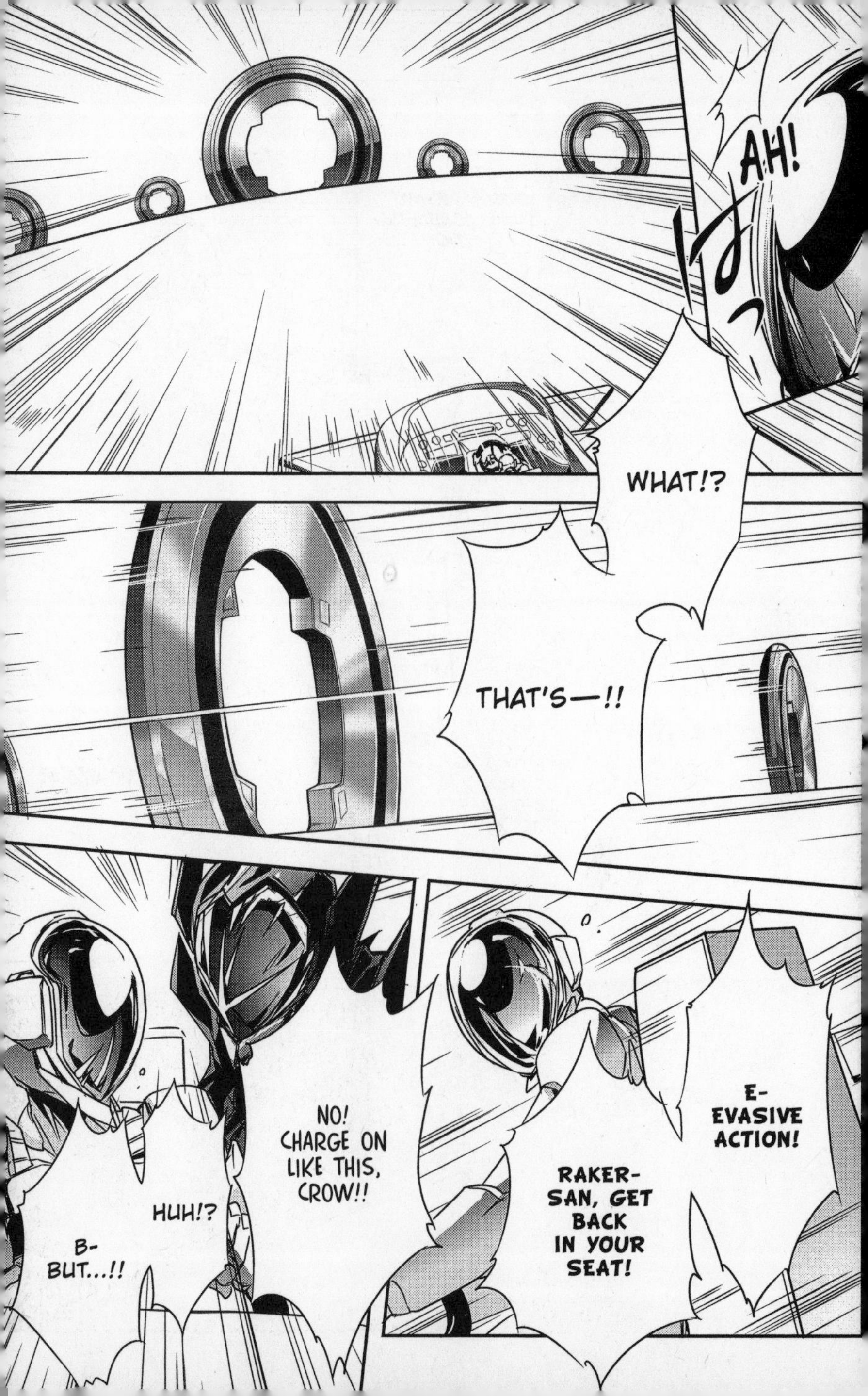
AH!
WHAT!?
THAT'S—!!
E- EVASIVE ACTION!
RAKER-SAN, GET BACK IN YOUR SEAT!
NO! CHARGE ON LIKE THIS, CROW!!
HUH!?
B- BUT...!!

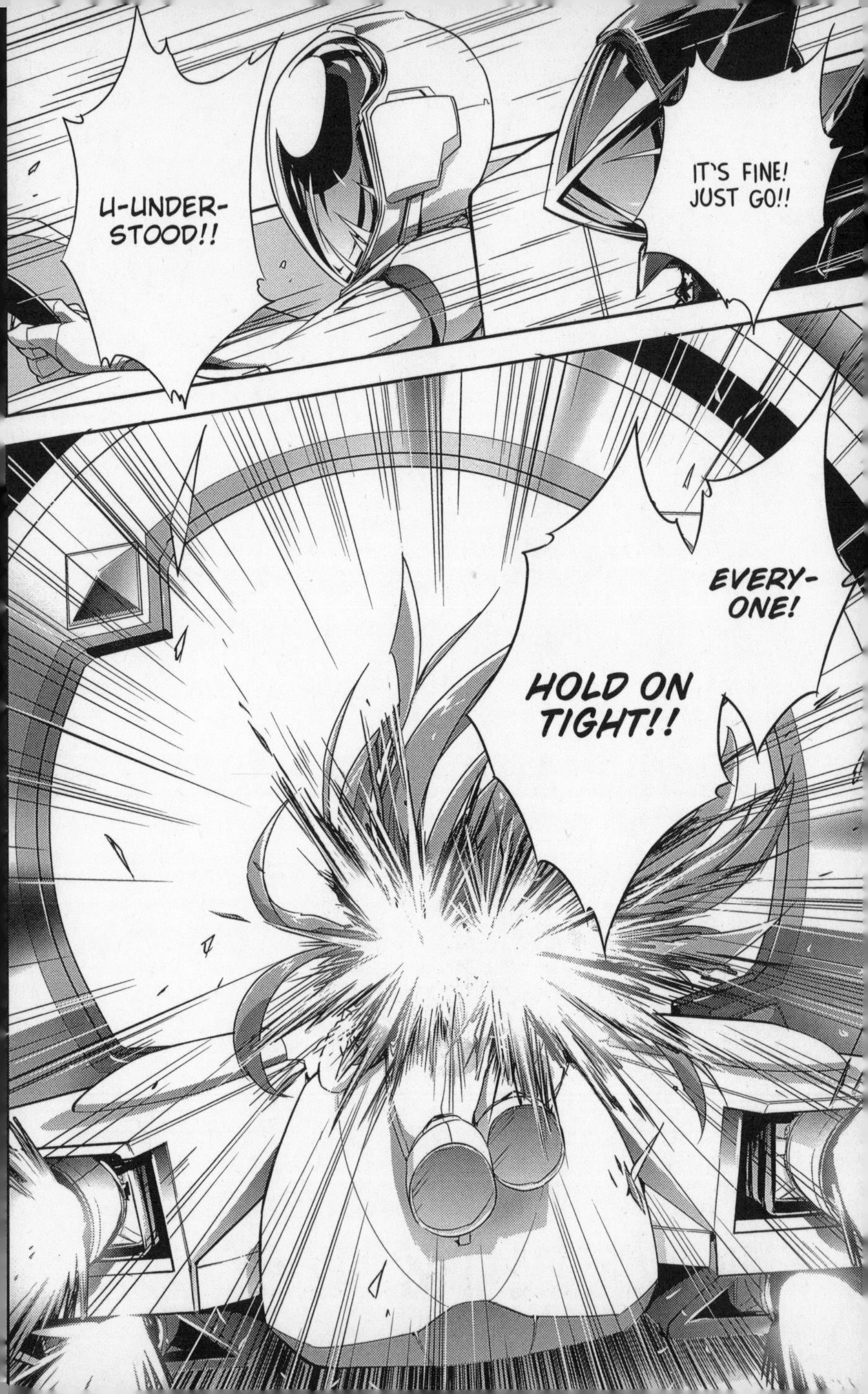
IT'S FINE! JUST GO!!
U-UNDER-STOOD!!
EVERY-ONE!
HOLD ON TIGHT!!

►►►ACCEL·WORLD

TO BE CONTINUED IN THE NEXT STAGE...!!

Duel avatar design assistance: Yosuke Kabashima, Noriyuki Jinguji, Takumi Sakura, Hiroyuki Taiga, Masahiro Yamane

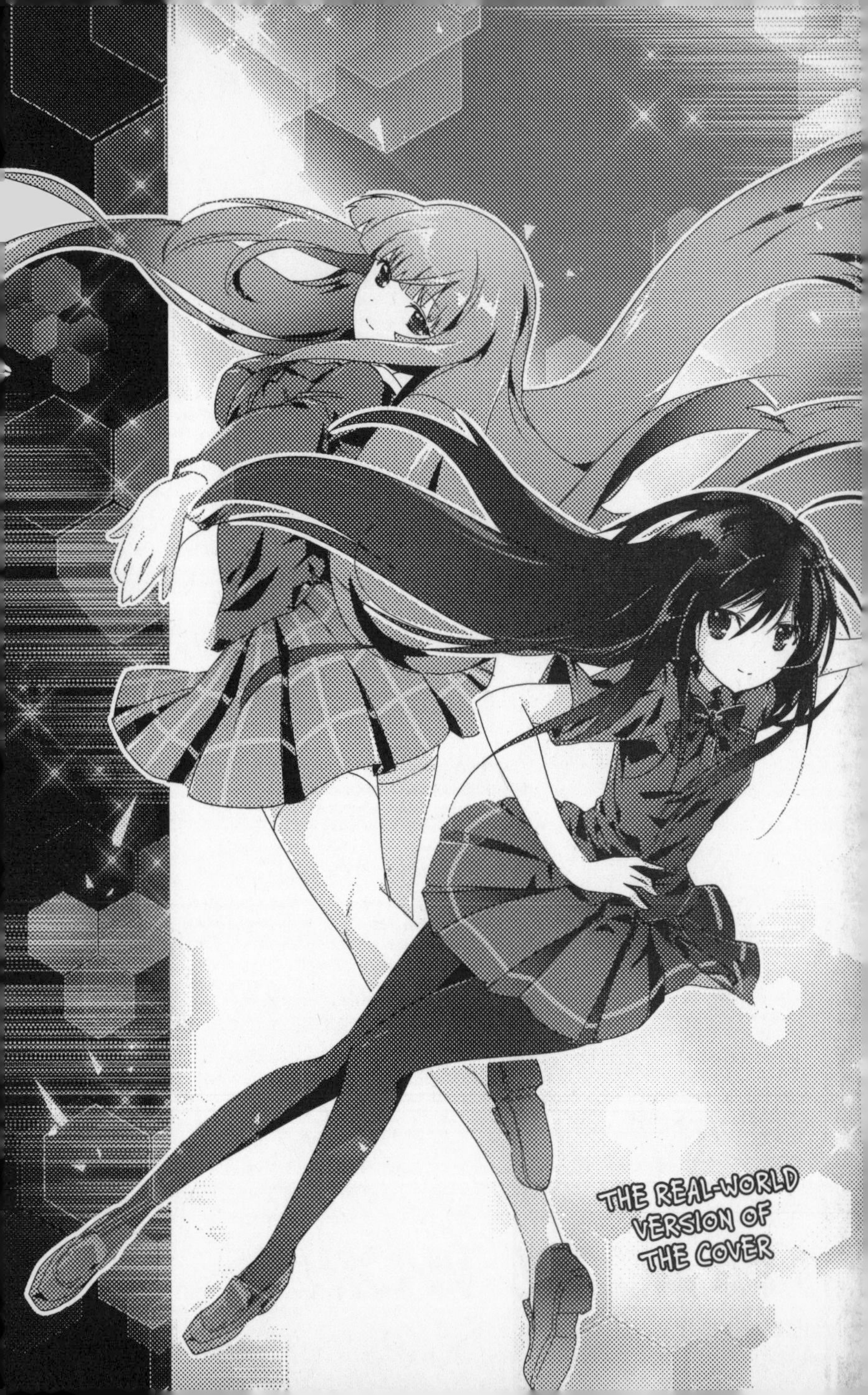
THE REAL-WORLD
VERSION OF
THE COVER

AFTERWORD

Thank you so much for picking up Volume 7 of the comics version of *Accel World*!

This volume picks up where the last one left off in Volume 5 of the original series: The Floating Starlight Bridge.

The prologue at the beginning of the book was not part of the serialization in Dengeki Bunko Magazine; it's completely new for this volume. I'm sure people who have read the original series already are thinking, "Wait. I don't remember a scene like this in the original."

Since I did a digest version in the comic of Volumes 3 and 4, I wanted to touch on the connection between Rust Jigsaw and the Acceleration Research Society once more, so I portrayed this scene as a prologue.

The author of the original series, Reki Kawahara-sensei, and his editor at Dengeki Bunko were kind enough to take time from their busy schedules to discuss the addition of this scene with me. Thank you so much!

Now then, this volume should be hitting the bookstores right around the time of the premiere of the new anime, *Accel World: Infinite Burst*, and the movie's theater run! I'm super excited about getting to see Haruyuki-kun and the others on the big screen!

I'd be delighted if we met again in the next volume. This has been Hiroyuki Aigamo!

■ ASSISTANTS
Hio-sama
Shige Edo-sama
Tsukikaname-sama
Yui Ito-sama
Motoko Ikeda-sama
Sakuraba-sama
Momoto-sama
Kusasora Yamano-sama
Ao Esaka-sama
Hanimaru-sama

■ SPECIAL THANKS
Reki Kawahara-sama
HIMA-sama
Ryuryuu Akari-sama
Ayato Sasakura-sama
Everyone on the Sunrise
  Anime staff
abec-sama
Chie Tsuhiya-sama
Kazuma Miki-sama

ACCEL WO

Original Story: Reki Kawahara
Character Design: HIMA

Translation: Jocelyne Allen
Lettering: Brndn Blakeslee

ACCEL WORLD
© REKI KAWAHARA / HIROYUKI AIGAMO 2016
All rights reserved.
Edited by ASCII MEDIA WORKS
First published in Japan in 2016 by KADOKAWA CORPORATION, Tokyo.
English translation rights arranged with KADOKAWA CORPORATION, Tokyo,
through Tuttle-Mori Agency, Inc., Tokyo.

English translation © 2017 by Yen Press, LLC

Yen Press
1290 Avenue of the Americas
New York, NY 10104

Visit us at yenpress.com
facebook.com/yenpress
twitter.com/yenpress
yenpress.tumblr.com
instagram.com/yenpress

First Yen Press Edition: March 2017

Yen Press is an imprint of Yen Press, LLC.
The Yen Press name and logo are trademarks of Yen Press, LLC.

Library of Congress Control Number: 2015952578

ISBN: 978-0-316-46920-3

10 9 8 7 6 5 4 3 2 1

BVG

Printed in the United States of America